AF651967

Cultivation of Plants and Soilless Gardening

Cultivation of Plants and Soilless Gardening

Subhash Meena

RANDOM

RANDOM PUBLICATIONS

NEW DELHI (INDIA)

Cultivation of Plants and Soilless Gardening

ISBN 978-93-5111-839-8
© Reserved

All Rights Reserved. No Part of this book may be reproduced in any manner without written permission.

Published in 2016 in India by

RANDOM PUBLICATIONS

4376-A/4B, Gali Murari Lal, Ansari Road
New Delhi-110 002
Phone : +9111-43580356, 011-23289044, 011-43142548
e-mail: sales@randompublications.com,
info@randompublications.com, randomexports@gmail.com

Type Setting by : Friends Media, Delhi-110089
Printed at : Replika Press Pvt. Ltd.

Preface

The science of soilless gardening is called hydroponics. It may sound like something devised in a modern laboratory, but it's been around for thousands of years.

Successful container gardening requires a potting medium that meets several of the plant's needs. The medium must be a stable reservoir of moisture and nutrients and remain loose enough to allow for root and water movement and the exchange of gases in the root zone. A growing medium must also have a pH (a measure of the alkalinity or acidity of a medium) that can support adequate nutrient uptake, and it must be free of soil-borne diseases, weed seeds, and toxins. Finally, a container medium must provide adequate anchorage and support for the roots while still being heavy enough to provide sufficient ballast to prevent plants from tipping over. A well-blended soilless medium can easily satisfy all these requirements and do so without the inherent problems and variability frequently encountered when field, or native, soils are used in containers.

Hydroponics is proved to have several advantages over soil gardening. The growth rate on a hydroponic plant is 30-50 percent faster than a soil plant, grown under the same conditions. The yield of the plant is also greater. Scientists believe that there are several reasons for the drastic differences between hydroponic and soil plants. The extra oxygen in the hydroponic growing mediums helps to stimulate root growth.

The physical and chemical properties of peat moss make it an ideal base for most soilless mixes because it can hold both water and air. It's light, but its fibrous structure allows it to hold 15 to 20 times its weight in water. The peat fibers also give it a large amount of pore space (80 to 90 percent of its total volume). It holds nutrients well, and it readily shares them with the roots, thanks to its slightly acidic pH. Horticultural-grade peats come from the decomposed remains of sphagnum moss species that have accumulated over centuries in peat bogs. They are not a renewable resource, however, and concerns about the sustainability of harvesting this product is a common topic of discussion among gardeners. Another type of peat that is used in soilless mixes is known as reed-sedge peat, but this material is generally inferior to sphagnum peat.

The book 'Hydroponics' (Soilless Gardening) is a subset of hydroculture, and it is a method of growing crop plants (Vegetables, fruits and flowers, etc.) using mineral nutrient solutions in water without soil.

– ***Author***

Contents

1

Introduction

The term potting soil has become something of a misnomer in today's world of container gardening. Most bags of potting soil contain no field soil but are composed of a variety of organic and inorganic materials and are referred to as soilless mixes.

Many excellent brands are readily available at chain stores and garden centers. If you have a clear understanding of the requirements for a good container medium and the various ingredients used in these products, choosing the right mix for your container plantings is in the bag.

Successful container gardening requires a potting medium that meets several of the plant's needs.

The medium must be a stable reservoir of moisture and nutrients and remain loose enough to allow for root and water movement and the exchange of gases in the root zone.

A growing medium must also have a pH (a measure of the alkalinity or acidity of a medium) that can support adequate nutrient uptake, and it must be free of soil-borne diseases, weed seeds, and toxins.

Finally, a container medium must provide adequate anchorage and support for the roots while still being heavy enough to provide sufficient ballast to prevent plants from tipping over. A well-blended soilless medium can easily satisfy all these requirements and do so without the inherent problems and variability frequently encountered when field, or native, soils are used in containers.

If you have a good mix, water will penetrate it quickly and drain freely from the bottom of the pot. When the excess water has drained away, air will fill the large pore spaces, but enough water will be retained in the smaller spaces to provide ample moisture for the plant.

In a poor mix, water may be slow to penetrate, the medium will become heavy and waterlogged, and a crust from algae or accumulated salts may form on the surface. Under these conditions, the roots become starved for oxygen, plant growth slows, foliage may begin to yellow, and plants often succumb to root rot.

ORGANIC INGREDIENTS HOLD WATER AND NUTRIENTS SOME ORGANIC INGREDIENTS, SUCH AS PEAT MOSS, PROVIDE NEEDED WATER-HOLDING CAPACITY, AND OTHERS, LIKE PINE BARK, CAN LEND A POROUS STRUCTURE TO AVOID COMPACTION.

Peat moss: The physical and chemical properties of peat moss make it an ideal base for most soilless mixes because it can hold both water and air. It's light, but its fibrous structure allows it to hold 15 to 20 times its weight in water. The peat fibers also give it a large amount of pore space (80 to 90 percent of its total volume). It holds nutrients well, and it readily shares them with the roots, thanks to its slightly acidic pH. Horticultural-grade peats come from the decomposed remains of sphagnum moss species that have accumulated over centuries in peat bogs. They are not a renewable resource, however, and concerns about the sustainability of harvesting this product is a common topic of discussion among gardeners. Another type of peat that is used in soilless mixes is known as reed-sedge peat, but this material is generally inferior to sphagnum peat. Composted pine bark: This material is a renewable resource and is one of the most widely used components in commercial container media, although barks from many other species are also processed for this purpose. Bark lacks the moisture-holding capacity of peat moss, but it can dramatically increase the porosity of a mix. Bark particles used in container media generally range in size from dustlike to about 3/8 inch in diameter.

Coir: Another renewable organic material is coir, a derivative of coconut hulls that shows promise as a peat substitute. Coir has exceptional water-holding capacity, and when mixed with pine bark, it can eliminate or substantially reduce the need for peat moss in a mix. Other sources of organic matter that can be used in soilless mixes include composted manures, leaf mold, and crop residues such as rice hulls.

BOTH ORGANIC AND INORGANIC INGREDIENTS SERVE A PURPOSE

Fig. Peat moss

Fig. Composted pine bark

Fig. Coir

INORGANIC INGREDIENTS IMPROVE DRAINAGE AND ADD WEIGHT

Inorganic ingredients improve drainage and add weight Inorganic ingredients like sand, vermiculite, and perlite generally lend porosity to a mix, but they can also help retain moisture and add weight or density.

Sand: This material can add needed weightto peat- and bark-based mixes and fill large pore spaces without impairing drainage. Coarse sand is preferred in most cases, and sand ground from granite is used in the best mixes. Fine sand with rounded grains like that found at the beach can actually reduce drainage when used in excessive amounts. Vermiculite: A mineral that has been heated until it expands into small accordion-shaped particles, vermiculite holds large amounts of both air and water. But it can easily be compacted, so avoid packing down mixes containing large quantities of it. Vermiculite can also retain nutrients and help a mix resist changes in pH.

Perlite: One of the more common ingredients in commercial potting mixes, perlite is an inert ingredient manufactured by heating a volcanic material to produce lightweight white particles. It promotes good drainage while holding nearly as much water as vermiculite. Other inorganic materials that are useful in potting media include polystyrene (plastic) beads and calcined clay, which is similar to kitty litter. Plastic beads are inert and serve only to promote drainage, but calcined-clay particles can actually improve the moisture- and nutrient-holding capacity of a mix.

Fig. Sand

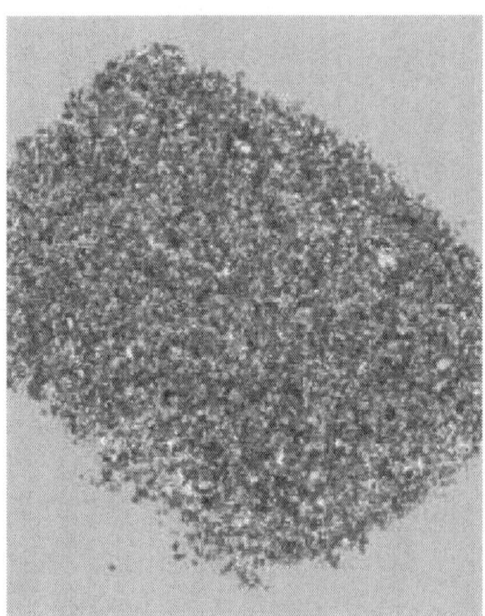

Fig. Vermiculite

The ideal mix: Generally, most container plants will thrive in a mix that contains about 40 percent peat moss, 20 percent pine bark, 20 percent vermiculite, and 20 percent perlite or sand.

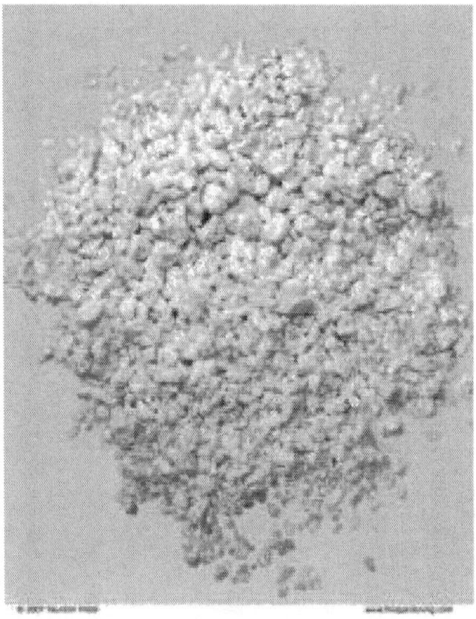

Fig. Perlite

SOILLESS MIXES LEAVE THE FERTILIZING

Soilless mixes have little natural fertility, so they need fertilizer, lime, and sometimes other materials added to them to give the plants nutrients. Many soilless mixes contain a "starter charge" of fertilizer that can satisfy the nutritional requirements of plants for a few weeks, but longer-term fertility maintenance can require the addition of liquid fertilizers on a regular basis. Another option is the application of a slow-release fertilizer, which provides a constant supply of available nutrients and can either be incorporated into the medium or simply top-dressed on the surface. The rate of nutrient release for most of these fertilizers is regulated by temperature, so plants receive more fertilizer when they are actively growing, and frequent watering will not leach the nutrients from the mix. Slow-release fertilizers are available in various formulations that can provide adequate nutrition for as short as three months or as long as two years.

Soilless mixes also have limited reserves of trace elements, so for best results, choose a fertilizer that also contains these micronutrients. Some mixes now come with slow-release fertilizers incorporated into the medium, and in these cases, the fertilizer analysis is usually included on the bag's label.

Most commercial mixes have ample lime added, so the pH should remain fairly stable over time. Soilless media perform well at a slightly acidic pH, so the lime requirements for these mixes are not as critical as for native garden soils. When in doubt about the fertility of a soilless mix, a soil test may be useful, but be sure to indicate that you have an artificial or greenhouse medium when submitting your samples. One positive trend in soilless media products is improved labeling on the bags. Many products now list all the ingredients and additives on the package (mixes with systemic insecticides added are always clearly labeled). If you have an understanding of what components do in a mix, then choosing the right product for your container gardening needs has never been easier.

SOILLESS POTTING MIX – WHAT IS A SOILLESS MIXTURE AND MAKING HOMEMADE SOILLESS MIX

Even with the healthiest of soils, dirt is still prone to carrying harmful bacteria and fungi. Soilless growing mediums, on the other hand, are usually cleaner and considered sterile, making them more popular with container gardeners.

WHAT IS A SOILLESS MIX?

Gardening with soilless potting mix does not include the use of soil. Instead, plants are grown in a variety of organic and inorganic materials. Using these materials rather than soil allows gardeners to grow healthier plants without the threat of soil-borne diseases. Plants grown in soilless mixes are also less likely to be bothered by pests.

TYPES OF SOILLESS GROWING MEDIUMS

Some of the most common soilless growing mediums include peat moss, perlite, vermiculite, and sand. Generally, these mediums are mixed together rather than used alone, as each usually provides its own function. Fertilizers are also commonly added to the mix, providing important nutrients.

- Sphagnum peat moss has a coarse texture but is lightweight and sterile. It promotes adequate aeration and holds water well. However, it's usually difficult to moisten on its own and is best used with other mediums. This growing medium is ideal for germinating seeds.

- Perlite is a form of expanded volcanic rock and is usually white in color. It provides good drainage, is lightweight, and holds air. Perlite should also be mixed with other mediums, like peat moss, since it does not retain water and will float to the top when plants are watered.
- Vermiculite is often used with or instead of perlite. This particular form of mica is more compact and, unlike perlite, does well at helping to retain water. On the other hand, vermiculite does not provide as good aeration as does the perlite.
- Coarse sand is another medium used in soilless mixes. Sand improves drainage and aeration but doesn't retain water.

In addition to these common mediums, other materials, such as bark and coconut coir, can be used. Bark is often added to improve drainage and promote air circulation. Depending on the type, it is reasonably lightweight. Coconut coir is similar to peat moss and works much the same way, only with less mess.

MAKE YOUR OWN SOILLESS MIX

While soilless potting mix is available at many garden centers and nurseries, you can also make your own soilless mix. A standard homemade soilless mix contains equal amounts of peat moss, perlite (and/or vermiculite), and sand. Bark can be used in lieu of sand, while coconut coir can replace peat moss. This is a personal preference. Small amounts of fertilizer and ground limestone should be added as well so the soilless mix will contain nutrients. There are numerous recipes for preparing soilless potting mixes online so you can easily find one to suit your individual needs.

USING SOIL AND SOIL MIXES

Well prepared garden soil is great for growing things in the ground but when it comes to growing things in containers, soil as you know it needs to be changed.

Soils for containers need to be well aerated and well drained while still being able to retain enough moisture for plant growth.

When choosing what to use to fill containers, never use garden soil by itself no matter how good it looks or how well things grow in it out in the garden. When put into a container both drainage and aeration are severely impeded, and the results are that plants grow poorly or not at all.

Soils for containers are always modified in some way to ensure proper drainage and aeration. Container soils are often referred to as soilless or artificial media, because they contain no soil at all. They are often composed of various things such as peat, vermiculite, bark, coir fiber (ground coconut hulls) in a variety of recipes depending on the manufacture and the type of plant material being grown. They can be found under a variety of trade names and in sizes ranging from a few quarts to bales that are many cubic feet in size. Sometimes the choice of media will be directed by what type of plants you are growing. Succulents, herbs, and perennials tend to prefer soils that are well drained and not retaining a lot of moisture over a long period of time. For them you might choose media that are courser in texture containing more bark, perlite or sand. For tropicals and foliage plants, you might choose a media with more peat and less course material as these plants tend to prefer moisture growing conditions.

When these mixes are used, they should be moistened slightly before planting. Fill a tub with the media, add water and lightly fluff the media to dampen it.

Garden soil can be used as a container media but it needs to be modified or amended. An acceptable soil based mix can be made by using one part garden soil, one part peat moss and one part perlite or coarse builders sand. Don't use fine beach sand or play sand.

This media has advantages and disadvantages. The disadvantage is that the soil you are using may contain insects, weed seeds and disease organisms. Soilless medias are generally free of these things. Soil based medias are heavier. This may be an advantage though especially if the containers are used in a very windy location and the extra weight will help keep the pot upright. Soil-based medias are also a bit more forgiving when it comes to water and fertility. They tend not to dry out as fast, and they also tend to hold on to nutrients longer. Because soilless medias can be a bit more costly, you could mix 25 percent soil with the soilless media to stretch your soilless media for a few more pots.

Also, can soilless media be reused from year to year? To a certain extent, yes. If the plants in the containers were healthy during the growing season with no major disease issues, you could remove the plant material at the end of the season and reuse the media next season. You may have to add some additional new media to fill the container. There will come a time when the media in the container will need to be replaced. Over the course of time, the organic materials that the soilless media is made from break down and decompose to the point where you will loose the drainage and aeration properties that are inherent in soilless container medias. When that happens, discard the media to the compost pile or to the garden and refill the container with fresh media.

There are also bagged products labeled as top soil that tend to be largely sedge peat. While they are inexpensive and look very good, once put into a pot they are poorly drained and poorly aerated. They can be used in combination with soilless media products or amended much the same way as if you were using garden soil. When filling containers with media, don't fill the pot to the top. Leave about a one inch space between the top of the soil and rim of the pot. This will help make watering the pot easier as it provides a place to "put water" and not have it run over the edge.

Filling very large containers can be costly especially when using commercially prepared media. To reduce the cost and also the weight of the container consider adding "filler" to the bottom of the container to take up space. Many things can be used, but they should be something that is inert, able to take up space and not break down over the course of the growing season. While there are inserts made for this purpose, there are a lot of home products that can be recycled for this use.

Items such as crushed aluminum cans, plastic milk jugs, and non-biodegradable "packing peanuts" are usually readily available. Fill the bottom one-quarter to one-third of the container with your choice of material. Lay a piece of landscape fabric over the top of the material and fill the rest of the container with media. The filler takes up space the landscape fabric keeps the soil from infiltrating the filler while allowing water to pass through, and there is still ample space for roots to grow.

SOILLESS MIXES & AMENDMENTS

The basic component of soilless mixes is sphagnum peat moss. The various amendments added to each mix include , coir, vermiculite, dolomitic limestone, fertilizer, trace elements, perlite, wetting agents, gypsum, rock wool, calcine clay, and pine bark. There are several manufacturers who blend these materials together to produce a range of special purpose mixes for greenhouses, nurseries, and gardeners. These mixes are quite variable across North America because of shipping costs. That is, the constituents are variable in nature, and there use will be heaviest in the region of their origin. Some of the popular brands include Terra-Lite, Metro Mix, Sunshine, and Pro-Mix. Each mix comes in several grades, the difference lying in the percentage of each of the amendments. This article is directed to recreational gardeners who are sowing seeds indoors or in a hobby greenhouse, are looking for the best seed sowing medium and the latest technique.

Germination mix, plug mix, and starter mix are the terms applied to mixes formulated for seed germination. Other formulations include growing mix, rock wool mix, bark mix (high porosity), and bark mix (low porosity). For your suitability testing of product, stick to those mixes labeled germination, plug, or starter. These mixes usually include the peat moss/bark/coir mixture plus perlite, vermiculite, dolomitic limestone, and a wetting agent. Some germination mixes will also include some fertilizer and trace elements. Fertilizer and trace elements are not required for seed germination. I prefer a mix without them, however I do use a weak fertilizer solution at initial sowing. The characteristics of a germination mix include a high water capacity (about 86%), an air capacity of 12 to 15%, and a Ph about 5.8 From this basic mix, you can custom make your own formulation.

BARK:

Southern pine bark and Northern softwoods are usually employed to increase bulk density and increase air space. In addition, bark will slightly reduce the water holding capacity of the mix, and there is some evidence that bark imparts some disease resistance. Bark is usually described as aged bark or as composted bark. Insufficient aging or composting could result in excessive heating of the mix or draw excessive nitrogen, but these materials are usually tested thoroughly before use by reputible companies. The fertilizer level of these mixes are usually amended with additional nitrogen. I do not use bark mixes for seed germination, but find them attractive for potting-on in several cases.

COIR:

(pronounced "choir" as in church choir) Coir dust is a by-product of the coconut fiber industry and is used in mixes to lessen the amount of peat required. It has a high air and water holding capacity. Its nutrient-holding capacity is a bit less than peat, but it does contain significantly higher levels of soluble salts. The use of coir dust as a component of germination and plug mixes is dictated by the high cost of shipping peat down South.

PERLITE:

Perlite is a natural heat expanded volcanic mineral that is chemically inert, and will not alter the nutrient quality or the Ph of the material with which it is mixed. The particles provide excellent drainage, while trapping air and water on their irregular surfaces. Perlite is usually sold in 4 cu. ft. bags for less than $10 by suppliers to the greenhouse and nursery industries, most of whom will also sell at retail. Perlite is available in fine, medium, and coarse grades.

The higher the total porosity of the mix, the greater the potential for providing water and air. Oxygen is essential to healthy root activity, but not more essential than moisture. Practical boundaries are 75% perlite/25% peat moss for lowest wet bulk density and 25% perlite/75% peat moss for highest wet bulk density. Finer grades of perlite decrease porosity of the mix, while coarse grades increase porosity. For ease of transplanting tender seedlings, adequate levels of aeration and moisture, I have been using the coarse grade of perlite. It provides the additional benefit of maximum root oxegenation.

Added to your germination mix, perlite will improve drainage and may reduce the cost of the overall mix. Outdoors, perlite performs similarly to help hold nutrients from leaching in sandy soil and to improve aeration and drainage in heavy clay soils. It can also be used as an insulating winter mulch if covered with about 2 inches of soil.

VERMICULITE:

Vermiculite is a mica-type material that is mixed and heated to cause the accordion like particles to expand. This expansion makes them capable of holding large amounts of plant available water and nutrients. As a seed covering, it helps maintain sufficient moisture at the growing medium surface for germination. Available in fine, medium, and coarse grades, I usually select the medium grade, but rarely have use for this material except in potted plants. Vermiculite is usually sold in 4 cu. ft. bags for less than $12. Caution: Vermiculite is available at home centers and building supply companies as an additive for plaster and insulation in walls and ceilings. Do not use these products for soil conditioning. Construction grades of vermiculite do not absorb water well and are not handled properly during the manufacturing process to maintain a sterile product. Make sure that the bag is labeled “horticultural.” There are three basic uses for vermiculite. Added to your germination mix, it will improve water retention and may reduce the cost of the overall mix. Finally, when added to sandy soil in the garden, water retention is greatly improved. I prefer to use this material in potted plants only or in situations where seedling development time is long, as in bulb forming plants.

WETTING AGENTS:

This is where the commercial mixes become distinguishable, one from another. Wetting agents are water absorbing polymers available in gel, liquid, or powder form. The amount of wetting agent added to your germination mix determines the ability of the mix to absorb water from the bottom. Watering seedlings from the bottom is one of several techniques used to reduce the incidence of damping-off. Therefore, I make bottom absorption my number one criteria in evaluating a commercial germination mix, and do not have to add wetting agents myself. They can be purchased to improve homebrew mixes, and make an excellent additive in gel form when repotting indoor plants. Peat and bark progressively lose their ability to retain and uniformly distribute water and chemicals to the rootzone. Wetting agents available from your distributor may include:

GRANITE GRIT:

Sifted crushed granite is used as a feed additive to help birds and poultry to grind their food (since they don't have molars). My feathered friends get theirs from the eave gutters where the grit from the roofing shingles tend to collect. It is sold in feed stores in three grades. Chick grit (or chicken starter grit) is the fine (smallest) grade. The bags are labeled "starter" or "fine", hence the name Chick grit. This is the size used as a seed topping. The next larger size is labeled "grower" or "special pullet". The largest size is about the size of a pea and carries the label "large" or "coarse" depending upon the supplier. Cost in the Chicago area is about $4.75 for 50 lb. bag. Chick grit is sometimes added to the germination mix to improve drainage, especially for alpines, but is usually used as a seed topping.

Other forms of chick starter grit are manufactured from oyster shell or calcium carbonate and can be used in the same manner, with some reservation as to longevity and the amount of long-term calcium release when the product is used for creating alpine soils. These are also offered in screened sizes and labeled in the same manner as granite grit. The "starter size" or "chick grit" of both of the above products is slightly smaller and lighter than granite grit, and therefore suitable for topping smaller seeds. Similarly, other products marketed under the names Terra-Green or Turface are inert sterile calcined mineral absorbent (high temperature processed ground up clay) which may be used as a seed topping or in mixes requiring "sharp" drainage. Certain grades of silica sand, bank sand, and kitty-litter are also used in these applications, but I would experiment with them very sparingly. A fine grade of aquarium gravel would be suitable too, but expensive. In some areas, granite grit may not be available due to freight costs, and you may find grit made from "quartzite". This substitute has proven itself the equivalent of granite grit in my own operation.

ADJUSTING YOUR MIX:

The germination mix I use is Sunshine #5 which is called a "plug mix". It contains sufficient wetting agent for excellent bottom absorption when watering. Regional distribution across North America may not be even. In every area, there will be at least one good brand which offers at least one formulation that will be satisfactory. Finding the best starter mix for you involves searching and testing. Many suppliers will release one lb. samples for this purpose.

Because these mixes are relatively expensive ($15 to $23 for 4 cu. ft. compressed bale) and because Canadian sphagnum peat moss is not a renewable resource, I prefer to cut the prepared mix with cheaper sterile additives which improve the mix to my needs while lowering the average cost, a little. I add four parts plug mix to two parts perlite and perhaps one half part vermiculite. Sometimes, the seeds have special requirements, and I will make up a special mix just for them. For example, when sowing Lisianthus, the seed company recommends three parts mix plus seven parts perlite. If I know in advance that a particular seedling is sensitive to damping-off, I will combine four parts mix with two or three parts perlite, and dispense with the vermiculite. Potted plants in the sun need more moisture retention, so I will increase the percentage of vermiculite, etc. Adjusting your basic mix is a matter of "feel" based on your experience. In some applications, I will add one or two parts of grit to the soil mix for plants requiring "sharp" drainage.

SEED SOWING TECHNIQUE:

The fewer the number of seeds you plan to start, the greater the number of seed starting systems available for purchase. As you increase your seed starting plans over the years, more and more of those seed starting systems become inadequate. The pots and trays that I use are suitable to the scale at which I operate, that is, the sowing of 300 to 400 packets of seed per year. There are recreational gardeners sowing anywhere from 1 to 2000 packets of seed per year. At some point, you will discover the need to sow seeds in communal rather than individual pots, especially where considerable numbers of seed types need conditioning before germination. Therefore, the method I describe is peculiar to the scale of my hobby, and may not be suitable for many gardeners.

My communal pots are 3.5 inch square pots which are four inches deep. The pot is filled with mix to a 3 inch depth, and tamped down lightly. Nine to thirty seeds are sown on top of the mix, and covered with 1/16th inch to 1/4 inch of grit, depending upon the diameter of the seed. Larger seeds get the heaviest topping. Seeds requiring light for germination are sown on top of 1/8 inch of grit, and watered into the topping and covered thinly with a very light dusting of oyster shell. The "starter" or chick grit size of oyster shell is basically powder. It has the advantage over silica sand in that it never cakes up. The pots are placed in a tepid water bath until the topping is fully moistened. Since these pots are disposable types, they are labeled on the sides with a pressure sensitive label showing plant identification, germination temperature, and growing-on temperature. The seeds are sown from the palm of my left hand. That is, the seed stock is placed there, and with the blade of a tiny pen knife, I pickup a one to four seeds at a time so that they can be distributed in the nine imaginary sowing squares in each pot. To control the distribution of very fine seeds, it is important to me to pick up exactly the number of seeds to be dropped into each sowing area. I never broadcast sow.

After germination, the pots are moved to the proper location for growing-on temperature. As soon as the seedlings have their first or second set of true leaves, depending upon vigor, they are transplanted to individual 2 1/4 inch seedling pots. When the leaves of each plant begin to interfere with plants in adjacent pots, the seedlings are transplanted to 3 1/2 inch, then 5 inch, 6 inch, or 8 inch pots as necessary to maintain constant vegetative growth until it is time for setting out. Additional grit is applied as topping with each transplant to prevent the growth of algae and mosses, and to protect the crowns of the seedlings from excessive moisture. In climates where algal growth on the seed topping is excessive, you can use a product called Agribrom misted onto the topping at the rate of 15ppm. The additional medium added during transplanting to accomodate larger pots is the same germination mix through transfer to 3 1/2 inch pots. For transfer to larger size pots the additional medium added during transplanting is potting mix. My potting mix is composed of 1/3rd germination mix plus 1/3rd compost plus 1/3rd garden soil. There are many variations of this practice for seed conditioning and special requirements.

After the first transplant, the seedlings need nutrients and trace elements. The trays are watered from a solution which I make up in 1/2 gallon plastic bottles containing one half tablespoon of household vinegar and 1/8th to 1/4 teaspoon of general purpose fertilizer. The purpose of the vinegar is to make a slight adjustment in Ph since my water supply tests out at 7.6 on average. Again, there are many variations on this practice based on the Ph preference of each type of plant. Seedling trays are moved to protected positions out of doors, under the carport, in the greenhouse, on the patio, etc. as soon as possible.

The following is excerpted from the practice of a popular nursery owner in Southern Illinois:

"I use Scott's Pro Metro Mix. I sift it for seed sowing to remove the large bark pieces through a 1/2 inch screen. Nothing added, unless I am doing alpines, in which case, I add 1/2 part grit. My transplant mix is one part Metro mix, one part peat, 1/2 part vermiculite, 1/2 part perlite, and one gallon of silica sand for each 3 cu. ft. bag of mix. For alpines, I add more perlite and some grit.

I use grit as a pot topping for seed growing. One of the main reasons is to control the various fungal diseases grouped under the general heading of damp-off. Seedlings come up through the grit easily, and since it dries quickly, and doesn't hold much moisture, the incidence of damp-off is much less than when using moisture retentive substances such as vermiculit or sphagnum. It also helps to control the growth of lichen and moss under the lights. I also use it on cuttings. In addition, I use grit as a top dressing on those plants that dislike moisture around the crowns. Most of those are rock garden plants.

If the seeds need light, just cover the post with a very light layer of grit, just until you can't see the soil. For very fine seeds, such as begonia or campanula, I sow the seeds on top, then use a fine mist sprayer to wash the seeds down into the grit. I also find it useful, when sowing like this, to sprinkle a very thin layer of white silica sand to help hold in moisture. Just as with other seed toppings, you can eventually tell by looking what pots need watering. The grit does not stay completely dry, and as with soil, changes color when the pots begin to get dry. I find that the watering is on a much more regular basis with grit as a topping. Almost all of the pots dry out in the same intervals. I end up watering indoor sown seedling pots about twice per month. I also mist them once a day with a mist setting on the hose sprayer to help break up the seed coats which sometimes prevent the cotyledons from getting free."

The following is the sowing procedure described by a nursery owner in Michigan:

"We sow almost everything in Sunshine mix which we mix with perlite, one part sunshine to two parts perlite. We fill flats in advance and water before we sow the seeds. All seed is sown directly on the surface and covered with a layer of chick starter grit, this goes a long way to prevent damping-off problems. Sow on the surface and cover to several times the thickness of the seed with fine thick grit; with very fine seed, pots should be gritted first and the seed should be sown on top of the grit and watered down into it.

Keep moist but do not over-water. Fungicides are no substitute for good culture and in general it is best to avoid them. We rarely have damping-off problems and do not routinely spray fungicides to prevent it. Chick grit and care in watering is the best prevention. Be sure to use a thick enough layer to inhibit moss growth.

Difficult species are almost always best sown in a minimally heated white, not clear, poly-covered greenhouse. Easy species can be done under clear poly or fluorescent lights. White poly-covered cold frames should work well on a small scale, or better still build a small Nearing Frame. Seeds that need multiple 40-70 cycles are best placed in the refrigerator vegetable drawer in a ziploc bag with sunshine mix. This works better than baggies and towel for most species. We routinely extend the cycle time on the species Norm Deno lists as multicycle germinators. This is very helpful.

Freezing is seldom necessary or helpful, it will crack seed coats but there are better ways to do it. Freezing in household freezers is much too abrupt and may rupture membranes killing the seed. If you must freeze, place seed in a coldframe outdoors in the fall. Seed can be stored in the freezer for extended periods but only if the moisture content is very low. In general this is not recommended. Remember for many species extended dry storage is actually beneficial with old seed germinating much better than fresh seed.

Seeds requiring GA3 can either be placed on coffee filters soaked in the appropriate concentration of GA3 (1000 ppm is a good place to start) and the seedlings pricked off as the radicle emerges, or sown in flats and misted with a one time application. You can also soak larger seeds until they swell and then sow out. Keep concentrations as low as possible to reduce stretch problems.

We fertilize young seedling with a soluble balanced fertilizer at every watering (250 ppm total nitrogen) which is higher than generally recommended but the plants thrive on it. No burn problems at all, with a bit more fertilizer most plants will be more likely to outcompete the mosses which generally dislike high fertility media. Water until runoff and let flats dry out between watering. Beware of high pH In the water. We killed a ton of stuff due to this. We now adjust our water pH to 5.6-6.0 by injecting battery acid directly into the irrigation water along with the fertilizer. Buy a portable pH pen – it's well worth the investment, pH-induced iron chlorosis is an insidious problem. Plants weakened by it quickly fall victim to fungus gnats and aphids. Algae and fungus gnat problems are also less severe if flats are allowed to dry out a bit, it's a very fine line.

Properly dry flats will be flattened when you water but show little sign of wilting before the water hits them, and will recover quickly with no tip burn. Be patient, the only thing to do with some species is to sow and wait for a couple of years. Don't kill shade-lovers by placing in full sun. Be careful of high light levels, even sun-tolerant plants may be sensitive as seedlings and it's easy to crispy the little ones. Many seeds will germinate immediately with the majority coming up a year or more later. Often the early germinators turn out to be the weakest plants. We often weed out the early stragglers to wait for the main flush of germination. Don't throw away seed pots for at least four years on the long germinators. Before you trash a pot dig around and find a seed and cut it in half — if it hasn't rotted then it will germinate eventually.

There are many formulas for success but the most important ingredient is patience. Don't let your seed pot dry to dust, and don't let them get soggy and moss covered — if they do carefully cut off the moss layer leaving the seed behind and regrit and wait some more. It in doubt about what to do, think about what would happen in nature and try to emulate it. This is a great help in determining whether to start cold or warm."

POTTING MIXES FOR ORGANIC GROWERS

Soilless potting mixes have long been used for greenhouse production of bedding plants, vegetable transplants and container-grown ornamentals. By avoiding the use of topsoil, the risk pathogenic microorganisms in this media may be reduced, avoiding problems with diseases like damping-off. In addition, topsoil is relatively heavy and dense so it can contribute to poor aeration and drainage in a potting mix. Soil-less mixes should be formulated to have optimal physical and chemical properties that promote germination and healthy seedling growth.

Qualities of a good mix. Poor performance in a potting mix is costly, since greenhouse space is expensive and so is having to toss out some seedlings or replant entirely. Optimal mix characteristics include the right density and porosity to provide good aeration and also good water holding capacity; proper pH and enough available nutrients to get plants off to a good start, and the absence of excess salts and plant pathogens. On organic farms, the mix must not contain any prohibited ingredients.

Organic vs. conventional mixes. Generally speaking, all soilless potting mixes contain a 'base' ingredient, usually sphagnum peat, or sometime coir. These provide a good physical environment for root growth but are relatively inert in terms of nutrient content and biological activity. Other materials may be added to improve drainage, adjust density and/or alter water holding capacity, such as perlite, vermiculite or builder's sand. Ground limestone may be needed to raise the pH. Fertilizers are added to provide available nutrients and obviously that's where conventional and organic mixes differ. In addition, organic mixes typically contain mature compost to provide slow release nutrients and contribute to good physical and biological conditions for plant growth, whereas conventional mixes rarely contain compost.

Issues with compost in potting mix. In some ways, compost is like snowflakes – no two batches of compost are exactly alike. So while compost usually adds value to a potting mix, it can also add a measure of uncertainty about performance that is not the case with conventional mixes. Immature compost in particular can harm seedlings by releasing ammonia, or tying up nitrogen, or stunting growth because of organic acids that have not fully decomposed. To avoid these problems it is important to use only mature compost, and to buy it from a reputable source or to carefully make your own using a consistent supply of high quality ingredients.

It's a good idea to keep organic potting mixes warm and moist for a week or two before planting into them. That allows microbial activity to kick in, and can reduce potential potting mix problems by allowing excess ammonium or organic acids to dissipate.

Compost is rarely used by itself as a potting medium. Compost alone does not have the optimal water holding characteristics, and soluble salt levels may be higher than optimal for potting mix. Plus, high quality compost can be relatively expensive so it makes sense to dilute it with other ingredients like peat. Organic potting mixes are typically made with 20% to 50% compost by volume, depending on the type of crop that will be grown in the mix, the container size, and the growing conditions.

Common potting mix ingredients. Sphagnum peat moss is a stable organic material that holds 15 to 30 times its weight in water and decomposes very slowly. It contains about 1% N but little is released because it breaks down so slowly. It has a pH of about 4 so lime must be added to the mix to along with sphagnum peat, at the rate of 8.5 lb. per cubic yard of peat to neutralize the acidity.

Coir comes from coconut husks and is a waste product of the coco fiber industry. It has physical properties much like peat but a higher pH of about 6. It holds up to nine times its weight in water. It can have a high salt content.

Limestone is either calcitic (high calcium) or dolomitic (high magnesium; both are used to increase the pH of a mix but dolomite is preferable for supplying both Ca and Mg.

Vermiculite helps hold water and fertilizer in the potting mix, and it also contains some calcium and magnesium. It has a pH near neutral. Vermiculite comes in different grades; medium grade is usually used for starting seeds, a coarse grade may be used for larger plants.

Perlite is a volcanic rock that has been heated and expanded. It is lightweight, sterile and has a neutral pH. It can be used to improve reduce the weight of a potting mix and increase its aeration and drainage.

Coarse washed sand also called builder's sand can be used to add air space to the potting mix and increase its weight. It has a neutral pH and provides almost no fertility to plants. Sand may be used when added weight is needed for growing tall or top heavy plants that might fall over if grown in a lightweight mix.

Fertilizers for organic mixes. In some cases, compost can provide adequate amounts of nutrients for transplant production but usually some fertilizer is added to the mix, especially if larger plants are to be produced or if small cell sizes are used that will require relatively high levels of available nutrients in order to sustain plant growth over time. Common organic fertilizers to provide phosphorus include bone meal, bone char or rock phosphate; potassium can be provided by potassium sulfate, sul-po-mag or greensand; magnesium can come from epsom salts or sul-po-mag. In some cases a blended fertilizer may be used such as pelletized chicken manure compost but such materials are usually reserved for field use rather than potting mix due to their slower nutrient availability.

Nitrogen availability. Assuring sufficient N in a form plants can use is often a concern with organic potting mix formulations, as N release may be quite variable depending on the compost that's used and the extent to which it is source of nitrogen. Most organic potting mixes are supplemented with fertilizers sources such as blood meal, crab meal, fish meal, or plant meals like alfalfa or soybean to provide additional N to feed plants for several weeks or months. Note that Chilean nitrate is expected to be prohibited for use in organic production sometime in 2012.

Some growers water with fish emulsion or other soluble organic N fertilizers to keep their transplants 'growing on' if a mix has run out of available nitrogen. Re-potting some plants, like tomato seedlings, into fresh mix is another way to keep them growing well.

When using blood meal, partially composted manure or poultry-manure based fertilizer be aware that these high N sources need some time to allow for microbial activity start breaking the organic forms of N and drive them to nitrate (the process called mineralization). If planted into too soon, when first wetted and just starting to break down, these materials may give off ammonia, organic acids and other compounds that can damage germinating seeds and young plants. It is best to moisten the potting mix at least a week or two before you plant into it, making sure it stays warm and allowing time for phytotoxic compounds to dissipate.

Many things can lead to poor germination, including a mix with excess salts, improper pH, unfinished compost, or nutrient imbalances. Old seeds, improper watering, and root disease can also be to blame.

Avoiding performance problems. While many growers have had success with compost-based potting mixes, the performance of such mixes, whether commercially produced or homemade, has sometimes been inconsistent. In the worst cases, growers have experienced significant financial loss due to poor seedling growth associated with a problem mix.

Poor seedling growth in compost-based mixes can result from low levels of available nutrients, high levels of soluble salts, excessive density of the mix, and/or the lingering presence of the harmful byproducts of initial decomposition mentioned above. In some cases the problem is not due to the mix but to management issues, like cold temperatures, improper watering or root disease.

Test your mix. It is a very good idea to test your organic potting mix well in advance of using it. Send a sample to a soil test lab at a land grant university or at a private company that specializes in horticulture. Do not request a regular field soil test, since potting mixes differ from field soil; they are much higher in organic matter and usually much higher in available nutrient content. A potting soil test will also measure soluble salts (electrical conductivity) and nitrogen in the nitrate and ammonium forms, which a field soil test doesn't.

ANALYSIS OF SATURATION EXTRACT

pH: 6.9
Soluble Salts (mS/cm): 2.27

Macronutrients	mg/L
Nitrate-N (NO3-N):	162
Ammonium-N (NH4-N):	3
Phosphorus (P):	8
Potassium (K):	112
Calcium (Ca):	211
Magnesium (Mg):	116
Sulfur (S):	96

Micronutrients	mg/L
Zinc (Zn):	0.04
Boron (B):	0.18
Manganese (Mn):	0.04
Copper (Cu):	0.10
Iron (Fe):	0.69
Sodium (Na):	83.19

Growers should use the low cost saturated media extract test (aslo called greenhouse media test), to get data on the pH, soluble salt, and nutrient levels of their potting mix well in advance of planting. Here are the results of one sample.

The soil test to use for potting mixes is the saturated media extract (SME), also called a greenhouse media test or soilless media test. Unlike field soil tests that extract nutrients with weak acid solutions, the SME sample is mixed with distilled water at a standard dilution and then analyzed. Since different labs may use different dilutions, stick with one lab. To get an accurate reading, be sure that the potting mix has been moist and warm for at least a week prior to sampling.

Most labs require a pint of mix to work with, and turnaround time is similar to a regular soil test, a week or two.

It's a good idea to test each batch of potting mix, and to be able to compare results from mixes that performed well to those that didn't. The cost is low, about \$15 or \$20 per SME sample.

Table 1. General information guidelines for greenhouse growth media analyzed by the Saturated Media Extract (SME) method.

Analysis	*CATEGORY*				
	Low	*Acceptable*	*Optimum*	*High*	*Very High*
Soluble Salt, mS/cm	0-.75	.75-2.0	2.0-3.5	3.5-5.0	5.0+
Nitrate-N, ppm	0-39	40-99	100-199	200-299	300+
Phosphorus, ppm	0-2	3-5	6-9	11-18	19+
Potassium, ppm	0-59	60-149	150-249	250-349	350+
Calcium, ppm	0-79	80-199	200+	-	-
Magnesium, ppm	0-29	30-69	70+	-	-

The information in this table was developed at Michigan State University in the 1980's. Keep in mind that some crops such as herbs are more sensitive to salts and require lower nutrient levels for good growth than other crops like tomatoes which can tolerate more salts and will respond to higher nutrient levels.

'Bioassays' are another way to test the quality of a potting mix. All you have to do is sow some fast-growing crops in the mix several weeks before you plan to use it. Cress, oats, beans are just a few to consider. Some growers also like to test their mixes with slower-growing crops. Onions can be useful for bioassays as they seem to require a very high quality mix for good germination and growth. It makes sense to include any key crops that you grow as part of your bioassay.

Compare potting mixes. Without a side by side trial, it's hard to evaluate the relative performance of your current potting mix. So even if you have one you like, plant a few trays of the same seeds using another potting mix brand or recipe. It may surprise you to see how poorly your plants do next to a different formulation.

If things go wrong. Go ahead and submit sample(s) for SME testing; better late than never. Having this data in hand is part of the process of elimination to identify the problem. Is the pH off? Are soluble salts too high? Is there sufficient available N for plant growth? Once you have that data in hand, contact your potting mix supplier and ask if others growers have reported problems. A good supplier will appreciate communication from their customers, and be able to provide technical advice.

"Buying potting mix from a company like ours means you are buying into a network of organic growers" says Karl Hammer, owner of Vermont Compost Company. "That has great value for both buyers and sellers of the product. Sometimes I get a call about a problem but when I follow up with other growers using the same mix to grow the same crops I find that they have no issues. Then it's probably related to a greenhouse management practice. In fact, ninety percent of the problems I see have to do with over-watering in short daylight and cold weather conditions. Overwatering cools the growing medium, reducing microbial activity and root growth, and it can leach out available nutrients. It's much better keep your growing medium on the dry side, and if possible, provide bottom heat. Over-the-top watering by hand with cold water creates a lot of plant growth problems in organic potting mixes."

WHY USE SOILLESS MIXTURES?

There's a lot of focus these days on grow mediums, and one common misconception for new growers centers upon soil and soilless mixtures. To start, real Earth topsoil is rarely used indoors anymore. Still, people refer to soil-replacements as soil, creating some confusion among newer growers. In reality these mediums are artificial soils – or soilless mediums.

Soilless mediums are mixtures that look and feel almost identical to real soil, but are usually peat- or sphagnum-based. These mixtures also have added organic amendments such as coco-coir, perlite or wood chips to help aerate the medium and retain moisture for plants. They also sometimes have mild organic nutrients, beneficial microbial agents, or mycorrhizae (fungi) added in for better plant health. The primary difference between soil and soilless mixtures comes down to their ability to retain water, oxygen and nutrient ions. These molecules all have electrical charges that help the root system absorb them as needed. These charges are often referred to as the CEC or "cation exchange capacity" (also referred to as EC, or electrical conductivity).

In the same way, grow mediums also have electrical charges. These charges in the medium will dictate how much nutrient and minerals the root system can absorb. In real soil, humus and certain other organic particles have high electrical charges or CEC. This means that the soil does not want to easily give up their minerals or moisture molecules to the plant.

As real soil dries out, it will retain water even more tightly. As plants need more water, soil begins to hold onto more of it and the plant must use extra energy to absorb it. This is not the case with soilless mediums.

Peat, sphagnum or coco-coir mixtures create soilless mediums that have extremely different CEC levels. In fact, most of them are inert, with zero CEC. This means that nutrients, water and gases such as oxygen (remember, the roots breath in O2, while the plant above ground breathes in CO2) are more readily available for uptake by the roots when the plant calls for them. It also means the plant will utilize more of what you feed your medium, converting nutrients and water into sugars during photosynthesis. Better uptake in the root zone results in better yields, as well as more resin and terpenoid production (i.e., higher potency and better flavor).

Best Uses for Soilless Mediums While soilless mixtures offer easy passage of nutrient solutions to the root system, this loss of buffering can be dangerous for grow systems that use heavy doses of nutrients. Still, these mediums offer better buffering than most hydroponic mediums such as Rockwool or clay-pellets. Because of this, soilless mediums are generally not recommended for big hydro set-ups such as flood-and-drain tables – not to mention, the medium is too unstable and fluid for such a system. Instead, these artificial soils are best suited for top-feed systems that utilize separate containers for each plant site.

Top-feed systems generally use stake emitters that plug easily into soilless mediums. These emitters may be drip-emitters or spray-emitters, drawing water from reservoirs like any hydroponic system would. Soilless mixtures are also great for smaller gardens at home where growers hand-water daily.

These mediums also over great flexibility and allow growers to customize their blends with various amendments. Many advanced growers and commercial operations tend to chose soilless mixtures as they can custom order mixtures or create their own easily at industrial facilities. Popular store brands of soilless mixes include Sunshine.

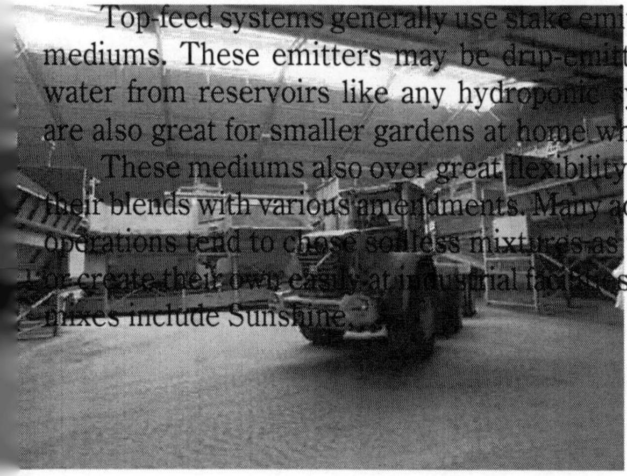

2

Hydroponic Gardening

INTRODUCTION TO HYDROPONICS

When most people think of gardening, soil comes to mind. But plants don't actually require it to survive. They mostly need the nutrients and minerals in the soil. Plants can grow in water, gravel, perlite, rice hulls, pine bark, cedar shavings, and other mediums, or even suspended in air.

The science of soilless gardening is called hydroponics. It may sound like something devised in a modern laboratory, but it's been around for thousands of years. The essential ingredient is an oxygenated mineral-nutrient solution that's circulated through plants' roots.

Some scholars theorize the ancient Hanging Gardens of Babylon, one of the Seven Wonders of the World, was a hydroponic system. The Aztecs grew maize, squash, beans, amaranth, tomatoes, chili peppers, and flowers in high-output *chinampas*, or floating gardens, which were hydroponic systems. A traditional hydroponics system is still in use on Myanmar's Inle Lake, and similar systems probably existed in ancient India, Greece, China, and Egypt.

In the early 1600s, the British scientist Sir Francis Bacon, father of the scientific method, conducted formal research on hydroponics, which he called "water culture." Laboratory experiments continued into the 20th century. In 1937, William F. Gericke applied the experiments to large-scale commercial applications, and the modern hydroponics movement was born.

Today many people identify hydroponics with marijuana growers, who've made use of the technology. But much of the world's greenhouse produce is now grown in hydroponics systems, including some of the lettuce, tomatoes, herbs, and veggies in many supermarkets' refrigerated cases.

WHY HYDROPONICS?

Growing food without dirt, earthworms, and, sometimes, sunshine may go against common ideas of where healthy food comes from. But hydroponics has taken off for good reason. It offers a number of benefits over traditional soil methods and it may even help solve some of the world's growing problems.

Water Conservation Agriculture currently uses 80 percent of the fresh water consumed in the U.S. and 60 percent of it worldwide. Meanwhile a water scarcity crisis currently plagues every continent, particularly arid regions such as the American West. With a name like hydroponics, it seems soilless systems would use a lot of water. However, on average, hydroponic systems use 10 times less water than soil agriculture because they recirculate fluids and cut waste. In the hope that soilless agriculture will help prevent worldwide water wars in the next century, the National Nuclear Security Agency built a hydroponics greenhouse in New Mexico's Sandia Laboratory to test the feasibility of growing forage crops for livestock with hydroponics.

LAND CONSERVATION

Water is not the only resource in short supply. Many countries, including Great Britain, may face a significant shortage of farmland in the next two decades. Some studies estimate crop yield must double by 2050 to meet projected demands, and scientists warn that will not happen if current trends continue. In the past we've cleared forests and grasslands to plant crops, with grave environmentalconsequences. What if there's a better way?

Some futurists, including microbiologist Dickson Despommier, are convinced hydroponics is the answer. In soilless systems, roots don't need to stretch out as much because they're supplied with all the nutrients they need. Crop yields are typically higher and more stable, and artificial lighting makes year-round crops possible. It currently takes a land area the size of Virginia to produce food for New York City. Despommier envisions cities feeding themselves with vertical skyscraper greenhouses. "If vertical farming in urban centers becomes the norm," Despommier says, "then one anticipated long-term benefit would be the gradual repair of many of the world's damaged ecosystems through the systematic abandonment of farmland."

LESS PESTICIDE USE AND RUNOFF POLLUTION

Agriculture is the leading cause of water quality problems in the U.S., and pesticides, including endocrine-disrupting atrazine, currently contaminate our watersheds and drinking water. Many hydroponic farmers use zero herbicides or pesticides, and any system with the potential to curb pesticide use is important. Because plants experience less stress and are fed optimally, they're healthy enough to resist any pests able to enter the greenhouse. Alternatively, organic methods can control pest infestations. Weeds are not an issue with hydroponics, since they need soil to grow.

FOOD SAFETY

We've all gotten used to headlines about deadly E.coli outbreaks. Twenty-three percent of foodborne illness deaths and 46 percent of foodborne illnesses are linked to eating produce, according to the Center for Disease and Prevention.

Soil polluted by livestock waste is often pinpointed as the cause. Because hydroponic systems are sterile and don't have soil to be contaminated, disease outbreaks are less likely, especially in clean, well-run systems. (However, hydroponics does not completely eliminate the risk of foodborne illness. Proper precautions are warranted.)

LOWER FOOD MILES

An eat-local movement has erupted across the country. Local produce is usually more nutritious, since vitamin content is depleted by light, temperature, and time. Moreover, local food doesn't require the expense and energy expenditure of long-distance trucking. But how can people grow food in dense urban centers or inhospitable climates? Hydroponics may be the answer.

Take Emory University for example. The lettuce the school used to serve in their cafeteria had been trucked 3,000 miles before the students ate it. Students built a hydroponics system and now greens are grown 10 feet from the salad bar.

A number of companies, including New York-based BrightFarms, grow tomatoes, greens, and herbs hydroponically on the roofs of grocery stores. The supermarkets sign a contract to partner with BrightFarms for ten years, and in exchange, they're able to sell the freshest, just-picked produce and eliminate some of their transportation costs.

Emory's experiment and the growing number of partnerships between hydroponics companies and supermarkets indicate soilless agriculture may provide more local food choices in the future.

HISTORY

The earliest published work on growing terrestrial plants without soil was the 1627 book *Sylva Sylvarum* by Francis Bacon, printed a year after his death. Water culture became a popular research technique after that. In 1699, John Woodwardpublished his water culture experiments with spearmint. He found that plants in less-pure water sources grew better than plants in distilled water. By 1842, a list of nine elements believed to be essential for plant growth had been compiled, and the discoveries of the German botanists Julius von Sachs and Wilhelm Knop, in the years 1859-65, resulted in a development of the technique of soilless cultivation. Growth of terrestrial plants without soil in mineral nutrient solutions was called solution culture. It quickly became a standard research and teaching technique and is still widely used today. Solution culture is now considered a type of hydroponics where there is no inert medium.

In 1929, William Frederick Gericke of the University of California at Berkeley began publicly promoting that solution culture be used for agricultural crop production. He first termed it aquaculture but later found that aquaculture was already applied to culture of aquatic organisms. Gericke created a sensation by growing tomato vines twenty-five feet high in his back yard in mineral nutrient solutions rather than soil. He introduced the term hydroponics, water culture, in 1937, proposed to him by W. A. Setchell, a phycologistwith an extensive education in the classics.

Reports of Gericke's work and his claims that hydroponics would revolutionize plant agriculture prompted a huge number of requests for further information. Gericke had been denied use of the University's greenhouses for his experiments due to the administration's skepticism, and when the University tried to compel him to release his preliminary nutrient recipes developed at home he requested greenhouse space and time to improve them using appropriate research facilities. While he was eventually provided greenhouse space, the University assigned Hoagland and Arnon to re-develop Gericke's formula and show it held no benefit over soil grown plant yields, a view held by Hoagland. In 1940, he published the book, *Complete Guide to Soil less Gardening,* after leaving his academic position in a climate that was politically unfavorable.

Two other plant nutritionists at the University of California were asked to research Gericke's claims. Dennis R. Hoagland and Daniel I. Arnon wrote a classic 1938 agricultural bulletin, *The Water Culture Method for Growing Plants Without Soil,*. Hoagland and Arnon claimed that hydroponic crop yields were no better than crop yields with good-quality soils. Crop yields were ultimately limited by factors other than mineral nutrients, especially light. This research, however, overlooked the fact that hydroponics has other advantages including the fact that the roots of the plant have constant access to oxygen and that the plants have access to as much or as little water as they need. This is important as one of the most common errors when growing is over- and under- watering; and hydroponics prevents this from occurring as large amounts of water can be made available to the plant and any water not used, drained away, recirculated, or actively aerated, eliminating anoxic conditions, which drown root systems in soil. In soil, a grower needs to be very experienced to know exactly how much water to feed the plant. Too much and the plant will not be able to access oxygen; too little and the plant will lose the ability to transport nutrients, which are typically moved into the roots while in solution. These two researchers developed several formulas for mineral nutrient solutions, known asHoagland solution. Modified Hoagland solutions are still used today.

One of the earliest successes of hydroponics occurred on Wake Island, a rocky atoll in the Pacific Ocean used as a refuelling stop for Pan American Airlines. Hydroponics was used there in the 1930s to grow vegetables for the passengers. Hydroponics was a necessity on Wake Island because there was no soil, and it was prohibitively expensive to airlift in fresh vegetables.

In the 1960s, Allen Cooper of England developed the Nutrient film technique. The Land Pavilion at Walt Disney World's EPCOT Center opened in 1982 and prominently features a variety of hydroponic techniques. In recent decades, NASA has done extensive hydroponic research for their Controlled Ecological Life Support System or CELSS. Hydroponics intended to take place on Mars are using LED lighting to grow in different color spectrum with much less heat.

ORIGIN

SOILLESS CULTURE

Gericke originally defined hydroponics as crop growth in mineral nutrient solutions. Hydroponics is a subset of soilless culture. Many types of soilless culture do not use the mineral nutrient solutions required for hydroponics.

Plants that are not traditionally grown in a climate would be possible to grow using a controlled environment system like hydroponics. NASA has also looked to utilize hydroponics in the space program. Ray Wheeler,a plant physiologist at Kennedy Space Center's Space Life Science Lab, believes that hydroponics will create advances within space travel. He terms this as a bioregenerative life support system.

TECHNIQUES

The two main types of hydroponics are solution culture and medium culture. Solution culture does not use a solid medium for the roots, just the nutrient solution. The three main types of solution cultures are static solution culture, continuous-flow solution culture and aeroponics. The medium culture method has a solid medium for the roots and is named for the type of medium, e.g., sand culture, gravel culture, or rockwool culture.

There are two main variations for each medium, sub-irrigation and top irrigation . For all techniques, most hydroponic reservoirs are now built of plastic, but other materials have been used including concrete, glass, metal, vegetable solids, and wood. The containers should exclude light to prevent algae growth in the nutrient solution.

STATIC SOLUTION CULTURE

In static solution culture, plants are grown in containers of nutrient solution, such as glass Mason jars (typically, in-home applications), plastic buckets, tubs, or tanks. The solution is usually gently aerated but may be un-aerated. If un-aerated, the solution level is kept low enough that enough roots are above the solution so they get adequate oxygen. A hole is cut in the lid of the reservoir for each plant. There can be one to many plants per reservoir. Reservoir size can be increased as plant size increases. A home made system can be constructed from plastic food containers or glass canning jars with aeration provided by an aquarium pump, aquarium airline tubing and aquarium valves. Clear containers are covered with aluminium foil, butcher paper, black plastic, or other material to exclude light, thus helping to eliminate the formation of algae. The nutrient solution is changed either on a schedule, such as once per week, or when the concentration drops below a certain level as determined with an electrical conductivity meter. Whenever the solution is depleted below a certain level, either water or fresh nutrient solution is added. A Mariotte's bottle, or a float valve, can be used to automatically maintain the solution level. In raft solution culture, plants are placed in a sheet of buoyant plastic that is floated on the surface of the nutrient solution. That way, the solution level never drops below the roots.

CONTINUOUS-FLOW SOLUTION CULTURE

In continuous-flow solution culture, the nutrient solution constantly flows past the roots. It is much easier to automate than the static solution culture because sampling and adjustments to the temperature and nutrient concentrations can be made in a large storage tank that has potential to serve thousands of plants. A popular variation is thenutrient film technique or NFT, whereby a very shallow stream of water containing all the dissolved nutrients required for plant growth is recirculated past the bare roots of plants in a watertight thick root mat, which develops in the bottom of the channel and has an upper surface that, although moist, is in the air. Subsequent to this, an abundant supply of oxygen is provided to the roots of the plants. A properly designed NFT system is based on using the right channel slope, the right flow rate, and the right channel length. The main advantage of the NFT system over other forms of hydroponics is that the plant roots are exposed to adequate supplies of water, oxygen, and nutrients. In all other forms of production, there is a conflict between the supply of these requirements, since excessive or deficient amounts of one results in an imbalance of one or both of the others. NFT, because of its design, provides a system where all three requirements for healthy plant growth can be met at the same time, provided that the simple concept of NFT is always remembered and practised. The result of these advantages is that higher yields of high-quality produce are obtained over an extended period of cropping. A downside of NFT is that it has very little buffering against interruptions in the flow, e.g., power outages. But, overall, it is probably one of the more productive techniques.

The same design characteristics apply to all conventional NFT systems. While slopes along channels of 1:100 have been recommended, in practice it is difficult to build a base for channels that is sufficiently true to enable nutrient films to flow without ponding in locally depressed areas. As a consequence, it is recommended that slopes of 1:30 to 1:40 are used. This allows for minor irregularities in the surface, but, even with these slopes, ponding and water logging may occur. The slope may be provided by the floor, or benches or racks may hold the channels and provide the required slope. Both methods are used and depend on local requirements, often determined by the site and crop requirements. As a general guide, flow rates for each gully should be 1 liter per minute. At planting, rates may be half this and the upper limit of 2 L/min appears about the maximum. Flow rates beyond these extremes are often associated with nutritional problems. Depressed growth rates of many crops have been observed when channels exceed 12 metres in length. On rapidly growing crops, tests have indicated that, while oxygen levels remain adequate, nitrogen may be depleted over the length of the gully. As a consequence, channel length should not exceed 10–15 metres. In situations where this is not possible, the reductions in growth can be eliminated by placing another nutrient feed halfway along the gully and halving the flow rates through each outlet.

AEROPONICS

Aeroponics is a system wherein roots are continuously or discontinuously kept in an environment saturated with fine drops (a mist or aerosol) of nutrient solution. The method requires no substrate and entails growing plants with their roots suspended in a deep air or growth chamber with the roots periodically wetted with a fine mist of atomized nutrients. Excellent aeration is the main advantage of aeroponics.

Aeroponic techniques have proven to be commercially successful for propagation, seed germination, seed potato production, tomato production, leaf crops, and micro-greens. Since inventor Richard Stoner commercialized aeroponic technology in 1983, aeroponics has been implemented as an alternative to water intensive hydroponic systems worldwide. The limitation of hydroponics is the fact that 1 kg of water can only hold 8 mg of air, no matter whether aerators are utilized or not.

Another distinct advantage of aeroponics over hydroponics is that any species of plants can be grown in a true aeroponic system because the micro environment of an aeroponic can be finely controlled. The limitation of hydroponics is that only certain species of plants can survive for so long in water before they become waterlogged. The advantage of aeroponics is that suspended aeroponic plants receive 100% of the available oxygen and carbon dioxide to the roots zone, stems, and leaves, thus accelerating biomass growth and reducing rooting times. NASA research has shown that aeroponically grown plants have an 80% increase in dry weight biomass (essential minerals) compared to hydroponically grown plants. Aeroponics used 65% less water than hydroponics. NASA also concluded that aeroponically grown plants requires ¼ the nutrient input compared to hydroponics. Unlike hydroponically grown plants, aeroponically grown plants will not suffer transplant shock when transplanted to soil, and offers growers the ability to reduce the spread of disease and pathogens. Aeroponics is also widely used in laboratory studies of plant physiology and plant pathology. Aeroponic techniques have been given special attention from NASA since a mist is easier to handle than a liquid in a zero-gravity environment.

PASSIVE SUB-IRRIGATION

Passive sub-irrigation, also known as passive hydroponics or semi-hydroponics, is a method wherein plants are grown in an inert porous medium that transports water and fertilizer to the roots by capillary action from a separate reservoir as necessary, reducing labor and providing a constant supply of water to the roots.

In the simplest method, the pot sits in a shallow solution of fertilizer and water or on a capillary mat saturated with nutrient solution. The various hydroponic media available, such as expanded clay and coconut husk, contain more air space than more traditional potting mixes, delivering increased oxygen to the roots, which is important in epiphytic plants such as orchids andbromeliads, whose roots are exposed to the air in nature. Additional advantages of passive hydroponics are the reduction of root rot and the additional ambient humidity provided through evaporations.

EBB AND FLOW OR FLOOD AND DRAIN SUB-IRRIGATION

In its simplest form, there is a tray above a reservoir of nutrient solution. Either the tray is filled with growing medium (clay granules being the most common) and planted directly or pots of medium stand in the tray. At regular intervals, a simple timer causes a pump to fill the upper tray with nutrient solution, after which the solution drains back down into the reservoir. This keeps the medium regularly flushed with nutrients and air. Once the upper tray fills past the drain stop, it begins recirculating the water until the timer turns the pump off, and the water in the upper tray drains back into the reservoirs.

RUN TO WASTE

In a run-to-waste system, nutrient and water solution is periodically applied to the medium surface. This may be done in its simplest form, by manually applying a nutrient-and-water solution one or more times per day in a container of inert growing media, such as rockwool, perlite, vermiculite, coco fibre, or sand. In a slightly more complex system, it is automated with a delivery pump, a timer and irrigation tubing to deliver nutrient solution with a delivery frequency that is governed by the key parameters of plant size, plant growing stage, climate, substrate, and substrate conductivity, pH, and water content.

In a commercial setting, watering frequency is multi factorial and governed by computers or PLCs. Commercial hydroponics production of large plants like tomatoes, cucumber, and peppers use one form or another of run-to-waste hydroponics. In environmentally responsible uses, the nutrient rich waste is collected and processed through an on site filtration system to be used many times, making the system very productive.

The majority of bonsai are now grown in soil-free substrates (typically consisting of akadama, grit, diatomaceous earth and other inorganic components) and have their water and nutrients provided in a run-to-waste form.

DEEP WATER CULTURE

The hydroponic method of plant production by means of suspending the plant roots in a solution of nutrient-rich, oxygenated water. Traditional methods favor the use of plastic buckets and large containers with the plant contained in a net pot suspended from the centre of the lid and the roots suspended in the nutrient solution. The solution is oxygen saturated by an air pump combined with porous stones. With this method, the plants grow much faster because of the high amount of oxygen that the roots receive.

TOP-FED DEEP WATER CULTURE

Top-fed deep water culture is a technique involving delivering highly oxygenated nutrient solution direct to the root zone of plants. While deep water culture involves the plant roots hanging down into a reservoir of nutrient solution, in top-fed deep water culture the solution is pumped from the reservoir up to the roots (top feeding).

The water is released over the plant's roots and then runs back into the reservoir below in a constantly recirculating system. As with deep water culture, there is an airstone in the reservoir that pumps air into the water via a hose from outside the reservoir. The airstone helps add oxygen to the water. Both the airstone and the water pump run 24 hours a day.

The biggest advantage of top-fed deep water culture over standard deep water culture is increased growth during the first few weeks. With deep water culture, there is a time when the roots have not reached the water yet. With top-fed deep water culture, the roots get easy access to water from the beginning and will grow to the reservoir below much more quickly than with a deep water culture system. Once the roots have reached the reservoir below, there is not a huge advantage with top-fed deep water culture over standard deep water culture. However, due to the quicker growth in the beginning, grow time can be reduced by a few weeks.

FOGPONICS

Fogponics is an advanced form of aeroponics which uses water in a vaporised form to transfer nutrients and oxygen to enclosed suspended plant roots. Using the same general idea behind aeroponics except fogponics uses a 5-10 micron mist within the rooting chamber and as use for a foliar feeding mechanism.

ROTARY

A rotary hydroponic garden is a style of commercial hydroponics created within a circular frame which rotates continuously during the entire growth cycle of whatever plant is being grown.

While system specifics vary, systems typically rotate once per hour, giving a plant 24 full turns within the circle each 24-hour period. Within the center of each rotary hydroponic garden is a high intensity grow light, designed to simulate sunlight, often with the assistance of a mechanized timer.

Each day, as the plants rotate, they are periodically watered with a hydroponic growth solution to provide all nutrients necessary for robust growth. Due to the plants continuous fight against gravity, plants typically mature much more quickly than when grown in soil or other traditional hydroponic growing systems. Due to the small foot print a rotary hydroponic system has, it allows for more plant material to be grown per sq foot of floor space than other traditional hydroponic systems.

SUBSTRATES

One of the most obvious decisions hydroponic farmers have to make is which medium they should use. Different media are appropriate for different growing techniques.

EXPANDED CLAY AGGREGATE

Fig. Expanded clay pebbles.

Baked clay pellets, are suitable for hydroponic systems in which all nutrients are carefully controlled in water solution. The clay pellets are inert, pH neutral and do not contain any nutrient value.

The clay is formed into round pellets and fired in rotary kilns at 1,200 °C (2,190 °F). This causes the clay to expand, like popcorn, and become porous. It is light in weight, and does not compact over time. The shape of an individual pellet can be irregular or uniform depending on brand and manufacturing process. The manufacturers consider expanded clay to be an ecologically sustainable and re-usable growing medium because of its ability to be cleaned and sterilized, typically by washing in solutions of white vinegar, chlorinebleach, or hydrogen peroxide (H_2O_2), and rinsing completely.

Another view is that clay pebbles are best not re-used even when they are cleaned, due to root growth that may enter the medium. Breaking open a clay pebble after a crop has been grown will reveal this growth.

GROWSTONES

Growstones, made from glass waste, have both more air and water retention space than perlite and peat. This aggregate holds more water than parboiled rice hulls. Growstones by volume consists of .5 to 5% Calcium carbonate. for a standard 5.1 kg bag of Growstones that's 25.8 to 258 grams of calcium carbonate. The remainder is Soda-lime glass.

COIR PEAT

Coco peat, also known as coir or coco, is the leftover material after the fibres have been removed from the outermost shell (bolster) of the coconut. Coir is a 100% natural grow and flowering medium. Coconut coir is colonized with trichoderma fungi, which protects roots and stimulates root growth. It is extremely difficult to over-water coir due to its perfect air-to-water ratio; plant roots thrive in this environment. Coir has a high cation exchange, meaning it can store unused minerals to be released to the plant as and when it requires it. Coir is available in many forms; most common is coco peat, which has the appearance and texture of soil but contains no mineral content.

RICE HUSKS

Parboiled rice husks (PBH) are an agricultural byproduct that would otherwise have little use. They decay over time, and allow drainage, and even retain less water than growstones. A study showed that rice husks did not affect the effects of plant growth regulators.

PERLITE

Perlite is a volcanic rock that has been superheated into very lightweight expanded glass pebbles. It is used loose or in plastic sleeves immersed in the water. It is also used in potting soil mixes to decrease soil density. Perlite has similar properties and uses to vermiculite but, in general, holds more air and less water. If not contained, it can float if flood and drain feeding is used. It is a fusion of granite, obsidian, pumice and basalt. This volcanic rock is naturally fused at high temperatures undergoing what is called "Fusionic Metamorphosis".

VERMICULITE

Like perlite, vermiculite is a mineral that has been superheated until it has expanded into light pebbles. Vermiculite holds more water than perlite and has a natural "wicking" property that can draw water and nutrients in a passive hydroponic system. If too much water and not enough air surrounds the plants roots, it is possible to gradually lower the medium's water-retention capability by mixing in increasing quantities of perlite.

PUMICE

Like perlite, pumice is a lightweight, mined volcanic rock that finds application in hydroponics.

SAND

Sand is cheap and easily available. However, it is heavy, does not hold water very well, and it must be sterilized between uses.

GRAVEL

The same type that is used in aquariums, though any small gravel can be used, provided it is washed first. Indeed, plants growing in a typical traditional gravel filter bed, with water circulated using electric powerhead pumps, are in effect being grown using gravel hydroponics. Gravel is inexpensive, easy to keep clean, drains well and will not become waterlogged. However, it is also heavy, and, if the system does not provide continuous water, the plant roots may dry out.

WOOD FIBRE

Wood fibre, produced from steam friction of wood, is a very efficient organic substrate for hydroponics. It has the advantage that it keeps its structure for a very long time. Wood fibre has been shown to reduce the effects of "plant growth regulators."

ROCK WOOL

Rock wool (mineral wool) is the most widely used medium in hydroponics. Rock wool is an inert substrate suitable for both run-to-waste and recirculating systems. Rock wool is made from molten rock, basalt or 'slag' that is spun into bundles of single filament fibres, and bonded into a medium capable of capillary action, and is, in effect, protected from most common microbiological degradation. Rock wool has many advantages and some disadvantages. The latter being the possible skin irritancy (mechanical) whilst handling (1:1000). Flushing with cold water usually brings relief. Advantages include its proven efficiency and effectiveness as a commercial hydroponic substrate. Most of the rock wool sold to date is a non-hazardous, non-carcinogenic material, falling under Note Q of the European Union Classification Packaging and Labeling Regulation (CLP).

SHEEP WOOL

Wool from shearing sheep is a little-used yet promising renewable growing medium. In a study comparing wool with peat slabs, coconut fibre slabs, perlite and rockwool slabs to grow cucumber plants, sheep wool had a greater air capacity of 70%, which decreased with use to a comparable 43%, and water capacity that increased from 23% to 44% with use. Using sheep wool resulted in the greatest yield out of the tested substrates, while application of a biostimulator consisting of humic acid, lactic acid and Bacillus subtilis improved yields in all substrates.

BRICK SHARDS

Brick shards have similar properties to gravel. They have the added disadvantages of possibly altering the pH and requiring extra cleaning before reuse.

POLYSTYRENE PACKING PEANUTS

Polystyrene packing peanuts are inexpensive, readily available, and have excellent drainage. However, they can be too lightweight for some uses. They are used mainly in closed-tube systems. Note that polystyrene peanuts must be used; biodegradable packing peanuts will decompose into a sludge. Plants may absorb styrene and pass it to their consumers; this is a possible health risk.

NUTRIENT SOLUTIONS

Plant nutrients used in hydroponics are dissolved in the water and are mostly in inorganic and ionic form. Primary among the dissolved cations (positively charged ions) are Ca (calcium), Mg^{2+} (magnesium), and $K+$ (potassium); the major nutrient anions in nutrient solutions are $NO^{"3}$ (nitrate), $SO^{2"}4$ (sulfate), and $H_2PO^{"4}$ (dihydrogen phosphate).

Numerous 'recipes' for hydroponic solutions are available. Many use different combinations of chemicals to reach similar total final compositions. Commonly used chemicals for the macronutrients include potassium nitrate, calcium nitrate, potassium phosphate, and magnesium sulfate. Various micronutrients are typically added to hydroponic solutions to supply essential elements; among them are Fe (iron), Mn (manganese), Cu (copper), Zn (zinc), B (boron), Cl (chlorine), and Ni (nickel). Chelating agents are sometimes used to keep Fe soluble, and humic acids can be added to increase nutrient uptake. Many variations of the nutrient solutions used by Arnon and Hoagland (see above) have been styled 'modified Hoagland solutions' and are widely used.

Variation of different mixes throughout the plant life-cycle, further optimizes its nutritional value. Plants will change the composition of the nutrient solutions upon contact by depleting specific nutrients more rapidly than others, removing water from the solution, and altering the pH by excretion of either acidity or alkalinity. Care is required not to allow salt concentrations to become too high, nutrients to become too depleted, or pH to wander far from the desired value.

Although pre-mixed concentrated nutrient solutions are generally purchased from commercial nutrient manufacturers by hydroponic hobbyists and small commercial growers, several tools exists to help anyone prepare their own solutions without extensive knowledge about chemistry. The free and open source tools HydroBuddy and HydroCal have been created by professional chemists to help any hydroponics grower prepare their own nutrient solutions. The first program is available for Windows, Mac and Linux while the second one can be used through a simple Java interface. Both programs allow for basic nutrient solution preparation although HydroBuddy provides added functionality to use and save custom substances, save formulations and predict electrical conductivity values.According to Kumar and Cho (2014) the hydroponics waste nutrient solution can be reused for growing commercially important crops and reuse of waste nutrient solution may control point source pollution.

The well-oxygenated and enlightened environment promotes the development of algae. It is therefore necessary to wrap the tank with black film obscuring all light.

Organic hydroponics uses the solution containing microorganisms. In organic hydroponics, organic fertilizer can be added in the hydroponic solution because microorganisms degrade organic fertilizer into inorganic nutrients. In contrast, conventional hydroponics cannot use organic fertilizer because organic compounds in the hydroponic solution show phytotoxic effects.

COMMERCIAL

Some commercial installations use no pesticides or herbicides, preferring integrated pest management techniques. There is often a price premium willingly paid by consumers for produce that is labelled "organic". Some states in the USA require soil as an essential to obtain organic certification. There are also overlapping and somewhat contradictory rules established by the US Federal Government, so some food grown with hydroponics can be certified organic. Most hydroponically grown produce cannot be sold as organic due to the fact that they do not use soil as a growing medium.

Hydroponics also saves water; it uses as little as D_{20} the amount as a regular farm to produce the same amount of food. The water table can be impacted by the water use andrun-off of chemicals from farms, but hydroponics may minimize impact as well as having the advantage that water use and water returns are easier to measure. This can save the farmer money by allowing reduced water use and the ability to measure consequences to the land around a farm.

To increase plant growth, lighting systems such as metal-halide lamp for growing stage only or high-pressure sodium for growing/flowering/blooming stage are used to lengthen the day or to supplement natural sunshine if it is scarce. Metal halide emits more light in the blue spectrum, making it ideal for plant growth but is harmful to unprotected skin and can cause skin cancer. High-pressure sodium emits more light in the red spectrum, meaning that it is best suited for supplementing natural sunshine and can be used throughout the growing cycle. However, these lighting systems require large amounts of electricity to operate, making efficiency and safety very critical.

The environment in a hydroponics greenhouse is tightly controlled for maximum efficiency, and this new mindset is called soil-less/controlled-environment agriculture (CEA). With this growers can make ultra-premium foods anywhere in the world, regardless of temperature and growing seasons. Growers monitor the temperature, humidity, and pH level constantly.

Hydroponics have been used to enhance vegetables to provide more nutritional value. A hydroponic farmer in Virginia has developed a calcium and potassium enriched head oflettuce, scheduled to be widely available in April 2007. Grocers in test markets have said that the lettuce sells "very well", and the farmers claim that their hydroponic lettuce uses 90% less water than traditional soil farming.

ADVANCEMENTS

With pest problems reduced, and nutrients constantly fed to the roots, productivity in hydroponics is high, although plant growth can be limited by the low levels of carbon dioxidein the atmosphere, or limited light exposure. To increase yield further, some sealed greenhouses inject carbon dioxide into their environment to help growth (CO2 enrichment), add lights to lengthen the day, or control vegetative growth, etc.

POTENTIAL DOWNSIDES OF HYDROPONICS

Any time people change conventional ways, especially those as embedded in our identities as food cultivation, controversy is inevitable. Hydroponics is no exception, and it does have some potential drawbacks that should be weighed with the benefits. (However, it's important to evaluate it in the context of the industrialized agricultural system we currently have, rather than an idealized one.)

Scientists are increasingly aware of the importance of the microbiomes in our soil. "There are millions of organisms in a couple cubic centimeters of soil," explains biologist Jeanne Romero-Severson, and we've been unable to grow 90 percent of them in the laboratory. Because we still don't fully understand the relationships between plants and soil microbes, it remains questionable whether we can reproduce them in a hydroponics system. For that and related reasons, a coalition of organic farmers oppose the USDA's decision to allow hydroponically grown produce to be certified organic.

Most hydroponic growers claim their greenhouse-grown veggies are as nutritious as, or more nutritious than, conventional veggies, although data is hard to come by.

There's a widespreadperception that hydroponic veggies are tasteless or watery, although the evidence is mostly anecdotal. In one blind taste test, hydroponically grown lettuce was rated as just as tasty as conventional or organic varieties. More nutritional analysis and taste testing on a variety of crops would be informative.

Several other issues may make hydroponics challenging or undesirable for some growers:

- It can be expensive. Growers, especially large-scale ones, must make an initial investment to buy pumps, pipes, basins, lights, air filters, and fans.
- Systems are made of fabricated materials, which require resources to build and maintain.
- Commercial nutrient solutions are often mined and produced in factories and they can be pricey.
- Systems, especially those with artificial lighting, can use a lot of electricity.
- Large systems require technical knowledge and careful monitoring.

Many of those challenges can be mitigated for small-scale home gardeners. Setting up a soilless system can be inexpensive and easy and it's an excellent way to understand the principles and potentials of hydroponics.

DIY HYDROPONICS FOR THE HOME GARDENER

The first and often most daunting decision for any gardener is what to grow. The best veggies to grow in any garden are the ones a person or family enjoys the most. But some plants tend to work better than others in small hydro-systems.

THE HISTORY OF HYDROPONICS

The word hydroponics comes from two Greek words, "hydro" meaning water and "ponics" meaning labor. The concept of soil less gardening or hydroponics has been around for thousands of years. The hanging Gardens of Babylon and The Floating Gardens of China are two of the earliest examples of hydroponics. Scientists started experimenting with soil less gardening around 1950. Since then other countries, such as Holland, Germany, and Australia have used hydroponics for crop production with amazing results.

THE BENEFITS OF HYDROPONICS

Hydroponics is proved to have several advantages over soil gardening. The growth rate on a hydroponic plant is 30-50 percent faster than a soil plant, grown under the same conditions. The yield of the plant is also greater. Scientists believe that there are several reasons for the drastic differences between hydroponic and soil plants. The extra oxygen in the hydroponic growing mediums helps to stimulate root growth. Plants with ample oxygen in the root system also absorb nutrients faster.

The nutrients in a hydroponic system are mixed with the water and sent directly to the root system. The plant does not have to search in the soil for the nutrients that it requires. Those nutrients are being delivered to the plant several times per day. The hydroponic plant requires very little energy to find and break down food. The plant then uses this saved energy to grow faster and to produce more fruit. Hydroponic plants also have fewer problems with bug infestations, funguses and disease. In general, plants grown hydroponically are healthier and happier plants.

Hydroponic gardening also offers several benefits to our environment. Hydroponic gardening uses considerably less water than soil gardening, because of the constant reuse the nutrient solutions. Due to lack of necessity, fewer pesticides are used on hydroponic crops. Since hydroponic gardening systems use no topsoil, topsoil erosion isn't even an issue. Although, if agricultural trends continue to erode topsoil and waste water, hydroponics may soon be our only solution.

GROWING MEDIUMS

The purpose of a growing medium is to aerate and support the root system of the plant and to channel the water and nutrients. Different growing mediums work well in different types of hydroponic systems. A fast draining medium, such as Hydrocorn or expanded shale works well in an ebb and flow type system. Hydrocorn is a light expanded clay aggregate. It is a light, airy type of growing medium that allows plenty of oxygen to penetrate the plant's root system. Both types of grow rocks can be reused, although the shale has more of a tendency to break down and may not last as long as the Hydrocorn. These grow rocks are very stable and rarely effect the pH of the nutrient solution.

Rockwool has become an extremely popular growing medium. Rockwool was originally used in construction as insulation. There is now a horticultural grade of Rockwool. Unlike the insulation grade, horticultural Rockwool is pressed into growing cubes and blocks. It is produced from volcanic rock and limestone. These components are melted at temperatures of 2500 degrees and higher. The molten solution is poured over a spinning cylinder, comparable to the way cotton candy is made, then pressed into identical sheets, blocks or cubes. Since Rockwool holds 10-14 times as much water as soil and retains 20 percent air it can be used in just about any hydroponic system. Although the gardener must be careful of the pH, since Rockwool has a pH of 7.8 it can raise the pH of the nutrient solution. Rockwool cannot be used indefinitely and most gardeners only get one use per cube. It is also commonly used for propagation.

Other commonly used growing mediums are perlite, vermiculite and different grades of sand. These three mediums are stable and rarely effect the pH of the nutrient solution. Although, they tend to hold too much moisture and should be used with plants that are tolerant to these conditions. Perlite, vermiculite and sands are very inexpensive options, and work charitably in wick systems, although they are not the most effective growing mediums.

NUTRIENTS

Most of the principles that apply to soil fertilizers also apply to hydroponic fertilizers, or nutrient solutions. A hydroponic nutrient solution contains all the elements that the plant normally would get from the soil. These nutrients can be purchased at a hydroponic supply store. Most are highly concentrated, using 2 to 4 teaspoons per gallon of water. They come in liquid mixes or powered mixes, usually with at least two different containers, one for grow and one for bloom. The liquids are the slightly more expensive and the easiest to use. They dissolve quickly and completely into the reservoir and often have an added pH buffer. The powered varieties are inexpensive and require a little more attention. They need to be mixed much more thoroughly and often don't dissolve completely into the reservoir. Most do not have a pH buffer.

Like soil, hydroponic systems can be fertilized with organic or chemical nutrients. An organic hydroponic system is considerably more work to maintain. The organic compounds have a tendency to lock together and cause pumps blockage. Some hydroponic gardeners simply supplement their hydroponic gardens with organic nutrients, using the chemical nutrients as the main food supply. This gives the plants a stable supply of nutrients without the high maintenance a hydro-organic system.

PH

Most plants can grow hydroponically within a pH range of 5.8 to 6.8, 6.3 is considered optimal. The pH in a hydroponic system is much easier to check than the pH of soil. Many hardware, pet, and hydroponic supply stores sell pH-testing kits. They range in price from $4.00 to about $15.00, depending on the range and type of test you prefer. Testing pH is easy and essential in a hydroponics system. If the pH is too high or too low the plant will not be able to absorb certain nutrients and will show signs of deficiencies. pH should be checked once a week. It is easy to adjust by adding small amounts of soluble Potash to raise pH, or phosphoric acid to lower pH. There are also several pH meters available. These give a digital reading of the pH in the system. The pH meter cost around $100 and are not necessary in most cases. Kit includes; 1 ounce of pH indicator solution, test vial, dropper, 8 ounces of pH down and 8 ounces of pH up. Contains Ph Up (add a little at a time when your nutrient pH is too low in order to raise the pH to the proper level), Ph Down (uses food grade ...

Hydroponic systems are characterized as active or passive. An active hydroponic system actively moves the nutrient solution, usually using a pump. Passive hydroponic systems rely on the capillary action of the growing medium or a wick. The nutrient solution is absorbed by the medium or the wick and passed along to the roots. Passive systems are usually too wet and do not supply enough oxygen to the root system for optimum growth rates.

Hydroponic systems can also be characterized as recovery or non-recovery. Recovery systems or recirculating systems reuse the nutrient solution. Non-recovery means just what it says. The nutrient solution is applied to the growing medium and not recovered.

THE WICK SYSTEM

The wick system is a passive non-recovery type hydroponic system. It uses no pumps and has no moving parts. The nutrients are stored in the reservoir and moved into the root system by capillary action often using a candle or lantern wick. In simpler terms, the nutrient solution travels up the wick and into the root system of the plant. Wick systems often uses sand or perlite, vermiculite mix and a growing medium. The wick system is easy and inexpensive to set-up and maintain. Although, it tends to keep the growing medium to wet, which doesn't allow for the optimum amount of oxygen in the root system. The wick system is not the most effective way to garden hydroponically.

THE EBB AND FLOW SYSTEM

The Ebb and Flow hydroponic system is an active recovery type system. The Ebb and Flow uses a submersible pump in the reservoir and the plants are in the upper tray. They work on a simple flood and drain theory. The reservoir holds the nutrient solution and the pump. When the pump turns on, the nutrient solution is pumped up to the upper tray and delivered to the root system of the plants. The pump should remain on for about 20 to 30 minutes, which is called a flood cycle. Once the water has reached a set level, an overflow pipe or fitting allows the nutrient solution to drain back into the reservoir. The pump remains on for the entire flood cycle. After the flood cycle the nutrient solution slowly drains back down into the reservoir through the pump.

During the flood cycle oxygen poor air is pushed out of the root system by the upward moving nutrient solution. As the nutrient solution drains back into the reservoir, oxygen rich air is pulled into the growing medium. This allows the roots ample oxygen to maximize their nutrient intake. Rockwool and grow rocks are most commonly used growing mediums in Ebb and Flow type systems. The Ebb and Flow is low maintenance, yet highly effective type of hydroponic gardening.

NUTRIENT FILM TECHNIQUE

The Nutrient Film Technique or NFT system is an active recovery type hydroponic system. Again, using submersible pumps and reusing nutrient solutions. The NFT uses a reservoir with a submersible pump that pumps the nutrient solution into a grow-tube where the roots suspended. The grow-tube is at a slight downward angle so the nutrient solution runs over the roots and back into the reservoir. The nutrient solution flows over the roots up to 24 hours per day.

Oxygen is needed in the grow-tube so capillary matting or air stones must be used. The plants are held up by a support collar or a grow-basket and no growing medium is used. The NFT system is very effective. Although, many novice hydroponic growers find it difficult to fine tune. It can also be very unforgiving, with no growing medium to hold any moisture, any long period of interruption in the nutrient flow can cause the roots to dry out and the plants to suffer and possibly die.

CONTINUOUS DRIP

The Continuous Drip system is an active recovery or non-recovery type system. This system uses a submersible pump in a reservoir with supply lines going to each plant. With drip emitter for each plant the gardener can adjust the amount of solution per plant. A drip tray under each row of plants, sending the solution back to the reservoir, can easily make this system an active recovery type. In the early days of hydroponics, the extra solution was leached out into the ground. Continuous Drip systems are often used with Rockwool. Although, any growing medium can be used with this system, thanks to the adjustment feature on each individual drip emitter.

The WaterFarm Module is built with high-impact plastic to assure a long service life. The WaterFarm unique square design allows growers to closely pack WaterFarm units to create large, high-density installations. The WaterFarm will grow small, medium, and...

BOTTOM OF FORM

Buying a System or Building a System

This is the most asked question relating to hydroponics. Should I buy one or build one? This author recommends a little of both. If you have an engineer's mind and dream of building your own hydroponic system, buy one first! Getting an inexpensive system will allow you to get your feet wet and give you a better understanding of how hydroponics works. The hands on experience is worth the cost of the system and chances are, you will be able to reuse the parts in that system when you set out to build your own.

If you would rather get right into building your own, do your research. Get all the information you can and don't rely on just one source. This is a constantly changing industry and there are many books still on the shelves that are already outdated. Building your own system can be very rewarding or extremely frustrating. It's mostly trial and error so, be patient.

Hydroponic gardening is the wave of the future. It is currently being studied in classrooms around the country, local horticultural societies and in government funded research at major universities and NASA. It is also becoming a popular hobby. Hydroponics is fun, exciting and easy to get involved in.

WHAT IS HYDROPONIC GROWING?

Hydroponics is a subset of hydroculture, which is the growing of plants in a soil less medium, or an aquatic based environment. Hydroponic growing uses mineral nutrient solutions to feed the plants in water, without soil.

For those of us who love growing plants these are exciting times indeed. We are no longer limited by climate or by season in the pursuit of our harmless pleasures. We can now grow virtually any plant at virtually any time of the year – the only limitation is our imagination. The simple, effective hydroponic systems now available, coupled with modern horticultural lighting, have transformed our hobby and freed us to grow our favourite plants where and when we choose.

TYPES OF HYDROPONIC SYSTEMS?

When you think of hydroponics, you instantly imagine plants grown with their roots suspended directly into water with no growing medium. However this is just one type of hydroponic gardening known as N.F.T. (nutrient film technique). There are several variations of N.F.T. used around the world and it is a very popular method of growing hydroponically. What most people don't realise is that there are countless methods and variations of hydroponic gardening.

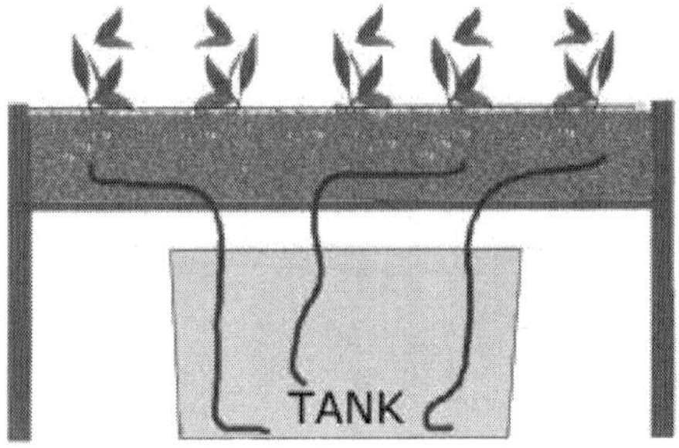

WICKS SYSTEM

Seen as the most simplistic hydroponic system. The Wick system is described as a passive system, by which we mean there are no moving parts. From the bottom reservoir, your specific Growth Technology nutrient solution is drawn up through a number of wicks into the growing medium. This system can use a variety of mediums, perlite, soil or coco.

What is best to grow in Perlite, Soil or Coco?

WATER CULTURE

This system is an active system with moving parts. As active hydroponic systems go, water culture is the simplest. The roots of the plant are totally immersed in the water which contains the specific Growth Technology nutrient solutions. An air pump with help oxygenate the water and allow the roots to breathe.

Note. Very few plants other than lettuce will do well in this type of system.

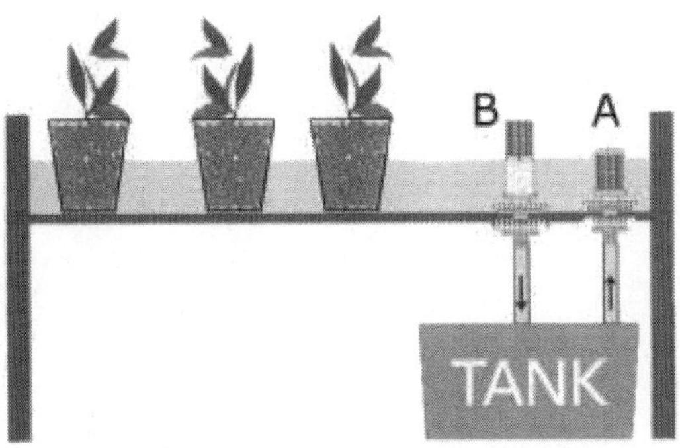

EBB AND FLOW SYSTEM (FLOOD AND DRAIN)

This hydroponic system works by temporarily flooding the grow tray. The nutrient solution from a reservoir surrounds the roots before draining back. This action is usually automated with a water pump on a timer.

DRIP SYSTEM (RECOVERY OR NON-RECOVERY)

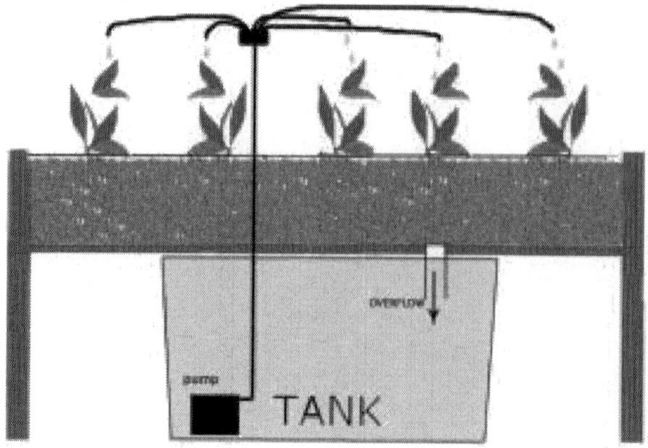

Dip systems are a widely used hydroponic method. A timer will control a water pump, which pumps water and the Growth Technology nutrient solutions through a network of elevated water jets. A recovery system will collect excess nutrient solution back into the reservoir. A non-recovery drip system will avoid this allowing the pH of the reservoir not to vary. If using a recovery system, be sure to check the pH level of the reservoir regularly and adjust using either pH UP or pH Down solutions on a more frequent basis.

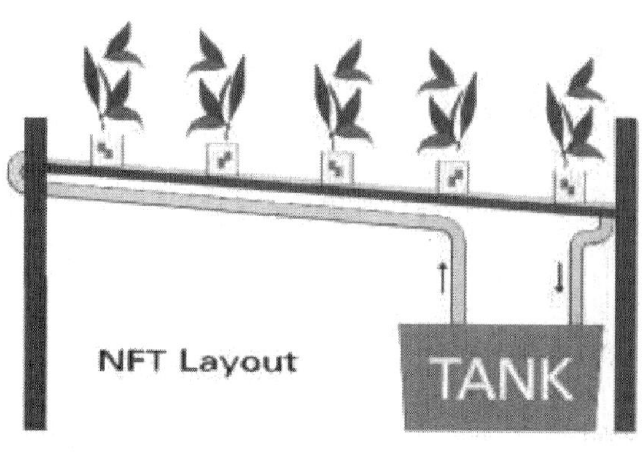

N.F.T SYSTEM

The N.F.T system is at the forefront of people's minds when hydroponics is mentioned. Nutrient Film Technique uses a constant flow of your Growth Technology nutrient solution (therefore no timer is required). The solution is pumped from a reservoir into the growing tray. The growing tray requires no growing medium. The roots draw up the nutrients from the flowing solution. The downward flow pours back into the reservoir to be recycled again. Pump and electric maintenance is essential to avoid system failures, where roots can dry out rapidly when the flow stops.

AEROPONIC SYSTEM

Aeroponic systems are seen to be a high tech method of hydroponic growing. Like the N.F.T system the growing medium is primarily air.

The roots hang in the air and are misted with nutrient solution. The misting of roots is usually done every few minutes. The roots will dry out rapidly if the misting cycles are interrupted.

A timer controls the nutrient pump much like other types of hydroponic systems, except the aeroponic system needs a short cycle timer that runs the pump for a few seconds every couple of minutes.

FUTURE OF HYDROPONICS

Hydroponics is a relatively new technology, evolving rapidly since its inception 70 years ago. From its origins in academic research, to its utilization in industry and government, hydroponics has found many new applications. It is a versatile technology, appropriate for both developing countries and high-tech space stations. Hydroponic technology can efficiently generate food crops from barren desert sand and desalinated ocean water, in mountainous regions too steep to farm, on city rooftops and concrete schoolyards and in arctic communities. In highly populated tourist areas where skyrocketing land prices have driven out traditional agriculture, hydroponics can provide locally grown high-value specialty crops such as fresh salad greens, herbs and cut flowers.

Like manufacturing, agriculture tends to move toward higher-technology, more capital-intensive solutions to problems. Hydroponics is highly productive and suitable for automation. However, the future growth of controlled environment agriculture and hydroponics depends greatly on the development of systems of production that are cost-competitive with those of open field agriculture. Improvements in associated technologies such as artificial lighting and agricultural plastics, and new cultivars with better pest and disease resistance will increase crop yields and reduce unit costs of production. Cogeneration projects, where hydroponic greenhouses utilize waste heat from industry and power plants, are already a reality and could expand in the next few years. Geothermal heat could support large expanses of greenhouses in appropriate locations.

It has been proposed that glasshouses located in deserts of the world could one day serve a dual purpose, where antenna could be embedded into the glass to receive energy radiation from an array of energy collectors in space, while at the same time facilitate hydroponic tomato production.

The economic prospects for controlled environmental agriculture and hydroponics may improve if governmental bodies determined that there are politically desirable effects of hydroponics that merit subsidy for the public good. Such beneficial effects may include the conservation of water in regions of scarcity or food production in hostile environments; governmental support for these reasons has occurred in the Middle East.

Another desirable societal effect could be the provision of income-producing employment for chronically disadvantaged segments of the population entrapped in economically depressed regions; such employment produces tax revenues as well as personal incomes, reducing the impact on welfare rolls and improving the quality of life.

Hydroponics is a technical reality. Such production systems are producing horticultural crops where field-grown fresh vegetables and ornamentals are unavailable for much of the year.

The development and use of controlled environment agriculture and hydroponics have enhanced the economic well being of many communities throughout the world.

GREENHOUSES

There are many factors to consider in determining the amount of greenhouse space you will need. Amount of investment capital, training, the type of business, environmental requirements, market, labor requirements and personal preferences must all be evaluated. You should also be aware of factors which are important in choosing a good building site, such as drainage, accessibility, available utilities and amount of sun exposure.

There are companies such as Crop King who sell greenhouse packages which contain everything needed for turnkey operation. Greenhouse tomatoes with indeterminate growth habits are best managed in houses with high roofs. The structural design of a greenhouse must provide protection from wind, rain, heat and cold. The structural supports must be of minimal size to permit maximum light transmission to the crop while still supporting the structure itself, heating and ventilation units and the weight of the crop which is trained to grow up a support system carried by the greenhouse frame.

Photo by M.Jensen

There are a variety of types of greenhouse covers. Glass is still a common glazing material. Large panes reduce the shading of the crop from the support frame. While shading may seem minimal in traditional greenhouses, it is estimated that every 1% decrease in light will result in a 1% decrease in yield.

Despite the common use of glass as a covering for greenhouses in Northwest Europe, glass remains inflexible, heavy, and expensive. Consequently, the hectarage of glasshouses on a world basis has remained static, (approximately 30,000 ha.) during the last 25 years. In contrast, the quantity of plastic used for greenhouses is increasing rapidly. Since polyethylene sheet film was first developed in England in 1938, it has been used widely in greenhouses because it is easy to work with and inexpensive. Worldwide, there are nearly 300,000 ha. of plastic greenhouses for growing high value horticultural crops.

Several other plastics have also been used for greenhouse glazings. Polyvinylchloride (PVC) has a very high emissivity for long wave radiation (similar to glass), which creates slightly higher air temperatures in the greenhouse during the night. The Japanese consider this improvement in thermal environment a benefit that outweighs the price advantage offered by the less expensive polyethylene (PE). The disadvantage of PVC is its narrow width as compared to PE, which may be manufactured in widths of up to15 meters. The narrow PVC sheets can be heat-welded together to form a large sheet, but this adds to the cost of the glazing material.

The large sheets of PE can be applied as an air-inflated "blanket" over a greenhouse: two sheets of PE are separated by air pressure maintained by a small continuously running fan. This arrangement provides approximately 30-40% heat savings during winter.

The double-layer, air-inflated roof has also proven valuable in regions with high winds or typhoons. It offers stability during these conditions, saving the greenhouse and the crop during times when structures covered only with one layer of plastic are often lost and the crops damaged or destroyed. PVC film is not suitable for air-inflated roofs because the air pressure stretches the film and reduces its structural strength. Because PVC film is not photodegradable, as is PE, environmental concerns about disposal may diminish the use of PVC in Japan in favor of PE, which is the predominant cover for greenhouses worldwide.

New materials such as double-skinned panels made of polycarbonate and acrylic are becoming increasingly popular. Unfortunately, their technical merit is offset by high costs, making them affordable only in the industrial nations of the world rather than in developing agricultural communities.

The ideal greenhouse "selective film" should do the following:

1. Transmit the visible light portion of the solar radiation spectrum, the only portion utilized by plants for photosynthesis.
2. Absorb the small amount of ultraviolet radiation in the spectrum and cause some of it to fluoresce into visible light, useful to plants.
3. Reflect or absorb infrared radiation , which plants cannot use and which cause greenhouse interiors to overheat.
4. Minimize costs, and have at least a 10 to 20 year useable life.

3

Transpiration in Water and Soil

A gentle breeze is relatively much more effective in increasing the transpiration rate than winds of greater velocity. Winds of very high velocity have been observed to have a retarding effect upon transpiration. This is probably due to closure of stomates under such conditions.

The effect of wind upon the transpiration of a leaf which is exposed to intense insolation is further complicated by the fact that a wind may have a cooling effect upon the leaves, due to their increased thermal emissivity under such conditions. Reduction in the temperature of a leaf, as we have already seen, exerts a decelerating effect upon transpiration. If conditions are such that this cooling effect of wind is predominant increased wind velocity may result in a diminution in transpiration rate.

SOIL CONDITIONS INFLUENCING THE AVAILABILITY OF WATER

Although transpiration can continue for short periods at rates considerably in excess of the rate of absorption of water, in general, if soil conditions are such that absorption of water is appreciably retarded, the rate of transpiration will soon show a corresponding retardation. The availability of soil water to the plant is therefore an important and, in fact, often the limiting factor in transpiration.

The principal soil factors which affect the rate of absorption of water by plants are:

- Available soil water,
- Soil temperature,
- Aeration of the soil, and
- Concentration of solutes in the soil solution.

All of these factors indirectly influence the rate of transpiration.

ATMOSPHERIC PRESSURE

It has been demonstrated experimentally that a reduction in atmospheric pressure results in an increase in the rate of transpiration. This result would be predicted theoretically since reduction in the density of the atmosphere would be expected to permit diffusion of water-vapour to occur into it more rapidly. In any given locality variations in atmospheric pressure are too slight to have any significant effect upon the rates of transpiration. Plants growing at high altitudes are subjected to distinctly lower atmospheric pressures thanthe plants of lowlands, and in comparative evaluations of the transpiration rates of species growing in these two types of habitats the influence of this factor must be considered.

TRANSPIRATION

A number of diverse species of plants growing under identical environmental conditions usually differ very greatly in transpiration rates. Physiological factors, such as differences in stomatal behaviour, cell sap concentration, colloid content of the cells, etc. are undoubtedly partially responsible for the fact that all plants do not lose water-vapour at the same rate even under the same environmental conditions. Structural differences, particularly in the leaves, also account in part for unlike rates of transpiration of different species growing in the same environment.

Many of the supposed effectsof structural differences in plants upon their transpiration rates are, however based solely on inferences, and not upon experimentally determined facts.

Many species which on the basis of their anatomy have been judged to have a low transpiration rate later were actually found to transpire very rapidly when environmental conditions were suitable. The following discussion of the anatomical features known or generally believed to influence the rate of transpiration will therefore be very brief.

THICKNESS OF THE CUTIN

It can be easily demonstrated that water vapourates more readily from uncutinized epidermal cell walls than from those which are coated with a layer of cutin. It is sometimes assumed, therefore that the thicker the layer of cutin on the outer walls of the epidermis of a leaf, the slower the rate of cuticular transpiration from that leaf. Actually,however, it seems obvious that any increased thickness in the cutin layer beyond that at which cuticular transpiration becomes negligible will have no appreciable influence on the rate of evapouration from the epidermal cell walls.

EPIDERINAL HAIRS

H airs are prominent features of one or both of the surfaces of the leaves of many species. Living hairs probably increase the rate of cuticular transpiration by increasing the exposed surface of the leaf. Many botanists have assumed that dead hairs reduce the rate of stomatal transpiration, particularly under conditions of intense sunlight or strong winds. In the former case it has been supposed that the whitish hairs reflect such a large proportion of the incident light that the leaf temperature is not as high as it otherwise would be, and that the rate of transpiration is correspondingly lower. In the latter case it has been supposed that the hairs impose a mechanical barrier to the effect of wind on transpiration. However, Sayre found that removal of the hairs from the leaves of the mullein had little effect upon the rate of stomatal transpiration under ordinary conditions of light intensity and wind velocity, although such treatment did result in an increase in cuticular transpiration.

RATIO OF INTERNAL TO EXTERNAL SURFACE IN LEAVES

Although transpiration rates are most frequently expressed in terms of the exposed area of the leaf surface, most of the water-vapour lost from leaves evapourates from the walls of the mesophyll cells which bound the intercellular spaces. The area of this internal evapourating surface in proportion to the external surface of a leaf varies greatly not only in leaves of one species as compared to those of another, but in leaves of the same species if they have developed under different environmental conditions.

Computations of the ratio of internal exposed surface to external exposed surface of leaves of a number of species have yielded values ranging from 6.8 to 31.3. In general the greater the proportion of palisade to sponge tissue the greater this ratio.The thickness of the leaf will also obviously be a factor influencing this ratio.The ratio is greater in sun leaves than in shade leaves of the same species; for the lilac the values are 13.2 and 6.8, respectively.

It has generally been supposed that the transpiration rates of leaves in which a relatively large area of mesophyll cell walls is exposed to the intercellular spaces as compared with the exposed epidermal area of the leaf are greater than in leaves in which the contrary condition obtains. Theoretically such an effect could be exerted only if the area of exposed mesophyll cell walls exercised a controlling influence upon the steepness of the vapour pressure gradient through the stomates.

When transpiration is relatively high a steeper vapour pressure gradient may be maintained by leaves possessing relatively extensive internal evapourating surfaces than by those which do not. The higher transpiration rate of sun leaves as compared with shade leaves on the same plant, which has been observed in some species, may be partly explainable on this basis.

SUNKEN STOMATES

The stomates of many species of plants are sunken below the general level of the epidermis. Since the length of a diffusion gradient is one of the factors governing its steepness, diffusion through a small opening is slower if the gas must pass through a relatively long tube before reaching the orifice, than if the diffusion is through a shorter tube. In leaves in which the stomates are not sunken the diffusion column is relatively short, amounting only to the diameter of the guard cells as seen in cross section, while in sunken stomates the column of gas may be longer by several times.

The diffusion of gases through such stomates is undoubtedly slower than through stomates of the ordinary type. This retarding effect of sunken stomates upon the rate of transpiration as compared with the stomates of the non-sunken type has been estimated by Renner to range from 30 to 70 per cent.

STRUCTURE AND DISTRIBUTION OF THE ROOT SYSTEM

Under some environmental conditions an individual plant of a given species will develop a greater leaf surface in proportion to the extent of its root system thanunder others. The latter type of structural development will, other conditions being equal, favour the maintenance of higher transpiration rates thanthe former.

The distribution of a root system in the soil sometimes influences rates of water absorption and transpiration. In a habitat where deep-rooted and shallow-rooted species are growing side by side the former may transpire more rapidly during drought periods than the latter because their roots penetrate to a soil horizon which still contains available water, while roots of the latter are in a moisture deficient soil. The completeness with which the soil mass is interpenetrated by roots may also influence rates of absorption and transpiration.

Thus Miller found that sorghum plants have almost twice as many fibrous roots as maize plants. Rates of absorption and transpiration can be better maintained, especially when the soil is relatively dry, by plants with the sorghum type of root system than by plants with the maize type of root system.

THE DAILY PERIODICITY OF TRANSPIRATION

All plants exhibit a daily periodicity of transpiration rate which varies somewhat with the species and is greatly influenced by the environmental conditions to which the plant is exposed. We shall first consider the transpiration periodicity upon a standard day as defined in the preceding chapter, since most experiments upon daily variations in transpiration rate have been conducted upon plants growing under approx-imately such conditions.

It should not be assumed, however, that under natural conditions the daily periodicity of transpiration usually or normally follows the trend. The daily periodicity of transpiration under these roughly defined conditions does, however, afford a convenient reference standard with which to compare the many variations which are manifested by this phenomenon.

The transpiration rate during the hours of darkness is generally low, and in most species water loss during this period may be regarded as almost entirely cuticular. It is not justifiable to assume that absolutely no stomatal transpiration occurs at night in any species unless this is definitely known to be true. In some species of plants, as we have already seen, nightstomatal opening is a common occurrence, while in others it occurs under certain environmental conditions. Even in those species in which the stomates are normally closed during the hours of darkness, a few may remain open.

The transpiration rate shows a rapid rise during the early morning hours followed by a slower but consistent increase which culminates in a point of maximum transpiration which occurs sometime during the mid-day hours. Following this peak of transpiration, the rate decreases usually consistently although often with an accelerated rate in the late after noon, until the low and virtually steady night rate is attained at approximately the termination of the daylight period.

The daily periodicity in the rate of stomatal transpiration in most species of plants can be interpreted almost entirely in terms of two variable factors:

1. The diffusive capacity of the stomates, and
2. The vapour pressure gradient between the intercellular spaces of the leaf and the outside atmosphere. In analyzing the daily periodicity of transpiration it is the diffusive capacity of the stomates in the aggregate (*i.e.* all of the stomates on a plant) which must be considered. The aggregate diffusive capacity of the stomates on a plant on which all of the stomates were half open, for example, would be much greater than that for a similar plant on which half of the stomates were fully open and half fully closed.

With the advent of daylight the stomates open over a period of time which varies in length according to the species and with environmental conditions. Some open earlier or more rapidly than others. The initial rise in the rate of transpiration in the morning is due to the opening of the stomates, resulting in a gradual increase in their aggregate diffusive capacity. As each stomate opens a vapour pressure gradient is established through it between the atmosphere of the intercellular spaces and the outside atmosphere. During the hours of darkness the leaf cells regain most or all of the water which they have lost during the preceding day, and thus attain approximately their normal turgidity.

This facilitates the evapouration of water into the intercellular spaces, so that when the stomates open in the morning be internal atmosphere of the leaf is usually saturated with water-vapour, or practically so. The vapour pressure of the intercellular spaces is therefore at the maximum possible for that leaf temperature. This is, on clear days, almost always in excess of the vapour pressure of the atmosphere when the stomates open, and often considerably so. Hence outward diffusion of water-vapour through the stomates usually begins as soon as they are open.

Once a stomate is well open, minor variations in the size of the stomatal aperture have little or no effect on the rate of water-vapour loss through it.The rate of transpiration continues to increase, however, for some time afterthe stomates, in the aggregate, have attained their maximum diffusive capacity. This is due to a gradual increase in the steepness of the vapour pressure gradient through the stomates. As the day progresses the temperature of both the atmosphere and the leaf increases; if the latter is in direct sunlight its temperature is invariably somewhat in excess of that of the atmosphere. On clear days, as previously described, the vapour pressure of the intercellular spaces usually increases relative to that of the atmosphere with a rise in temperature.

The steepness of the vapour pressure gradient between the internal atmosphere of the leaf and the external atmosphere therefore usually increases progressively during the earlier part of the day, and this is the important factor accounting for a rise in the transpiration rate once the stomates have attained approximately their maximum diffusive capacity. Almost from the moment when the stomates begin to open in the morning a train of events is set in operation in the plant which ultimately causes a reduction in the rate of transpiration.

During approximately the first half of the day, however, these factors are more than offset by the factors resulting in an increase in the rate of transpiration. In most plants, while transpiration is occurring rapidly, the rate of absorption of water does not keep pace with the rate at which water-vapour is lost from the leaves. This results in a reduction in the water content of the entire plant, and especially that of the leaves. In more extreme cases wilting results, but under standard day conditions the leaves seldom pass beyond the stage of incipient wilting which corresponds only to a partial loss of turgor by the leaf cells.

PERIODICITY OF TRANSPIRATION

Decrease in the water content of the leaf cells also results in a rise in their diffusion pressure deficit, and a correlated decrease in their vapour pressure. A fully turgid cell (*i.e.* one with a diffusion pressure deficit of zero) has an equilibrium vapour pressure equivalent to that of pure water regardless of its osmotic pressure.

At 20 C. this is 17.54 mm. Hg. If the diffusion pressure deficit of the mesophyll cells of a leaf at this temperature were raised to 100 atmos., a value which can be attained in only a very few species of plants, their vapour pressure would decrease by only about 1.27 mm. Hg. Since the vapour pressure of the cell walls, with which the vapour pressure of the intercellular spaces tends to be in equilibrium, in turn tends to be in equilibrium with that of the cell sap, it would appear that an increase in the diffusion pressure deficit of the mesophyll cells has only a very slight influence upon vapour pressure conditions in the intercellular spaces.

However, certain other factors must be taken into consideration in evaluating the effect of a diminished leaf water content upon the vapour pressure of the intercellular spaces. Decrease in the water content of the leaf cells involves a reduction in the quantity of water in the cell walls as well as in other parts of the cell. Water undoubtedly passes through cell walls principally through the intermicellar material. The principal effect of a decrease in the quantity of water in the walls is a shrinkage in the volume of the hydrophilic intermicellar material and a resulting contraction in diameter of the intermicellar capillaries.

This probably results in a decrease in the permeability of the walls to water. Hence, under such conditions, water often may not pass across the walls with sufficient rapidity that an equilibrium vapour pressure is maintained between the cell sap and the outer surface of the cell walls. When the water content of a leaf is low the vapour pressure of the cell wall surface in contact with the intercellular spaces may therefore be less than the vapour pressure of the water in the cell sap. Any such reduction in the vapour pressure of the intercellular spaces results in decreasing the steepness of the vapour pressure gradient between the intercellular spaces and the outside atmosphere, and hence decreases the rate of transpiration.

The experimental results of That indicate that the vapour pressure of the intercellular spaces is often at less than a saturation value. During the course of a day, however, the steepness of the vapour pressure gradient through the stomates may be decreased in still another and perhaps more important way. When the stomates open in the morning the vapour pressure gradient between the saturated internal leaf atmosphere and the outside atmosphere is short and hence steep, being approximately equal in length to the depth of the guard cells. For some time after the stomates open essentially such a condition is probably maintained. As the day advances the rapid loss of water-vapour molecules out of the interc-ellular spaces, perhaps coupled with a gradual reduction in the vapour pressure of the cell walls makes it less and less likely that a condition of saturation can be maintained throughout the intercellular spaces.

The zone in which a vapour pressure inequilibrium with the water in the mesophyll cell walls is maintained almostcertainly retreats more and more deeply into the intercellular spaces. Eventually it may be restricted to a thin layer just above the evapourating surfaces of the mesophyll cell walls. This gradual lengthening of the vapour pressuregradient through the stomates is probably an important factor in bringing about a reduction in the rate of transpiration during the afternoon hours.

It has frequently been observed in studies of transpiration periodicity that the transpiration rate often begins to decrease during the midday period before any appreciable change occurs in the area of the stomatal apertures. This indicates that the initial reduction in transpiration rate is induced by some other factor than a change in the diffusive capacity of the stomates. As the preceding discussion has shown this other factor is almost certainly a reduction in the steepness of the vapour pressure gradient through the stomates.

By late afternoon the air temperature and the intensity of the solar radiation begin to decrease appreciably, thus inducing a decrease in the temperature of the leaf. This lowering of the leaf temperature may further decrease the vapour pressure of the intercellular spaces, and hence further depress the steepness of the vapour pressure gradient, since temperature changes have very little influence on the vapour pressure of the outside atmosphere under standard day conditions.

Thus the effect of a reduction in the vapour pressureg radient through the stomates in decreasing the rate of transpiration, which first becomes apparent during the midday period, continues with augmented effect as the hours of darkness approach. Continued diminution in the leaf water content due to the excess of transpiration over absorption eventually results also in a diminution of the turgor of the guard cells due to a decrease in the water content of the leaf.

This results in a gradual closure of the stomates. Some of the stomates on a plant probably begin to close even before the time at which the peak of the transpiration rate is attained. In all likelihood stomates near the margin or tip of a leaf begin to close before those in the middle since the effects of deficiency of water usually appear first in these regions of a leaf. With an increasing leaf water deficit more and more of the stomates on the plant close.

This soon results in a reduction in the aggregated iffusive capacity of the stomatal population of the plant. As the afternoon advances more and more of the stomates become completely closed, resulting in a progressive diminution in diffusive capacity. This gradual closing of the stomates, resulting in an increasingly larger proportion of them being closed as the day advances, is the principal factor reducing the rate of transpiration during the latter part of the day. The effect of this factor and that of a decreased steepness of the vapour pressure gradient overlap during a large part of the afternoon.

Finally, by late afternoon, complete closure of essentially all of the stomates has occurred. Stomatal transpiration is terminated at that time and during the hours of darkness the rate of water loss from the plant is controlled by factors influencing the rate of cuticular transpiration. Under environmental conditions deviating very greatly from those which were postulated in the preceding discussion, transpiration periodicity curves may be entirely different from those. Variations in temperature, light intensity, humidity, and soil water supply may all markedly influence both the trend of transpiration periodicity, and the magnitude of the daily water loss.

Low temperatures may result in a complete elimination of stomatal transpiration by inducing stomatal closure. Low light intensities, such as those existing on cloudy days, are unfavourable to stomatal opening in most species. The stomates seldom open completely under such conditions and the period during which they are open is usually of shorter duration than on clear days. Furthermore, the vapour pressuregradient through the stomates is seldom as steep on such days as on clear bright days, since leaf temperatures never appreciably exceed atmospheric temperatures except when exposed to direct sunlight, and atmospheric vapour pressures are usually higher during cloudy days than on clear days at the same season of the year. The magnitude of transpiration under such conditions is usually greatly reduced, and transpiration periodicity curves plotted for plants exposed to such conditions usually present a somewhat fore shortened and greatly flattened appearance.

A deficient soil water supply is most commonly the factor which causes marked departures from the type of transpiration periodicity already considered, especially during the summer months. The effect of a gradual diminution in soil water content upon transpiration periodicity. A reduction in soil water content has two pronounced effects upon the daily march of transpiration. The total daily magnitude of water loss is decreased, and the peak of the transpiration curve often occurs somewhat earlier in the day than under conditions of abundant soil water supply. Since, even in temperate regions, periods of decreased soil water supply are of common occurrence during the summer months, and in many habitats are the rule rather than the exception for many species of plants much of the time.

Internal factors may also be responsible for transpiration periodicities of a different trend from those which have already been discussed. In some species of plants, as has already been described, the stomates remain open to a greater or lesser extent during the hours of darkness. Such plants have higher transpiration rates at night than those in which the stomates are closed. In some species of cacti there is a complete inversion of the usual transpiration periodicity curve, transpiration rates being regularly greater at night than in the daytime. This appears to be due to complete or nearly complete stomatal closure during the hours of daylight, while the stomates are, as a rule, open at night.

TEMPERATE REGIONS TRANSPIRATION

In temperate regions transpiration occurs predominantly during the warmer months of the year and especially during those periods of the warm season when the soil water supply is abundant. Among the deciduous group of woody perennials, the branches are defoliated during most of the autumn, all of the winter, and the earlier part of the spring.

Although the twigs and branches which remain exposed to the atmosphere are completely encased in corky layers of bark and the buds are enclosed within cutinized bud scales some water loss occurs from such species even during the winter months. Young twigs lose water under such conditions faster than older ones. Winter transpiration rates of deciduous woody plants are always negligible in comparison with summer rates. In evergreen species of either the needle-leaved or broad-leaved type the transpiration rates are usually not appreciably different at most times during the winter from the transpiration rate of deciduous trees at that season. This is probably due principally to the fact that the low temperatures of the winter prevent opening of the stomates although the relatively low leaf water contents characteristic of this season may also be a factor in maintaining the stomates in a closed condition. Mild periods of any considerable duration often have a detrimental effect upon evergreen species during the winter months. The warm air temperatures induce stomatal opening, and a relatively high rate of transpiration ensues.

The soil is apt to be deficient in water at such times, or even if present, that in the surface layers may remain frozen during a period of warm air temperatures. Even if neither of the foregoing conditions exists, the soil temperatures will be low, and this greatly retards the rate of absorption of water.

The combined effect of a relatively high transpiration rate and relatively low absorption rate results in a gradual desiccation of the leaves and branches of the plant. This diminution in the water content of the aerial organs during warm periods in winter is more severe in windy weather and is more likely to occur if a sequence of mild days follows immediately after a cold spell. If severe enough this desiccation will result in the death of some of the branches, or in extreme cases of the entire tree or shrub. This is one cause of the phenomenon known as winter-killing. Winter-killing due to desiccation of the tissues should not be confused with cold injury due to low temperatures which is an entirely different phenomenon.

DOWNWARD MOVEMENT OF WATER

There are a number of experiments on record which indicate that downward movement of water can occur in stems. For example, Dixon found that if the tip of the leaf of a potato plant be cut off under an eosin solution the liquid will descend through the xylem tissue of the leaf, petiole, and stem, and eventually reach the under ground organs. In general, however, such an effect is to be expected only when an internal water deficit exists in a plant.

The cohesion theory of the movement of water will account equally well for the conduction of water in either the upward or the downward direction through the plant. If conditions are ever such that the diffusion pressure deficit of the cells of roots or some other basal organ of a plant exceeds that of the apical parts of the same plant a reversal of the direction of movement of water in the xylem will occur. Although downward movement of water can be readily induced in plants under certain experimental conditions, such movements of water are probably of infrequent occurrence in intact plants.

SOILS AND SOIL WATER RELATIONS

Most vascular plants are rooted in the soil from which they obtain both water and mineral salts. The entrance of water from the environment into any of the organs of a plant is called the absorption, intake, or uptake of water. In most vascular species the quantity of water absorbed through organs other than the roots is of negligible importance. Any thorough consideration of the entrance of water into roots requires a consideration of the properties of soils, particularly as they affect the movement of water from the soil into the root.

CONSTITUTION OF THE SOIL

The soil matrix which is the habitat of most roots is an extremely complex system. In general five different components of this system are distinguished:1. The Mineral Matter of the Soil.The parent substance of practically all soils is rock, of which there are numerous varieties. By various weathering processes rock strata are reduced to fragments of diverse sizes and these compose the bulk of most soils. The rock particles in soils may vary in size from stones and gravel down to sub-microscopic particles of colloidal clay.

The mineral portion of the soil is customarily classified into several fractions depending upon the size of the particles. Such classifications usually disregard the very large particles of the soil (rock fragments, pebbles, etc.). The proportions of the different fractions present are very different in different kinds of soils.The clay fraction of the mineral portion of soils requires special consideration. Unlike the coarser fractions which are composed of small fragments of unmodified rock minerals such as quartz, feldspar, and mica, the clay portion of soils is made up almost entirely of the products of chemical weathering of the rock minerals and hence differs not only in its physical state, but in its chemical composition from the particles in the coarser fractions.

Most of the particles in the clay fraction are of colloidal dimensions and exhibit the characteristic properties of colloidal systems. The particles of the clay complex, like those of many other colloidal systems, retain water by imbibition, *i.e.* within the structure of the particle. On the contrary the sand and silt particles of the soil retain water only on their surfaces. The presence of a considerable proportion of clay in a soil therefore endows it with a high water retaining capacity. Changes in the water content of colloidal clay result in marked changes in its volume. One result of such changes in volume is the commonly observed cracking of a soil rich in clay upon drying. The plasticity and cohesiveness of soils are also due very largely to the colloidal clay present.

Like other colloidal systems colloidal clay is markedly sensitive to the influence of electrolytes. The micelles of colloidal clay usually bear a negative charge when in contact with water. In the presence of calcium ions the individual clay particles are more or less completely flocculated into compound particles. Much of the colloidal clay in most soils exists as enveloping films around the larger soil particles and is also closely associated with organic material in the soil. Flocculation of the clay particles therefore usually results in the formation of compound granules including sand and silt particles and organic matter in addition to the clay.

These are called soil crumbs. For agricultural purposes a well developed granular structure of the soil is highly desirable since such a structure favours both a high moisture-retaining capacity and a good aeration of the soil. Calcium soils, that is, those with a high calcium content, are in general the most suitable and most valuable for agricultural purposes partly because calcium favours the development of a crumb structure. In the presence of an excess of univalent cations ($Na+$, etc.), on the other hand, a greater proportion of the clay fraction of the soil disperses into its ultimate particles, and the soil has a single grain structure.

In this condition the soil is in the least desirable structural condition for agricultural purposes. Many soils contain hydrogen ions in excess. Such soils often develop a good crumb structure, but the crumbs are less stable than those developed in a calcium soil. The addition of lime improves the physical structure of such soils. The crumb structure of a soil, especially in its surface layers, can also be destroyed by purely mechanical effects, such as trampling,or beating by heavy rains. The Organic Matter of the Soil.

Most soils contain organic matter which has been derived principally from the partial decomposition of plant residues. Small quantities may also originate from animal residues and excretions. The proportion of organic matter present may vary from almost none as in some sand deposits to 95 per cent or better in some peat soils. In ordinary agricultural soils the amount present seldom exceeds 15 per cent. In forests organic matter comes from falling leaves, dead branches and trunks of woody plants, roots which die and decay underground, and from dead herbaceous vegetation. In grasslands the underground roots and rhizomes as well as the aerial parts of the plants all contribute their quota to the organic matter of the soil. In well managed agricultural soils attempts are made to maintain the organic matter content by supplying them with organic fertilizers.

The organic matter is the seat of most of the microbiol-ogical processes occurring in the soil. One of the most important of these is the oxidation of the organic matter, a process due largely to the metabolic activities of bacteria and fungi, although a limited amount of purely chemical decomposition probably also occurs. Under conditions which are exceptionally favourable for the activities of microorganisms the organic matter of the soil is oxidized completely and disappears.

For this reason the organic matter of soils in tropical regions, particularly when under cultivation, is very low. Even in more temperate regions cultivation of the soils generally results in a rapid reduction inorganic matter content, due principally to the better aeration induced by till age. As a result of the decay process there is present in most soils organic matter in various stages of decomposition. A large proportion of the organicmaterial which is added to some soils survives in the form of a dark-colouredamorphous substance called humus.

Humus is composed principally of the degradation products of the cellulose and lignin derived from plant remains.

The accumulation of humus in soils is furthered by conditions unfavourable to the oxidative decomposition of organic matter. The decomposition of organic matter in bogs, ponds, swamps, and water-logged soils under conditions which are largely if not entirely anaerobic results in the production of relatively large quantities of humus, frequently of the type which is called peat. Where the organic matter supplied is distinctly acid, as under coniferous forests, or heath plants, humus usually accumulates as a definite layer at the surface. Decomposition of the organic remains under these conditions is largely effected by fungi. In prairie and steppe regions, where a grassland vegetation is predominant, humus usually accumulates in considerable quantities as a result of the decay of both underground and aerial organs of plants.

The amount of humus which accumulates in any soil depends upon the relative rates of the addition of organic residues and of its disappearance as a result of oxidation. Soils with a low humus content may result from a sparse contribution of organic matter, as in desert or semi-desert regions, or from a rapid oxidation of organic material which prevents accumulation of humus even when the supply of organic residues to the soil is large.

This latter condition obtains in many tropical and sub-tropical soils. Humus is essentially colloidal in its properties and possesses an even greater imbibitional capacity than the colloidal clay particles of the soil. The plasticity and cohesiveness of the colloidal organic matter, while considerably less than that of the colloidal clay, is much greater than that of the non-colloidal fractions of the soil. Humus is rather inert chemically, its influence on the soil being largely a physical one. Its presence in soils favours a looser structure and hence better aeration, a higher water holding capacity and a reduction in cohesiveness as compared with heavy clay soils.

Since the clay fraction and the humus are the two essentially colloidal fractions of the soil, and are associated in an intimate physical relationship many soil scientists refer to these two soil fractions, considered jointly, as the colloidal complex of the soil. A large part of this colloidal complex occurs in many soils, as films enveloping the larger soil particles. The relation of these films to the maintenance of the crumb structure of the soil has already been mentioned. Many other important soil properties are either due to or greatly influenced by the colloidal complex.

SOIL WATER AND THE SOIL SOLUTION

Water is universally a component of soils, although the amount present may vary from the merest trace to a quantity sufficient to saturate the soil, *i.e.* completely fill all of the spaces between the soil particles. Dissolved in the soil water are varying quantities of numerous chemical compounds. These originate principally from the dissolution or chemical weathering of the rock particles, from the decomposition of organic matter, from the activities of microorganisms, and from reactions between the roots of plants and the soil constituents. It is thus more accurate to speak of the soil solution than of the soil water, although in discussions of the water relations of soils it is often a common practice to disregard the presence of solutes in the soil water.

The concentration of the soil solution in any given soil varies with the proportion of water present. While in most soils the soil solution is very dilute, in saline and alkaline soils it maybe so concentrated that only a few species of plants can survive with their roots in contact with it. The principal cations found in the soil solution are Ca_{11}, Mg_{11}, K1, Na1, Al^{+1+}, and Fe^{111} (or Fe^{++}); the principal anions are HCO_3Th $P0_4$, Cl, $N0_3$, $S0_4$, and 5i03. Other solutes too numerous to mention may also occur in the soil solution but are usually present only in very low concentrations. Soil water relations receive a more detailed discussion later in this chapter.

THE SOIL ATMOSPHERE

The irregularity of the soil particles in size shape, and arrangement insures the existence of a certain amount of space between them, even in the most tightly packed soils. This is termed the pore space of a soil. The pore space of soils varies from approximately 30 per cent of the volume of the soil in sandy soils to about so per cent of the volume in clay soils, or even higher in soils which are very rich in organic matter. The pore space of any given soil depends upon the physical and chemical conditions to which the soil is subjected. Conditions favouring a crumb structure of a soil, for example, usually result in an increase in its pore space.

The interstitial spaces of a soil may be occupied entirely by air, as indesiccated soils, entirely by water, as in saturated soils, or, as is most usually true, partly by water and partly by air. The relative proportions of water and air present in any given soil vary depending upon the water content of the soil.

The air present in the soil is generally referred to as the soil atmosphere.The soil air usually contains a higher concentration of carbon dioxide and a lower concentration of oxygen than the above ground atmosphere. Concentrations of carbon dioxide as high as 5 per cent have been recorded for the soil atmosphere; such values are far in excess of the average value of 0.03 per cent for the air. The accumulation of carbon dioxide in soils is due more to the metabolic activities of micro-organisms than to respiration of soil animals and the underground portions of vascular plants. Except in very dry soils the soil atmosphere is usually saturated or nearly so with water-vapour.5. Soil Organisms.

The soil flora includes bacteria, fungi, and algae. The bacteria are generally the most abundant of all the living organisms present in any soil. Among them are the nitrifying, sulfofying, nitrogen fixing, ammonifying, and cellulose decomposing bacteria. The bacteria accomplishing the oxidative decomposition of cellulose and similar compounds are the most important agents in the production of humus. The numbers of bacteria present vary greatly from soil to soil, and in any one soil vary with seasonal and other fluctuations in soil conditions. Most soils contain between two million and two hundred million individual bacteria per gram of soil. The number of bacteria decreases rapidly with increasing depth, sub soils being sterile or practically so.

In general an abundant representation of most species of bacteria is favoured in soils by warm temperatures (3 - 400 C.), good aeration, and a good but not superabundant water supply. A high calcium content of the soil is also favourable to the development of most species of bacteria, apparently because it favours a granular structure of the soil, thus improving aeration. Some species of bacteria, on the other hand, are anaerobic,and thrive when aeration of the soil is deficient. The denitrifying bacteria and certain of the nitrogen-fixing bacteria (Clostridiurn spp.) are examples of anaerobes. Fungi are, in general, most abundant in soils of acid reaction. In such soils they largely replace bacteria as agents of decomposition of organic matter.

The soil fauna includes protozoa, nematodes, earthworms, insects, insect larvae, and burrowing species of the higher animals. The earthworms are generally credited with having the most important effects on soil structure, at least in many soils. Their activities result principally in a general loosening of the soil, which facilitates both aeration and distribution of water. Many of the other soil animals have similar effects on the structural organization of the soil.

SOIL WATER RELATIONS UNDER FIELD CONDITIONS

In a region of moist climate, if a hole be dug or bored into the ground at almost any place where the soil is deep enough a level at which the soil is completely saturated with water will be encountered at some depth or other. Water will stand in this hole up to this level of complete saturation which is called the water table. In river valleys or in close proximity to large bodies of water the water table will usually be reached at a depth of only a few feet under the soil surface. Even in regions of arid climate there are some local situations in which a water table is present.

The depth of the water table in any locality usually fluctuates, sometimes very markedly, with seasonal and periodic changes in the relative rates of rainfall, evapouration, transpiration and other factors. Relatively impermeable soil layers sometimes impede downward percolation of water sufficiently to cause the development of temporary water tables which may be far above the level of the true water table. Such temporary water tables have essentially the same effects on soil water relations as true water tables, except that their influence is often only a transient one.

For many years an important role was ascribed to the capillary rise of the water from the water table into the soil above in maintaining the moisture conditions within that soil. Recent investigations have shown, however, that the importance of this source of water in soils has been overemphasized. Experiments upon the rise of water through columns of soil indicate that water seldom rises through the soil by capillarity from the water table at an appreciable rate for heights of more than a few feet. In a typical loam soil the absolute maximum capillary rise of water is about 8 feet. Such capillary rise as does occur takes place most slowly, but to the greatest height in clay soils, and most rapidly but to lesser heights in sandy soils, loam soils occupying an intermediate position.In many soils the water table lies so far below the soil surface that it has little or no effect on the soil moisture conditions in the soil layers which are penetrated by the roots of most plants.

Generally speaking even in loam or clay loam soils, a capillary rise of water from a zone of complete saturation is probably ineffective in providing the roots of most species of plants with any considerable part of the water which they absorb unless the water table is within about 15 feet of the surface. Some of the more deeply rooted species may obtain some water from a water table located at depths as great as about 30 feet, but the presence of a water table at greater depths than this is an egligible factor in supplying the roots of any species of plants with water. A capillary rise of water from a water table is usually an important source of water for plants in such locations as river bottom lands or in fields or forests in close proximity to ponds or lakes. In many and perhaps most agricultural soils in moist climate regions plants obtain some water from the water table at least during the earlier part of the growing season.

However the widespread practice of drainage of agricultural regions has often resulted in such a marked lowering of the water table as to greatly reduce the possibility that capillary rise of water from below will supply crop plants with any significant part of the water which they absorb. The other important source of soil water is that part of the precipitation usually rain, although often melting snow or ice, which percolates downward into the soil. In dry regions this is the only source of water available to plants.

Even in more humid regions this is the principal or only source of available soil water in most soils during the dry season of the year. Not all of the rain which falls on the surface of a soil penetrates into it. Some maybe lost by surface run-off and a portion usually evapourates before it can sink into the soil. The proportion of the precipitation which is lost in the run-off is in general much less with open, porous soils such as those found in most forests than with those of a lower porosity.

A smaller proportion of the water is lost in the run-off when it falls as a gentle rain than when it comes as sudden downpour. The proportion of the precipitation which is lost by evapouration from the surface layers of the soil depends in part on the colour, texture porosity, and other properties of the soil, and in part on the temperature and vapour pressure of the atmosphere, as well as upon the impinging solar radiation.

Let us now consider how percolating rainwater becomes distributed in as oil. We will assume that the soil under consideration is approximately air dry, that it is essentially homogeneous to a depth of several feet, and that Let us now assume that another two inches of rain falls on this same soil before any appreciable amount is lost from its upper layers by evapouration or transpiration. After a new equilibrium has been attained the upper foot of soil will not have increased in water content, but a layer of the soil approximately two feet in depth will now be moistened up to its field capacity. In other words addition of a second increment of water equal in volume to the first does not increase the water content of the already moist layer of the soil above its field capacity, but results, due to further capillary movement, in raising to its field capacity a second layer of soil, lying directly under the zone which had been moistened by the addition of the first increment of rain, and approximately equal to it in thickness.

Although the exact mechanics of the distribution of water under these conditions is probably more complicated, the effect produced is as if the second increment of water simply flows through the moist blanket of soil, after which it is distributed to the dry soil layer underneath by capillarity. Successive rainfalls would thus continue to deepen the layer of soil which has been moistened up to its field capacity. If the water table is not too deep, and if sufficient rainfall penetrates the soil, not too much of which is utilized by plants growing thereon, eventually the entire soil from its surface down to the water table will be moistened up to its field capacity. A zone several feet in height just above the water table may be enriched somewhat above field capacity by upward capillary movement from the water table.

If additional water is applied to the soil, after the entire soil mass down to the water table has attained its field capacity, this water percolates down through the soil under the influence of gravity and becomes apart of the ground water. Such conditions obtain in many of the soils of more humid regions at least during the wetter seasons of the year, provided that the water table is not located at too great a depth. This downward percolation of water to the water table is an important factor in influencing its depth below the soil surface, which usually fluctuates considerably from season to season.

In the preceding discussion we have assumed, in the interests of simplicity a homogeneous soil. However, most soils consist of a vertical succession of several distinct horizons, each with more or less distinctive physical and chemical properties. Even after long continued disturbance of a soil by plowing or other cultural activities at least some semblance of the original soil stratification usually persists. In the horizons below those reached by the plow the original structural organization of the soil is usually maintained practically intact. Although the individual horizons of a soil are often fairly homogeneous within themselves, each such horizon in a given soil may have a distinct field capacity of its own.

The water contents of the different horizons, even after an equilibrium in the capillary distribution of water has been attained, may therefore be very different. A somewhat erratic distribution of rainfall to an underlying soil often results from cracks or channels which are opened into the soil by one agency or another. Many soils crack upon drying, sometimes to depths of several feet. Such cracks often facilitate a mass flow of rainwater to a considerable depth in the soil. Similarly in forest soils the decomposition of roots may leave channels through which water flows down into the deeper layers of the soil. The burrows of animals may also facilitate the entry of water into a soil.The presence of rock strata, or of relatively impervious layers of soil close to the surface, will also modify very markedly the simple picture which has been presented of soil water conditions.

LABORATORY MEASUREMENTS OF SOIL WATER RELATIONS

The problem of the water relations of soils has been approached both from the standpoint of laboratory and field studies. Some of the broader generalizations resulting from field studies have been just described. Of the numerous laboratory measurements of the water relations of soils which have been devised, only a few of the better known will be discussed. Water Content. The water content of a soil is commonly expressed as the percentage of water present in terms of the dry weight of the soil. It is measured by drying a sample of the soil in an oven to constant weight at (usually) 105^0C. and assuming that the loss in weight represents water.

There is however nothing critical about the temperature 105^0C. The relation between the water content as determined by this method and the temperature at which the soil is dried is a linear one over a wide range of temperatures extending on both sides of this point. This shows that there is no especial significance to be attached to the amount of water which is lost from a soil when dried at this temperature. There is also a small error in such determinations due to some decomposition of organic matter at this temperature. Determinations of the total water content of the soil contribute very little to an understanding of the absorption of water from the soil by plants. As will be shown later the amount of water available to plants may be very different in two soils of identical water contents.

WATER RETAINING CAPACITY

One of the most familiar laboratory determinations of soil water is that of the so-called water retaining capacity (also called moisture holding capacity, water holding capacity, water capacity,etc.). This determination is usually made as follows: A shallow cylindrical pan with a perforated bottom is filled with dry soil, immersed in water to the depth of a few millimeters, and allowed to stand until it becomes saturated. The soil is then allowed to drain free of all the water which will drip out under the influence of the pull of gravity. The water content of the soil after it has been subjected to this treatment, determined by the usual method of oven-drying, is regarded as its water retaining capacity.

It has often been assumed that a determination such as that just described is an indication of the amount of water which would be held by that soil in the field in opposition to the pull of gravity but such an assumption is entirely unjustified. In the first place in making such determinations the vessel is filled with the soil in such a way that the distribution of particles in the soil mass is very different from that which obtains in the field. This error is sometimes minimized by cutting out a core of soil in the field by means of a steel cylinder and using this core for a determination of the water retaining the plant. Since no water is added to the soil the plants eventually pass into a state of permanent wilting due to the loss of water by transpiration. As soon as this occurs a sample of the soil is removed and its water content is determined by the oven-drying method. Prior to extensive determinations of wilting percentages it was supposed that plants differed very markedly in their capacity to reduce the water content of a soil.

It was assumed, for example, that species which could endure drought conditions could deplete the moisture content of a soil to a lower percentage before showing permanent wilting than could those species which were soon injured or killed when subjected to drought. Extensive investigations have shown, however, that hydrophytes, mesophytes, and xerophytes all reduce the water content of a given type of soil to about the same value before the condition of permanent wilting is induced. The value of the wilting percentage for each species was determined by calculating the ratio of the individual determination to the mean of all determinations made with that soil. The values given in this table are the average mean ratios for a number of determinations on each species.

While the wilting percentage for a given soil shows no appreciable variation when measured by means of different plants growing in it, the value varies greatly with the type of soil. The percentage of water remaining in a soil when permanent wilting of the plants growing in it occurs ranges from approximately 5 to 10 per cent for sandy loams, from about 10 to 15 per cent for silty loams, and from about 1 to 20 per cent in clay loams. According to Caidwell (1913) and Shive and Livingston (1914) a greater percentage of water is left in the soil at permanent wilting if the plants are transpiring rapidly than if they are transpiring slowly. Veihmeyer and Hendrickson however, record that the wilting percentage of a given soil as determined with sunflower plants shows very little difference over a wide range of climatic conditions. In general this quantity seems to be controlled almost entirely by soil conditions and is only slightly influenced by the species of plant used, or by the climatic conditions to which that plant is exposed.

The significance of the wilting percentage lies in the fact that it is essentially a measure of that fraction of the soil water which is unavailable forplants. However, it should not be assumed that absolutely all movement of water into the roots has ceased when the soil water content has been reduced to its wilting percentage. Wilted plants continue to reduce the water content of the soil but at such a slow rate that restoration of turgidity is impossible since the rate of transpiration even from a wilted plant exceeds the rate of absorption of water from a soil which is at its wilting percentage or lower.

Actually, plants in the field often exhibit permanent wilting at soil water contents somewhat in excess of the wilting percentage as determined by the usual technique. In laboratory determinations of the wilting percentage the plants are ordinarily rooted in relatively small containers in which the soil mass becomes effectively penetrated by roots resulting in a fairly uniform reduction in the water content of the soil. In the field, however, such conditions do not often prevail. The soil is usually less effectively penetrated by the root systems of the plant growing therein, and some portions of the soil may be less completely depleted of water than others before permanent wilting ensues. Although the soil in the immediate vicinity of the absorbing zone of each root is at the wilting percentage more remote portions of the soil may still be at the field capacity. Hence the average water content of such a soil at permanent wilting may be considerably in excess of the wilting percentage as determined by the usual laboratory procedure.

THE DIFFUSION PRESSURE DEFICIT OF THE WATER IN SOILS

In preceding discussions of the water relations of plant cells and tissues it has been shown that the most significant unit for the expression of the dynamics of water relations of plant cells is the quantity which has been termed in this book the diffusion pressure deficit. Since all problems of the absorption of water by plants involve a consideration of the relation of the water in the soil and the water in the plant, it is desirable that this concept of the diffusion pressure deficit of water be extended to the soil water if the absorption of water is to be interpreted in terms of dynamic units.

One of the first successful attempts to measure the retentive capacity of the soil for water was made by Shull. In an ingenious approach to this problem air-dry seeds of the cocklebur (Xanthium pennsylvanicurn) were used as the instrument for measuring the diffusion pressure deficit ofthe soil. Seeds of this species were first placed in salt solutions of various osmotic pressures and the percentage of water which had been imbibed when an equilibrium was attained in each solution was first determined.

Once the percentages of water held by these seeds when in equilibrium with solutions of different osmotic pressures had been determined, the diffusion pressure deficit of any medium in which they might be immersed could beme asured. For example, if some of these seeds were immersed in a medium of unknown osmotic pressure (diffusion pressure deficit) until a dynamic equilibrium was established, after which it was determined that their moisture content was 32.8 per cent, a diffusion pressure deficit of 26.6 atmos. was indicated for the medium. This principle was applied to the measurement of the diffusion pressure deficit of soils at different water contents.

A sample of soil at a known water content was shaken with some ofthe seeds until an equilibrium was attained, after which the water content ofthe seeds was determined. With an increase in the soil water content its diffusion pressure deficit decreases. In the range of low water contents a small increase in water content corresponds to a very large decrease in the diffusion pressure deficit ofthe soil. As the water content of the soil is increased further the diffusion pressure deficit continues to decrease but at a progressively slower rate. Diffusion pressure deficit values for soil water may be calculated from the results of a number of other types of determinations.

Among these are vapour pressure measurements determinations of the freezing point depression of the soil, and measurements of the amount of water retained by a soil in equilibrium with tensions of a known magnitude. Each of these methods is suitable only for a certain range of soil water contents. The first can be used satisfactorily only with relatively dry soils, the last with relatively wet soils, and the second only over an intermediate range of soil water contents. From data obtained by one or more of these methods it is possible to construct for any soil a water content-diffusion pressure deficit curve. Most ofthe important soil water relation scan be interpreted in terms of such curves. Such a curve is characterized by an abrupt rise in diffusion pressure deficit in the region of low soil water contents.

The position of the wilting percentage is just to the right of the sharp inflection which occurs in the curve. The diffusion pressure deficit of the soil water at the wilting percentage lies within a range of 412 atmos. Experimentally determined values for this quantity vary slightly depending uponthe method used for their measurement.

The position of the wilting percentage makes understandable the fact that all species of plants seem to be able to reduce the soil water content of any given soil to approximately the same percentage before they pass into a state of permanent wilting. As shown by this curve reduction of the water content of the soil by only a very small percentage below that of the wilting percentage results in a very rapid rise in the diffusion pressure deficit of the soil. Plants can only obtain water when the diffusion pressure deficit of the soil water is less than that of the peripheral cells in the absorbing zone of the root.

Except in halophytes the diffusion pressure deficit of root cells probably seldom exceeds 25 atmos. and is usually considerably less. The diffusion pressure deficit of the water in a soil will attain an equilibrium with a plant in which a diffusion pressure deficit of 25 atmos. has developed in the root cells at only a slightly lower soil water content than with a plant in which the diffusion pressure deficit of the root cells is only 5 atmos. Hence wilting percentages as determined with different species of plants are all approximately the same since the actual differences in wilting percentages usually don't exceed the experimental errors inherent in the method of determining this quantity.

To the right of the point corresponding to the wilting percentage the slope of the curve is very gradual. The field capacity corresponds to a diffusion pressure deficit of about one atmosphere, indicating that plants have very little difficulty in absorbing water at soil moisture contents corresponding to this value the preceding discussion has been based on the assumption that the soluble salt concentration of the soil is not sufficient to have an appreciable effect on the diffusion pressure deficit of the soil water.

In any soil heavily charged with soluble salts, as for example alkali soils, the diffusion pressure deficitof the water may range up to 100 atmos. or even higher, due to the osmotic effect of the dissolved salts. The curve expressing the soil water content-diffusion pressure deficit relationship in such a soil would not approach very closely to the zero axis, even in soils which are nearly or entirely saturated but would level off at a value corresponding to the osmotic pressure of the soil solution.

THE MOVEMENT OF WATER THROUGH THE PLANT

Most terrestrial plants obtain the water which is necessary for their existence from the soil. An overwhelmingly large proportion of the water which is absorbed by the roots of land plants is lost in the process of transpiration. Smaller quantities are utilized in growth and in photosynthesis and in some species limited amounts of water may be lost by guttation.

Water must therefore move through the intervening tissues and organs from the absorbing regions of the root to the tissues in which it is utilized, or from which it passes out of the plant. The process whereby water moves through the plant is often termed the conduction, transport, or translocation of water.

In herbaceous species and many shrubby plants the distance throughwhich water moves in passing from the root tips to the leaves is usually not more than a few feet. Even in such plants appearances are sometimes deceptive, as some herbaceous and shrubby species such as alfalfa may have such deep root systems that some of the absorbed water often ascends for distances as great as twenty or more feet before it reaches the level of the soil surface. It is in trees, however, in which the most striking illustrations of the upward movement of water occur. The tallest tree of which we have an authentic record is a specimen of the Coast Redwood which has attained a height of 364 feet.

Many other individuals of this species and of several others, including the Big Trees of California, the Douglas Firs (Pseudotsuga mucronata) of the Pacific Northwest, and the Blue Gums (Eucalyptus) of Australia exceed 300 feet in height. Trees ranging from 100 to 200 feet in height were of common occurrence in the virgin forests of eastern North America. Since the root systems of trees always penetrate at least a few feet into the ground the actual vertical distance through which at least a part of the water absorbed is elevated is always more than the height of the tree. In trees, therefore, water must ascend to heights ranging up to nearly 400 feet above the level of water absorption.

The mechanism by which this feat is accomplished in tall trees has been the subject of much experimentation, and even more speculation. The ensuing discussion of the ascent of sap through plants will be presented largely in terms of its movement through trees, principally because much of the experimental work on this problem has been performed on woody species. Any explanation of this phenomenon which can be shown to be adequate for tall trees should also prove satisfactory for vascular species of lesser stature.

THE PATH OF WATER THROUGH THE PLANT

Water enters the plant through the epidermal cells and root hairs at or near the tips of the roots and crosses the cortex, endodermis, and a part of the pericycle before it finally enters the lumina of the vessels or tracheids of the root xylem. At this point its upward movement begins. The xylem tissue is continuous from just back of the root tips, through the roots, into and through the stems, the petioles of leaves, and ultimately, usually only after much branching, terminates in the mesophyll of the leaf.

The xylem tissue through which the water moves is thus a continuous unit system within the body of the plant. Along most of its course water moves en masse through the vessels or tracheids of the xylem. At the termination of the xylem ducts in the leaves the water passes into the adjacent mesophyll cells. In the mesophyll of the leaves it moves from cell to cell, eventually most of it being lost from the cells by ognized at least since the time of the girdling experiments of Malpighi in 1671. Girdling (or ringing) a stem, so that all of the tissues external tothe xylem are removed, does not prevent movement of water to organs attached to that stem above the ring. On the contrary cutting through the xylem tissue of a stem results in almost immediate wilting of leaves attached to the stem above the ring.

MECHANISM OF THE MOVEMENT OF WATER

Since the mechanism of the movement of water can scarcely be understood intelligently without some knowledge of the anatomy of the tissues through which it moves, a brief review of stem structure is desirable before proceeding further with a discussion of this process. Stems vary greatly in their structure, every species possessing some anatomical features which are peculiar to itself. Nevertheless certain general patterns of tissue arrangement have been found to prevail, and the stem structure of most species will approximate one or another of these general arrangements.

The corn stem represents an herbaceous monocot type of structure while that of the tulip poplar is typical of woody dicot stems. The structure of woody stems cannot properly be appreciated merely from a consideration of one year old stems. The primary tissues of such stems develop from tissues formed at the apical growing tip during growth of the stem in length. Nearly all perennial stems also grow in diameter as a result of the development of secondary tissues from the cambium.

By successive stages of division, enlargement, and differentiation of cambium cells additional layers of xylem (secondary xylem) are laid down on the inner face of the cambium, and new layers of phloem tissue (secondary plzloem) on its outer face Hence after a few years the great bulk of any woody stem is composed of secondary tissues. Secondary xylem and secondary phloem also develop from the cambium in most herbaceous dicot stems but in such species the cambium in any one of phloem and xylem elements from the cambium.

- A cambium initial,
- Division of cambium cell,
- Outer cell resulting from division becomes a phloem element,
- Another division of the cambium cell,
- Outer cell resulting from second division becomes a xylem element.

Actually several xylem or several phloem elements are often formed successively. Upon maturation most of the xylem and phloem elements acquire sizes and shapes which are very different from those of the cambium initials from which they originate. Stem is never active for more than one growing season. The spring formed xylem tissue, as viewed in cross section is usually distinctly different in aspect from that formed later in the season.

In many angiosperms the springwood contains more and larger vessels and the cell walls are generally thinner than in the subsequently produced summer wood. In the conifers the spring formed tracheids are thinner-walled and of larger cross-sectional diameter than those formed later in the growing season. The transition from spring to summer wood is often a very gradual one. On the other hand the more open xylem tissues formed each spring abut directly upon the denser tissues which were produced during the preceding summer, thus giving rise to an abrupt line of demarcation between the zones of xylem formed in any two successive seasons. The result of this growth behaviour is that a cross section of the trunk or a branch of any tree appears as a system of concentric layers, the so-called annual rings, each representing an annual increment of growth. In rare cases no annual rings nor more than one annual ring may be produced in a season, but usually each ring represents the xylem produced by the activity of the cambium during one season.In many woody species as the xylem tissues increase in age important changes occur in the colour, composition, and structure of the various elements, resulting in the conversion of sapwood into heartwood. As sapwood ripens into heartwood the walls of any remaining living cells of the xylem become increasingly lignified death of these cells soon following. The water content of the tissues is generally reduced and such compounds as oils, resins gums, and tannins accumulate in the cells or cell walls. The darker colouration of the heartwood of most species as compared to the sapwood is due to such accumulations. In mature trees the heartwood becomes merely a central supporting column surrounded by a cylinder of sapwood which varies in thickness from a few to many annual layers, depending upon the species and the environmental conditions under which the tree is growing.

In some species (apple, elm) the heartwood remains virtually saturated Tangential section of a small portion of the wood of whitepine (Pinus strobus). The vertically oriented elongated elements are tracheids. Bordered pits show in sectional view in the tracheid and marginal ray cells. Simple pits show in sectional view in other ray cells. Half-bordered pits show between marginal ray cells and other ray cells.

The water in the heartwood of such species as apple and elm appears to be largely static and is not directly involved in translocation. Coincident with the development of secondary xylem, secondary phloem tissues also develop from the cambium. Cork cambiums are also initiated in the bark which produce cork layers. Profound modifications therefore occur in the outer tissues as well as in the xylem of woody stems as they grow older.

A somewhat more detailed concept of the structure of the cells and elements of the stems of angiosperms through which the movement of water occurs is presented which represent longitudinal tangential and radial sections from the xylem of a tulip tree which may be taken as representative for this group of plants. The xylem tissues of the wood of angiosperms are composed of vessels tracheids, fibres of several types, wood parenchyma, and xylem ray cells. There is a tremendous variability in the proportional distribution and arrangement of these tissues according to species.

The most characteristic elements of the xylem tissue of angiosperms are the vessels. These are, in general, more or less tubular structures which may extend through many feet of the xylem. In some species cross walls, usually perforated, are of frequent occurrence in vessels, in others such cross walls are infrequent or lacking. In diameter they may range in trees from about 20 to about 400. In vines they may be as much as 700 in diameter. The vessels branch extensively in certain regions of the plant, especially at nodes within the leaf lamina, and at the points in the root systems where rool branching occurs.

The vessels of the proto xylem (the first cells of the xylem to mature during the ontogeny of a growing stem or root tip) have cellulose walls which are reinforced by distinctive lignified thickenings which appear as rings, spirals,or other characteristic patterns. The vessels that develop later in the ontogeny of any growing tip have lignified, usually pitted walls which lack any of the thickenings which distinguish the walls of the vessels of the protoxylem.

Pits normally occur in all parts of vessel walls which are contiguous with other vessels or cells. These pits consist essentially of thin areas in the walls. The walls of the vast majority of plant cells are pitted. The architecturally distinct type known as the bordered pit.

ANATOMY OF STEM

Tracizeids are found in wood of many but not all species of angiosperms. They are typically more or less spindle-shaped cells with thick walls which are almost always lignified. As viewed in cross section they are usually angular. Mature tracheids contain no protoplasm and hence are non-living like the xylem vessels. The largest tracheids are about 5 mm. in length, and about 30 in diameter, although most of them are smaller. The walls of tracheids are pitted like those of vessels. Tracheids are water-conducting cells but in most angiosperms they are relatively of much less importance as channels throughwhich water moves than the vessels.

Tracheids are developed from the cambium by a process essentially similar to that by which vessel segments are formed, except that the size and shape of the resulting cells is different, and that there is no coalescence of the individual elements such as occurs in the formation of vessels. The xylem of the angiosperms also contains fibres of various types, which in general are similar to the tracheids in structure except that usually they have thicker walls, smaller lumina, and fewer and smaller pits. Fibre cells are non-living and their walls are lignified. Because of their thick walls and small lumina the fibres do not play an important part in the movement of water through stems.

The xylem tissue of practically all angiosperms also contains wood parenchyma cells which, unlike the elements already described, remain alive for some time after their differentiation. Usually death of the wood parenchyma cells does not occur until the wood of which they are a part is converted into heartwood. Wood parenchyma cells are generally somewhat elongate, and roughly four-angled in cross section. They occur in the xylem as vertical series of cells placed end to end. The strands of wood parenchyma thus produced often extend for a long distance in a vertical direction through the wood.

The distribution of the wood parenchyma strands throughout an annual ring of xylem tissue varies with the species. In some they are more or less scattered through the xylem, in others they occur only in the last layer or two of cells which are produced in the summer woodin other words at the termination of the seasons growth and in others only in contact with the vessels, or in contact with other wood parenchyma cells which are themselves in contact with the vessels. All of the xylem elements previously described are oriented with their long axes in a vertical direction.

In addition to this vertical system there is also present in the xylem a transverse, radiating system in which the long axis of the cells is at right angles to the long axis of the stem. These transversely oriented tissue units are known as vascular rays. In the stems of most species they are continuous from the outer extremity of the phloem through the cambium into the xylem, which they penetrate to a greater or lesser distance. The portion of the vascular ray found in the xylem is termed the xylem ray; that found in the phloem the pliloem ray.

Xylem rays may vary from one to many cells in thickness and likewise in height, certain types usually being characteristic of any one species. The cells of the xylem rays,like those of the wood parenchyma, usually remain alive until the woody tissue is converted into heartwood. The cells of the xylem ray are typically elongate and more or less angular in cross section.

The xylem rays probably serve as routes along which lateral movement of water occurs from the xylem to the cambium and phloem, and along which translocation of soluble foods takes place from the phloem to the living cells of the xylem. The living ray cells are in contact at various points with the strands of living wood parenchyma cells. The vertically oriented wood parenchyma strands and transversely oriented xylem ray strands thus form a unit system of living cells within the woody cylinder.

Hence there is present a continuous inter meshing network of living cells throughout the greater mass of non-living vessels, tracheids, and fibres in the younger portions of any woody angiosperm stem. There are probably few if any of the conducting elements vessels and tracheids which are not in contact at one or more points with this continuous system of living cells. The wood of the gymnosperms is simpler in its structure than that of the angiosperms, this group of woody species also showing, in general, a greater uniformity in stem structure than the latter group. The only cell types universally present in the wood of coniferous trees are the tracheids and woodray cells. Wood parenchyma cells are also present in the wood of most species of conifers, while in many species tracheid-like fibre cells are also present. The most important distinction between the wood of conifers and that of angiosperms is the total absence of vessels in the former.

The tracheids are the distinctive element in conifer wood, constituting as they do the great bulk of all the woody tissues present in such species. In conifers the tracheids form a densely packed type of woody tissue, composed of interlocking cells. Vertically contiguous tracheids always overlap along their tapering portions. Movement of water and solutes from one tracheid to another is facilitated by means of the bordered pits in the adjacent walls. Because of the numerous cross walls in a xylem tissue composed almost entirely of tracheids, water encounters a greater resistance in moving through such tissues than in traversing woody tissues which contain vessels. Nevertheless it is interesting to note that the tallest trees in the world are conifers in which all movement of water occurs through tracheids.

Theories of the Mechanism of the Movement of Water through Plants. A number of different theories of the mechanism by which the ascent of water is brought about iii plants have been suggested, and it is probable that more than one mechanism is involved in this process.

The present state of our knowledge justifies a discussion of only three possible mechanisms:

1. That ascent of sap is caused by the vital activities of living cells, principally those in the stem,
2. That this process occurs according to a mechanism described in the cohesion of water theory, and
3. That upward movement of water occurs as a result of root pressures. In passing, it should be noted that neither atmospheric pressure nor capillarity can account for the rise of sap in plants, although both of these processes are recurringly suggested as being involved in this process. Atmospheric pressure could never account fora rise of more than about 10 metres, and most mature trees attain a greater height than this. The capillary rise of water in tubes 10 in diameter is only about 3 metres, and few if any of the conducting elements have as small a diameter as this.

The mechanism of the movement of water through the plant is inextricably bound up with the mechanism of the absorption of water, so the following discussion will necessarily treat to some extent of both of these processes. Vital Theories. While the vessels and tracheids through which longitudinal transit of water occurs are non-living, they are always in more or less intimate contact with living cells. Suggestions have therefore been made from time to time that the motive power causing movement of water is furnished by the living cells of the stem. The most recent advocate of such a theory is Bose. As an example of the vital theories of the ascent of sap we may consider the proposals advanced by Godlewski in 1884. He considered that conduction of water occurred as a result of periodic changes in the osmotic pressure of the living cells present in the xylem (especially the wooJ ray cells). Upon increase in their osmotic pressure water was supposed to move into the cells from bordering xylem elements.

Upon decrease in osmotic pressure water was supposed to move back into a xylem duct. In the xylem duct it was supposed that water would move upward until it came in contact with another living ray cell because of a lower air pressure in the upper than in the lower part of the vessels. The ascent of water in stems was thus supposed to be brought about by a number of repetitions of this same process. There is little or no direct evidence in support of this or any of a number of more or less similar theories which have been suggested.

The experiments of Strasburger demonstrated quite clearly that the primary mechanism of the rise of sap in trees operates independently of the living cells of the stem. He performed many experiments upon the movement of water through woody stems in which the living cells had been killed by one method or another. In one experiment, for example, he used a 75 -year -old oak tree about 22 metres in height. This was sawed off close tothe ground and the cut end transferred to a solution of picric acid, which is toxic to living cells.

The picric acid solution slowly moved up the stem. Fuchsin, added to the liquid in which the base of the tree was immersed 3 days after the picric acid, also ascended to the top of the tree through tissues in which the living cells had been killed by the picric acid. Water also continued to ascend through similar stems after they had been completely killed by exposure to a temperature of 900 C. Similar experiments have been performed by later investigators. All of these investigators have confirmed Strasburgers results that water would continue to ascend for some time through stems, segments of which had been exposed to one treatment or another which would kill all living cells present. In all experiments of the type just described, it has been observed that the leaves at the top of a stem, part or all of which has been killed, sooner or later wilt and wither, although this effect is by no means an immediate one,often appearing only after several days. Proponents of the vital theories have accepted this as evidence that the living cells of a stem are essential for the passage of water through it. Dixon however, considers that this delayed lethal effect on the leaves is due to either or both of two causes.

Killing of the stem tissues often causes the formation of substances which plug up the vessels or tracheids, thus impeding the upward movement of water. Furthermore, death of the cells in the treated regions causes the release into the conducting channels of toxic compounds which, when transported to the eaves, cause death of the leaf cells. There is still some doubt, however,whether all of the retardation in rate of translocation as a result of such experiments can be explained in these two ways. The possibility remains open that the living cells of the xylem may in some way be necessary to the maintenance of the water-conducting capacity of the xylem, or even that they may contribute in some way to the lifting of water through stems.

In general, the evidence appears to be quite conclusive that the living cells of the stem do not furnish the principal mechanism which causes the upward transport of water in stems. On the contrary, as shown in the subsequent discussion, the living leaves or stem tips at the top of the plant appear to be absolutely necessary for the ascent of water through stems. Root Pressure. That a slow exudation of sap often occurs from the cut surface of a stem is well known. Such sap exudations are often ascribed to the development of a pressure in the dilute sap of the xylem vessels resulting from the operation of some as yet not fully understood mechanism in the root cells. Hence the name root pressure. It is generally considered that such pressures may occur in intact plants as well as in those which have been cut into. It is probable that not all of the phenomena which have been classed under the name of root pressure are due to the operation of the same physiological mechanism. Some sap exudations seem to come from the cambium or phloem rather than from the xylem. It seems quite certain that some of the sap exudations from the xylem occur from the living wood parenchyma or woodray cells rather than from the vessels, or at least that the exudation is greatly influenced by the activity of such cells.

Hence the living cells of the stemas well as those of the root are probably involved in many root pressure phenomena. James and Baker go so far as to regard the subjection of the sap in vessels to a pressure as an exceptional occurrence in plants, but this seems to be an extreme point of view, and will not be followed in this discussion. Because of the unsettled state of our knowledge regarding this phenomenon it will be necessary to use the term root pressure in a very uncritical sense. The magnitude of root pressures is commonly determined by attaching a manometer to the cut surface of the plant from which the bleeding is occurring. With only a few rare exceptions the exudation pressures which have been recorded for plants do not exceed 2 atmos., and most of them are less than this. According to White individual excised roots of tomato plants exude sap from their basal ends with a pressure of more than 6 atmos.

It has not yet been shown, however, that such pressures operate for any considerable distance through plants. In general there is no correlation between the pressure with which the sap is exuded from cut stems and the volume of sap flow. In some species relatively large volumes of sap may be exuded under a relatively low pressure, in others exactly the opposite relation may exist. Some of the woody plants in which bleeding from cut surfaces occurs,commonly ascribed in part or entirely to root pressure, are the sugar maple,box elder, dogwood, hornbeam (Ostrya), sycamore, birches, currant, and grape. Such exudation of sap under pressure usually occurs only during the seasons of the year when the plant bears no foliage, and most commonly in the early spring months.

The popular concept of a rise of sap in woody plants in the spring is largely based on the observation of such phenomena. Exudation of sap under pressure can also be demonstrated in many species of herbaceous plants especially if potted plants are used and the soil is flooded with water before the demonstration is attempted. The sap which moves through woody plants in the spring and, less abundantly, in the autumn under the influence of root pressures contains appreciable concentrations of carbohydrates as well as traces of mineral salts. In contrast with this is the condition of the xylem sap in the summer at which season it contains traces of mineral salts, but practically no soluble carbohydrates.

It has sometimes been claimed that root pressures are adequate to account for the rise of water in herbaceous plants and in low shrubs or trees,and that they may even play a very considerable part in the ascent of sap in taller trees. While it is undoubtedly true that root pressure does, in some species of plants, under certain conditions, account for the movement of some water in an upward direction through plants, this process is inadequate to account for the translocation of any considerable amount of water through plants. In the first place there are many species in which this phenomenon has never been observed.

In the second place, the magnitude of the pressure developed is seldom sufficient to force water to the top of any except relatively low-growing species of plants. Neither is the rate of flow, as it occurs inmost species, anywhere near rapid enough to compensate for the known rates of transpiration. Finally, and this is perhaps the most fundamental objection to the idea that root pressures play a very prominent part in the ascent of sap in plants; they are usually negligible, in temperate regions at least,during the summer period when transpiration is most rapid. During periods of rapid transpiration, the cut surfaces of plants not only fail to exude sap, but will usually absorb water if it is supplied at the cut surface.

The trunks of many species of deciduous trees exhibit a marked seasonal variation in water content. A minimum water content is attained during middle or late summer and the trunks gradually fill up during the fall and spring. Often there is a temporary shrinkage in their water content during the winter months but the main period of diminishing trunk water content occurs in the spring and summer. Some authorities even speak of a seasonal rise and fall in the water table of a tree trunk, and consider that intercellular spaces as well as cells become occupied with water during this process. Root pressure undoubtedly accounts at least in part for such seasonal replenishments of the store of water in tree trunks.

The living cells of the xylem probably play an active part in this process. It is possible that there may be slowly ascending streams of water in the living cells of the xylem which operate entirely independently of the water columns in the vessels or tracheids. Hence the same portions of the xylem which at times contain gases may at other seasons be occupied by water. The trunks of many conifers show no marked seasonal variations in water content; this is possibly correlated with the lack of appreciable root pressures in such species. The Cohesion of Water Theory. The leading advocate of this theory has been Dixon who has performed much of the experimental work upon which it is based.

A number of other workers, notably Askenasy and Renner have also contributed important theoretical and experimental evidence in support of this theory. Molecules of water, although ceaselessly in motion, are also attracted to each other by strong cohesive forces. In masses of liquid water the existence of such cohesive forces is not obvious, but when water is confined in long tubes of small diameter the existence of attractive forces between water molecules can often be demonstrated. If the water at the top of such a tube be subjected to a pull the resulting stress will be transmitted all along the column of water, due to the mutual attraction between the molecules.

The water conducting system of plants constitutes just such a system, enclosing continuous thread-like columns of water which extend from the top to the bottom of the plant. A stress applied at any point to this system will be propagated to all its parts. The application of such a stress stretches the water into taut threads, throwing it into a condition of tension, which is the equivalent of negative pressure. According to this theory forces develop in the upper parts of plants, and especially in the leaves, which cause the rise of water through the plant. As evapouration proceeds from the walls of the mesophyll cells into the intercellular spaces the diffusion pressure deficit of the mesophyll cell walls increases. Water therefore moves into the walls from the adjacent protoplasm,this resulting in turn in the movement of water from the cell sap into the protoplasmic layer. The resulting increase in the diffusion pressure deficitof the cell sap is in turn propagated to the protoplasm and the cell sap in all parts of the cell. The osmotic pressures of the leaf cells are generally high enough that diffusion pressure deficits of sufficient magnitude to account for movement of water to the top of the plant can develop in them without a complete loss of turgor by the leaf cells.

If the cell is in direct contact with one of the branches of the xylem ducts which ramify throughout the lamina of the leaf, water will move from the vessel or tracheid into the cell this results in the development of tension in the water column terminating in this xylem element. The diffusion pressure deficit of the water in the conducting elements will be increased by the amount of this tension. Water under a tension (negative pressure) of 10 atmos., for example, has a diffusion pressure just 10 atmos. less than that of pure water at the same temperature which is not under tension. In other words its diffusion pressure deficit is 10 atmos. If the cell from which evapouration is occurring is not in direct contact with a xylem element a gradient of diffusion pressure deficits, gradually increasing in magnitude from cell to cell in the direction in which the water is moving, is established between the xylem element and the cell from which evapouration is occurring. The tension developed in the conducting elements is transmitted along their entire length to their lower termination just back of the root tips and probably, very often at least, across the root tissues as well. The magnitude of the tension which develops in the xylem conduits is increased by conditions which favour a rate of water loss from the leaves considerably in excess of the rate at which water enters the roots from the soil. The movement of water across the cells of the root from the soil into the lower ends of the water-conducting elements must be considered as an integral part of the translocational process. At their lower terminations thexylem vessels or tracheids are in contact with the pericycle, or more rarely,directly with the endodermal cells of the root. Water moves from the adjacent root cells into the conducting elements because the tension (diffusion pressure deficit) developed in these elements exceeds the diffusion pressure deficit of the cells of the root.

When the tension in the water columns is relatively low a gradient of diffusion pressure deficits will be established across the root cells similar to those which are established in the leaf mesophyll cells when water is moving through them. The diffusion pressure deficits will increase from cell to cell along this gradient in the direction in which water is moving, *i.e.* from the periphery of the root towards the xylem.

Since, however, the osmotic pressures of root cells are usually lower than those of the mesophyll cells it is probable that the tension developed in the water columns often exceeds the highest osmotic pressures of any of the root cells through which water passes on its way from the soil to the xylem. Under such conditions the volume of water in the root cells may continue to diminish even after their turgor has been reduced to zero. As a result the walls of the cell are pulled inwards due to the adhesion between them and the contracting mass of water.

The counter pull exerted by the elastic walls of the cell will stretch the encompassed mass of water and throw it into a state of tension. Whenever a tension of sufficient magnitude has been generated in the conducting elements, therefore,the water in the root cells may also pass into a state of tension. Even under such conditions a gradient of diffusion pressure deficits would be established across the root, but the mechanism responsible for the development of this gradient would be more complicated than were no tension generated in the cells. When the water in a cell is under tension its diffusion pressure deficit is equal to its osmotic pressure plus the tension to which the water is subjected. Regardless of the exact mechanism involved, the essential fact is that the development of tensions in the water columns induces the establishment of a gradient of diffusion pressure deficits, increasing consistently from cell to cell across the root from its peripheral cell layer to the conducting elements and water will move along this gradient from the epidermal layer to thexylem tissue.

Water enters the peripheral cells of a root whenever the diffusion pressure deficit of water in the soil is less than that of the water in the epidermal cells and root hairs in the absorbing zone of the root. In most trees practically all upward movement of water occurs in the vessels or tracheids of a few of the outermost annual rings of the sapwood and in some species, especially those with ring-porous wood is almost entirely confined to the outermost ring. As is well known, in some species of trees (beech, sycamore, etc.) the heartwood of the trunk may disappear completely by decay. The fact that such hollow trees continue to live and thrive is conclusive evidence that the heartwood plays no essential role in the upward movement of water in such species.

The water-conductive system of plants should be regarded as a unit system; the individual threads or columns of water not operating separately but each as a part of a more or less complicated meshwork. The air-plugged tracheids or vessel sections become merely islands in the meshwork of intact water columns, and the capacity of the tissues as a whole to conduct water, although somewhat impaired by the presence of air in some of the conducting elements, is by no means destroyed.

MAGNITUDE OF THE COHESIVE FORCE OF WATER

If water is to move through the xylem ducts as postulated by this theory, its cohesive force must be of sufficient magnitude to resist the stresses which are imposed upon it.The maximum height to which water ever moves in plants does not exceed 400 feet. This height is equivalent to about 2 atmos. which represents the maximum stress which the water columns could develop as a result of their own weight. Water, however, encounters a certain amount of resistance in moving through the conducting tissues. The greater the velocity of the current of water, the greater the resistance which it will encounter.

Dixon has shown that at the velocity corresponding to usual rates of transpiration this resistance is approximately equal to the pressure required to support water for the height of the plant. He used the wood of the yew for his determinations, in which higher values for resistance would be expected than in non-conifers in which most water traverses vessels rather than tracheids. For high rates of conduction Huber estimates the resistance to be several times as great as this. Accepting Dixons estimates as an average value,the required cohesive force of water must be doubled, giving a value of 24 atmos.

To this must be added the resistance normally encoun-tered by water in crossing the tissues of the root and the mesophyll cells of the leaves which is equivalent to only a few atmospheres. The estimated minimum cohesive force required to lift water to the tops of the tallest tree is therefore about 30 atmos. Even if we assume a resistance three times as great as that found by Dixon, the value of the necessary cohesive force becomes only about 50 atmos. Values experimentally determined for the cohesive force of water range up to 350 atmos. Dixon obtained values as high as 207 atmos. for sap centrifuged from branches of holly (hexaquifoliurn) The cohesive force of water is therefore much in excess of the minimum required for the lifting of water to the tops of even the tallest trees.

Although the estimates given in the preceding paragraph represent the minimum cohesive force actually required for the movement of water to the top of tall trees, many botanists believe that when an internal water deficit exists in plants, tensions as great as 100 atmos. or even more may develop in the water columns of at least some species of plants. One of the most ingenious methods of studying the cohesion of water employs the sporangia of the ferns for this purpose. Around the edge of a fern sporangium occurs a ring of dead, thick walled cells, known as the annulus. As the sporangium matures water is gradually lost from the cells of the annulus by evapouration. Because of the powerful adhesion between the cell walls and water, the resulting shrinkage in the volume of water in each of these cells results in the thin outer wall of each cell being drawn inward, while the ends of the thicker lateral walls are pulled towards each other.

This results in tearing open the weak side ofthe sporangium, and eventually, in a complete inversion in the position of the annulus, exposing the spores on its outer surface. The annulus is now in a condition similar to that of a highly strained spring.

THE MOVEMENT OF WATER THROUGH THE PLANT

Eventually the cohesive force of the water in the cells of the annulus is exceeded, the water ruptures, and the annulus recoils suddenly into approximately its original position, scattering the spores into the atmosphere by its violent rebound. The cohesive force of the water in cells such as these can be measured by allowing the annuli to come to equilibrium with known vapour pressures, and determining the highest vapour pressure at which rupturing of the water occurs. The osmotic pressure corresponding to this vapour pressure is equal to the cohesive force of the water in the annulus cells. Such measurements indicate the cohesive force of the water in these cells to be, at a minimum, between 300 and 350 atmospheres.

The first experiment of this type was performed by Askenasy. As evapouration proceeds from the porous clay cup of this apparatus water moves up the vertical glass tube, followed by mercury from the reservoir. If the demonstration is successful the mercury will continue to rise above the level to which it will stand in a barometer. The water is now being pulled up the tube, a phenomenon which is possible only because of its cohesive force. The water in the tube is thus thrown into a state of tension which is transmitted to the mercury column below it, due to the relatively enormous adhesive force between water and mercury.

The forces exerting this pull originate at the evapourating surface of the cup, and are due to the adhesive and cohesive forces operative in the maintenance of innumerable microscopic menisci in the pores of the clay cup. That succeeded in demonstrating a rise of mercury to a height of 226.6 cm. in such an apparatus. This is approximately three times as high as a column of mercury will be supported by atmospheric pressure acting alone. While the maximum tension developed in the water column in these experiments does not exceed two atmospheres, the demonstration graphically illustrates a physical system which is analogous to that which is believed to operate in the plant. Experiments similar to that just described have also been performed using small branches or twigs of plants as an evapourating surface instead of a porous clay surface.

These are attached at the upper end of a glass tube in place of the clay cup; otherwise the set-up for such an experiment is similar to that just described. While it has not been possible to obtain as great a rise of mercury in these experiments as when a porous clay evapourating surface isused, upward traction of mercury for distances well in excess of atmospheric pressure can be demonstrated if a suitable technique is followed.

DEVELOPMENT OF TENSION IN THE WATER COLUMNS

Convincing evidence that the water in the xylem vessels is often in a state of tension has been obtained by direct observations of vessels under a microscope. The stems of some species of herbaceous plants, especially the Cucurbits, are especially suitable for such observations.

Such a stem of an intact, rapidly transpiring plant can be fastened in position across the stage of a microscope and, by careful dissection, vessels examined individually. If one of the vessels under observation be jabbed with the point of a fine needle, an immediate jerking apart of the water column at the point of the rupture will be seen to occur, indicating that the water in the intact vessel was actually in a state of tension. Interesting evidence that the water in the xylem ducts of woody stemsis, at times at least, under tension has been obtained by means of an instrument known as the dendrograph. This is a self-recording instrument which measures variation in the diameters of tree trunks.

It is so constructed that its sensitivity is very great and that its recordings are not influenced by temperature effects upon the instrument. Dendographs are used principally to measure periodic variations in the diameter growth of trees. However, even in trees in which diameter growth has ceased, slight diurnal periodic variations in the diameter of trees have been found to be of regular occurrence. A record of the periodic variations in the diameter of a tree trunk for aperiod of several days at a season when little diameter growth was occurring. The trunk attained its minimum diameter during the transported through plants, be they the tallest of trees or herbs only a few feet in height.

It is also generally agreed that root pressures play a minorrole in this process at least under certain conditions and in some species.There is no doubt that living cells are involved in the phenomena generally described under the term root pressure and there is at least a possibility that living cells of the xylem are in some way essential to the maintenance or operation of the cohesion mechanism.

RATES OF MOVEMENT OF WATER THROUGH PLANTS

The rate which water ascends through the xylem ducts may vary from a movement so slow as to bealmost imperceptible to a speed of at least 75 cm. per minute. By rate is meant the length of the water column which will move past a given point in one minute. In general daily variations in the rate of ascent of water closely parallel daily variations in transpiration rate.

LATERAL MOVEMENT OF WATER

A cell to cell lateral movement of water in a radial direction undoubtedly occurs along the vascular rays in the stems of most species of plants. In woody stems there is probably also a lateral movement of water around the stem in a tangential direction. Except in trees in which the grain of the wood is twisted, the conducting vessels on one side of the tree generally connect with branches on that side of the treeat their upper extremity, and with roots on the same side of the tree at their lower extremity.

If no lateral movement of water occurred in woody stems,it would be expected that removal of the roots from one side of a tree would result in a dearth of water, or perhaps even death of the leaves or brancheson that side of the tree. Experiments have been performed on apple, peach, oak, and other woody species in which the roots on one side of the plant were removed in an attempt to determine whether or not lateral movement of the water occurs.

Although the water content and growth of the plants treated in this manner diminished there was no difference in the moisture content of the leaves on the two sides of the tree. Neither did the leaves on the side from which the roots had been removed show any greater tendency to wilt on clear warm days than those on the other side. These results indicate very strongly that lateral movement of water occurs in woody stems, and that the water conductive system of plants acts as a unit system.

4

Crops Root Development

Enough work has been done to show clearly that among garden crops root adaptations frequently occur. These will be pointed out in the following chapters, although a mere beginning has been made. The field is enormously large and difficult but one rich in possibilities. It seems entirely probable that some of the best-yielding crops are able to outstrip others largely because of their greater efficiency in securing a greater and more constant supply of water and nutrients. On the other hand, the failure of a crop to thrive in a particular soil may be due to a lack of adaptation of its root system to the environment imposed upon it. Both of these conditions are illustrated by the growth of flax in India.

The agriculture in many of these areas is ancient, there have been few innovations, and the soil conditions have had time to impress themselves on the varieties of crops cultivated. A condition of equilibrium between the type of plant and the soil has been obtained, as there has been ample time for the operation of natural selection. When we compare the root system of linseed from the black-soil areas with that of the varieties grown on the Gangetic alluvium, striking differences appear. The roots produced on the black soils (of the Peninsula) are deep, somewhat sparse, and are well adapted to ripen the plant quickly with the minimum of moisture.

The type of gearing fits the soil. On the alluvium, where moisture is more abundant and where the aeration of the subsoil is poor, the root system is superficial but at the same time well developed. On the intermediate types of soil linseed produces a type of root about halfway between that of the black soils and of the alluvium. Once more the root system is found to fit the soil type. Further when we grow side by side on the alluvium these three classes of linseed, there is little or no adaptation of the roots to the new conditions, but the three types behave very much as they would in their native habitat.

The deep, sparse root system of the black soil areas is developed in the alluvium, although it is fatal to the well-being of the crop. When, the experiment is reversed and the types which suit the alluvium are grown on the black soils, there is again little or no adaptation to fit the new conditions. The linseed crop consists of a large number of varieties which differ from one another in all sorts of characters, including the extent and distribution of the roots. The root systems of the varieties are just as characteristic and just as fixed as the differences in the seed and other aboveground characters of these plants. A similar state of affairs obtains in other crops like wheat... and the opium poppy, and is probably universal all over India. Thus the differences between the root systems of varieties have been clearly shown and the economic significance illustrated.

Vegetable growing is an important phase of agriculture and one that is increasing at a rapid rate. In the United States practically every kind of soil is used for growing vegetables. Among the dozens or sometimes hundreds of varieties of the various vegetable crops, some undoubtedly have root systems more suited to a given soil environment than others. If the highest possible production is desired, attention should be given to selecting the variety that is not only climatically adapted but also best fitted to a particular soil, modified as favourably as lies within the power of the grower.

It seems certain that a large part of the success in connection with the improvement of varieties consists in better adapting the absorbing system to the soil. As stated by one who has extensively worked on plant selection, breeding, root investigations, and other phases of agronomic science, "The more I learn about cultivated plants the more I am convinced that the future lies in the root-soils relation and in matters which influence it." An intimate knowledge of the habits of growth of the root systems of vegetable crops will enable the grower to space plants to better advantage. It should also permit him to intercrop or grow in succession such crops or mixtures that the soil volume will have a better distribution of roots and thus permit of methods of more intensive cultivation. Similarly, by means of proper crop rotations and occasionally cultivating very deeply rooting crops, the subsoil may be kept in good condition and the effects of drought mitigated.

INTRODUCTION TO ROOT

In vascular plants, the root is the organ of a plant body that typically lies below the surface of the soil. This is not always the case, however, since a root can also be aerial (that is, growing above the ground) or aerating (that is, growing up above the ground or especially above water). Furthermore, a stem normally occurring below ground is not exceptional either. So, it is better to define root as a part of a plant body that bears no leaves, and therefore also lacks nodes. There are also important internal structural differences between stems and roots.

The two major functions of roots are:

1. Absorption of water and inorganic nutrients and
2. Anchoring of the plant body to the ground.

In response to the concentration of nutrients, roots also synthesise cytokinin, which acts as a signal as to how fast the shoots can grow. Roots often function in storage of food and nutrients. The roots of most vascular plant species enter into symbiosis with certain fungi to form mycorrhizas, and a large range of other organisms including bacteria also closely associate with roots.

FUNCTIONS OF ROOT GROWTH

Early root growth is one of the functions of the apical meristem located near the tip of the root. The meristem cells more or less continuously divide, producing more meristem, root cap cells (these are sacrificed to protect the meristem), and undifferentiated root cells. The latter become the primary tissues of the root, first undergoing elongation, a process that pushes the root tip forward in the growing medium. Gradually these cells differentiate and mature into specialized cells of the root tissues. Roots will generally grow in any direction where the correct environment of air, mineral nutrients and water exists to meet the plant's needs. Roots will not grow in dry soil. Over time, given the right conditions, roots can crack foundations, snap water lines, and lift sidewalks. At germination, roots grow downward due to gravitropism, the growth mechanism of plants that also causes the shoot to grow upward. In some plants (such as ivy), the "root" actually clings to walls and structures.

Growth from apical meristems is known as primary growth, which encompasses all elongation. Secondary growth encompasses all growth in diameter, a major component of woody plant tissues and many nonwoody plants. For example, storage roots of sweet potato have secondary growth but are not woody. Secondary growth occurs at the lateral meristems, namely the vascular cambium and cork cambium. The former forms secondary xylem and secondary phloem, while the latter forms the periderm.

In plants with secondary growth, the vascular cambium, originating between the xylem and the phloem, forms a cylinder of tissue along the stem and root. The cambium layer forms new cells on both the inside and outside of the cambium cylinder, with those on the inside forming secondary xylem cells, and those on the outside forming secondary phloem cells. As secondary xylem accumulates, the "girth" (lateral dimensions) of the stem and root increases.

As a result, tissues beyond the secondary phloem (including the epidermis and cortex, in many cases) tend to be pushed outward and are eventually "sloughed off" (shed).

At this point, the cork cambium begins to form the periderm, consisting of protective cork cells containing suberin. In roots, the cork cambium originates in the pericycle, a component of the vascular cylinder. The vascular cambium produces new layers of secondary xylem annually. The xylem vessels are dead at maturity but are responsible for most water transport through the vascular tissue in stems and roots.

TYPES OF ROOTS

A true root system consists of a primary root and secondary roots (or lateral roots). The primary root originates in the radicle of the seedling. It is the first part of the root to be originated. During its growth it rebranches to form the lateral roots. It usually grows downwards.

Generally, two categories are recognized:

1. *The taproot system*: The primary root is prominent and has a single, dominant axis; there are fibrous secondary roots running outward. Usually allows for deeper roots capable of reaching low water tables. Most common in dicots. The main function of the taproot is to store food.
2. *The diffuse root system*: The primary root is not dominant; the whole root system is fibrous and branches in all directions. Most common in monocots. The main function of the fibrous root is to anchor the plant.

Specialized Roots

The roots, or parts of roots, of many plant species have become specialized to serve adaptive purposes besides the two primary functions described in the introduction.

- Adventitious roots arise out-of-sequence from the more usual root formation of branches of a primary root, and instead originate from the stem, branches, leaves, or old woody roots. They commonly occur in monocots and pteridophytes, but also in many dicots, such as clover (Trifolium), ivy (Hedera), strawberry (Fragaria) and willow (Salix). Most aerial roots and stilt roots are adventitious. In some conifers adventitious roots can form the largest part of the root system.
- *Aerating roots (or pneumatophores)*: Roots rising above the ground, especially above water such as in some mangrove genera (Avicennia, Sonneratia). In some plants like Avicennia the erect roots have a large number of breathing pores for exchange of gases.
- *Aerial roots*: Roots entirely above the ground, such as in ivy (Hedera) or in epiphytic orchids. They function as prop roots, as in maize or anchor roots or as the trunk in strangler fig.
- *Contractile roots*: They pull bulbs or corms of monocots, such as hyacinth and lily, and some taproots, such as dandelion, deeper in the soil through expanding radially and contracting longitudinally. They have a wrinkled surface.
- *Coarse roots*: Roots that have undergone secondary thickening and have a woody structure. These roots have some ability to absorb water and nutrients, but their main function is transport and to provide a structure to connect the smaller diameter, fine roots to the rest of the plant.

- *Fine roots*: Primary roots usually <2 mm diameter that have the function of water and nutrient uptake. They are often heavily branched and support mycorrhizas. These roots may be short lived, but are replaced by the plant in an ongoing process of root 'turnover'.
- *Haustorial roots*: Roots of parasitic plants that can absorb water and nutrients from another plant, such as in mistletoe (Viscum album) and dodder.
- *Propagative roots*: Roots that form adventitious buds that develop into aboveground shoots, termed suckers, which form new plants, as in Canada thistle, cherry and many others.
- *Proteoid roots or cluster roots*: Dense clusters of rootlets of limited growth that develop under low phosphate or low iron conditions in Proteaceae and some plants from the following families Betulaceae, Casuarinaceae, Eleagnaceae, Moraceae, Fabaceae and Myricaceae.
- *Stilt roots*: These are adventitious support roots, common among mangroves. They grow down from lateral branches, branching in the soil.
- *Storage roots*: These roots are modified for storage of food or water, such as carrots and beets. They include some taproots and tuberous roots.
- *Structural roots*: Large roots that have undergone considerable secondary thickening and provide mechanical support to woody plants and trees.
- *Surface roots*: These proliferate close below the soil surface, exploiting water and easily available nutrients. Where conditions are close to optimum in the surface layers of soil, the growth of surface roots is encouraged and they commonly become the dominant roots.
- *Tuberous roots*: A portion of a root swells for food or water storage, *e.g.* sweet potato. A type of storage root distinct from taproot.

"Pneumatophores" Water even after air has been bubbled through it contains less than one-thirteenth the oxygen as air. some swamp plants such as black mangrove devolop spongy roots called pneumatophores which go above waters surface and enhance gas exchange.

Rooting depths

The distribution of vascular plant roots within soil depends on plant form, the spatial and temporal availability of water and nutrients, and the physical properties of the soil. The deepest roots are generally found in deserts and temperate coniferous forests; the shallowest in tundra, boreal forest and temperate grasslands. The deepest observed living root, at least 60 m below the ground surface, was observed during the excavation of an open-pit mine in Arizona, USA. Some roots can grow as deep as the tree is high. The majority of roots on most plants are however found relatively close to the surface where nutrient availability and aeration are more favourable for growth. Rooting depth may be physically restricted by rock or compacted soil close below the surface, or by anaerobic soil conditions.

Root Architecture

The pattern of development of a root system is termed 'root architecture', and is important in providing a plant with a secure supply of nutrients and water as well as anchorage and support. The architecture of a root system can be considered in a similar way to above-ground architecture of a plant - *i.e.* in terms of the size, branching and distribution of the component parts. In roots, the architecture of fine roots and coarse roots can both be described by variation in topology and distribution of biomass within and between roots. Having a balanced architecture allows fine roots to exploit soil efficiently around a plant, but the 'plastic' nature of root growth allows the plant to then concentrate its resources where nutrients and water are more easily available. A balanced coarse root architecture, with roots distributed relatively evenly around the stem base, is necessary to provide support to larger plants and trees.

Evolutionary History

The fossil record of roots - or rather, infilled voids where roots rotted after death - spans back to the late Silurian, but their identification is difficult, because casts and molds of roots are so similar in appearance to animal burrows - although they can be discriminated on the basis of a range of features.

Economic Importance

The term root crops refers to any edible underground plant structure, but many root crops are actually stems, such as potato tubers. Edible roots include cassava, sweet potato, beet, carrot, rutabaga, turnip, parsnip, radish, yam and horseradish. Spices obtained from roots include sassafras, angelica, sarsaparilla and licorice.

Sugar beet is an important source of sugar. Yam roots are a source of estrogen compounds used in birth control pills. The fish poison and insecticide rotenone is obtained from roots of Lonchocarpus spp. Important medicines from roots are ginseng, aconite, ipecac, gentian and reserpine. Several legumes that have nitrogen-fixing root nodules are used as green manure crops, which provide nitrogen fertilizer for other crops when plowed under. Specialized bald cypress roots, termed knees, are sold as souvenirs, lamp bases and carved into folk art. Native Americans used the flexible roots of white spruce for basketry.

Tree roots can heave and destroy concrete sidewalks and crush or clog buried pipes. The aerial roots of strangler fig have damaged ancient Mayan temples in Central America and the temple of Angkor Wat in Cambodia. Vegetative propagation of plants via cuttings depends on adventitious root formation. Hundreds of millions of plants are propagated via cuttings annually including chrysanthemum, poinsettia, carnation, ornamental shrubs and many houseplants.

MODIFYING THE ROOT ENVIRONMENT

In both field and garden the part of the plant environment that lies beneath the surface of the soil is more under the control of the plant grower than is the part which lies above. He can do relatively little towards changing the composition, temperature, or humidity of the air, or the amount of light. But much may be done by proper cultivation, fertilizing, irrigating, draining, etc. to influence the structure, fertility, aeration, and temperature of the soil.

Thus, a thorough understanding of the roots of plants and the ways in which they are affected by the properties of the soil in which they grow is of the utmost practical importance. Before other than an empirical answer can be given to the questions as to what are the best methods of preparing the land for any crop, the type of cultivation to be employed, the best time or method of applying fertilizers, the application and amount of water of irrigation, kind of crop rotations, and many other questions, something must be known of the character and activities of the roots that absorb water and nutrients for the plant and the position that they occupy in the soil.

ADAPTATION OF ROOTS TO ENVIRONMENT

By more or less profound modifications of their root system, many plants become adapted to different soil environments, others are much less susceptible to change. Among forest trees, for example, the initial or juvenile root system of each species follows a fixed course of development and maintains a characteristic form for a rather definite period of time following germination. The tendency to change when subjected to different external conditions becomes more pronounced as the seedlings become older. But some species thus subjected exhibit much earlier tendencies to change than others and a widely different degree of flexibility is also shown. Hence, certain species, *e.g.*, red maple (*Acer rubrum*), because of the great plasticity of their root systems, are able to survive, at least for a time, in various situations from swamps to dry uplands.

Native herbaceous species usually show great plasticity of root habit, successfully adapting themselves to considerable differences in soil environment.

The plant on the left was excavated in the Great Plains of Colorado. Maximum branching occurred in the third and fourth foot, although the taproot reached a depth of more than 7 feet. The plant on the right, with a shallower but much more finely branched root system, was excavated from a "half-gravel slide" in the Rocky Mountains of Colorado.

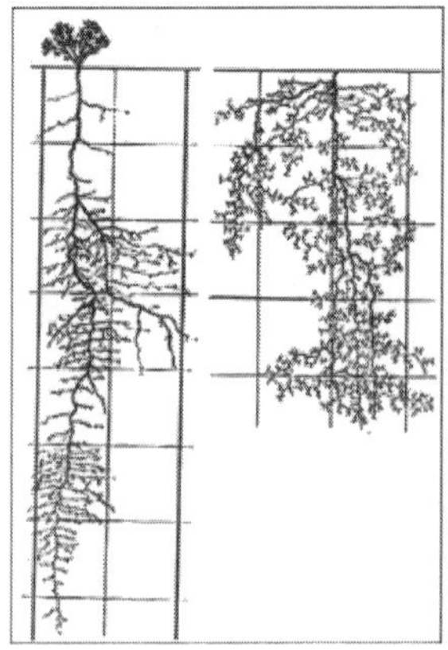

Fig. 2.1 A spurge (*Euphorbia Montana*) Showing Differences in Root Habit Resulting from Environment.

The wide range in soil and agricultural conditions under which vegetable crops are grown renders them particularly suitable both for the investigations of their root habits and also for a study of the agricultural significance of the differences encountered.

CONDITIONS FOR ROOTS GROWTH

Since roots, like aboveground parts of plants, are greatly modified by environment, a brief statement will be given of the conditions under which the crops were grown.

SOIL

The vegetable crops at Lincoln were grown in a fertile, dark-brown, Carrington silt loam. Preceding them white clover had been raised for 2 years. This was followed by a crop of maize. The soil was not only in an excellent condition as regards tilth but also was well supplied with humus. In general, it may be said that the soils of eastern Nebraska have a sufficient supply of all the essential nutrients to insure good crop yields, except that, owing to the systems of cropping, there may be a deficiency in available nitrates. The area was only slightly rolling, the general slope being towards the south. As usual, some differences in soil texture were found in excavating the root systems in different parts of the area. The following description of the soil profile represents an average condition.

The surface 12 to 14 inches was a mellow, very dark silt loam from which the roots were readily removed. At greater depths it intergraded into a dark-coloured, clay subsoil. This became quite sticky when wet and hard when dry. It exhibited a columnar or jointed structure, especially below 18 inches, cracking badly when it shrank upon drying. Roots were removed with much more difficulty from this soil layer. At about 3 feet in depth the subsoil became much lighter yellow in colour and graded rather abruptly into an easily worked, quite mellow, friable soil type approaching loess in many of its physical properties. This extended beyond the depth of greatest root penetration, *i.e.,* over 12 feet. It was characterized by rusty streaks and numerous small calcareous areas and concretions. Earthworm burrows penetrated the soil to depths of 8 feet or more and numerous old-root channels extended almost as deeply. In many places extensive surface cracks reached depths of 4 to 5 feet. They were sometimes 1 inch in width. These crevices had been formed during past years of drought and were filled with rich, black, surface soil which had been washed or blown into them. Cultural operations in a large measure had also undoubtedly contributed to the filling.

NUMBER AND SIZE OF PLATS

The crops, in nearly all cases, were grown in triplicate plats so that early, midsummer, and later examinations could be made without disturbing the areas in which the plants were to make further growth. The plats, although somewhat variable in size, were in all cases large enough to permit of normal field development, each group of plants being entirely surrounded by plants of its kind. For example, the plats of lettuce, radishes, and onions were 12 feet long and 10 feet wide, the plants in the central portion of each plat being used for a single root study. In the case of the tomato, cabbage, eggplant, and other crops where each plant occupied considerable space, the plats were proportionately larger so that the plants examined were grown under the ordinary competitive conditions and mutual environment of garden crops.

TILLAGE

The field was plowed 8 inches deep early in the spring after all cornstalks, stubble, and dried weeds had been carefully removed. This was followed by repeated harrowing until an excellent, firmly compacted, moist seed bed of good soil structure was formed. On areas not immediately planted, weeds were removed by raking and hoeing. After the seeds were sown or the seedlings transplanted, further cultivation was done very shallowly with rake or hoe so as not to disturb the roots. Cultivation and weeding were repeated, as in ordinary gardening, when needed to prevent the growth of weeds and to keep the surface soil in a good condition of tilth. At no time did cultivation extend to greater depths than 1 inch.

PRECIPITATION

The rainfall of 19.2 inches during the 6 months of the growing season was 2.3 inches below the normal, with periods of moderate drought occurring in May and again in July. April with a deficiency of 1.2 inches had three well-distributed showers. In May efficient rains occurred on the eighth and fifteenth, with a monthly deficiency of 3 inches. June was a wet month with a total of 6.6

inches of precipitation, mostly in seven well-distributed rains. This was 2.3 inches above the mean. July had four rains during the latter half of the month and a total precipitation 1.8 inches below the mean. Five well-distributed showers fell in August, an excess of 1.2 over the mean. September had only 0.2 inch above normal, the rains also being well distributed.

SOIL MOISTURE

It is a well-established fact that rainfall is only a very general indicator of soil moisture, since many other factors both climatic and edaphic intervene between precipitation and water available for plant growth.

Hence, a study of the soil moisture in several of the plats was made from time to time throughout the growing season. Ideally this should have included determinations for each kind of crop at frequent intervals. Owing to the laborious task of excavating roots this was not attempted.

Table. Approximate Available Soil Moisture

		Cabbage				Beets		
Depth, Feet	**May 29**	**June 10**	**June 24**	**Aug. 4**	**May 29**	**June 10**	**June 30**	**Aug. 13**
0.0–0.5	7.6	5.4	13.1	12.5	13.0	8.8	14.9	17.5
0.5-4.0	9.0	8.0	12.5	3.4	12.5	10.2	12.6	12.8
1–2	12.3	8.9	10.4	4.0	10.0	8.0	10.4	1.6
2–3	7.5	7.2	9.3	2.9	5.6	3.8	9.7	1.0
3–4		9.6	7.7	4.0		3.9	10.0	2.1
4–5		9.0					11.6	2.6
5–6								6.7
6–7								9.0

	June 17	July 13		July 25	Aug. 22		Aug. 29	Cct. 5	
Depth, Feet	Peas	Lettuce	Radish	Sweet Corn	Sweet Corn	Cucumber	Rutabaga	Rutabaga	Parsnip
0.0–0.5	18.8	2.4	3.8	0.3	12.4	18.1	1.6	5.2	12.3
0.5-4.0	13.5	5.4	7.5	0.4	10.7	14.8	0.3	4.0	9.7
1–2	7.1	6.9	8.3	2.1	4.7	12.4	0.7	4.5	8.0
2–3	4.2	8.4	8.3	2.4	2.4	9.3	2.7	2.4	6.9
3–4	4.2	9.1	7.9	3.4	3.4	7.1	2.5	2.2	5.0
4–5		10.5	11.7	4.3	3.8			11.4	5.0
5–6								17.4	

An examination of Table shows that in both the cabbage and beet plats sufficient water was available until the middle of August to promote a good growth. On July 25 sweet corn, which uses water in large amounts, had rather thoroughly depleted its supply of soil moisture, especially in the surface soil, but later in the season sufficient water was again present to promote normal development. Differences in the degree of soil-moisture depletion by the various crops will be discussed when the root habits of the crops are considered.

TEMPERATURE

The temperature of the air is an important factor not only directly in promoting metabolic processes but especially in connection with root studies in modifying humidity and affecting transpiration. The amount of water lost from the aboveground parts reflects itself in the development and extent of the absorbing organs. Table gives the average day temperatures for the several weeks. These data were obtained in the usual manner from the records of a thermograph placed in an appropriate shelter in the field. It records the shade temperature at a height of 5 inches from the soil surface. The average daily temperatures are also included. Except for a few extremely hot days, temperatures throughout were very favourable for growth.

Table. **Air Temperatures in Degrees Fahrenheit During 1925**

Week ending	May	May	May	June	June	June	June	July		
	13	20	27	3	10	17	24	1		
Average day	57.3	61.9	67.9	78.0	80.0	81.5	82.8	77.3		
Average daily	49.5	57.5	60.0	74.6	74.3	77.9	78.7	72.1		
Week ending	**July**	**July**	**July**	**July**	**Aug.**	**Aug.**	**Aug.**	**Aug.**		
	8	15	22	29	5	12	19	25	Average day	88.4
90.1	82.0	78.2	74.0	77.4	81.2	79.4	Average daily		82.5	84.5
76.0	74.1	64.8	73.2	76.8	74.8					

A continuous record of soil temperatures at a depth of 6 inches was obtained from May 16 to Aug. 25. During May the temperature ranged between 58 and 82°F., except on May 17 when a temperature of 50°F. was reached. The daily variation never exceeded 15°F. and was usually about 10°F. In June a variation from 62 to 90°F. was found, although the daily range did not usually exceed 12°F. But on one day a range of 19°F. was recorded. The soil at this depth was warmest at 6 p.m. and coldest at 8 a.m. This condition held throughout the summer. It represented a lag of nearly 4 hours behind the maximum and minimum air temperatures, respectively. Throughout July the temperature varied between 65 and 94°F. The daily range was usually through 15°F. (maximum, 18°F.), the highest and lowest temperatures occurring as in June. In August a temperature range from 61 to 89°F. was found, the daily range being slightly greater than for July.

The soil above 6 inches was not only much warmer at. times but also subject to greater temperature fluctuations than at greater depths. Thus roots lying close to the surface of the soil were subject to the influence of an environment which was quite different from that affecting those growing more deeply. It seems probable that surface-soil temperatures never became so high as to be injurious to root growth but that the absence of roots or their death in the shallowest soil was due to lack of a sufficient supply of moisture. 15,174 Soil temperatures are also of great importance because of their relation to disease-producing organisms that may greatly limit successful crop production.

HUMIDITY

The loss of water through transpiration is directly controlled in a large measure by the amount of moisture already in the air. This is also an important factor governing the evaporation of water directly from the surface soil. Consequently, a record of relative humidity was obtained by means of a hygrograph appropriately sheltered with the recording apparatus about 5 inches above the soil surface.

Table. Relative Humidity in Per cent, 1925

Week ending	May	May	May	June	June	June	June	
	13	20	27	3	10	17	24	
Average day	56.9	58.9	44.0	59.5	53.5	67.5	74.8	
Average daily	65.0	67.0	55.2	65.2	62.0	75.8	81.6	
Week ending	**July**	**July**	**July**	**July**	**Aug.**	**Aug.**	**Aug.**	**Aug.**
	1	15	22	29	5	12	19	25
Average day	54.7	51.8	41.7	54.2	53.1	70.2	56.7	54.8
Average daily	66.4	61.6	55.6	63.1	63.8	78.6	67.3	63.1

EVAPORATION

Evaporation was measured by Livingston's standardized, non-absorbing, white, cylindrical atmometers. These were placed in a bare area in the field with the evaporating surface at a height of 2 to 4 inches above the surface of the soil.

Table. Average Daily Evaporation

May Jun 17	May 30 17-24	June Jul 11	Jun24- 11-22	July 22-29	July Aug 5	Jul 29- 5-12	Aug 12-25	Aug 25-29	Aug 16-30
43.7	32.0	22.0	43.5	43.7	35.5	31.5	19.3	25.4	35.0

CONDITIONS FOR GROWTH AT NORMAN, OKLA

The greater portion of root studies in Oklahoma was made during 1926. Some work was also done the preceding growing season and the root growth of several crops was followed during the intervening winter. Where root excavations were made in Oklahoma this is so stated in the text.

SOIL

The crops were grown in a fine sandy loam soil that had been heavily manured for a number of years and used for growing vegetables. It was in excellent condition as regards tilth and amount of humus. The area was level and the soil quite uniform throughout. The surface foot had a reddish-brown colour, was quite sandy in texture but rather compact, and contained enough clay to exhibit a tendency to bake when it dried after heavy rains.

In the second foot it was a light-chocolate brown and contained more clay. When dry, it became quite hard, especially at a depth of 18 to 24 inches. The greater sand and smaller clay content of the soil prevented it from cracking and. fissuring as did the soil at Lincoln.

This, as will be shown, had a marked effect upon general root habit and branching. Roots penetrated the 18- to 24-inch soil layer with some difficulty, especially when it was rather dry. This was shown by their tortuous courses.

The third foot consisted of a reddish-yellow sandy clay. It contained numerous, small, black concretions of iron 1 to 2 millimeters in diameter. After long periods of drought it became very hard. The next 18 inches were much sandier and had more and larger concretions but showed no change in colour. At greater depths the soil became still sandier, was mottled with reddish-brown spots, and contained many concretions. At 7 to 8 feet it was very compact. Table shows the sizes and proportions of the various soil particles at the several depths together with the hygroscopic coefficients.

Table. **Mechanical Analyses and Hygroscopic Coefficients of Soil.**

Depth of Sample, Feet	Fine Gravel Per cent	Coarse Sand, Per cent	Medium Sand Per cent	Fine Sand Per cent	Very Fine Fand Per cent	Silt Per cent	Clay Per cent	Hygro-scopic Coeffi-cient
0.0-0.5	0.00	0.66	2.28	14.01	47.14	19.84	16.07	5.2
0.5-1.0	0.00	0.65	1.70	7.54	47.14	22.50	20.46	6.7
1-2	0.00	0.55	1.97	8.66	41.56	19.59	27.67	8.5
2-3	0.00	0.41	1.35	6.55	29.45	27.96	34.26	9.7
3-4	0.00	0.61	2.42	12.05	33.78	20.96	30.16	9.2
4-5	0.00	1.07	3.66	16.33	36.67	12.96	29.30	8.9
5-6	0.00	1.08	3.94	18.31	36.30	13.39	26.97	8.5

METHOD OF PLANTING AND TILLAGE

The field was plowed to a depth of 8 inches late in March. Repeated disking and harrowing resulted in a good, compact seed bed. All of the crops were planted by hand, each in four to eight rows, 3.5 feet apart in order to permit of cultivation with a horse-drawn harrow. Shallow cultivation was given after each rain to prevent the formation of a surface crust and also to kill weed seedlings. A mulching fork, supplemented by a hoe when necessary, was used near the plants. In this manner a surface mulch 1 to 1.5 inches deep was maintained but in no case was a cultivation deeper. A good supply of moisture was present just below the mulch during almost the entire growing season.

PRECIPITATION

The rainfall of 11.5 inches during the period when the crops were grown was 3.6 inches below the mean. April with 1.9 inches had a deficiency of 1.3 inches and no efficient rainfall after the tenth. May had 2.3 inches which was somewhat (3.1 inches) below the normal amount. No efficient rain fell between May 8 and 30. During June precipitation was 1.6 inches less than the mean. A precipitation of 2.2 inches, however, was fairly well distributed throughout the month. July had 5.1 inches rainfall, 2.4 inches above the mean, little moisture falling after the thirteenth.

SOIL MOISTURE

Notwithstanding the rather limited rainfall, a good supply of water was present throughout the entire growing season. The fine sandy loam soil of the level field, loose from the cultivation of the previous season, had been thoroughly wet by the fall and winter rains.

Water had entered the deeper subsoil and moistened it beyond the depth of greatest root penetration. Most of this water was retained in the spring and supplemented by rains in March. Thus, although the summer rainfall was light, a good supply of moisture was present throughout the entire growing season. Since soil samples were taken from the middle of the area between the rows, the earlier determinations represent the total available moisture. Later the widely spreading roots extended into these areas and the water supply was considerably reduced.

Table. Average Approximate Available Soil Moisture

foot	0.0 to 0.5 foot	0.5 to 1.0 feet	1 to 2 feet	2 to 3 feet	3 to 4 Date
Mar. 11	8.6	11.5	10.5	5.3	7.8
Mar. 18	10.6	12.2	10.1	7.5	8.3
Mar. 25	10.2	10.4	9.0	7.8	7.6
Apr. 1	14.6	15.5	12.3	9.0	7.7
Apr. 8	11.6	13.3	10.7	8.9	8.7
Apr. 15	13.9	13.9	12.2	10.3	9.5
Apr. 22	10.9	11.0	11.2	9.6	10.3
Apr. 29	9.8	12.3	10.1	9.0	10.1
May 6	13.6	14.0	11.9	10.5	9.9
May 13	14.5	14.0	11.5	7.2	10.6
May 20	10.1	12.9	10.8	9.8	9.3
May 27	15.3	10.6	10.3	9.4	10.2
June 3	9.4	11.2	10.6	9.5	9.3
June 10	3.5	7.2	5.7	7.8	7.9
June 17	6.4	13.5	10.7	10.5	10.3
June 24	8.9	11.3	9.9	9.3	9.4
July 1	7.0	6.5	9.0	7.0	8.7

July 8	12.1	7.1	8.1	6.2	7.3
July 15	8.0	4.0	8.0	5.4	7.7
July 22	4.3	3.4	5.9	5.3	8.1

An examination of Table shows that the soil was moist when the crops were planted and that sufficient water was available at all times to promote a good growth.

That conditions of soil moisture in the plats of pepper and Swiss chard were representative for the crops as a whole was shown by frequent soil sampling among the roots of other vegetables. In nearly every case very similar results were obtained.

This, however, was to be expected, since the root habits of both pepper and Swiss chard are representative and their aboveground transpiring parts moderately extensive. The excellent moisture content in the surface 6 inches was undoubtedly in part due to the soil mulch preserved at all times.

RELATION OF ABSORBING AREA TO SOIL MOISTURE

In one experiment Nebraska White Prize dent corn of the *F*1 generation from two pure-line parental strains and, consequently, of similar hereditary constitution was grown for 5 weeks in fertile loess soil with original water contents of 9 and 19 per cent, respectively, above the hygroscopic coefficient. The plants were in the eighth-leaf stage when the roots were examined. In the more moist soil the area of the tops, including the stem and both surfaces of the leaves, was 82 per cent of that of the roots. But in the drier soil the tops had only 46 per cent as great an area as the roots. In other words, the absorbing area of the roots (exclusive of root hairs which covered the entire root system) was 1.2 times as great as the area of the tops in the more moist soil and 2.2 times as great in the drier soil.

The total length of the main roots in the two cases was about the same, as was also their diameter. In neither case did the main roots make up more than 11 per cent of the total absorbing area. In the drier soil 75 per cent of the area was furnished by the primary laterals and the remaining 14 per cent by branches from these. But in the more moist soil the primary branches furnished only 38 per cent of the root area. It seemed as though the plant had blocked out a root system quite inadequate to meet the heavy demands for absorption made by the vigorous tops, and as the soil became drier the remaining 51 per cent of the area was furnished by an excellent development of secondary and tertiary branches. Maize, in loess soil with only 2 to 3 per cent of water in excess of the hygroscopic coefficient, had, in proportion to the length of the main roots, about one-third more laterals than it had in a similar soil of medium water content. Moreover, the absorbing area in comparison to tops was greater.

Similar top-and-root area relations have been found to hold for other plants when grown in like soils of different water content. Numerous experiments have shown that root extent is greater in dry Soil. 68 Because of the difficulty of recovering the root system in its entirety from the soil and the onerous task of measuring the length and diameter of all its parts, but few data are available. For example, a plant of maize only in the eighth-leaf stage has from 8,000 to 10,000 laterals arising from the 15 to 23 main roots. Usually the relations are stated in the ratio of the dry weight of roots to tops, an expression difficult of interpretation in terms of function. The larger, thicker, and heavier roots are least significant, the delicate branchlets, too often lost in such determinations, being of greatest importance although adding little to weight.

MIDSUMMER GROWTH

The plants had a height of about 4.5 feet and were very leafy. The parent stalk had usually given rise to two to four tillers but sometimes there were as many as six. The very numerous leaves, averaging 2.5 feet long and 3.5 inches wide at the base, offered a very large area for food manufacture and transpiration. For example, one plant with four tillers had a leaf surface of 20 square feet. The tassels were about half out.

The root system had made a really wonderful growth and was clearly in a state of very rapid development. After considerable study a plant with four tillers was selected as typically representative, and was fully examined and described. There were 45 roots of larger diameter, 3 to 4 millimeters. These were older and longer than the others. Another lot of 15 roots were about, 1.5 millimeters in diameter and also extended widely. In addition there were 33 young roots of a diameter of 1.5 to 3.5 millimeters and of an average length of 4 inches (varying from 1.2 to 8.5 inches). Finally, 29 smaller, fine roots only 0.5 millimeter thick and about 2 inches long arose from the root crown. It is impossible to represent all of these in detail in the most carefully executed drawing. But at least the principal features can be clearly portrayed.

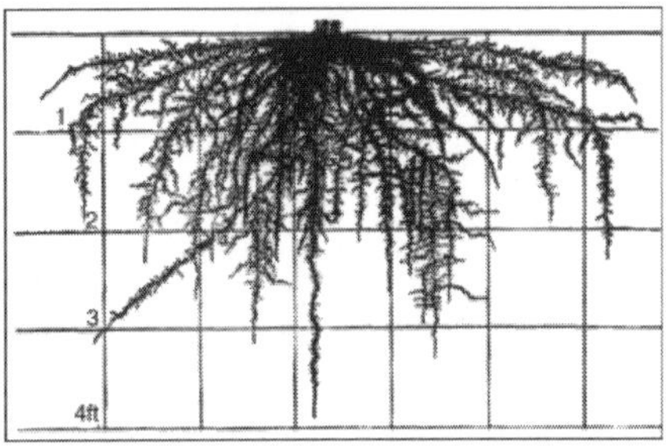

Fig. 3.2 Root System of Sweet Corn 8 Weeks Old.

The primary root (often erroneously called temporary), which could still be easily identified, pursued an obliquely downward and outward course, ending 28 inches horizontally from the base of the stalk and at a depth of 37 inches. Only a few roots penetrated deeper. One, however, was found near the 4-foot level, but the usual depth of maximum penetration scarcely exceeded 3 feet.

The working level was at a depth of 2 feet and a maximum lateral spread of 3 feet had been attained. The working level, or the working depth, means that to which many roots penetrate and at which much absorption must occur. The thorough occupancy of even the surface 3 inches of soil and the competition of the roots between the 42-inch rows may be plainly seen. The lax, meandering course of the longer main roots of the adventitious or secondary root system was such as to ramify the soil completely from the surface to directly beneath the plant. These strong, tough roots were 3 to 4 millimeters in diameter at their origin and maintained a diameter of 1.5 to 2 millimeters to their tips. They were extremely well branched. Only the 3 to 5 inches of the rapidly growing root ends were free from branches. The branches were usually most numerous and often longest throughout the first few feet of their course. Here they were frequently distributed 18 to 25 per inch, but they were profuse throughout, *i.e.,* 8 to 12 per inch. All of the branches are not shown in the drawing. These were variable in length, the usual length of the shorter ones ranging from 0.2 to 2 inches. But branches 6 inches to 2 to 3 feet long were also common. The shorter rootlets were often unbranched, but longer ones (mostly those over 1 inch in length) were rebranched with 20 branches, 0.1 to 1 inch long, per inch. These longer sublaterals were again rebranched. Often the larger branches on the main roots were 1 to 1.5 millimeters thick and branched like the main root. Thus, dense masses of roots and rootlets ramified the soil.

The root network was especially dense within a radius of 6 to 10 inches from the plant. Here, in addition to the older roots, new surface roots were formed. For example, one of these only 7.5 inches long was 5 millimeters thick. It tapered-to a tip 2 millimeters in diameter. There was a total of 63 branches, many of which were profusely rebranched as shown in Fig. 3.3 roots of this general type were found near the base of the plant, and some actually had 40 branches per inch! Some aerial roots, as yet without branches, extended 2 to 4 inches into the rootfilled soil. All of the surface roots were very turgid and brittle. In fact, the denseness and abundance of the rapidly growing roots can scarcely be overemphasized.

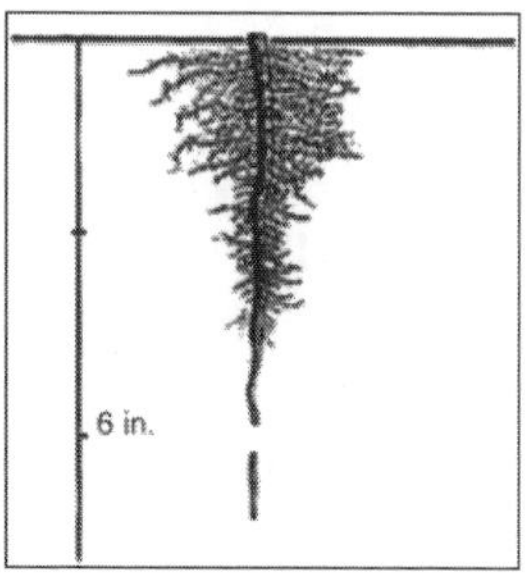

Fig. 3.3 One of the Younger and Shorter but Densely Branched Roots of Corn.

MATURING PLANTS

Late in August a final examination was made. The plants had an average height of 5.3 feet; some stalks were 6.5 feet tall. The leaves had not increased in average size but there were more of them owing to the development of the tillers, some of which were now as large as the parent plant. Only a few of the basal leaves had deteriorated and the plants were in good condition. The one selected for detailed study had five stalks and seven ears. The kernels were well filled but the husks were only beginning to dry.

The root system had developed proportionately to the tops. Branchlets extended to the root tips and indicated that growth was practically complete. The surface area delimited at the former examination (approximately 3 feet on all sides of the plant) had not been greatly extended, but the soil volume, of which this was one end, had been greatly extended in depth. A working level of 50 inches was found and numerous roots ended between 60 and 68 inches, which was the maximum depth.

After continued study a typical plant was selected and its root system worked out in the usual manner. A total of 78 main roots (*i.e.*, roots of large diameter, 3.5 millimeters or more) arose from the base of this plant and 123 smaller ones. Those of the latter group ranged from 0.5 to 2 millimeters thick. Nine of the large main roots extended outward 18 to 42 inches from the base of the plant in the surface soil and then, turning downward, reached depths of 3 to 5 feet.

Twenty-five main roots (20 to 30 on other plants) extended outward only a short distance from the base of the plant or, more usually, ran obliquely downward in such a manner that even at their ends (at depths of 3.5 to 5 feet) they were only 12 to 18 inches from a vertical line from the base of the plant. Figure 3.4 shows that some of these more vertically descending roots were half grown at the earlier examination. But many more of them had developed at this time.

The remainder of the large roots consisted of prop roots and others with a large diameter (not infrequently 5 millimeters) which mostly extended only a short distance, usually not over 12 inches, from the base of the plant. As regards the remaining very numerous but smaller roots, these extended outward almost entirely in the surface foot of soil. Here they ended at distances of 3 to 24 inches from the base of the plant. Thus, the surface soil, especially the first 10 inches and within a radius of 9 inches from the crown, was filled with a dense tangle of roots, a network so complex and so profuse that there seemed actually to be more roots than soil. Certainly no moisture could evaporate from this soil volume. Indeed it seems many more roots were present than were necessary to exhaust it of its water and readily available nutrients! Figure 3.4 shows a surface view of this root complex, the soil having been removed and the roots exposed to a depth of 12 inches.

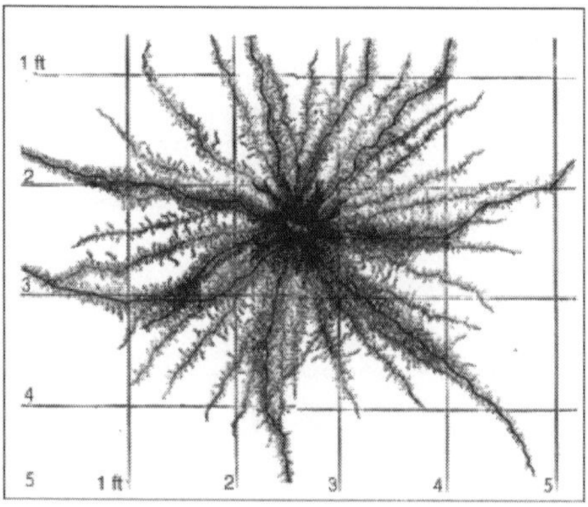

Fig. 3.4 Roots of a Mature Plant of Sweet Corn Found in the 12 inches of Surface Soil.

As regards degree of branching, it was indeed profuse. On the main, long, widely spreading roots, laterals occurred as before at the rate of 8 to 12 branches per inch, but 30 branches per inch were not uncommon. Even at depths of 4 feet or more 5 to 10 short branches per inch were usual. The branches, moreover, were, in general, longer than at the earlier examination; in fact long branches (over 5 inches) were much more numerous, and the network of branches due to rebranching much more profuse. Similar branching occurred on the long, rather vertically descending main roots, but these, like the others, were less profusely branched below 3 feet.

From the tough, yellowish, cord-like roots many long branches filled the soil. Some of these in the deeper soil were quite yellow in colour. Branching of the finer surface laterals occurred at the rate indicated in the drawing. Here also the length of the branches and their degree of rebranching are shown in detail.

If one can visualize the root system of the sweet-corn plant, he will see the surface 12 inches of soil near the plant filled with a tangled root mass even to within 1 inch of the soil surface. Extending beyond this to distances of 18 to 42 inches, main horizontal roots pursue their course. From these long branches extend into the deeper soil and finally the main roots themselves turn downward and penetrate deeply. Below the 10-inch level, roots are still abundant, but not so dense, until the working level at 50 inches is reached. Still deeper roots are fewer but occasionally occur at a depth of 68 inches. The main vertical roots penetrating downward, spreading 12 inches or more on all sides of a vertical line from the base of the plant, go thoroughly fill the soil that in comparison there seems to be more or less of a gap between this soil volume and that so completely occupied by the main horizontal ones. In some plants this is less pronounced since, as in field corn, the roots spread at wider angles and thus thoroughly occupy this portion of the soil volume.

ROOTS AND PLANTS

The roots of monocotyledonous plants differ in their development from those of dicotyledons. The single primary root of the onion, lasts but a short time, and is succeeded by others which do not arise as branches upon the primary one, but spring from the very short stem of the plant. Roots which arise on stems and leaves, or on various parts of the roots of plants, but not in acropetal succession are described as adventitious. They are very common upon all monoco-tyledonous plants of the farm and garden, and may be considered the chief ones which such plants possess.

In wheat, the embryo within the grain possesses three roots; in barley, five or six. Young barley plant show- use during the earlier stages of growth. Although common upon monocotyledons adventitious roots are not confined to this class. Examples are abundant upon many kinds of dicotyledonous plants.

Good instances are met with on the underground stems of mint, potato and hop, and on the runners of the strawberry, stems of creeping crowfoot and white clover, as well as many others. They are generally produced at the joints where leaves grow upon the stem, and may arise in some plants from internal causes apart from any external influences; in other instances their development depends upon contact of the stem with water or moist soil.

Almost all parts of certain plants may be made to produce them, and the propagation of plants Buch as gooseberries, currants, roses and hops by means of slips and cuttings depends upon their development. Pieces of stem cut off just below a leaf, and placed in moist earth soon develop adventitious roots near the cut end. Advantage is taken of their formation in the propagation of plants by means of layers. Examine the roots upon any cuttings or slips which can be obtained, and observe whether they arise on the cut surface or at a point some distance away from it. Usually adventitious roots are thin and fibrous, but those of the dahlia are tuberous. The complete root-systems of plants vary enormously in extent, but in all cases the total length is much greater than is usually anticipated.

That of an ordinary oat plant, although not spreading through more than a cubic yard or two of soil, measured in one instance over one hundred and fifty yards in length. A tree uprooted by the wind exposes to view a small number of stout roots similar to the thicker branches of the crown, and from these are given off a larger number of a finer texture. By far the greater bulk, however, which the tree possessed remain in the ground in the form of extremely fine rootlets or fibrils extending outwards generally as far, or a little farther, than the branches and leaves of the tree, but in some instances to much greater distances. Not only do the roots grow out horizontally and near the surface of the soil, but they extend downwards as well. In isolated instances, where an adequate supply of air has been maintained along open cracks and fissures, roots have been found to descend many yards into the ground, but in general the roots of the tallest trees rarely go down more than seven or eight feet. The want of air and presence of noxious substances in the lower regions of the soil checks further growth in this direction.

With many plants almost every cubic inch of soil immediately beneath their shade contains fine delicate rootlets, and the extent of their root-branching is very rarely realised on account of the ease with which these hair-like fibrils are broken off when the plant is pulled up or disturbed. Many forest trees have a natural habit of sending their roots several feet into the soil Examples of fruit-trees belonging to this class, and requiring a deep soil for proper growth, are the cherry and wild pear. Some trees, such as larch, keep their root-system nearer the surface, spreading out more horizontally in the ground. The quince, used as a stock on which to graft pears, has roots which remain in the upper regions of the soil. Similar surface-rooting habit is very marked in the ' Paradise' apple on which apples are grafted, and in Prunus Mahaleb upon which cherries are often grafted. The root-system of wheat penetrates more deeply than that of barley; the mangel sends its fine rootlets more extensively into the deeper layers of the soil than cabbage or turnip red clover roots more deeply than white clover, and almost all plants have distinct and peculiar habits in this respect.

The character and extent of root-development is not, however, altogether dependent upon the species of the plant concerned, but is materially influenced by external circumstances, such as the texture of the soil, and the amount of water in it. In deep open soils and loose sands the root-system of a plant is much larger than that of a similar plant grown in compact heavy ground. In soils which are not water-logged, increase of moisture up to a certain extent increases the branching of the root, and excellent examples of the influence of water, coupled with good air supply, are seen in well managed plants in pots, and also among plants growing near wells and in drain pipes; the latter in some instances become completely blocked by the large number of fine rootlets of trees growing in their neighbourhood.

The root-system is also considerably modified by the totyl amount and kind of the manures or food-materials present in the soil. Up to a certain point an increase of nutrient substances increases root-development; an excess hinders it.

Mutilation influences the development of the root-system. If the growing-point of the tap root of a cabbage or tree is cut off its further elongation is prevented, but the secondary roots make up for the loss by more vigourous growth and often many adventitious roots arise near the cut end. In order to properly cultivate plants of all kinds it is very important to study the habit or manner of branching of their roots and the relative proportions of the thick tap and secondary roots to the fine ramifications to which they give rise and which spread through the soil in all directions.

The proportion of root-system below ground to the branches and leaves above is also worthy of attention. The adaptability of plants to the various kinds of soils, their need of water, the cultivation which the ground should have and the rational application of manures to the plant are best understood and appreciated after a careful study of these points. Tap-rooted crops, such as sugar-beet, mangel, carrot, and parsnip, require the soil to be well-worked to some considerable depth. Surface-rooting plants, such as barley, can be grown upon comparatively thin soils. The same is true of pears grafted on the quince and apples on the Paradise stock, and such plants respond more quickly to, and are more benefited by, top-dressings of soluble manures than plants with a deeply-penetrating root-system.

KINDS OF PLANTS AND CROPS

ALFALFA

Leaf Spot (Pseudopeziza medicaginis): Small black spots on the leaves. Causes the leaves to turn yellow and fall.

Control: Frequent close mowing usually holds the disease in check.

Dodder (Cuscuta epithymum): A tangled mat of yellow threads entwining the alfalfa stems. Usually appears in spots in the field and spreads from these points. Is easily spread by the rake, and especially in seed. Dodder is not a fungus, but a specialized parasitic plant of the morning-glory family.

Control: As soon as discovered, cover the infested spot with straw and oil and burn. Screen the alfalfa seed to remove seed of . dodder. Make a screen 12 inches square by 3 inches deep with a 20 X 20 mesh wire-cloth made of No. 34 steel wire. Sift each half pound of seed vigorously for one half minute. Almond. Blight (Coryneum beyerinkii).

APPLE

Blight: The same disease as Pear Blight.

Bitter-rot or Ripe-rot (Glomerella rufomaculans): Produces a browning and drying of the fruit. Progressing in concentric rings from a central point. Attacks nearly mature fruit. Also occurs on limbs, where it produces a canker scarcely distinguishable.

Control: Trim out all cankers early in the spring, and remove all mummied apples from the trees. In addition to the sprayings for apple scab, make three, four, or five sprayings with bordeaux mixture, 3-3-50, according to the severity of the disease and the character of the summer as regards rainfall.

Black-rot of fruit: Fruit stage of the New York apple-tree canker disease, which see.

Blotch (Phyllosticta solitaria): Attacks fruit, twigs, and leaves. Blotches a quarter of an inch or more in diameter appear on the fruit. These often coalesce, and the fruit often cracks deeply. Scurfy cankers are formed on the twigs while very small; circular spots a quarter of an inch in diameter are formed on the leaves. Ben Davis is especially susceptible.

Control: Careful pruning to remove cankered twigs. Spray as for apple scab and bitter rot.

Control: Smooth cankers in bark of trunk and limbs usually indicate blight, rough ones New York apple-tree canker.

Collar-rot: A dead area in the bark near the ground ; often girdles the tree. Cause not known. May be started in some cases by the fire-blight organism, in others by winter injury. Common on King, Baldwin, and Ben Davis.

Remedy: As soon as noticed, cut away dead bark and wood to the living healthy tissue. Swab the wound with a solution of corrosive sublimate, 1:1000, and paint over with a lead paint which is free from turpentine. Slit the callus on the edge from year to year to make it spread faster, and keep dead wood well protected with paint.

Apple-tree Canker (Sphceropsis malorum): The fungus causing the disease attacks limbs, causing roughened cankers and often girdling the limb ; attacks leaves, causing a reddish brown leaf-spot, and on the fruit produces a black rot. Abundant on Twenty Ounce.

Control: Remove and burn old cankers. Clean out and disinfect small cankers as for collar-rot. Soak old limbs well with spray mixture when spraying for scab. Spraying as for apple scab usually controls black rot of fruit, though in the Ozark region a late spraying may be advisable for leaf-spot. Cultivate thoroughly.

Powdery Mildew (Sphcerotheca leucotricha): Attacks nursery stock, covering the leaves with a grayish white, powdery mildew. Also on leaves and twigs of new growth in the orchard, often causing the leaves to fall.

Remedy: Lime-sulfur, 1-40, as applied for scab is a specific.

Rust (Gymnosporangium macropus): A bright yellow rust appearing on the young leaves and fruit. Enfeebles the whole tree and produces one-sided fruits. It is known that one stage in the cycle of the fungus is the cedar apple, which occurs on the red cedar. Apples are always infected from the cedar, never from apple to apple. *Control:* Destroy red cedars in the neighborhood, also wild apples and hawthorns. Spray thoroughly in the spring as for scab.

Scab (Venturia incequalis): Olive green, brownish or blackish scab-like spots on leaves and fruit. Arrests growth, and often causes distortion. In severe cases may make the leaves and young fruit fall. Makes leaves susceptible to spray injury. The fungus is known to be dependent upon weather conditions. The fungus winters regularly on the dead fallen leaves. In the milder climate of Virginia, the fungus may winter on the twigs.

Control: Rake and burn leaves, or plow under very early (before blossom buds open). Spray with lime-sulfur 32° Beaume, 1-40, or bordeaux, 3-3-50:

- When blossom buds show pink, but before they open;
- When the majority of petals have fallen;
- Tthree weeks after b depending upon the weather;
- If a late attack is feared, spray thoroughly before the fall rains begin.

ASPARAGUS

Rust (Puccinia asparagi): A rust of the tops, which is often so severe as to kill them, thus interfering with root development.

Control: Three weeks after cutting stops dust the young tops with dry sulfur at the rate of 11/2 sacks of sulfur per acre. This should be done very early in the morning while the dew is still on, and only on a dewy morning. In a month or less make another application, using 2 sacks of sulfur per acre. The sulfur must go on in a dusty, smoky cloud and form a covering over all the growth. Flowers of sulfur is more satisfactory for this work, and is less expensive in the long run. Dusting machines may be obtained on the market.

BEAN

Anthracnose or Pod-spot (Colletotrichum lindemuthianum): Reddish-brown scab-like spots appearing on stems, pods, and veins of leaves, particularly on yellow-podded snap beans. The fungus grows through the pod and into the young bean seed. It lies dormant in the seed, and becomes active when the bean is planted.

Control: Select pods which are free from the spots and save the seed for planting. Such seed will grow a clean crop. If disease appears in the garden, it can be controlled by thoroughly hand spraying the vines from beneath as well as above, repeating the operation every ten days as long as necessary.

Blight {Bacterium phaseoli): A bacterial disease. Causes large, papery spots on leaves and watery spots on pods. *Control:* As for Anthracnose.

BEAN, LIMA

*Blight (Phytophthora phaseoli):*Attacks the pods in August and September, covering them with a white, felted coating. It also attacks shoots and leaves.

Control: Spray with bordeaux, 4–4–50, beginning about August first, and making applications at intervals of ten days or two weeks.

Beet. Heart-rot (Phoma betae): Leaves appear spotted late in July, then wilt, and finally a dry heart rot appears.

Control: Destroy infected plants. Practice long rotation. Treat seed with formalin, 1 pint in 30 gallons of water.

Leaf-spot (Cercospora beticola): Ashen gray spots with reddish borders occurring on leaves. In advanced stages, leaf becomes much cracked and torn.

Control: Spray with bordeaux mixture, 4–4–50, at frequent intervals.

Scab (Oospora scabies): Fungus produces a scabby patch on the root. The same disease as potato scab. *Control:* Avoid planting beets after potatoes for several years.

Crown-gall or Root-gall (Bacterium tumefaciens): A bacterial disease which soon ruins the bushes.

Treatment: Plow up and burn all bushes in a diseased patch. Plant clean roots in a new place.

CABBAGE

Club-root or Club-foot (Plasmodiophora brassicae): A contorted swelling of the roots of cabbage in the seed bed or field, preventing the plant from heading and causing it to assume a sickly color. Occurs on many allied plants—turnips, cauliflower, Brussels sprouts, chard, radish, wild mustard, etc.

Control: Destroy affected seedlings. Rotate crops, and do not follow with other susceptible crops. Keep down weeds on which disease occurs. Lime the soil at least eighteen months before planting to cabbage, using at the rate of two tons of quicklime to the acre.

Black-rot (Bacillus campestre): The bacteria causing this disease get into the sap tubes, turn them black, and cause the leaves to drop, thus preventing heading.

Control: Practice crop rotation. Soak the seed for fifteen minutes in a solution of mercuric chloride, one tablet in a pint of water.

CARNATION

Rust (Uromyces caryophyllinus): Produces brown, powdery pustules on stems and leaves.

Control: Take cuttings only from healthy plants. Pick off diseased leaves. Spray once in two weeks with a solution of copper sulfate, 1 pound to 20 gallons. Keep water from leaves, and grow the plants at as low temperature as is compatible with best development.

Stem-rot (Rhizoctonia and Fusarium): The former produces a sudden wilting of the plant, and the stems are soon dead and dry. The latter produces a slow rot of the heart, one branch dying at a time. The treatment is the same.

Control: In the field change the location every year. In the greenhouse sterilize the soil with steam.

CELERY

Early Leaf-blight (Cercospora apii): A spotting and eventual blighting of the leaves early in the summer. Begins in the seed-bed. It is favored by hot weather, either wet or dry. *Control:* Spray with ammoniacal copper carbonate, 5-3-50, beginning in the seed bed and keeping the new growth covered throughout the season. *Late Blight (Septoria petroselini var. apii):* A fungous disease, appearing late in the season, causing a blight of the foliage, and often destructive after the celery is stored. *Control:* As above, except that spraying should be continued up to harvesting time. In either case, the disease is practically controlled by growing the plants under half shade. Cherry.

Brown-rot (Sclerotinia fructigena): Attacks flowers, leaves, and fruit. The flowers die and decay, the leaves become discolored with irregular brown spots, and the fruit rots on the tree. Attacks also peaches, plums, and apples.

Control: Spray with bordeaux mixture, 4-4-50, or lime-sulfur, 1-40, (a) just before the blossom buds open; (b) just after the blossoms fall; (c) make one or two more applications at intervals of ten days.

Powdery Mildew (Podosphaera oxycanthae): Attacks leaves and twigs, often causing defoliation. Serious on nursery stock. Spraying as for brown rot usually controls this trouble. If it appears, spray with lime sulfur, 1-40, or dust heavily with powdered sulfur.

Leaf-spot (Cylindrosporium padi): A fungous disease in which the leaves become thickly spotted with reddish or brown spots and fall prematurely. The spots often drop out, leaving shot holes.

Control: Spray with lime sulfur, 1-40, or with bordeaux mixture, 4-4-50, as for brown rot. Winter Injury.—Trees so injured make a scant growth; many leaves turn yellow and fall about picking time; gum exudes at the crotches and about the trunk; sometimes the bark on the stock is entirely killed, in which case the tree languishes and finally dies.

Control: It is thought that heavy applications of highly nitrogenous fertilizers in late summer favor winter injury. Do not stimulate the tree to too active wood development. Cut out the gum pockets and cankers, and paint them with a heavy lead paint.

COTTON

Anthracnose (Colletotrichum gossypii): Forms black or purplish colored spots on bolls. Disease also occurs on seed leaves and on the leaves and stems. Select seed from fields free from the disease. Rotate crops. Use disease-resistant varieties.

Root-rot (Ozonium omnivorum): Easily recognized by the sudden wilting and dying of the plants in the field.

Control: A combination of rotation of crops and deep fall plowing is effective.

Wilt (Fusarium vasinfecta): Causes a gradual wilt and eventual death of leaves and stems.

Control: Rotate crops. Secure seed of wilt-resistant varieties of cotton.

CRANBERRY

Blast or Scald (Guignardia vaccinii): The fungus causes a blast of the flowers and very young fruits, and attacks older fruits, causing them to appear scalded or watery.

Control: Spray five or six times with bordeaux mixture, 5–5–50, to which has been added 4 pounds of resin fish oil soap, making the first application just before the blossoms open. Long lines of hose are most satisfactory for this work, and the spraying must be done thoroughly.

Rot. (Acanthorhynchus vaccinii): A disease which cannot be distinguished from scald with the naked eye.

Control: As for Scald. Hypertrophy (Exobasidium oxycocci).—Appears on the young leaves soon after the water has been let off in the spring. The axillary leaf buds are attacked and produce short shoots with rather close, enlarged, swollen, and distorted leaves which are pink or light rose color. The production of fruit is prevented or reduced.

Control: Early spraying with bordeaux mixture has been advised.

CUCUMBER

Blight or Mildew (Pseudoperonospora cubensis): A blighting and premature yellowing of the foliage.

Control: Spray with bordeaux mixture, 5–5–50. Commence to spray when the plants begin to run, and repeat every ten to fourteen days throughout the season.

Wilt (Bacillus tracheiphilus): This is a disease caused by bacteria that get into the sap tubes of the leaf and stem, clog and destroy them, causing the plant to wilt. The bacteria are distributed chiefly by the striped cucumber beetle.

Control: Control the striped beetle. Gather and destroy all wilted leaves and plants.

Wilt (caused by malnutrition): Excessive fertilizing with highly nitrogenous fertilizers will sometimes produce a peculiar curling and wilting of the leaves.

CHESTNUT

Bark Disease (Diaporthe parasitica): A fungous disease, attacking the bark of the American chestnut. Limbs and trunk are girdled, and the tree dies. The disease is present in many of the nurseries.

Control: Inspect nursery stock very carefully, especially about pruned stubs. Discard diseased trees. Make a careful examination of old trees, especially about old wounds and pruned stubs. If the disease is present, clean out the diseased wood with a gouge, and coat heavily with gas-tar. If the disease has progressed far, cut off diseased limbs or the whole tree and burn at once. Keep all wounds and pruned stubs covered with gas-tar.

CHRYSANTHEMUM

Leaf-spot (Septoria chrysanthemi): First appears as dark brown spots, which increase in size until the leaf dies. *Control:* Pick and burn diseased leaves. Spray the plants with bordeaux mixture, 4-4-50.

Rust (Puccinia chrysanthemi): Reddish brown rust pustules on the leaves.

Control: Avoid wetting the foliage when watering. Spray as for Leaf Spot.

CORN

Ear-rot (Diplodia zeae): Several other organisms may cause an ear rot, but this is the more common one. The ear is imperfectly developed, soft, and overrun with a whitish mold. In many cases the husks and silk are also involved.

Control: Destroy old infected ears and stalks. Practice a rotation which will exclude corn for two years from or near the given plat of ground.

Rust (Puccinia maydis): Reddish pustules on the blades. Common on some varieties of sweet corn.

Control: No satisfactory method of control is known.

Smut (Ustilago zeae).—Attacks stalks, ears, and tassels, producing abnormal boils or outgrowths. Will infect at actively growing points at any time.

Control: Rotate crops. Do not manure corn ground. Cut out smut and burn it. Soaking seed is of no avail.

CURRANT

Anthracnose (Glaeosporium ribis): Small dark brown spots, chiefly on the upper surface of the leaf. The leaves finally turn yellow, and fall in July or August.

Control: Thorough applications of bordeaux mixture, 5-5-50.

Leaf-spot (Septoria ribis, Cercospora angulata etc.): Whitish spots with black centers. Appears in midsummer, and causes defoliation.

Control: Thorough applications of bordeaux mixture, 5-5-50.

Wilt or Cane-blight: A destructive fungous disease which causes the canes to die suddenly. Character of the wilting much like that produced by the cane-borer. *Control:* No satisfactory method known. The most that can be done is to go over the patch three or four times during the summer, cut out and burn the blighted canes.

Ginseng. Blight (Alternaria panacis): Papery brown spots on the leaves, which spread until the whole leaf is involved. Also attacks the seed heads, producing a blast.

Control: In the spring before the plants come through the ground spray the soil thoroughly with copper sulfate, 1 pound to

10 gallons of water. As the plants are breaking through the soil, spray with bordeaux, 3–3–50. Spray repeatedly while the plants are coming through the ground, making a special effort to cover the stems. Keep all growth covered with spray throughout the summer. Spray the seed heads thoroughly just after the blossoms fall, and again when they are two-thirds grown. Destroy all diseased tops. *Fiber Rot (Thielavia basicola):* Commonly called rust or rusty root, from the characteristic appearance. The plants eventually wilt and die.

Control: Treat the soil with acid phosphate at the rate of 1000 pounds to the acre. Dip the roots in bordeaux mixture, 3-3-50, before planting.

Mildew (Phytophthora cactorum): Attacks tops shortly after they come up.

Control: Thorough spraying early, as for blight, will control this disease.

Wilt (Acrostalagmus sp.): A sudden wilting of the whole plant, caused by the action of the fungus in the sap tubes of the root.

Control: Remove the wilted plants as soon as discovered in order to prevent further spread.

Root-rot: Caused by various soil organisms. Favored by wet, soggy soil.

Control: Underdrain the soil thoroughly. Golden-seal. - Consult treatments under Ginseng.

GOOSEBERRY

Mildew (Sphaerotheca mors-uvce): A powdery mildew attacking the fruit and young growth of English varieties of gooseberpy.

Control: As soon as the leaves begin to unfold, spray with potassium sulfid, 1 ounce to 2 gallons of water.

Rust (AEcidium grossularice): Orange-colored rust pustules on the fruit and under side of the leaves.

Control: Early spraying as for Mildew. Keep down sedges and grasses.

GRAPE

Anthracnose (Sphaceloma ampelinum): Occurs on the fruit as a definite dark brown spot with a lighter auriole ; on canes as deep pits with an elevated red margin, and on veins of the leaves, causing the leaves to crimp. Occurs on all varieties, especially Roger's hybrids. Not so abundant as formerly.

Control: It is said that an early spraying before the buds open with sulfate of iron, 100 pounds to 50 gallons of water, is very important. Later sprayings for black rot will also be effective in preventing spread.

Black-rot (Guignardia bidwellii): The most serious disease of grapes east of the Rocky Mountains, especially southward. Attacks all green parts. Produces a brown circular spot on leaves, a black, elongated, sunken pit on petioles, canes, etc., and on the berry a brown rot with shriveling and wrinkling ; finally the berry becomes black and hard.

Control: This disease may be controlled by timely applications of bordeaux mixture, 4–4–50. It is of great importance that spraying be done before rain storms, as the berry enlarges so rapidly.

Spray:

- When the third or fourth leaf has unfolded ;
- As soon as the blossoms have fallen;
- When the berries are the size of a pea ;
- In about two weeks. In a wet season make two more applications.

After July 20 make the bordeaux 4–2–50, or use ammoniacal copper carbonate. In case of dense foliage all applications except the first two should be made by hand. Attach trailers to the sprayer, and have two men following to apply the spray directly to the clusters. About ten acres can be sprayed in a day, and the total cost of labor and material should not exceed 75 cents per acre for each application.

California Vine-disease: An obscure disease, which destroyed thousands of acres of vines in California. Cause not known, and at present practically unknown and of no importance economically.

Crown-gall or Black Knot (Bacterium tumefaciens): A tu-merous, gnarled outgrowth on roots and stems, especially on European varieties. Frost injury often forms an infection court for the bacteria.

Control: Grub out and burn infected vines.

Downy Mildew or Leaf-blight (Plasmopara viticola): Appears in white frost like patches on under side of leáf, the upper side of the leaf showing a yellowish discoloration ; gradually spreads to all parts of the leaf causing it to dry up. Attacks the berry, which remains hard and white or gray. Worst on hybrids with vinifera blood ; especially common on Delaware and Roger's hybrids. Widespread in North America.

Control: Spray as for Black-rot.

Necrosis or Dead-arm Disease (Fusicoccum viticolum): Attacks shoots, and progresses from there to the old wood, causing a dry rot and eventual death of the vine.

Control: Inspect canes at trimming time, and use care not to leave those on which the brownish black spots are present. Train up renewals from the root, and cut off the old stem below the diseased area.

Treatment as for black-rot is efficacious.

Shelling or Rattles: Cause unknown. The berry breaks squarely off at its juncture with the pedicle. The leaves on such vines usually turn reddish brown about the margin. Powdery mildew is sometimes responsible for shelling.

Control: No method is known. Hollyhock.

Anthracnose (Colletotrichum malvarum): Angular brown spots on leaves and stems which spread, killing the entire leaf.

Control: As for Rust. *Rust (Puccinia malvacearum):* Attacks all parts of the plant, causing reddish brown pustules on affected parts ; later leaving deep pits ; may entirely destroy the leaves. It is abundant on the common mallow or "cheeses."

Control: Eradicate the mallow ; pick off diseased leaves in the fall, and burn all litter. Repeat in the spring, and spray new growth thoroughly with bordeaux mixture, 4-3-50. Spray every week until the flower-stalks are well developed. Lettuce. *Leaf Perforation (Marssonia perforans):* Dead areas in the leaves which finally drop out. Also on veins of the leaves.

Downy Mildew (Bremia lactucce): Yellow spots on the upper surface of the leaf, accompanied by a frosty growth on the opposite side.

Control: Destroy infected plants. Keep water from the leaves ; furnish water by means of subirrigation.

Drop or Rot (Sclerotinia libertiana): Base of the leaves or stem rots off, allowing leaves to drop.

Control: Sterilize the soil with steam before planting.

Rosette (Rhizoctonia sp.): A rotting or damping-off of the stem. Late affected plants have a rosetted appearance.

Control: Start seed in steam-sterilized soil, and transfer to beds that have been sterilized with steam, as for Drop.

MUSKMELON

Anthracnose (Colletotrichum lagenarium): Dead spots on the leaves and stems and sunken pits on the fruit. Thorough and frequent spraying with bordeaux mixture will hold this disease in check.

Downy Mildew: The same disease as on cucumbers. Often very destructive.

Control: A satisfactory method is not known. Spraying as for cucumber mildew has not proved effective.

Nursery Stock: Foliage on young trees is apt to be attacked by various leaf-spot fungi. The damage comes in reducing growth, thus often making seconds. Several applications of bordeaux mixture to keep the new growth protected are beneficial.

OATS

Rust (Puccinia coronata): A red rust of the blades.

Control: There is no known method of control.

ONION

Mildew (Peronospora schleideniana): Causes a wilt or blight of the leaves.

Control: Spray with bordeaux mixture, 5–5–50, to which has been added one gallon of resin-sal-soda sticker. The first application should be made when the third leaf has developed, and the application should be repeated every ten days until the crop is harvested.

Smut (Urocystis cepulae): Forms black pustules on the leaves and bulbs. Seedlings may be killed outright.

Control: Onions from sets or from seed started in soil free from the disease seldom have the smut. Practice crop rotation. Drill into the soil with the seed 100 pounds of sulfur and 50 pounds of air-slaked lime to the acre.

Pea. Mildew (Erysiphe polygoni): A powdery mildew on pods and leaves.

Control: Dust dry sulfur over the plants, repeating the operation if necessary.

Pod Spot and Leaf-spot (Ascochyta pisi): Black circular spots on stems, leaves, and buds. The fungus grows through the pod into the seed, and is thus carried through the winter.

Control: Select pods free from spots, and save the seed from these for the next year's planting. On a large scale have a clean seed garden in which to grow clean seed for the following year.

Peach. Blight (Coryneum beyerinkii): A spotting, gumming and death of the buds and twigs, particularly in the lower part of the tree. The fruit drops. Especially serious in California.

Control: For California conditions two applications of spray are made:

- In November or December
- In February or March.

This also controls leaf-curl. Bordeaux mixture, 5–5–50, or lime-sulfur, 1-10, may be used.

Brown-rot (Scerotinia fructigena): Causes a rot of the fruit, and often runs down the spur, forming a canker in the limb. Also produces brownish irregular spots on the leaves.

Control: Spray with self-boiled lime-sulfur, 8-8-50, adding 2 pounds of arsenate of lead. Spray first about time shucks are shedding from young fruit; second, two to three weeks later, and third, about one month before the fruit ripens. Omit the arsenate of lead from the third spraying. On early maturing varieties two applications may be sufficient. Spraying within a month of picking time is apt to leave the fruit spotted. It is especially important that sprayings be made before a continued storm period. Destroy rotten peaches. The rotten ones on the ground are as great a menace (especially if plowed under) as. those on the tree, as the fungus winters readily on the fallen mummies. Brown-rot also occurs on cherries, plums, apricots, and sometimes on apples and pears.

Leaf-curl (Exoascus deformans): Causes the leaves to crimp and curl and often to turn bright red. Also causes shoots to swell and become distorted.

Control: In an infected orchard more than 90 per cent of the curl can be controlled the first year. The second year control should be complete. The secret of control of leaf-curl lies largely in the thoroughness with which the work is done. A number of spray substances may be used. A single thorough application before the buds swell in the spring is sufficient. Every bud must be covered and from all sides. Lime-sulfur as applied for San Jose scale will control curl. Commercial lime-sulfur, 1-20; bordeaux mixture, 4–4–50; or a simple solution of blue vitriol in water, 2–50, are all specifics.

Little-peach.: A disease that in its early stages resembles yellows. It differs from yellows in producing small fruit that matures later than normally. Fruit does not have the small red spots characteristic of yellows, nor are there slender sickly branches. The cause of this disease is unknown. Apparently spreads more rapidly than yellows and commonly destroys the affected tree sooner.

Powdery mildew (Sphcerotheca pannosa). - A whitish powdery growth on the young shoots and leaves, and whitish spots on the fruit.

Control: Self-boiled lime-sulfur as for Rot.

Root-gall, Root-Knot, Crown-gall, Hairy-root (Bacterium tumefaciens).—Hairy roots or tumerous outgrowths on the roots and root crowns ; sometimes occurs on trunks and limbs. Primarily a nursery disease. Does not seem to be a serious disease on peaches in the North, but is reported as very serious in the South. Attacks a wide range of orchard plants, including apple, pear, brambles, grape, etc.

Control: Reject all stock showing symptoms.

Rosette.—An obscure southern disease of peach trees and some kinds of plums, characterized by bunchy growths containing very many rolled and yellowish leaves which fall prematurely. The tree dies the first or second year. There is no premature fruit as in yellows. It is often accompanied by gummosis of the roots. The disease is communicable by budding, and it may enter through the roots.

Scab or Black-spot (Cladosporium carpophilum): Black scablike spots on the fruit, often causing it to crack deeply.

Control: Self-boiled lime-sulfur, as applied for Brown-rot.

Yellows: A fatal disease of peaches ; also attacks nectarine, almond, apricot, and Japanese plum. Cause unknown. The first symptom in bearing trees is usually the premature ripening of the fruit. This fruit contains definite small red spots, which extend towards the pit. The second stage is usually the appearance of " tips," or short, late, second growths upon the ends of healthy twigs, and which are marked by small, horizontal, usually yellowish leaves. The next stage is indicated by very slender shoots, which branch the first year and which start in tufts from the old limbs, bearing narrow and small yellowish leaves. Later the entire foliage becomes smaller and yellow. In three to six years the tree dies. The disease spreads from tree to tree. It attacks trees of any age.

Preventive: Pull up and burn all trees as soon as the disease appears. Trees may be reset in the places from which the 1 yellows " trees were taken. Laws aiming to suppress the disease have been enacted in most peach-growing states, and the enforcement of them will keep the disease well under control.

PEAR

Blight (Boxillus amylovorus): A very serious bacterial disease. Bacteria winter just at the edge of the dead wood in trees blighted the previous year. With the advent of warm spring days they ooze through the bark in sticky drops and are carried by bees and flies to blossoms. The blossoms blight, and the spur may also blight. Plant-lice carry bacteria from blighted blossoms to spurs and shoots. If a spur becomes blighted, the bacteria may spread in the bark of the limb, causing a depression or canker. This may girdle the limb and cause its death. The leaves turn black and stick tenaciously, even through the winter. Succulent water sprouts are very apt to blight and cause large cankers. Generally distributed in North America, and known only in America. Attacks apple, quince, mountain ash, hawthorn; the Spitzenburgh is specially liable to attack.

Control: Clean up hedgerows of hawthorn, old blighted pear trees and apple trees. In early spring cut out the blight of the previous year and disinfect the stubs with corrosive sublimate, 1-1000. Clean out cankers with a sharp knife, and disinfect. Paint over with lead paint. At blossoming time make a systematic daily inspection for blossom blight, and break it out. Watch for blight in the shoots. When it appears get a long-handled pruning-hook, fasten a sponge near the knife, and saturate it with corrosive sublimate solution, 1-1000. Clip out the blighted twigs, cutting five or six inches below the blight, and sop the pruned stub with the sponge. During a blight epidemic, drop all other work. The work must be done systematically and persistently, or not at all. One week's work may save the pear crop and the pear trees.

Leaf-blight and Cracking of fruit (Fabrea maculata): Attacks nursery stock of pears and quinces, beginning as small circular brown spots on the leaves. These spread, and if numerous cause the leaf to fall. The same disease produces a black spot or pit on the fruit.

Control: In nurseries spray with bordeaux mixture, 4-4-50. In the orchard spray as for pear scab, with perhaps one additional application.

Leaf-spot (Mycosphaerella sentina): Small lecticular spots with white centers on leaves. Spots become so numerous as to cause defoliation. The fungus is known only on leaves, and it winters on them.

Control: Burn fallen leaves. Spray as for Scab.

Scab (Venturia pyrina): Greenish brown or black spots on leaves and fruit, arresting growth and often causing fruit to crack. Severe on Flemish Beauty. Often attacks pedicles of fruits and causes them to drop, and may even cause defoliation. Is different from apple scab, but behaves much like it. Differs especially in the fact that the fungus winters on the twigs as well as on fallen leaves.

Control: Owing to the nearness of the fungus (on the twigs) and the slowness with which the pear-leaf unfolds, two applications of spray before the blossoms open are sometimes necessary, and one immediately after they fall. Use lime-sulfur, 1-50, or bordeaux, 3-3-50.

Rust (Gymnosporangium globosum): Having the same habits and appearance as apple rust.

Control: Owing to the nearness of the fungus (on the twigs) and the slowness with which the pear-leaf unfolds, two applications of spray before the blossoms open are sometimes necessary, and one immediately after they fall. Use lime-sulfur, 1-50, or bordeaux, 3-3-50.

PLUM

Black-knot (Plowrightia morbosa). -A black tumerous swelling from one to several inches in length, appearing on the limbs and twigs of American plums and sour cherries. Point of attack is usually under a bud or in crotches. Confined to America. A very serious disease. In some regions it has destroyed the plum industry. It was once supposed to be caused by an insect.

Control: Burn all affected parts in the fall. Cut several inches below the swelling. A badly infected tree should be cut down at once, as there is no hope of saving it. Many states have a law requiring the destruction of affected trees.

Leaf-rust (Puccinia pruni-spinosce): Small circular powdery spots of yellowish brown on the under surface of the leaves, and reddish spots on the upper surface directly above them.

Control: Early spraying with bordeaux, 3-3-50, or self-boiled lime-sulfur, 8-8-50.

POTATO

Early blight (Alternaria solani): A blight of foliage beginning as an even circular spot and coming early in the season, usually in July. Progresses slowly. This disease does not attack the tubers.

Control: Bordeaux mixture at intervals of ten days, beginning when plants are 6-8 in. high.

Late blight and Potato-rot (Phytophthorainfestans): The fungus winters in the tuber, which shows a faint pinkish tinge and a dry rot. Diseased tubers are planted, the fungus fruits on the cut surface and its swarm spores pass through the soil-water to the leaves which touch or are buried in the soil. An extensive irregular blighted area covers the leaf, the under surface of which may have a mildewy appearance. The disease spreads very rapidly. Later spores are washed down to the tubers and infect them.

Control: Can be controlled successfully by the use of bordeaux mixture, 5-5-50. It is always profitable to spray at least three times, and in a wet season six or more applications should be made. As the vines increase in size, greater quantities of spray and more nozzles must be used. Use from 40 to 100 gallons of spray mixture per acre.

Dry-Rot and Wilt (Fusarium oxysporum): A dry rot of the tuber in storage and wilt of plants in the field. Can be detected in the seed tuber before there is any external appearance by examining a section near the stem end. A black ring or chain of dots near the surface is indicative of the rot. Infection frequently takes place through wounds.

Control: Reject all diseased tubers for seed. Practice a rotation in which potatoes are not grown on the soil for at least two years.

Scab (Oospora scabies): A scabby and pitted roughness of potato tubers. Lime, ashes or manure added to the soil increases the amount of scab by favoring the growth of the fungus. It has become one of the serious diseases of the potato.

Control: Do not plant on land which has grown scabby potatoes. Plant clean seed. If only scabby seed is at hand, soak the uncut tubers in a solution of formalin, 1 pint in 30 gallons of water, for two hours. Drain, cut, and plant in clean soil. Use the formalin solution over and over. The same fungus also attacks beets.

PUMPKIN

Quince. Black-rot (Sphaeropsis malorum): A trouble which usually appears at the blossom end of young quince fruits, causing them to become black and hard, with a dry rot of the tissue.

Rust: The organism causing this disease is of the same habit and nature as that causing apple rust.

RADISH

White rust or Mildew (Albugo candidus): A whitish powdery growth on the leaves and petioles, often causing distortion.

Control: Steam-sterilize the soil before planting.

RASPBERRY

Anthracnose (Glaeosporium venetum): Circular or elliptical, gray scab-like spots on the canes.

Control: Avoid taking young plants from diseased plantations. Remove all diseased canes as soon as the fruit is picked. Practice frequent rotation.

Crown-gall or Root-call (Bacterium tumefaciens): Tumerous outgrowths on the roots, especially on red varieties. It is contagious and destructive.

Control: Never set plants which have galls on the roots. Avoid setting on infested land.

Red or Orange rust (Gymnoconia interstitialis): A dense red powdery growth on the under side of the leaves of black varieties and of blackberries. The fungus hibernates in the roots.

Control: Dig up and destroy infected plants.

Rice. Blast, Blight or Rotten-neck (Piricularia oryzae): An extensive paling and drying of leaf and stem, and a partial failure of the heads to fill.

Control: The selection of early maturing varieties is advisable. Burn stubble and trash left in the fields.

ROSE

Black leaf-spot (Actinonema rosae): Attacks the full-grown leaves, first appearing as small black spots, but later covering nearly or quite the whole surface with blotches. The spots have frayed edges.

Control: Spray with ammoniacal copper carbonate, beginning with the first appearance of the spots and continuing at intervals of one week until under subjection.

Mildew (Sphaerotheca pannosa): A white powdery mildew on the new growth.

Control: For greenhouse roses keep the steam pipes painted with a paste made of equal parts lime and sulfur mixed with water. Out-of-door roses should be dusted with sulfur flour or sprayed with potassium sulfid, 1 ounce to 3 gallons of water. Spinach.- There are numerous fungous diseases of this crop, but a practical method of control has not been developed. The best that can be done is to rotate crops.

STRAWBERRY

Leaf-spot or leaf-blight (Mycosphaerella fragarice): Small purple or red spots appearing on the leaves. They increase in size and make the leaf appear blotched. The fungus passes the winter in the old diseased leaves that fall to the ground.

Control: In setting new plantations remove all diseased leaves from the plants before they are taken to the field. Soon after growth begins, spray the plants with bordeaux mixture, 4-4-50. Make three or four additional sprayings during the season. The following spring spray just before blossoming, and again in ten to fourteen days. If the bed is to be fruited again, mow the plants and burn over the bed as soon as the crop is off.

Mildew (Sphaerotheca castagnei): A whitish cobweb-like mildew on fruit and leaves, causing the latter to curl.

Control: Spraying as for leaf-spot ; dusting with sulfur flour.

SWEET-POTATO

Black-rot (Ceratocystis fimbriata): Causing black shank of the plant and a black rot of the tuber. The spots on the tuber are greenish black, from a quarter of an inch to four inches in diameter and extending for some distance into the tissue.

Control: Never use affected potatoes from which to grow sprouts. Steam-sterilize the soil in the hotbed. Practice rotation.

Rots: The sweet-potato is susceptible to a large number of rots, soft, dry, hard, white, etc. In practically all cases the organism producing the disease is an inhabitant of the soil. The best method of preventing these diseases is to use perfectly sound potatoes for sprouts and plant on soil which has not grown sweet-potatoes for several years.

TOBACCO

Root-rot (Thielavia basicola): A rot of the main root and dwarfs the plants. Occurs both in seed-bed and field.

Control: Steam-sterilize the seed-bed by the inverted pan method. Rotate crops. Avoid liming, and add acid fertilizers.

Wilt (Bacterium solanacearum): A wilt of the plants caused by bacteria.

Control: Very difficult to control, as the organism lives in the soil for years. Never plant on land known to be diseased. Do not cultivate related plants, as potato, tomato, egg plant, or pepper, on the same soil. Transplant early, and avoid breaking the roots. Where tobacco is grown under shade (as is now a common practice) the soil should be steam-sterilized.

TOMATO

Bacterial Wilt (Bacterium solanacearum): A wilt of the plants caused by bacteria.

Control: Very difficult to control, as the organism lives in the soil for years. Never plant on land known to be diseased. Do not cultivate related plants, as potato, tomato, egg plant, or pepper, on the same soil. Transplant early, and avoid breaking the roots. Where tobacco is grown under shade (as is now a common practice) the soil should be steam-sterilized.

Blight or Scab {Cladosporium fulvum): Soft brown irregular spots on the under surface of the leaves. The upper surface becomes spotted with yellow. The leaves finally wither and die. Most serious in the greenhouse.

Control: In mild cases the disease can be prevented by picking off the affected leaves. In severe cases spray with bordeaux mixture, 4-4-50, at intervals of ten days.

Downy mildew (Phytophthora infestans): The same fungus that causes Potato-blight.

End-rot: Not well understood, and no method of control is known.

Leaf-spot (Septoria lycopersica): A serious disease attacking leaves and stems. At first small spots appear, which spread until the whole leaf is consumed. (In severe cases the fruit may also be attacked.

Control: Spray with bordeaux mixture, 4-4-50, making the first application two weeks after the plants are set out, and repeating every two weeks throughout the growing season. *Control:* A diseased condition of forced tomatoes characterized by rolled or curled leaves, distended veins, and by swollen areas having a frosty appearance on leaf veins, petioles and stem. This condition may be brought about by insufficient light, too much water in soil, excessive fertilization, high soil temperature. *Prevention:* Avoid conditions favorable for the disease. Provide good ventilation in forcing-house; in field, cultivate deep and avoid topping plants.

VIOLET

Leaf-spots and leaf-blights: A number of different organisms are responsible. Usually not very destructive.

Control: Destroy affected plants; use fresh soil for new plantings; spray the foliage in the summer and fall with bordeaux mixture, 4-4-50.

Root-rot (Thielavia basicola): The same as the root-rot of tobacco. The plants make poor growth, owing to the fungus on the roots.

Control: Start in steam-sterilized soil, and transfer to sterilized beds..

ROOT OF A SEEDLING BEAN GROWN

On the root of a seedling bean grown on damp flannel or blotting-paper is seen a fine white silky band of hairs. These are called root-hairs, and they are never present at the extreme tip of the root but arise at some distance behind its growing point. As the root elongates the root-hairs on the older parts die and turn brown, but others are produced on the younger parts, so that no matter what the length or size of the root may be for a short distance behind its tip it is clad with these delicate transparent hairs.

When secondary roots make their appearance hairs are produced upon them in the same manner and follow the same order of development as those upon the primary root. Their size and abundance are dependent on the species of the plant, and the amount of moisture surrounding the root. Plants growing in very wet situations or completely in water have few or no root-hairs.

In very dry soils their development is checked, the greatest abundance being met with in moderately damp soils. A good supply of lime is found to increase the number and length of the root-hairs of many plants. The hairs are hollow tube-like structures and should not be confused with fine small rootlets.

They are outgrowths from the surface of the root, and as long as they last are concerned with the absorption of water and various ingredients in solution from the soil. Upon plants growing in the ground the root-hairs are very intimately in contact with the particles of soil and are of so delicate a nature that it is practically impossible to remove a plant without destroying them.

INTERRELATIONS OF PLANT, SOIL, AND CLIMATE

In considering the importance of root relations in crop production, it should be clearly kept in mind that the plant, the soil, and the climate form a closely interlocking system of which no part should be overlooked or overemphasized. It is now rather generally recognized that climate and vegetation are the most important factors determining the character of the mature soil. 148 "The features assumed by the soil in its development from infancy, through youth, maturity, and old age, vary with the environment, especially with the climate and the vegetation." The effect of both climate and soil on the growth of aboveground plant parts has long been known. It has only recently been clearly demonstrated that the environmental factors which affect the root are not only those of the soil immediately about it but also those affecting the shoot which is rightly a part of the complex. Through the shoot the root system is influenced by the aerial environment. 23,103 The amount of light or the degree of humidity, temperature, etc. and the effect of these upon food manufacture, water loss, and other activities affect root development. In fact there is a rather close correlation between shoot and root development.

The complex relationship of plant, soil, and climate may be further illustrated in the use of fertilizers. They modify the habit of growth as well as the composition of the plant. For example, phosphates, when applied to soil upon which wheat or certain root crops are grown, promote deeper root penetration. This results in a greater water and nutrient supply for the plant. Earlier development and ripening may be promoted or drought mitigated. Soils thus fertilized will produce crops under an environment perhaps otherwise quite unfavourable. Vegetable production should be studied from the point of view of how roots and shoots of plants grow, and use should be made of the plant itself for indicating the direction of future research. An adequate discussion of the environment of roots (the soil), how roots are built to perform their work, and root habits in relation to crop production has been so recently given in "Root Development of Field Crops" that further statement seems unnecessary. For a general discussion of the effects of irrigation, drainage, water content, aeration, temperature, nutrients, tillage practice, plant disease, and related phenomena upon root habit and their significance in crop production, the reader is referred to the same volume.

ACTIVITIES OF ROOTS IN SUBSOIL

The great extent of the root systems of most vegetable crops and their usual thorough occupancy of the subsoil may at once arouse interest concerning the importance of the deeper soil layers. Experiments have shown that the roots of crops are active in the absorption of both water and nutrients even to the maximum depth of penetration. 174,165 Nutrients, when available, are taken from the deeper soils in considerable quantities, although to a lesser extent than from the soil nearer the surface which the roots occupy first and, consequently, at least in annual crops, where they absorb for the longest time. The deeper portions of the root system are often particularly active as the crop approaches maturity. Nutrients absorbed by them may produce a pronounced effect both upon the quantity and the quality of the crop yield.

METHOD OF ROOT STUDY

In the present studies the direct method of root examination has been employed. It has been used by the writer and his coworkers in the excavation of hundred of root systems during the past 14 years and has proved very satisfactory. By the side of the plants to, be examined, a long trench is dug to a depth of about 5 feet and of convenient width. This affords an open face into which one may dig with hand pick and ice pick and thus uncover and make a careful examination of the entire root system. This apparently simple process, however, requires much practice, not a little patience, and wide experience with soil structure.

In every case several plants were examined at each stage of development to insure an adequate idea of the general root habit. As the work of excavation progressed, the trench was deepened, if necessary, so that finally the soil underlying the deepest roots was removed. Frequently, the trenches reached depths of 6 to 11 feet.

Fig. 2.2 Trench used in the Study of Root Systems.

In this case 3-year-old trees were being excavated. They did not extend deeper (5 to 8 feet), however, than many vegetable crops of a single season's growth.

Upon excavating the roots, detailed notes and careful measurements were made in the field. After several plants were examined, these notes were studied and any point that remained indefinite was at once clarified by further study. This method leads to a high degree of accuracy.

Drawings of the root systems were made in the field on a large drawing sheet with pencil and later retraced with India ink. They were made simultaneously with the excavation of the roots and always by exact measurements. In the drawings the roots are arranged as nearly as possible in a vertical plane; that is, each root is placed in its natural position with reference to the surface of the soil and a vertical line from the base of the plant. In some cases the drawings represent the roots in their natural position in the surface foot of soil.

In every case it was sought to illustrate the average condition of root development rather than the extreme. Although the drawings were made on a large scale, the rootlets were often so abundant that it was quite impossible to show the total number.

Such drawings, however, carefully executed, represent the extent, position, and minute branching of the root system even more accurately than a photograph, for under the most favourable conditions, especially with extensive root systems, the photograph is always made at the expense of detail, many of the finer branches and root ends being obscured.

VEGETABLE CROPS PRODUCTION

The plant is the most important agent in crop production. Soils, cultivation, fertilizers, irrigation, and other factors, in a sense, are all more or less subsidiary. Soils are modified by cultivation, by adding manure or other fertilizers, by drainage or irrigation, and in other ways with the express purpose of changing the environment so as to stimulate plants to increased productivity. Hence, it is not surprising that from time immemorial extended observations and, later, experiments have been made upon the aerial growth of crops under varying conditions.

In fact an almost bewildering array of literature has resulted. But quite the converse is true of the underground parts. The root development of vegetable crops has received relatively little attention, and indeed accurate information is rarely to be found. The roots of plants are the least known, least understood, and least appreciated part of the plant. This is undoubtedly due to the fact that they are effectually hidden from sight. Notwithstanding the extreme difficulty and tediousness of laying the roots bare for study, it is not only remarkable but also extremely unfortunate that such investigations have been so long neglected.

It clearly seems that a thorough understanding of the activities of plants both aboveground and belowground and the ways in which these activities are favourably or unfavourably modified by various cultural practices should be basic for scientific crop production. Yet almost countless field experiments, selections, breeding, and testing of varieties, etc. have been carried on in all parts of the world with little or no knowledge as to the behaviour of that very essential portion of the plant, the absorbing system.

Similarly, in the study of soils, the greatest attention is given to the problems of the physics, chemistry, and bacteriology of this substratum and rather largely to the cultivated portion of the surface only. The soil, barring the living organisms which it supports, is perhaps the most complex, the most interesting, and the most wonderful thing in nature. Surely it should receive thorough investigation. But a study of the soil and the way in which its various relations affect yield without a consideration of the essential, intermediary absorbing system is more or less empirical. A complete, scientific understanding of the soils-crops relations cannot be attained until the mechanism by which the soil and the plant are brought into favourable relationships, the root system, is also understood.

The student of plant production should have a vivid, mental picture of the plant as a whole. It is just as much of a biological unit as is an animal. The animal is visible as an entity and behaves as one. If any part is injured, reactions and disturbance of the whole organism are expected. But in the plant, our mental conception is blurred by the fact that one of the most important structures is underground. Nor is the plant usually treated as an entity; it is often mutilated by pruning, cutting, and injuring the root system, frequently without much regard to the effect upon the remaining portion.

CLIMATE CHANGE ON CROP PRODUCTION

At the basis of any understanding of climate impacts on agriculture lies the biophysical sciences. The rates of most biophysical processes are highly dependent on climate variables such as radiation, temperature, and moisture, that vary regionally. For example, rates of plant photosynthesis depend on the amount of photosynthetically active radiation and levels of atmospheric carbon dioxide (C02). Temperature is an important determinant of the rate at which a plant progresses through various phenological stages towards maturity. The accumulation of biomass is constrained by the availability of moisture and nutrients to a growing plant.

Numerous studies have examined the impacts of past climatic variations on agriculture using case studies, statistical analyses and simulation models. Such studies have clearly demonstrated the sensitivity of both temperate and tropical agricultural systems and nations to climatic variations and changes. In the temperate regions, the impacts of climate variability, particularly drought, on yields of grains in North America and the Soviet Union have been of particular concern because of their effects on world food security.

In the tropics, drought impacts on agriculture and resulting food shortages have been widely studied, especially when associated with the failure of the monsoon in Asia or the rains in Sudano-Sahelian Africa. In the temperate regions, climatic variations are associated with economic disruptions; in the tropics, droughts bring famine and widespread social unrest.

THE BIOPHYSICAL IMPACT OF CLIMATIC CHANCES ASSOCIATED WITH GLOBAL WARMING

It is frequently assumed that global change will bring higher temperatures, altered precipitation, and higher levels of atmospheric C02. What might these changes mean for the biophysical response of agricultural crops?

Interactions with thermal regimes. Higher temperatures in general hasten plant maturity in annual species, thus shortening the growth stages during which pods, seeds, grains or bolls can absorb photosynthetic products. This is one reason yield are lower in the tropics. Because crop yield depends on both the rate of carbohydrate accumulation and the duration of the filling periods, the economic yields of both temperate and tropical crops grown in a warmer and C02-enriched environment may not rise substantially above present levels, despite increases in net photosynthesis.

Because temperature and tropical regions differ in both current temperature and the temperature rise predicted for climate change, the relative magnitudes of combined C02 and temperature effects will likely be different in the different regions. In the mid-latitudes, higher temperatures may shift biological process rates towards optima, and beneficial effects are likely to ensue. Increases in temperature will also lengthen the frost-free season in temperate regions, allowing for longer duration crop varieties to be grown and offering the possibility of growing successive crops (moisture conditions permitting). In tropical locations where increased temperatures may move beyond optima, negative consequences may dominate.

Both the mean and extreme temperatures that crops experience during the growing season will change in both temperate and tropical areas. Extreme temperatures are important because many crops have critical thresholds both above and below which crops are damaged. Prolonged hot spells can be especially damaging. Critical stages for high temperature injury include seedling emergence in most crops, silking and tasseling in corn, grain filling in wheat, and flowering in soybeans. In general, higher temperatures should decrease cold damage and increase heat damage. Agro-climatic zones are expected to shift poleward as lengthening and warming growing seasons allow new or enhanced crop production (soil resources permitting).

Changes in hydrological regimes. The hydrological regimes in which crops grow will surely change with global warming. While all GCMs predict increases in mean global precipitation (because a warmer atmosphere can hold more water vapor), decreases are forecast in some regions and increases are not uniformly distributed. The crop water regime may further be affected by changes in seasonal precipitation, within-season pattern of precipitation, and interannual variation of precipitation. Increased convective rainfall is predicted to occur, particularly in the tropics, caused by stronger convection cells and more moisture in the air.

Too much precipitation can cause disease infestation in crops, while too little can be detrimental to crop yields, especially if dry periods occur during critical development stages. For example, moisture stress during the flowering, pollination, and grain-filling stages is especially harmful to maize, soybean, wheat and sorghum.

The amount and availability of water stored in the soil, a crucial input to crop growth, will be affected by changes in both the precipitation and seasonal and annual evapotranspiration regimes. Some GCMs predict mid-continental drying the Northern Hemisphere and other GCM predictions have been interpreted to suggest that the rise in potential evapotranspiration will exceed that of rainfall resulting in drier regimes throughout the tropics and low to mid-latitudes. Because the soil moisture processes are represented so crudely in the current GCMs, however, it is difficult to associate much certainty with these projections.

Global climate change is likely to exacerbate the demand for irrigation water. Higher temperatures, increased evaporation, and yield decreases contribute to this projection. However, supply of needed irrigation water under climate change in uncertain. Where water supplies are diminishing, such as the Ogallala Aquifer in the United States, extra demand might require that some land be withdrawn from irrigation.

Physiological effects of CO2. The study of agricultural impacts of trace gas induced climate change is complicated by the fact that increasing atmospheric CO_2 has other effects on crop plants besides its alteration of their climate regime. These are often called "fertilizing" effects, because of their perceived beneficial physiological nature. Specifically, most plants growing in enhanced CO_2 exhibit increased rates of net photosynthesis. The higher photosynthesis rates are then manifested in higher leaf area, dry matter production, and yield for many crops. In several cases, high CO_2 has contributed to upward shifts in temperature optima for photosynthesis and to enhanced growth with higher temperatures; other studies, however, have not shown such benefits.

CO_2 enrichment also tends to close plant stomates, and by doing so, reduces transpiration per unit leaf area while still enhancing photosynthesis. The stomatal conductances of 18 agricultural species have been observed to decrease markedly (by 36%, on average) in an atmosphere enriched by doubled CO_2. However, crop transpiration per ground area may not be reduced commensurately, because decreases in individual leaf conductance tend to be offset by increases in crop leaf area. In any case, higher CO_2 often improves water-use efficiency, defined as the ratio between crop biomass accumulation or yield and the amount of water used in evapotranspiration. Increases in photosynthesis and resistance with higher CO_2 have been shown to occur at less than optimal levels of other environmental variables, such as light, water, and some of the mineral nutrients.

Temperate crops may benefit more from increasing CO_2 than tropical crops. In crop species with the C_3 pathway characteristic of non-tropical plants (*e.g.*, wheat, soybean, cotton) CO_2 enrichment has been shown to decrease photorespiration, the rapid oxidation of recently formed sugars in the light, a process which lowers the efficiency of overall photosynthesis. C_4 crops, which are particularly characteristic of tropical and warm arid regions (*e.g.*, maize, sorghum, and millet), are more efficient photosynthetically under current CO_2 levels than C_3 plants (because they fix CO_2 into malate in their mesophyll cells before delivering it to the RuBP enzyme in the bundle-sheath cells). Because of this CO_2-concentrating and photorespiration-avoiding mechanism, experimental data show that C4 plants are less responsive to CO_2 enrichment.

The physiological effects of high levels of atmospheric CO_2 described above have been observed under controlled experimental conditions. In the open field, however, their magnitude and significance are still largely untested, and their importance relative to the predicted large-scale climatic effects uncertain. Greenhouse and field-chamber environments tend to be much smaller, less variable, and more protected from wind than field conditions. Furthermore, physiological feedback mechanisms such as starch accumulation or lack of sink (that is, growing, storing, or metabolizing tissue) for the products of photosynthesis may limit the extent to which the "fertilizing" CO_2 effects may be realized.

Finally, if trace gas emissions continue to grow unchecked, their climate warming effect is projected to continue even up to 2000 ppm, but the beneficial boost to photosynthesis appears to level off at about 400 ppm for C_4 crops and about 800 ppm for C_3 crops.

Soils. Climate change will also have an impact on the soil, a vital element in agricultural ecosystems. Higher air temperatures will cause higher soil temperatures, which should generally increase solution chemical reaction rates and diffusion-controlled reactions.

Solubilities of solid and gaseous components may either increase or decrease, but the consequences of these changes may take many years to become significant. Furthermore, higher temperatures will accelerate the decay of soil organic matter, resulting in release of CO_2 to the atmosphere and decrease in carbon/nitrogen ratios, although these two effects should be offset somewhat by the greater root biomass and crop residues resulting from plant responses to higher CO_2.

In temperate countries where crops are already heavily fertilized, there will probably be no major changes in fertilization practices, but alterations in timing and method (*e.g.*, careful adjustment of side-dress applications of nitrogen during vegetative crop growth) are expected with changes in temperature and precipitation regimes. In tropical countries, where fertilization level is not always adequate, the need for fertilization will probably increase. Sea level rise, another predicted effect of global warming, will caused increased flooding, salt-water intrusion, and rising water tables in agricultural soils located near coastlines. This is particularly crucial in tropical countries such as Bangladesh, with large agricultural regions and high rural population located near current sea level.

Pests. Pests are organisms that affect agricultural plants and animals in ways considered unfavourable. They include weeds, and certain insects, arthropods, nematodes, bacteria, fungi, and viruses. Because climate variables (especially temperature, wind and humidity) control the geographic distribution of pests, climate change is likely to alter their ranges. Insects may extend their ranges where warmer winter temperatures allow their over-wintering survival and increase the possible number of generations per season. Pests and diseases from low latitude regions, where they are much more prevalent may be introduced at higher latitudes. As a consequence of pest increase, there may be a substantial rise in the use of agricultural chemicals in both temperate and tropical regions to control them.

TEMPERATURE CONTROL IN CROP PRODUCTION

Microclimate

Greenhouse (British "glasshouse," often a misnomer in this plastic age) production is the obvious example of microclimate temperature control. But greenhouse production has its own considerable expertise and literature. Thus, the examples of greenhouse research cited here are included only to illustrate specific situations in which individual control of air and soil temperatures is important. Even outdoors, although climate (including temperature) is usually regarded as beyond the control of man, localized temperature control is sometimes effective on a microclimate scale.

Vancouver, Canada, is a few miles north of the 49th parallel, about 60 miles farther north than Minot, North Dakota, with its legendary harsh winter temperatures. But constant foehn winds off the Pacific Ocean make Vancouver winters mild and wet, although sunshine is scant. When I had a garden there in the late 1940s, a neighbor used to say that I "cheated God" to bring in my lettuce and tomatoes earlier than anyone else.

The bed in which the vegetables grew was banked towards the south at approximately 50 degrees, and the area between the plants was covered with flat stones, gathered from the nearby beach, to maximize soil heating from the weak late winter–early spring sun.

This management was, of course, an extreme example of microclimate modification for crop production. Nevertheless, it was no more than ingenious growers have done to survive inhospitable climates throughout the ages, as with pre-Columbian Andean potato growers. In recent years, the native peoples of the Andean Altiplano have learned to revive the methods of their ancestors, growing potatoes on high narrow beds at the foot of mountain slopes. On freezing nights, the cold air settles between the raised beds without damaging the aerial parts of the plants, whose subterranean portions are protected by the latent heat of the water accumulated in the troughs between the beds, an ancient example of sophisticated microclimate control.

Poinsettia is typical of an ornamental grown for a specific date; unless the plants are marketable at Christmas, their value drops dramatically. Growth of the plants can be sharply reduced by too cool air temperatures. Maintaining temperatures in a greenhouse in very cold weather is very expensive. However, it has been found that raising soil temperature to 23°C (which is much cheaper to do) could counteract the adverse effects of air temperature as low as 11.5°C.

Sometimes the reverse modification is needed. Flowering of *Alstroemeria* (lily-of-the-Incas) was stimulated by cooling the root zone with 10°C circulating water. There was also an interaction with light, supplementary lighting being essential in winter but harmful in spring and summer. A beneficial lowering of root zone temperature explained an anomalous result with azaleas pot-grown outside on either clamshell mulch or black polyethylene. Placing the pots close together increased growth of azaleas in black pots but not in white pots. The beneficial effect was traced to a decrease in root zone temperatures by shading when the plants in black pots were placed close together.

Another unexpected root zone temperature effect was traced to the chilling effect of cold greenhouse irrigation water in winter. The effect was noted with roses and chrysanthemums and was sufficient to affect turgidity, stomate opening, and flowering. Such unforeseen deleterious temperature effects are particularly easy to overlook when they involve the temperatures of soil rather than air.

Root zone heating usually involves use of expensive fuel. This potential cost was halved in an ingenious system of pumping comparatively warm water from a well 100 m deep and circulating it through buried pipes.

Temperature, of course, affects more than plant growth. It is sometimes necessary to tread a fine line between temperatures optimum for growth and those that initiate or increase fungal attack. This can be a problem for Florida foliage growers in warm weather, as shown in a study of aerial blight (*Rhizoctonia solani*) infection of Boston fern (*Nephrolepis exalta*). Some plant quality had to be sacrificed if potting medium and air temperatures were to be regulated to restrict development of the pathogen.

Given sufficient irrigation water, many deserts will blossom as the rose. But sometimes the desert sun is too hot, with consequent potential for crop damage. An obvious remedy is to spray the crop with an overhead irrigation system.

The cooling effect of such sprinkling is sharply dependent on initial air temperature. A California study reported the following (the results have been converted from Fahrenheit to Celsius):

Macroclimate temperature Lowered by

32°C 2–3°C

38°C 5°C

39°C 7.5°C

In addition to other benefits, the water spray at 39°C was reported as being successful in reducing excessive "June drop" of small fruitlets. But such spraying of water in extremely hot weather can cause localized injury due to the "lens effect" of standing drops of water on the leaves. Lens effect injury can be avoided, and better temperature reduction obtained, by using nozzles that emit a fine mist instead of streams of water.

Microclimate is being modified on a very large scale. Whole hectares are commonly covered with plastic sheeting, which may be black, white, or transparent. Plastic covering may be spread over raised beds, with the plants inserted through holes in the plastic; it may lie over individual rows secured along the sides, with or without some form of framing; or it may be used as "floating row covers," supported by the crop itself and rising as it grows. Sometimes such plastic covering serves essentially for weed and soil moisture control. Often, however, some degree of temperature elevation is sought, and air and soil temperatures are commonly included in research reports. The elevation of temperature under plastic film will depend on both the climate and the type of plastic. In sunny climates, temperature rise may be sufficient to provide effective disinfestation of pathogenic fungi.

Sunshading

Another form of large-scale microclimate control is by shading. A practice that started as "slat houses" for orchids and "cloth houses" for high-quality tobacco has developed into very considerable industries, usually growing ornamentals. A high proportion are foliage plants, grown under coarse-woven plastic material developed to give certain "percentages" of shade. Obviously, any modification of insolation (irradiance) also modifies temperature. It is remarkable that although research reports commonly pay considerable attention to the expression of the exact degree of shade, temperature differences are often not mentioned. It can be very helpful to include temperature as a variable, as demonstrated in a study of disease intensity under different levels of shade. Research workers in this field are urged to routinely measure and report the temperature variations that inevitably accompany any modification of irradiance. Shade conditions can be expected not only to lower daytime temperatures but also to raise night temperatures, particularly under cold night–clear sky conditions, in which ground-to-sky radiation can cause a very rapid, possibly harmful, drop in temperature near the ground. Similarly, the use of spectral filters can be expected to modify not only light quality but also temperature.

Freeze Protection

The first, most obvious, and least expensive protection against freeze injury is to select a planting site where injurious freezing is unlikely to occur. Because this is often not possible, freeze protection measures may be necessary. Burning fossil fuels should be regarded as a last resort—the fuels themselves are very expensive, and their use is often environmentally questionable. Only too often, freeze protection methods are ineffective because of ignorance of the following basic thermodynamic and meteorological principles.

1. Cold air will roll down a slope until arrested by some physical barrier, which then forms a "frost pocket."
2. Hot air rises vertically. It cannot be made to move up a slope.
3. Radiated heat travels in all directions uniformly but only in line-of-sight (straight) lines. Thus, to be warmed by irradiation from a heat source (such as an orchard heater), a plant must be able to "see" the heat source. Because radiated heat, like all forms of radiation, is

subject to the inverse square law (*i.e.*, intensity decreases proportionately to the square of the distance traveled), radiation warming decreases sharply with distance from the heat source.

4. The total heat content of a mass of air depends not only on its temperature (sensible heat) but also on its latent heat, the two together approximating its total energy content or enthalpy. Thus, total heat content can be very much greater for moist air than for dry air at the same temperature. Putting this in a different way: air masses at the same atmospheric pressure and conditions of 15°F (9.4°C) and 100% RH, 20°F (6.7°C) and 40% RH, and 25°F (3.9°C) or 0% RH all have the same heat content of approximately 5.5 Btu per pound of dry air (ca. 3 kg cal kg1).
5. The latent heat of evaporation is approximately 7.5 times as great as the latent heat of freezing. Thus, when spraying irrigation water for freeze protection (a common practice for Florida strawberries and various other crops), it is essential to freeze at least 7.5 times as much water as is evaporated. In calm or near-calm weather, this is no problem. Continuing to spray after the onset of a brisk breeze, however, can be disastrous. An ingenious application of this principle is to use such evaporative cooling to delay the blooming of fruit trees until the danger of a blossom freeze is over. The blooming of apple trees was delayed by as long as 17 days by use of thermostatically controlled sprinkling whenever prebloom temperatures exceeded 7°C (44.6°F).
6. Smoke from burning oil or other fuel does *not* form a protective shield. It used to be believed (particularly in California) that "smudge pots" could create a low cloud that reflected heat back to the crop below. It is now known that the smoke particles are not in a size range suited to reflect infrared emissions. It is, however, possible to generate very fine water fog with droplets of the appropriate size. An added benefit is that any fog droplets that freeze give off latent heat to the surrounding atmosphere.
7. Freezes are classified as "convection freezes" or "advection freezes." Convection freezes occur with calm air and cloudless skies, conditions in which the earth is radiating heat to the sky, with consequent rapid cooling of the air near the ground. For orchard crops, it is beneficial to have bare ground to radiate ground heat to the trees. Weeds or cover crops trap such radiated heat at the expense of the trees. Convective conditions commonly result in atmospheric inversions, in which the lower air is colder than that at 10–30 m above the ground. In such conditions, "wind machines" mounted on tall towers or pylons can be beneficial. Helicopters have sometimes been used to achieve

the same effect, particularly to prevent dangerously cold air from accumulating in the "frost pocket" hollows.

In an advective freeze, a wind strong enough to disrupt normal convection patterns freezes crops on the exposed higher ground, with much less freeze injury in the valleys and lowlands. Wind machines are worse than useless in an advective freeze, but rows of heaters placed at right angles to the wind direction can benefit crops for a considerable distance downwind. A deadly interaction among temperature, humidity, and wind speed can occur in an advective freeze. Tender leaves and shoots can be killed, not by freezing, but by desiccation, if wind speed is high enough when the temperature approaches the freezing point of plant tissues under conditions of very low humidity (which frequently occur).

For further information on methods and principles of freeze protection, readers are referred to an extensive chapter on freeze protection.

Incidental Effects of Temperature

Old Ecclesiastes said, "Of the making of many books there is no end," and a number of them probably could be written on the incidental effects of temperature. However, only a very few examples can be cited here to indicate how often temperature is an unforeseen or unplanned-for variable.

Temperature can move in mysterious ways, its wonders to perform, through its subtle influence on the activity of growth regulators. As noted earlier, fruit setting in tomato plants is inhibited by too high temperatures. A role for growth regulators in this high-temperature inhibition is indicated by a report that relative levels of gibberellin and auxinlike growth regulators were sharply affected at high temperatures.

On a purely physical basis, temperature can be expected to affect gas diffusion rates, hence rates of photosynthesis and leaf respiration. However, not only can the physical effects of temperature be complicated by the metabolic effects of temperature on rates of photosynthesis and respiration, but such gas exchange is reported to be affected by an interaction between temperature and humidity.

Exact control of temperature is routine, but equivalent accuracy in control of humidity can be difficult, and exact simultaneous control of temperature and humidity can be very challenging indeed. Vegetable transplants usually benefit from hardening by controlled temperature and/or moisture stress before being planted out in the field. This does not appear to be the case for sweet potato transplants, which are vine cuttings rather than seedlings. Transplants held at 13–18°C were reported to have greatly increased vitality and ultimately higher yields compared with transplants held at an ambient temperature of 26.7°C. (That "26.7°C ambient" temperature is curiously exact and is possibly a translation from "ca. 80°F ambient.") A particularly intriguing example of an unexpected temperature effect is reported in a study of male sterility in the common bean (*Phaseolus vulgaris* L.). When, in the course of an atypically cool summer, unexpected fertility was noted in supposedly male sterile plants, research was transferred to growth chambers.

A day/night temperature regime of 30/18°C for an average of 12 days was sufficient to cause most unstable steriles to produce sterile buds. Day/night conditions of 18/7°C for an average of 14 days were effective in converting sterile to partially sterile phenotypes. Both temperature-stable and temperature-unstable genotypes were identified; this is an excellent example of valuable research findings achieved by following up on a temperature-related anomaly revealed in a field study.

The literature abounds in such examples. Many mysteries would be elucidated if research workers routinely reported temperatures (whether controlled or not) and included such data in their research reports. Subsequent research workers, if alert to the multitudinous roles of temperature, will then be in a position to carry the research further, perhaps with the advantages of better funding or instrumentation.

5

Potato

INTRODUCTION TO POTATO

POTATO BLIGHT

The attack on potato leaves starts as a rule at the edge or tip of a leaflet as a light-green spot, which quickly becomes brown and limp, and later blackish-brown and dry. Under damp conditions the brown spots have a marginal zone of fine white mould, composed of conidiophores and conidia of the fungus, which burst through the skin of the leaf 2-3 days after infection. There are at first a few scattered spots, usually on the lower leaves; but others quickly follow and the whole potato haulm may be destroyed in about a week.

The diseased leaves have a characteristic sickly sweet smell which can often be detected at some distance from a diseased crop. Brown streaks develop too on the stems and even the flowers and berries may be attacked.

Potato blight on under-side of the leaf. Tubers attacked by potato blight show leaden or dull purplish-grey, slightly sunken spots or irregular blotches in the skin. When they are cut through, rusty-brown streaks are seen growing from the skin into the flesh. In time the whole tissue becomes destroyed by a rather dry brown rot. Commonly, however, P. infestans is quickly followed by secondary fungi, especially species of Fusarium and bacteria, which obscure the symptoms of blight and may cause an evil-smelling soft wet rot to supervene. In all its stages the blight fungus needs oxygen and it cannot penetrate rapidly into the flesh by itself. The secondary invaders feed on the starch grains that the blight fungus has only superficially attacked. P. infestans conidia may be formed on diseased tubers.

The most important source of infection every summer is certainly slightly infected seed tubers. These may give rise to:

- Quite a normal sprout,
- Infected sprouts which soon die or
- Infected sprouts which come above ground, bear conidia and thus infect the lower leaves of the crop.

The potato blight fungus can also grow out from diseased tubers and small dead shoots into the soil where it lives for a time, and may produce conidia which are splashed on to the leaves by rain.

The appearance of the fungus in a crop from diseased seed tubers has been doubted but was seen by de Bary. Severely attacked tubers are readily destroyed by bacteria and millipedes, and sprout feebly or not at all. It is only those tubers which are slightly infected which are able, when planted, to produce shoots that come above ground. In June and July spread of infection from these diseased sprouts to lower leaves of the crop proceeds unnoticed.

These centres of infection form starting points for the incredibly rapid blazing up of the disease which occurs when conditions become favourable to it in July and August. It may be supposed that it will break out at many places at the same time if the conidia are carried a short distance by the wind. It may be of importance whether the early potatoes lie on the windward or leeward side of the late varieties. Sometimes one may notice that a hedge has afforded a certain amount of shelter and that blight has started opposite a gateway or other gap in the hedge. Small potato patches in town gardens become attacked at the same time as fields in the country.

In experiments with cultures in sterilized soil or manure, where the blight fungus encounters no competition from other organisms, it has survived the winter out of doors. The possibility of it overwintering in ordinary field or garden soil is very small but it must be remembered that there are always some groundkeeper tubers not killed by frost and the fungus may naturally survive the winter in some of those.

Heaps of chats discarded when the crop was graded or left on the site of an old pit are another possible source of infection. If the potato tops are killed early by blight and the tubers are left to ripen in the soil a very small crop is obtained but the tubers do not become infected, provided they were covered by a good thick layer of soil.

If blight attack comes late, retarded by weather conditions or by spraying, so that the tops are still green and bear fresh blight spots when the crop is lifted, there is great danger of the tubers becoming infected, especially in wet weather. Liability of the tubers to become infected depends partly on the variety, partly on the soil. Haulm and soil remain infectious for 10, possibly 20, days after the haulm has died. Haulm cut down by frost is at once freed from infection.

ALTERNARIA BLIGHT

This leaf spot disease is known and feared under the name " early blight " because it tends to appear earlier than true potato blight, called there " late blight." It is due to the mould Alternaria solani, formerly called Macrosporium solani Ell. & Mart., which causes leaf spotting also on tomato and egg plant. More or less circular brown or blackish spots appear on the potato leaves from

July onwards. They are limited by the leaf veins though in severe outbreaks several spots may become united. Under a lens the spots are seen to be marked with darker, irregularly concentric lines, hence the name " target spot" sometimes applied to them. In damp weather a fine olive-brown mould may appear on the surface. Some varieties show considerable resistance to the disease and only very small brown spots develop on their leaves. This is the form of Alternaria blight usually seen in Britain, where, indeed, the disease is regarded as of no economic importance and where conidia are seldom to be found on the spots. It seems clear, in fact, that not all the " target spot " on potato leaves in this country is attributable to Alternaria infection. Very early spraying with Bordeaux mixture prevents an outbreak of Alternaria blight; according to one investigator Burgundy mixture is even more effective.

Where the disease has been prevalent care should be taken that the tubers do not become infected by spores from the haulm at lifting, and to store them in a dry cool place. The optimum temperature for Alternaria rot of the tubers is 60° F. and its growth ceases at 41° F. Alpha, Bravo, King Edward, Majestic, Kerr's Pink, Edzell Blue and Up-to-Date are all susceptible; Juli is fairly resistant and Golden Wonder more so. This fungus causes a minor leaf spot disease which in some parts of Europe causes premature withering of potato haulm in severe seasons. The leaf spots appear from July onwards; they are at first yellow, then brown on the upper surface, and are tinged greyish-purple with the conidia on the under-side of the leaf. The routine sprays against potato blight control this disease as well.

SEED-PIECE DECAY OF POTATO

Fusarium dry rot is an important postharvest disease of potato tubers that causes significant losses in storage and transit of both seed tubers and those for table consumption. It is also a major cause of seed-piece decay after planting.

SYMPTOMS

Infected tubers usually develop a dry rot, but a moist rot may occur if secondary infections with soft-rot bacteria also are involved. Surfaces of infected tubers are sunken or wrinkled, and rotted tissues appear brown or gray to black. A white or pink mold is sometimes visible on tuber surfaces. When tubers are cut, internal cavities within rotted tissues may contain white, yellow or pink molds. In storage, blue, black, purple, gray, white, yellow, or pink spore masses may develop in these internal cavities. After low-temperature storage, internal tissues often will become firm and dry or even powdery.

Causal Organisms

Fusarium dry rot is caused by several species of the soilborne fungus Fusarium. These fungi are common in most soils where potatoes are grown and survive as resistant spores free in the soil or within decayed plant tissues. Although some infections may develop on tubers before harvest, most infections occur as the fungus enters tubers through harvest wounds. Small, brown lesions appear at wound sites 3-4 weeks after harvest and continue to enlarge during storage, taking several months to develop fully.

The disease develops fairly rapidly at temperatures above 50 F, but lesions will cease enlarging below 40 F. The fungus is only dormant at these low temperatures, however, and will resume growth when tubers are warmed.

Fusarium seed-piece decay is really the same disease. Seed tubers may be infected prior to shipment.

Decay during transit or storage often accounts for poor quality seed tubers. When these Fusarium fungi are present on seed pieces or in the soil, poor stands may result, especially if cut surfaces of seed pieces are not properly healed. Fusarium seed-piece decay begins as reddish-brown to black depressions on cut surfaces.

These may expand to cover the entire seed piece and often result in a slimy rot when infection by secondary soft-rot bacteria follows.

- Harvest tubers only after the vines are completely dead to ensure skin maturity.
- Take all precautions when harvesting and handling tubers to minimize cuts and bruises.
- Hold newly harvested potatoes at 55-60 F with 90-95 per cent relative humidity for the first 1-2 weeks to promote wound healing. After this curing period, lower the temperature of table stock to 38-40 F for long-term storage.
- Plant only certified, disease-free seed tubers. If possible, use whole (B-size) seed tubers that do not have to be cut into seed pieces before planting.
- When receiving seed tubers in bags, do not stack more than five bags high. With bulk or bagged seed, store at 40-45 F until 2-3 weeks before planting. Then allow seed potatoes to warm prior to cutting.
- Treat cut seed pieces with recommended fungicide dressings immediately after cutting.
- Plant treated cut seed pieces immediately or store them at 55-60 F and 95-99 per cent relative humidity to hasten healing of cut surfaces. Condensation on surfaces of seed pieces must be avoided.

STOLON CANKER OF POTATO

Rhizoctonia stem and stolon canker, also called black scurf, is an extremely common problem on potatoes that can result in delayed emergence, reduced stands and poor tuber quality.

SYMPTOMS

Rhizoctonia canker often goes unnoticed until harvest when tubers are found to be covered with small brownish-black fungal bodies (sclerotia) that look somewhat like bits of black soil that will not wash off. These may vary in size from a pinhead to as large as a pea.

When introduced into soil, these structures can survive and germinate the following spring to attack young shoots, roots, stolons, and tubers of the new crop. In many cases, weak, spindly-looking or late-emerging plants may be the result of an attack by this fungus. The first sprouts are often killed before they reach the surface, resulting in the emergence of a weaker secondary sprout. Dry, sunken, brownish lesions developing on the base of the stem below the soil line are evidence of the stem canker phase of this disease. The lesions may girdle the stem or large cankers may interfere with movement of nutrients from the leaves to the tubers. In such cases, vines become yellow to reddish purple; the leaves begin to curl upward; the stalks swell, particularly at the nodes; and often small purplish tubers form where leaves branch from stems.

During midseason under a dense canopy of foliage, the fungus may develop a white, powdery mold growth on stems, extending just above the soil line. Cankers that form on stolons may prune off young developing tubers. This disease may lead to russeting or surface cracking of mature tubers and sometimes shallow, brown lesions will form around lenticles. Low soil temperatures in the fall favour formation of sclerotia on tubers.

Causal Organism

This disease is caused by the fungus Rhizoctonia solani which can survive in the soil for many years, even under relatively dry conditions. Rhizoctonia causes disease in a wide variety of crops, but the strains found in association with potato generally do not attack and reproduce on other plant species. The fungus survives in soil associated with decomposing plant residues.

In addition, the sclerotia can survive on infected tubers and can persist free in soil for extended periods. Emerging sprouts are usually attacked by fungus present on the seed tubers. Once green leaves develop on sprouts, stem tissues are much less susceptible to infection.

Stem cankers, stolon infections, and sclerotia on tubers usually develop when these tissues grow in proximity to sources of the Rhizoctonia fungus in soil. Cool (55-60 degree F), moist soils are optimal for infection. Sclerotia form on the surfaces of mature tubers under cool, moist conditions, generally after the vines have begun to die.

- Use a crop rotation with corn, grasses, and cereal grains. If this disease has been severe, 3-5 years should elapse between potato crops.
- Plant certified seed tubers that are free of Rhizoctonia on the skin.

- Use planting practices that promote rapid emergence: Avoid planting in heavy, poorly-drained soils. Plant seed potatoes when soil is warm (above 60 degree F). Cover seed tubers with no more than 2 inches of soil.
- Harvest tubers promptly after vines are dead to avoid the development of sclerotia on the surfaces of tubers while still in the soil.

MOSAIC VIRUS DISEASES OF VINE CROPS

Mosaic diseases of vine crops are caused by at least five different viruses:

- Cucumber mosaic virus (CMV),
- Squash mosaic virus (SQMV),
- Watermelon mosaic virus-2 (WMV-2),
- Zucchini yellow mosaic virus (ZYMV)
- Papaya ringspot virus-watermelon isolate (PRSV-W).

All five of these viruses can infect all cultivated vine crops (squash, melons, gourds, cucumbers, pumpkins) and under ideal conditions can cause a high rate of crop failure and severe economic losses.

SYMPTOMS

As the names imply, all five viruses cause a mottling of foliage called mosaic. This is characterized by the presence of intermingled patches of normal and light green or yellowish coloured plant tissue.

Depending on environmental conditions, mosaic symptoms can range from mild to severe and be visible on both leaves and fruit. The younger the plant when infected, the more severe the symptoms as the plant matures. In some cases, plants infected at the seedling stage may collapse and die. Plants infected at the flowering stage may not set fruit or young fruits may abort. If plants are more mature when infected they do not show severe mosaic and may still produce marketable fruit. The most dramatic symptoms are often associated with infected fruit. Fruit symptoms can range from subtle colour change to severe deformation. It is not uncommon to have two or more viruses infecting the same plant and in these cases symptoms may be much more severe than if the plant were infected with only one virus. It is nearly impossible to distinguish between any of the five viruses based only on visible symptoms.

Because of this, it is important to have suspect plants sent to a diagnostic clinic capable of using specialized techniques to identify the viruses that are present. Proper disease management depends on knowing which specific virus is involved.

Disease Cycle and Transmission

All five vine crop mosaic viruses are transmitted by insects. CMV, ZYMV, WMV-2 and PRSV-W are transmitted primarily by the green peach aphid and the melon aphid. SQMV is transmitted by the striped cucumber beetle and spotted cucumber beetle and also through seed, but only at a very low rate. In most cases these insects acquire the virus by feeding on weeds or other vine crops that are infected.

The insects then feed on noninfected vine crops and in the process of this feeding transmit the virus to the host plant. In the case of the green peach and melon aphid, the insect carries the virus on its probing mouthparts and the aphid only needs to probe the plant to transmit the virus. Feeding by the aphid is not necessary. Once the insect probes one plant, it can move onto the next, probing and infecting as it goes.

The more aphids present, the quicker and more complete the virus spread. By this process, large acreages can become infected quickly.

- Plant varieties with resistance to these viruses whenever possible. The availability of varieties with virus resistance varies depending on the virus and the vine crop in question. Major seed producers list resistant varieties in their seed catalogs.
- Control weeds which could harbor the viruses from areas around production fields. Pokeweed is a primary weed in the area which harbors many plant viruses. Weeds also serve as hosts for insects that transmit the viruses.
- Since the virus is moved about by insects it would seem logical that insect control would be a primary method of virus control. However, in this case it is not that simple. Since aphid vectors need only probe the plant to transmit the virus, insect control is not really that effective in controlling the virus. Even if the aphid were to die immediately following probing, virus transmission would still take place. To control the insect effectively insecticides would need to be applied on a daily basis. The economics of this may not be feasible. Aphids also move long distances with weather fronts making local control difficult.

TUBERS IN POTATO

Scab is a disease of potato tubers that results in lowered tuber quality due to scab-like surface lesions. There are no above-ground symptoms. Two forms of scab occur. Common scab occurs in all production areas and is most severe in soils with a pH above 5.5. Another less common form, called acid scab, is important in acidic soils.

SYMPTOMS

Scab symptoms are quite variable. Usually, roughly circular, raised, tan to brown, corky lesions of varying size develop randomly across tuber surfaces. Sometimes scab develops as a rather superficial layer of corky tissues covering large areas of the tuber surface. This is called russet scab. Pitted scab can also occur where lesions develop up to 1/2 inch deep. These deep lesions are dark brown to black, and the tissues underneath are often straw-coloured and somewhat translucent. More than one of these lesion types may be present on a single tuber.

Although scab symptoms are usually noticed late in the growing season or at harvest, tubers are susceptible to infection as soon as they are formed. Small brown, water-soaked, circular lesions are visible on tubers within a few weeks after infection.

Mature tubers with a well-developed skin are no longer susceptible, but existing lesions will continue to expand as tubers enlarge. Thus disease severity increases throughout the growing season. Scab is most severe when tubers develop under warm, dry soil conditions.

Coarse-textured soils that dry out quickly are therefore more conducive to scab than are fine-textured soils. A few other conditions can be confused with scab. White, enlarged lenticles, which frequently occur on potato tubers harvested from wet soil, can be mistaken for scab.

Usually this condition will disappear when tubers are dried. Patchy russeting, checking, or cracking of tuber surfaces caused by the fungus Rhizoctonia also may be confused with russet scab.

A totally different but uncommon disease called powdery scab, caused by the fungus Spongospora subterranea, causes very similar scab-like symptoms. Laboratory examination may be necessary to identify these diseases.

Causal Organisms

Scab is caused by a group of filamentous bacteria called actinomycetes that occur commonly in soil. In soils with a pH above 5.5, Streptomyces scabies is usually responsible for common scab, and is capable of causing all the types of scab lesions. It is commonly introduced into fields on seed potatoes, and will survive indefinitely on decaying plant debris once the soil is contaminated.

Because the organism can survive passage through the digestive tract of animals and be distributed.

TUBER SOFT ROT OF POTATO

Blackleg, aerial stem rot, and tuber soft rot are all similar diseases caused by several types of soft-rot bacteria. Blackleg and tuber soft rot occur wherever potatoes are grown. Aerial stem rot is also widespread, but is most severe under sprinkler-irrigation.

SYMPTOMS

Blackleg begins from a contaminated seed piece, but the symptoms can occur at several stages of plant development. In severe cases, entire seed pieces and developing sprouts may rot in the ground prior to emergence, resulting in a poor stand. Blackleg often develops after plants are well up or even in flower. In this case, stem bases of diseased plants typically show an inky-black to light-brown decay that originates from the seed piece and can extend up the stem from less than an inch to more than two feet. Leaves of infected plants tend to roll upward at the margins, become yellow, wilt, and often die. Aerial stem rot (also called bacterial stem rot or aerial blackleg) is initiated by soft-rot bacteria from sources external to the seed piece. Stem infection can occur through wounds or through natural openings such as leaf scars. Lesions on diseased stems first appear as irregular brownish to inky-black areas.

These enlarge into a soft, mushy rot that causes entire stems to wilt and die. Potato tubers with soft rot have tissues that are very soft and watery, and have a slightly granular consistency. The diseased tissue is cream- to tan-coloured, and often has a black border separating diseased from healthy areas. In the early stages, soft-rot decay is generally odorless, but later a foul odor and a stringy or slimy decay usually develop as secondary decay bacteria invade infected tissues. Most internal tuber tissues may be consumed by soft rot organisms, sometimes leaving only a shell of skin remaining in the soil.

Causal Organisms

Blackleg, aerial stem rot, and tuber soft rot are caused by two closely related bacteria, Erwinia carotovora subsp. atroseptica and Erwinia carotovora subsp. carotovora. E. c. carotovora is very common and has an extensive host range, including most fleshy vegetables. It survives readily in soil and surface waters such as rivers, lakes, and even oceans. These bacteria are capable of multiplying and persisting in the root zones of many host and nonhost crop and weed species. In contrast, E. c. atroseptica is associated mostly with potatoes.

These bacteria do not survive well in soil for more than one year, unless they are contained within diseased tubers or other potato plant debris.

Blackleg is usually caused by E. c. atroseptica carried on contaminated seed tubers. Most lots of seed tubers are contaminated to some degree, but the bacteria are usually dormant and do not cause disease unless environmental conditions are favourable.

In contrast, aerial stem rot is usually caused by E. c. carotovora contained in infested soil or introduced to the crop by irrigation water, wind-blown rain, and insects. Tuber soft rot can be caused by either of these soft-rot bacteria. Moisture and temperature are the two critical factors in initiation and development of soft-rot diseases.

High soil temperatures and bruising of seed tubers favour seed-piece decay and pre-emergence blackleg. Blackleg in growing plants is favoured by cool, wet soils at planting followed by high temperatures after emergence. Dense plant canopies and long periods of leaf wetness favour infection of aerial plant parts.

Although tuber soft rot can occur at any temperature above 50 degree F, disease develops best above 75 degree F. Oxygen depletion in tubers also favours soft rot. When seed pieces in soil or tubers in storage become covered with a film of water, the tissues rapidly become depleted of oxygen. This also may be induced by soil flooding or improper drying of washed tubers. Once it starts, tuber soft rot can proceed rapidly in storage. "Wet" areas may develop in the piled tubers that flow onto ones below, spreading the bacteria. Heat, coupled with condensation on tuber surfaces, can further adversely affect storage conditions, resulting in accelerated "melt" of the pile.

- Plant only certified, disease-free seed tubers. If possible, use whole (B-size) seed tubers that do not have to be cut.
- When receiving seed tubers in bags, do not stack more than five bags high. With bulk or bagged seed, store at 40-45 F until 2-3 weeks before planting, then warm to 55-60 prior to cutting.
- Clean all equipment used for cutting seed tubers thoroughly and then sanitize with an appropriate disinfectant.
- Treat cut seed pieces with recommended fungicide dressings immediately after cutting.
- Plant treated cut seed pieces immediately if soil temperatures are 55-65 degree F at planting depth. Seed pieces can be held 1-2 weeks at 55-60 degree F and 95-99 per cent relative humidity to hasten healing of cut surfaces. Condensation on surfaces of seed pieces must be avoided.
- Do not irrigate fields until plants are well emerged. Avoid using surface water for irrigation.
- During crop growth, monitor irrigation and nitrogen fertility to minimize excessive vine growth that will promote leaf wetness within the plant canopy.
- Harvest tubers only after the vines are completely dead to ensure skin maturity. Low spots in the field should be left unharvested if significant waterlogging has occurred.
- Take all precautions to minimize cuts and bruises when harvesting and handling tubers.
- Hold newly harvested potatoes at 55-60 F with 90-95 per cent relative humidity for the first 1-2 weeks to promote wound healing. After this curing period, lower the temperature of table stock to 38-40 F for long-term storage. Never wash tubers prior to storage.

BACTERIAL RING ROT OF POTATOES

Bacterial ring rot is an important disease of potatoes and is one of the main reasons for rejection of seed potatoes from certification programmes. This disease is particularly serious because it has the potential to spread quickly throughout a farm and may lead to severe losses if left unchecked. Ring rot was originally found in Germany in the late 1800's. The causal bacteria were introduced into the United States in the early 1930's and by 1940 were found throughout the country.

SYMPTOMS

Severe ring rot can result in wilting of leaves and stems along with yellowing and death of leaves. Lower leaves usually wilt first, are slightly rolled at the margins, and are paler green than healthy leaves. As wilting progresses, leaf tissues between veins become yellow. In the later stages of disease, margins of lower leaves die and become brittle and eventually entire stems yellow and die. Frequently, only one or two stems in a hill will develop symptoms and, in some cases, there are no above-ground symptoms at all.

Ring rot derives its name from a characteristic breakdown of the vascular ring within the tuber. This often appears as a creamy-yellow to light-brown, cheesy rot. The symptom is most frequently observed when a diseased tuber is cut crosswise at the stem end. In severe cases, the vascular ring may be separated, and a creamy or cheesy exudate can be forced out from this tissue when the tuber is squeezed.

On the outer surface, severely diseased tubers may show slightly sunken, dry, cracked areas. Infected tubers are often invaded by secondary decay organisms which may lead to complete breakdown. Symptoms of ring rot in the vascular tissue of infected tubers are often less obvious t, appearing as only a broken, sporadically appearing dark line, or as a continuous, yellowish dis-colouration. Because of this, laboratory tests should always be performed to confirm a diagnosis of ring rot.

Causal Organism

Ring rot is caused by the bacterium Clavibacter michiganense subsp. sepedonicus. Ring-rot bacteria survive between seasons mainly in infected seed tubers. They are also capable of surviving 2-5 years in dried slime on surfaces of crates, bins, burlap sacks, or harvesting and grading machinery, even if exposed to temperatures well below freezing. Survival is longest under cool, dry conditions. Ring-rot bacteria do not survive in soil in the absence of potato debris, but can survive from season to season in volunteer potato plants.

Wounds are necessary for penetration of the bacteria into seed pieces. The pathogen is easily transmitted from diseased tubers to healthy seed pieces during the seed-cutting process. A knife that cuts one infected tuber can spread these bacteria to the next 20-100 seed pieces. Likewise, the bacteria may be spread during planting, particularly if a picker-type planter is used. Ring-rot bacteria can be moved in irrigation water and by chewing insects, such as

Colorado potato beetles and flea beetles. After the bacteria become established in a plant, they multiply and move throughout the plant via the water-conducting tissues. Fortunately ring-rot bacteria are capable of causing disease only in potato, although they may be able to colonize roots of sugar beets.

- Plant only certified disease-free seed tubers. Certified seed potatoes are produced under regulations mandating zero tolerance for ring rot. Although use of certified seed tubers will not guarantee total freedom from ring rot bacteria, it is the best assurance.
- Discontinue use of any lot of seed tubers in which ring rot is found. Seed lots known to be contaminated with ring-rot bacteria should never be planted.
- Before handling seed tubers, all containers, tools, knives and mechanical cutters, planters, and other equipment should be thoroughly washed with a detergent solution, rinsed, and then sanitized with a disinfectant (for current recommendations,
- If ring rot is confirmed to be present, a thorough cleanup must be undertaken. Dispose of all infected tubers away from potato production areas. Clean all surfaces of storages and equipment to remove all mud, dirt and debris and then wash with a strong detergent in hot water applied by a high-pressure washer. After cleaning, sanitize all storages and equipment with a disinfectant. Do not plant potatoes for two seasons in any field in which ring rot has been found.

POTATO PINK ROT, PYTHIUM LEAK AND SEED-PIECE DECAY

Pink rot and Pythium leak, sometimes collectively called water rot; occur sporadically wherever potatoes are grown. These diseases are a problem of mature tubers at harvest and in storage. They are most serious when warm, wet soil conditions persist during tuber formation and at harvest. When newly-planted seed pieces are exposed to these conditions, Pythium seed-piece decay also can be severe. Major problems with these diseases are usually associated with excessive rainfall or irrigation either early or late in the season, especially on poorly-drained soils.

SYMPTOMS

Pythium seed-piece decay often results in delayed emergence and poor stands. Infected seed pieces become a soft, watery mass in the soil. Symptoms of pink rot in mature plants include brown or blackened roots or stolons, and in severe cases, leaf chlorosis, stunting, wilting, and even plant death. Tubers develop pink rot mostly through diseased stolons, but occasionally infections occur at buds or lenticels. Decay spreads through infected tubers with the advancing margin of the rot usually sharply defined by a dark line, which may be visible through the skin. Eyes of infected tubers are often dark brown.

Decaying tubers remain intact, but are spongy and odorless. If squeezed, a clear liquid will exude. When infected tubers are cut open, the internal tissues turn salmon pink after a 15-20 minute exposure to air, then later become brownish-black. Pythium leak usually develops through harvest wounds in tuber surfaces and begins as a discoloured, watersoaked area. As with pink rot, the advancing margin of infection is usually bounded by a dark line. Infected tissues are extremely watery, and appear brown or gray. Severely rotted tubers are of a uniform texture resembling a soft, watery paste.

Causal Organisms

Pink rot is caused by several species of the soilborne fungus Phytophthora while Pythium leak and seed-piece decay are caused by several species of the closely related soilborne fungus Pythium. These fungi are widely distributed in both water and soil, and their behaviour is similar. They survive in soil within decaying plant material, or as resistant spores free in the soil. In warm, moist soil, these fungi produce swimming spores that move in water films.

Roots can be infected by Phytophthora at almost any stage of plant growth, but symptoms are more severe on younger roots. Both groups of fungi infect tubers through wounds, but Phytophthora generally infects tubers before harvest, often through stolons. Infection by Pythium usually occurs through harvest wounds, especially at temperatures above 70 degree F. Seed pieces can be infected by Pythium as soon as they are planted.

- Select areas with well-drained soils for planting potatoes.
- Use a crop rotation away from potatoes for at least 4 years if pink rot or leak has been severe. This may reduce the amount of fungus surviving in the soil.
- Delay planting for at least 2 weeks after plowing down green vegetation as this may temporarily stimulate populations of Pythium fungi.
- Avoid planting in soils colder than 45 degree F or warmer than 70 degree F.
- Avoid harvesting infested fields when soils are especially wet or soil temperatures are below 50 degree F or above 65 degree F. Stop irrigation well in advance of harvest.
- Avoid bruising tubers during harvest by adjusting equipment properly, keeping digger chains fully loaded and minimizing drops to 6 inches or less. Do not leave harvested tubers lying on warm, moist soils for any length of time as infection with Pythium may occur quickly.
- Leave low spots in fields unharvested if they have been waterlogged and much rot is present.
- Keep tubers cool and as dry as possible during harvest, loading, transit and storage.

- Grade out infected tubers as much as possible before placing harvested tubers in storage.
- Store lots of harvested tubers containing many infected tubers separately from healthy lots. Good airflow through the pile should be provided to dry out leaky tubers. Lots with significant amounts of disease should be marketed as soon as possible as they will not store well.

DISEASE IN POTATO

Wart disease increases rapidly on land where potatoes are frequently grown, as in gardens md allotments, and in a space of 2-3 years it may attain such proportions as to ruin the crop. Direct losses of crop from the disease on an agricultural scale have been small but stringent quarantine regulations against it hamper export of produce from infected districts and discourage the cultivation of susceptible varieties. Hence the regulations which aim at excluding wart disease from countries in which it does not yet occur cannot be held to be unreasonable.

On several occasions the disease has been brought in with small consignments of potatoes among immigrants' luggage or by small-scale commercial traffic across a frontier. Only plants of the nightshade family, Solanaceae can be attacked by this fungus. Tomatoes develop swellings on roots and stem, and under experimental conditions small warts on the leaves also. Henbane and a number of species of Solanum develop small swellings on the roots and eventually small galls on the stems.

It has not proved possible to infect thorn apple (Datura stramonium], deadly nightshade (Atropa belladonna) or any kind of tobacco. In a wet season warts may be found on the stems and lowest leaves of potatoes, and even on the inflorescence, but as a rule the attack is confined to the tubers and is first noticed at digging.

The stolons may be affected but the roots are never attacked. As a rule growth of the haulm is normal and unchecked. The warts on the tubers start as tiny white granular swellings growing out from the eyes.

They quickly enlarge into cauliflower-like structures which may be larger than the tuber itself. Above ground they are light green, below ground at first white, then brown. Old warts decay and turn black and even at the normal lifting time many will be partially rotten, or break off and decay in the soil, leaving only a small scar on the tuber.

Occasionally new small outgrowths may develop in the clamp around the scars, giving a disease picture like that of powdery scab. Powdery scab infection of the sprouts occasionally produces swellings simulating wart disease, as may also irregular second-growth, covered with scab. Sometimes microscopic examination is necessary to distinguish between these diseases.

The swellings of crown gall also resemble those of wart disease but the former is known on potato only from artificial inoculations. The wart disease swellings contain a vast number of minute, brown, thick- walled resting sporangia which become liberated into the soil as the tissues decay. When they germinate a number of extremely minute, mobile swarm spores emerge and swim about until they meet a young potato tuber. They then penetrate the skin of an eye and settle down inside the potato cells. Here in a fortnight clusters of from 1 to 7 summer sporangia are formed which liberate hundreds more swarm spores.

These are partly responsible for multiplying the number of infected cells on and around the developing wart, partly for infecting other tubers. Second generations of summer sporangia form during the summer, and their development requires 10-20 days. They do not overwinter but are replaced in the mature wart by the thick-walled winter sporangia, formed after a kind of sexual process. These not only survive the winter but remain alive in the soil for very many years; they are not destroyed even when an infected potato is eaten and digested by an animal.

The formation of warts is due to the potato cells being stimulated to abnormal growth and multiplication by the fungus cells which invade them. The wart disease organism is one of the most primitive of fungi and never develops any kind of mycelium.

COMMON SCAB

The disease called common scab of potato is caused by the ray fungus Actinomyces scabies, which also attacks beet, carrot, radish, swede and turnip. Care is needed to distinguish between it and powdery scab.

The ray fungi are generally regarded as being somewhat intermediate in structure between bacteria and fungi. Several hundred species occur in soils, where they play a large part in the breakdown of decaying organic matter; others live in water and a few cause disease in animals. Potato scab appears as rough, scabby spots on the otherwise smooth skin of the tubers. The spots may grow together and the whole surface of the tuber may be covered by them.

If careful examination is made when the layer of cork begins to form in the skin the first signs of disease will be detected as small grey-brown spots under the lenticels where the fungus is stimulating the living cells to production of additional layers of cork. The outer cork is burst open and the new cork follows suit, producing the scabby outer surface of the lesion. The more prone the variety is to cork formation the scabbier it will be.

Roots and stolons of potato may be slightly attacked. Tubers that protrude above ground are not affected, nor do scabs increase in the clamp. Tubers are the most readily infected; if they have a long growing period, the period during which they become scabby is increased, hence, perhaps, the various reports that " spraying induces scab." A strong earthy smell due to the presence of the actinomycete is peculiar to common scab; powdery scabs have no such smell. The fungus may overwinter either in the soil or in the scabs on tubers. It can survive on cellulose and similar plant products in the soil for years at a time. Several instances have been reported in which disinfected tubers planted in freshly broken forest soil produced scabby crops.

On the other hand an interval of several years between potato crops has sometimes led to a striking reduction in the amount of scab. The fungus reproduces simply by its fine hyphae breaking up to form spores, easily disseminated in soil and water. Manure may be regarded as infected if it comes from farms where scabby potatoes are used raw as fodder. Infection may also be spread by compost and, of course, by planting infected tubers.

VARIETAL SUSCEPTIBILITY

No potato variety completely resistant to common scab is known and on soil favourable to the fungus all varieties are attacked to about the same extent. Early varieties tend to escape infection, probably because the cork layer in their skin is formed before the soil becomes warm enough to suit the fungus. Main crop varieties do show some differences in susceptibility, probably associated in part with the size and texture of their lenticels.

Breeding for scab resistance is in progress in Minnesota where the possibility of physiological races of the fungus is also under investigation. Disinfection of the tubers is effective in destroying the scab fungus on them but is only of value when they are to be planted on scab-free soil, or in soil treated with sulphur or otherwise disinfected.

Digging in grass cuttings may be effective in gardens or allotments provided they are available in sufficient quantity. Up to a stone per square yard has been recommended. On a field scale ploughing in rye or other green manure in the spring may be helpful.

Consistent use of sulphate of ammonia instead of chili saltpetre will gradually reduce the amount of scab, but one must be careful that the soil is not made too acid for other crops that need lime.

Combined use of dung and sulphate of ammonia has proved helpful. The proprietary preparation Bayer P. at the rate of about 1 oz. per square yard or 54 Ib. per acre, dug well in before the potatoes are planted, may greatly reduce both common scab and stem canker.

It works very well when used with sulphate of ammonia. Liming may be necessary because of other crops in the rotation, but it is well to have the soil analysed and to apply only the lime requirement. Where it is important to obtain a crop of smooth tubers a piece of ground may be kept unlimed for potato production. Continuous cropping with potatoes is liable, however, to lead to trouble from other diseases and especially from root eelworm.

POTATO WART DISEASE

Wart disease increases rapidly on land where potatoes are frequently grown, as in gardens md allotments, and in a space of 2-3 years it may attain such proportions as to ruin the crop. Direct losses of crop from the disease on an agricultural scale have been small but stringent quarantine regulations against it hamper export of produce from infected districts and discourage the cultivation of susceptible varieties. Hence the regulations which aim at excluding wart disease from countries in which it does not yet occur cannot be held to be unreasonable.

On several occasions the disease has been brought in with small consignments of potatoes among immigrants' luggage or by small-scale commercial traffic across a frontier. Only plants of the nightshade family, Solanaceae can be attacked by this fungus. Tomatoes develop swellings on roots and stem, and under experimental conditions small warts on the leaves also. Henbane and a number of species of Solanum develop small swellings on the roots and eventually small galls on the stems.

It has not proved possible to infect thorn apple (Datura stramonium], deadly nightshade (Atropa belladonna) or any kind of tobacco. In a wet season warts may be found on the stems and lowest leaves of potatoes, and even on the inflorescence, but as a rule the attack is confined to the tubers and is first noticed at digging.

The stolons may be affected but the roots are never attacked. As a rule growth of the haulm is normal and unchecked. The warts on the tubers start as tiny white granular swellings growing out from the eyes.

They quickly enlarge into cauliflower-like structures which may be larger than the tuber itself. Above ground they are light green, below ground at first white, then brown. Old warts decay and turn black and even at the normal lifting time many will be partially rotten, or break off and decay in the soil, leaving only a small scar on the tuber.

Occasionally new small outgrowths may develop in the clamp around the scars, giving a disease picture like that of powdery scab. Powdery scab infection of the sprouts occasionally produces swellings simulating wart disease, as may also irregular second-growth, covered with scab. Sometimes microscopic examination is necessary to distinguish between these diseases.

The swellings of crown gall also resemble those of wart disease but the former is known on potato only from artificial inoculations. The wart disease swellings contain a vast number of minute, brown, thick- walled resting sporangia which become liberated into the soil as the tissues decay. When they germinate a number of extremely minute, mobile swarm spores emerge and swim about until they meet a young potato tuber. They then penetrate the skin of an eye and settle down inside the potato cells. Here in a fortnight clusters of from 1 to 7 summer sporangia are formed which liberate hundreds more swarm spores. These are partly responsible for multiplying the number of infected cells on and around the developing wart, partly for infecting other tubers. Second generations of summer sporangia form during the summer, and their development requires 10-20 days. They do not overwinter but are replaced in the mature wart by the thick-walled winter sporangia, formed after a kind of sexual process. These not only survive the winter but remain alive in the soil for very many years; they are not destroyed even when an infected potato is eaten and digested by an animal.

The formation of warts is due to the potato cells being stimulated to abnormal growth and multiplication by the fungus cells which invade them. The wart disease organism is one of the most primitive of fungi and never develops any kind of mycelium.

COMMON SCAB

The disease called common scab of potato is caused by the ray fungus Actinomyces scabies, which also attacks beet, carrot, radish, swede and turnip. Care is needed to distinguish between it and powdery scab.

The ray fungi are generally regarded as being somewhat intermediate in structure between bacteria and fungi. Several hundred species occur in soils, where they play a large part in the breakdown of decaying organic matter; others live in water and a few cause disease in animals. Potato scab appears as rough, scabby spots on the otherwise smooth skin of the tubers. The spots may grow together and the whole surface of the tuber may be covered by them.

If careful examination is made when the layer of cork begins to form in the skin the first signs of disease will be detected as small grey-brown spots under the lenticels where the fungus is stimulating the living cells to production of additional layers of cork. The outer cork is burst open and the new cork follows suit, producing the scabby outer surface of the lesion. The more prone the variety is to cork formation the scabbier it will be.

Roots and stolons of potato may be slightly attacked. Tubers that protrude above ground are not affected, nor do scabs increase in the clamp. Tubers are the most readily infected; if they have a long growing period, the period during which they become scabby is increased, hence, perhaps, the various reports that " spraying induces scab."

A strong earthy smell due to the presence of the actinomycete is peculiar to common scab; powdery scabs have no such smell. The fungus may overwinter either in the soil or in the scabs on tubers. It can survive on cellulose and similar plant products in the soil for years at a time. Several instances have been reported in which disinfected tubers planted in freshly broken forest soil produced scabby crops.

On the other hand an interval of several years between potato crops has sometimes led to a striking reduction in the amount of scab. The fungus reproduces simply by its fine hyphae breaking up to form spores, easily disseminated in soil and water. Manure may be regarded as infected if it comes from farms where scabby potatoes are used raw as fodder. Infection may also be spread by compost and, of course, by planting infected tubers.

VARIETAL SUSCEPTIBILITY

No potato variety completely resistant to common scab is known and on soil favourable to the fungus all varieties are attacked to about the same extent. Early varieties tend to escape infection, probably because the cork layer in their skin is formed before the soil becomes warm enough to suit the fungus. Main crop varieties do show some differences in susceptibility, probably associated in part with the size and texture of their lenticels.

Breeding for scab resistance is in progress in Minnesota where the possibility of physiological races of the fungus is also under investigation. Disinfection of the tubers is effective in destroying the scab fungus on them but is only of value when they are to be planted on scab-free soil, or in soil treated with sulphur or otherwise disinfected.

Digging in grass cuttings may be effective in gardens or allotments provided they are available in sufficient quantity. Up to a stone per square yard has been recommended. On a field scale ploughing in rye or other green manure in the spring may be helpful. Consistent use of sulphate of ammonia instead of chili saltpetre will gradually reduce the amount of scab, but one must be careful that the soil is not made too acid for other crops that need lime.

Combined use of dung and sulphate of ammonia has proved helpful. The proprietary preparation Bayer P. at the rate of about 1 oz. per square yard or 54 lb. per acre, dug well in before the potatoes are planted, may greatly reduce both common scab and stem canker.

It works very well when used with sulphate of ammonia. Liming may be necessary because of other crops in the rotation, but it is well to have the soil analysed and to apply only the lime requirement. Where it is important to obtain a crop of smooth tubers a piece of ground may be kept unlimed for potato production. Continuous cropping with potatoes is liable, however, to lead to trouble from other diseases and especially from root eelworm.

METHODS OF SPREAD AND REQUIREMENTS FOR INFECTION

The most important and most dangerous means by which infection spreads is the transport of seed potatoes, not only diseased tubers but healthy potatoes from infected land, which may carry resting sporangia in the soil adhering to them. Potato peelings in kitchen waste added to compost heaps or manure and dung of animals fed on raw potatoes may also carry infection.

The fungus may be carried from infected land in soil on carts, tools, boots, and the feet of domestic animals and poultry. Soil particles transported by storms, or floods, or by crows and other wild birds may also spread the disease.

Resting sporangia can germinate over a wide temperature range (40 to 86° F.) but best at 66-68° F. Presence of oxygen and nitrates encourages germination. Invasion of the host cells by the swarm spores also occurs over a wide temperature range (45-86° F.), best at 60-68° F., and oxygen is needed for this process. Soil reaction seems to have little effect on infection. It occurs over the whole range between pH 3.9 and 7.5, even pH 5 is said to be quite favourable.

Soils more acid than these are seldom cultivated and one can feel no assurance that infection will not occur on soils more alkaline than 7.5. No essential difference has been found between infection on clay and sandy soils. Extreme drought may completely prevent outbreak of potato wart disease.

On the other hand the warts become particularly large with a heavy fall of rain. Plants that mature early or form no tubers owing to virus disease, etc., may escape attack, as may very early varieties. Resting sporangia in the soil survive longest when the ground is under permanent grass or is left unbroken for other reasons. After a severe outbreak infection has been proved to persist in the soil for 12-16 years. Wart disease is easily and completely controlled by growing immune varieties. No potatoes from an infected crop may be sold for planting and no tubers visibly affected with wart disease may be sold for any purpose. Only approved immune varieties of potato may be grown on land where wart disease has occurred at any time.

In a scheduled Protected Area the only potatoes allowed to be planted are tubers from a crop certified to conform to official standards of purity and health and to have been grown on land free from wart disease.

It is also forbidden to remove rubbish or compost from such places or to dispose of manure. Export of tubers from boroughs where infected areas occur is also prohibited. There is no practicable method of destroying wart disease resting sporangia in a field soil. On a very small scale soil can be disinfected by steaming; baking the soil is not effective. Treatment of soil with 5 per cent formalin for 24 hours also kills the sporangia.

Incorporation of sulphur in the soil also has some effect but only in large quantities which make the soil sour and are unreasonably expensive. Implements used on infected land may be disinfected by dipping in 2 per cent formalin solution, but disinfection of potato " seed " has not proved effective. Cooking of potatoes used as fodder helps to prevent contamination of manure and is, in any case, required by the Wart Disease Order as far as infected tubers are concerned.

POWDERY SCAB

Powdery scab, sometimes known also as corky scab, first appears on the skin of potato tubers as pale little pimples. Either before or after lifting, the skin over the pimple splits and falls off, exposing a snuff-brown powder composed of the spore balls of the fungus.

For a considerable time the individual powdery scab remains as a shallow crater-like hollow, filled with brown powder and fringed by the loose edges of burst skin. Under good cultural conditions the scab seldom exceeds, but in potatoes grown in wet land or which have made considerable second growth, large open scabs and cankers may be formed, especially on the ends and protuberances of the tuber.

In such extreme forms of the disease microscopic examination may be needed for confident diagnosis. Corticium solani may be found in the wounds and various other secondary organisms may enter and set up a rot. In exceptional circumstances the fungus may continue its activity on tubers in the clamp and stimulate them to production of irregular tumour-like outgrowths closely resembling those of wart disease. Spongospora subterranea also attacks the roots of potatoes, and less often of tomato, causing irregular white nodules.

It is doubtful if these cause any damage to the plant but they contain spores which are liberated into the soil when the roots decay and thus add to the reservoir of infection in the ground. S. subterranea is one of the most primitive fungi, a relative of the fungus which causes club root in cabbages. Its spores, which are stuck together in peculiar sponge-like balls, can remain alive in the soil for 4-5 years at least and are easily spread to new localities in soil on tubers or by adhering to roots of transplants. When they germinate they liberate swarm spores which penetrate either the roots through root hairs or the tubers through lenticels or small wounds. Cultural conditions.

Powdery scab is found on both sides of the Atlantic and in the potato-growing districts, but is only of importance where there is a heavy rainfall and on ill-drained soils. In dry soils a reasonably clean crop may be lifted even though grown from infected tubers.

No varieties are immune from the disease but there is some difference in susceptibility, said to be correlated with the thickness of the cork layer in the skin of the tuber. Liming is said to make the trouble worse, and application of sulphur at the rate of 3-6 cwt. per acre checks it.

Where the disease is prevalent, soil drainage should be made as efficient as possible and the rotation should be arranged to leave 4-5 years between potato or tomato crops. Soil disinfection is impracticable in the field. Diseased tubers should not be returned to the land but may be cooked and used for fodder.

Manure from animals fed on raw infected potatoes will contain undamaged spores and should not be used for potato fields, nor should potato peelings and similar kitchen refuse be put in the compost heap. Disinfection may be practised where infected tubers have to be used on land free from the disease. They may be dipped for 3 hours in formalin solution, 1 pint of formalin in 30 gallons water, or 1: 2,000 corrosive sublimate solution. Moistening the tubers and rolling them in powdered sulphur may also be effective. Spores of closed scabs still in the pimple stage may not be killed by any of these methods.

Secondary Scab Injury

Both in common and powdery scab, especially when associated with second growth, the damage is often increased by the activity of a number of insects and other pests, such as the larvae of Sciara flies, wood lice, and millipedes which penetrate the outer layers of the tuber flesh by way of the scabs and cracks and convert it into a dry crumbling crust. The stem eelworm Anguillulina dipsaci produces extreme crust-like rotting of this kind. Secondary fungi may also play a part; even dry rot often starts at a powdery scab lesion. When storage conditions are too damp, or too warm, soft-rotting bacteria obtain easy access to the damaged tissue and the whole tuber decays.

VERTICILLIUM WILT

The symptoms of Verticillium wilt in potato usually develop only after the haulm has attained a normal size, though in extreme cases it may be stunted, with all the leaves rolled, and yields a negligible crop. More often, from July onwards, the leaves become limp and turn yellow at the tips and edges. Often one side of the leaf turns yellow and dies. Finally the leaves die and hang down brown and shrivelled against the stem, so that the whole plant gradually dries from below upwards.

Characteristic of the disease is the brown stain in the woody strands, often extending throughout the whole haulm. In autumn a delicate velvety white mould of conidiophores may appear on the base of the dying plants, and finally the stem may be blackened by the minute resting bodies of the fungus. Tubers on infected plants are usually also infected from the stolons, and if one slices them at the heel end the vascular bundles will be found to be brown, often far into the flesh. Brown vascular bundles occur also in Fusarium wilt, black-leg and other diseases, including leaf roll, and some forms of slight frost damage.

There is no natural separating layer between the tuber and the stolon so that when the crop is lifted a small wound is inevitably made at the heel end which takes a little time to heal. Before the cause of potato leaf roll was understood it was frequently confused with Verticillium wilt and there was consequently a tendency to exaggerate the prevalence and importance of the latter disease.

EFFECT OF ENVIRONMENT

Verticillium wilt is widespread on both sides of the Atlantic but in warm climates it tends to be superseded by Fusarium wilt. High temperatures check the growth of the fungus but the drought and excessive transpiration accompanying them usually kill all the infected potato plants. Experiments have indicated that heavy nitrogenous manuring increases the susceptibility of the crop; soil reaction has little effect. Provided a normal rotation of crops is practised the disease is unlikely to become prevalent. Crops containing many infected plants should be used for ware only.

If a few plants show Verticillium wilt in a crop grown for " seed " they should be dug out and burnt, preferably with those on each side in the drill as otherwise a few infected tubers may be left and lifted with the crop.

Also neighbouring plants may have become infected by root contact and if this occurs late in the season they may not show distinctive symptoms before the haulm begins to ripen off.

FUSARIUM WILT

It is associated with a brown discolouration of the vascular bundles throughout the plant, as in Verticillium wilt; indeed, the two diseases can only be distinguished with certainty by isolation of the fungus in pure culture. The FusaHum enters the tubers along the vascular bundles from the stolons and in the worst cases it grows through them all round the tuber so that a brown ring is visible when it is cut in half. During the winter the fungus slowly grows into the flesh and may cause rotting of the whole tuber.

If those only slightly infected are planted they give rise to infected shoots which grow only into small stunted plants. Fusarium oxysporum requires a fairly high temperature; it makes scarcely any growth at 48° F. and its optimum lies between 77° and 86° F. In cool climates it is only likely to be troublesome in potatoes forced under glass. Warm, damp soils favour infection but drought hastens the death of the infected plant. Trouble is not likely to arise even in forced potatoes if they are raised from " seed " from a normal field crop. If the disease does occur potatoes should not be grown in the same soil for several years.

BLACK DOT

This very common fungus may damage potato haulm in dry seasons. The stems are attacked just below soil level, and become marked or even girdled by dark-brown or blackish lesions from which the skin breaks away. Girdling of the stems leads to yellowing and rolling of the leaves and premature dying of the haulm. The fungus is common on the tubers where it causes silvery grey patches covered with tiny black dots like those of silver scurf. It may also girdle the stolons and penetrate some distance up the stems along the vascular bundles.

The tiny black sclerotia, sometimes bearing conidia on their surface, may be found on any of the diseased tissues. King Edward, Red King and Doon Star are considered to be susceptible varieties. The fungus is cosmopolitan and has been described under several other names, of which Vermicularia variant

Ducom. is that most used on the Continent. It is regarded as a serious parasite in France but is of little consequence in cooler climates. The fungus is better known as a parasite of tomato and egg plant.

DRY ROT

During storage of potatoes numerous species of Fusarium may gain access to the flesh of damaged tubers, sometimes through wounds but mainly through tissues already killed by blight. Dead patches of tissue caused by sun scald or damaged by disinfectant or other chemicals may also afford entry to weak parasites. Susceptibility of the tubers to these rots increases during the winter. True dry rot, however, is caused mainly by one easily recognized species of Fusarium coeruleum, so-called because its conidial pustules instead of being salmon pink have more or less of a blue tint. They may be covered with a white or pinkish spore powder but if this is rubbed off the blue colour will be found in the base of the pustules. It also sometimes appears in the mycelium, lining cavities in the rotting flesh. F. coeruleum is an active parasite though it may often gain access to the tuber through a scab wound or a bruise.

The first sign of dry rot is a brown patch on the skin, which rapidly increases in size, becomes slightly sunken and surrounded by concentric wrinkles. The underlying flesh is deeply penetrated by a soft brown rot, full of cavities lined with white or blue mycelium, and giving off a peculiar sweetish smell. In time the rot destroys the whole tuber which becomes hard, dry, shrivelled and very light in weight. The characteristic conidial pustules burst through the dead skin.

BLACK SCURF AND STEM CANKER

This, one of the commonest and most cosmopolitan of fungi, was first recognized in connection with potatoes, with which it is almost invariably found. But it also attacks many other plants, cabbage, tomato, wheat, lettuce, asters, though sometimes in the form of a specialized strain more or less adapted to a particular host, and has been found on many weeds such as buttercup, shepherd's purse, field thistle, plantain, etc. It can also live freely in the soil. More recent studies have made it possible to sub-divide this very large genus into a number of smaller more clearly denned genera.

When this is done C. solani falls in the genus Pellicu-laria and some authors think it identical with a fungus described earlier under the name Hypochnus filamentosa Pat., hence it has been re-christened Pellicularia filamentosa. This name has not yet, however, been generally accepted.

On potato tubers one often finds hard scurfy patches to which the soil adheres. When the tubers are washed these patches show up as dark-brown or black spots and lumps. They are the sclerotia of C. solaniy sometimes described as "The dirt that won't wash off." They are attached to the skin by very fine hyphae and can be scratched off with the finger nail, leaving the uninjured skin of the tuber beneath. Apart from making ware potatoes a little unsightly this phase of the fungus's life history does no immediate damage. Occasionally it has been found to attack tubers through the lenticels before they are lifted, causing small shallow brown pits rather like those of pit rot. When "seed" tubers carrying C. solani sclerotia are planted, however, the fungus becomes active again and many cause more or less serious injury to the sprouts. It may be found on the young sprouts even in the chitting boxes but most damage is done after planting. Then sunken brown spots appear on the sprouts below soil level. Or the tip of the shoot may be killed before it emerges above ground; it then puts out a side shoot which may escape or may also be killed.

In the worst cases groups of such dead shoots are found with the result that blanks occur in the potato drill. Later in the summer the fungus causes dry, brown, sunken wounds on the underground parts of the stems. If these are deep and girdle the stems the haulm may be weakened and the leaves roll, somewhat as in primary leaf roll though less stiffly. When the starch cannot reach the tubers, green aerial tubers are produced in the axils of the leaves. Brown lesions also appear on the stolons, which may be killed. The plant then forms merely a cluster of small angular tubers round the base of the haulm. The roots too may be attacked, especially the fine absorbing rootlets.

In all these brown sunken lesions only the mycelium of the fungus, or occasionally Rhizoctonia sclerotia, can be found. But at the base of vigourous haulms where the air remains moist the fungus covers the stems just above soil level with a white powdery film, sometimes extending up them to a height of 6 inches. This film consists of a layer of basidia and basidiospores. No harm seems to be done to the plants by this sporing stage of the fungus but it offers special possibility for its spread by means of wind-blown spores. The effect of an attack on yield of tubers varies greatly from practically nothing to severe losses where the fungus has caused extensive gaps in the drills.

Conditions of Growth

Potato sprouts may be infected partly from the see"d tubers, partly from the soil. The fungus seems to thrive in all cultivated soils, is not much affected by soil reaction and can grow over a wide range of temperatures. The rate at which the tubers sprout determines the severity of the disease in spring because the damage is greater when potatoes are planted early in cold soil; nevertheless early planting generally pays! As a rule lavish use of dung and artificial manures helps the crop.

SILVER SCURF

Sometimes silvery patches of skin are noticeable on potato tubers, especially when they are washed. The underlying tissue may be quite normal or a little darker than usual. Silver scurf is seldom seen at lifting time but develops in the clamp and may be regarded as a slight blemish rather than a disease. In wet clamps the condition may be widespread and extensively affected tubers may tend to shrivel if stored afterwards in a dry place.

Otherwise no real harm is done. Under warm, damp conditions a black velvety layer of short conidiophores and conidia appears on the silvery patches, springing from very tiny black specks in the skin, rather like the tiny sclerotia of Colletotrichum atramen-tarium. No control measures are normally called for, but if the fungus becomes undesirably prevalent a longer interval between potato crops should be tried, as infection of the tubers is derived from the soil.

PINK ROT

The fungus, which occurs in the soil, may attack the underground parts of the haulm and the stolons, sometimes causing the plants to wilt, but this usually happens only at the end of the season. Losses from the disease are due to infection of the tubers.. This occurs normally at the heel end while they are still attached to the parent plant, but the fungus may also sometimes gain access through an eye or a wound. Inside the tuber it causes rather a rapid rot but the diseased potato remains fairly firm until it is completely killed. When squeezed, however, sap generally oozes from it.

If an infected tuber is cut and exposed to the air the flesh turns pink in a few minutes and within half an hour the whole diseased portion becomes salmon-coloured. Later it slowly turns purplish-brown or blackish-brown. Similar colouration may occasionally occur in healthy tubers or in those attacked by black-leg. The infected tubers decay fairly quickly and are not likely to survive until planting time, hence there is little risk of spreading the disease with the " seed." As the causal organism is a soil-borne water-mould, thorough drainage of potato fields is desirable and a long rotation should help to prevent infection of the soil being built up to a dangerous level. All infected tubers should be destroyed, not dug or ploughed back into the land.

JELLY-END ROT

This is a physiological disorder associated with a form of second growth, especially in Arran Pilot. When second growth occurs evenly over the rose end of the tuber, so that it becomes abnormally elongated, the tissue at the heel end loses its starch and becomes soft, flabby and shrunken. Ultimately it usually shrivels up and falls off leaving an irregular scar.

WET ROT

Even at lifting, tubers may be found that are completely soft and rotten; as a rule they are from a black-leg plant or have been suffocated by flooding or puddling of the soil. Potatoes that have been attacked by blight and black-leg or have been damaged during lifting and bruised by rough handling in transit, packed tightly in railway vans or in a ship's hold, or stored under ill-ventilated conditions, may be transformed in a few days into a rotten mess. Numerous species of bacteria may play a part in this decay. If heating in the clamp is discovered in time and ventilation is supplied many of the tubers will merely develop black-heart. If not, and the temperature continues to rise, the potatoes will be suffocated and afterwards reduced to a soft, stinking, slimy mass by the common putrefactive bacteria that cannot attack living tissues.

VIRUS DISEASES

Virus diseases occur wherever potatoes are grown, though they only spread rapidly in climates favourable to their insect vectors, hence potatoes grown in some mountainous countries and in exposed wet maritime districts can be kept free from viruses without great difficulty. In commercial potato fields the virus-infected plants occur scattered throughout the crop because they arose from tubers which were already infected when they were planted. Secondary spread of the diseases within the crop is usually evident only late in the season or only in plants grown from the harvested tubers the following year.

In lowland districts the decline in productivity resulting from virus infection would render potato production uneconomic if fresh " seed " tubers were not secured every few years from a suitable " seed " producing region. Tubers from a diseased plant mostly contain the virus or viruses that have attacked it but a few may sometimes escape infection. Once a tuber has become infected, it, and the plant grown from it, always remain diseased. Hence the primary source of potato virus disease is the planting of diseased tubers. It is impossible to tell from its appearance or by any chemical test whether a tuber is virus-infected or not.

The symptoms caused by infection by a potato virus vary greatly, partly according to the variety of potato infected, partly according to the time elapsed since infection (symptoms in the second years are often very different and more severe than those in the season of infection) and partly according to environmental conditions, for heavy manuring, especially with nitrogen, and warmth may " mask " the symptoms in the haulm.

Carriers, varieties which can be or always are infected with a particular virus without showing any symptoms, are common among potato varieties. In practice potato virus diseases are usually referred to one of four categories, irrespective of the particular virus present. These are leaf roll, mild mosaic, severe mosaic and aucuba mosaic. This is the most destructive of all potato virus diseases and the most difficult to control. Rolling of the leaves may also be caused by drought, waterlogging, fume damage, Corticium solani, black-leg, insect damage to the stem, eelworm and the like, but in all these cases the rolled leaves are limp or at least pliable, and usually it is the upper young leaves that are affected.

In true leaf roll, derived from a diseased tuber, the lower leaves are rolled, point more or less upwards and are stiff and hard. Mild mosaic is defined as a mild light and dark green mottle, in which the leaves are neither distorted nor reduced in size. It may be so faint as to be visible only on a cloudy day or when the leaf is held to the light. Often it is clearest in the young haulm, and less apparent in late summer and autumn. Mottling may also result from manganese or magnesium deficiency, but then the whole haulm is usually affected throughout a field or in considerable parts of it. Aucuba mosaic, so called from a fancied resemblance to the variegated leaf of Aucuba japonica, is recognized by clearly defined, bright yellow spots scattered over the lowest leaves.

The leaves are not distorted and are of normal size, and the plant seems to suffer little from the disease. Somewhat similar variegation may result from spring frosts. This includes all diseases of the mosaic type in which the surface of the leaves is roughened, crinkled, streaked with dark lines, distorted or reduced in size and in which the haulm is more or less stunted, especially in the year after infection.

OTHER VIRUS DISEASES OF THE HAULM

Paracrinkle is a peculiarly severe form of crinkle caused in the stock when a scion of King Edward potato is grafted on certain other varieties. All King Edward plants contain the para-crinkle virus without suffering any ill effect from it. Paracrinkle is purely a laboratory disease; it has never been seen in the field and no means of transmitting it other than grafting has yet been discovered. Top necrosis begins by the appearance of numerous small brown dead spots on the youngest leaves. These rapidly spread and the shoot dies back from the tip. If any tubers were formed before the plant died, corky spots develop in them during storage and they either die before planting or, at best, give a weak shoot which soon dies.

Top necrosis is very seldom seen in a field crop but it is of practical importance in two ways. In the first place different potato varieties react by top necrosis to different viruses. Hence grafting scions from a plant under examination to a selected number of indicator varieties is a standard method of identifying the viruses it contains. This method is particularly valuable in detecting "carried" viruses. Secondly, because the progeny of a plant that reacts by top necrosis are all killed, this is a self-eliminating disease. A virus cannot be perpetuated in a potato variety in which it causes top necrosis. Hence much attention has been paid to breeding new potato varieties which react by top necrosis to as many viruses as possible.

VIRUS DISEASE OF THE TUBERS

Net necrosis is the name given to a fine brown network in the flesh of the tuber. This is a reaction of certain varieties, notably Golden Wonder, in the year they become infected with leaf roll. That is, tubers with net necrosis produce plants with primary leaf roll but these do not, as a rule, yield more tubers showing net necrosis. A somewhat similar brown network may be the result of slight frosting of the tuber.

Tuber blotch refers to small brown spots or blotches in the flesh of the tuber, rather like those known as internal rust spot. The condition may be a result of infection with Solanum Viruses. Potato varieties all react in much the same way to Solanum Virus, the cause of leaf roll, though the symptoms are more pronounced in some, e.g. President, than in others like Great Scot.

Their reaction to Solanum Virus 2 also differs in intensity rather than in kind. They react very differently, some by top necrosis, others by a mild mosaic or by showing no symptoms of disease at all.

METHODS OF SPREAD AND REQUIREMENTS FOR INFECTION IN POTATO

The most important and most dangerous means by which infection spreads is the transport of seed potatoes, not only diseased tubers but healthy potatoes from infected land, which may carry resting sporangia in the soil adhering to them. Potato peelings in kitchen waste added to compost heaps or manure and dung of animals fed on raw potatoes may also carry infection.

The fungus may be carried from infected land in soil on carts, tools, boots, and the feet of domestic animals and poultry. Soil particles transported by storms, or floods, or by crows and other wild birds may also spread the disease.

Resting sporangia can germinate over a wide temperature range (40 to 86° F.) but best at 66-68° F. Presence of oxygen and nitrates encourages germination. Invasion of the host cells by the swarm spores also occurs over a wide temperature range (45-86° F.), best at 60-68° F., and oxygen is needed for this process. Soil reaction seems to have little effect on infection. It occurs over the whole range between pH 3.9 and 7.5, even pH 5 is said to be quite favourable.

Soils more acid than these are seldom cultivated and one can feel no assurance that infection will not occur on soils more alkaline than 7.5. No essential difference has been found between infection on clay and sandy soils. Extreme drought may completely prevent outbreak of potato wart disease.

On the other hand the warts become particularly large with a heavy fall of rain. Plants that mature early or form no tubers owing to virus disease, etc., may escape attack, as may very early varieties. Resting sporangia in the soil survive longest when the ground is under permanent grass or is left unbroken for other reasons.

After a severe outbreak infection has been proved to persist in the soil for 12-16 years. Wart disease is easily and completely controlled by growing immune varieties. No potatoes from an infected crop may be sold for planting and no tubers visibly affected with wart disease may be sold for any purpose. Only approved immune varieties of potato may be grown on land where wart disease has occurred at any time. In a scheduled Protected Area the only potatoes allowed to be planted are tubers from a crop certified to conform to official standards of purity and health and to have been grown on land free from wart disease. It is also forbidden to remove rubbish or compost from such places or to dispose of manure. Export of tubers from boroughs where infected areas occur is also prohibited. There is no practicable method of destroying wart disease resting sporangia in a field soil. On a very small scale soil can be disinfected by steaming; baking the soil is not effective. Treatment of soil with 5 per cent formalin for 24 hours also kills the sporangia.

Incorporation of sulphur in the soil also has some effect but only in large quantities which make the soil sour and are unreasonably expensive. Implements used on infected land may be disinfected by dipping in 2 per cent formalin solution, but disinfection of potato " seed " has not proved effective. Cooking of potatoes used as fodder helps to prevent contamination of manure and is, in any case, required by the Wart Disease Order as far as infected tubers are concerned.

POWDERY SCAB

Powdery scab, sometimes known also as corky scab, first appears on the skin of potato tubers as pale little pimples. Either before or after lifting, the skin over the pimple splits and falls off, exposing a snuff-brown powder composed of the spore balls of the fungus.

For a considerable time the individual powdery scab remains as a shallow crater-like hollow, filled with brown powder and fringed by the loose edges of burst skin. Under good cultural conditions the scab seldom exceeds, but in potatoes grown in wet land or which have made considerable second growth, large open scabs and cankers may be formed, especially on the ends and protuberances of the tuber. In such extreme forms of the disease microscopic examination may be needed for confident diagnosis. Corticium solani may be found in the wounds and various other secondary organisms may enter and set up a rot. In exceptional circumstances the fungus may continue its activity on tubers in the clamp and stimulate them to production of irregular tumour-like outgrowths closely resembling those of wart disease. Spongospora subterranea also attacks the roots of potatoes, and less often of tomato, causing irregular white nodules. It is doubtful if these cause any damage to the plant but they contain spores which are liberated into the soil when the roots decay and thus add to the reservoir of infection in the ground. S. subterranea is one of the most primitive fungi, a relative of the fungus which causes club root in cabbages. Its spores, which are stuck together in peculiar sponge-like balls, can remain alive in the soil for 4-5 years at least and are easily spread to new localities in soil on tubers or by adhering to roots of transplants. When they germinate they liberate swarm spores which penetrate either the roots through root hairs or the tubers through lenticels or small wounds. Cultural conditions.

Powdery scab is found on both sides of the Atlantic and in the potato-growing districts, but is only of importance where there is a heavy rainfall and on ill-drained soils. In dry soils a reasonably clean crop may be lifted even though grown from infected tubers. No varieties are immune from the disease but there is some difference in susceptibility, said to be correlated with the thickness of the cork layer in the skin of the tuber. Liming is said to make the trouble worse, and application of sulphur at the rate of 3-6 cwt. per acre checks it.

Where the disease is prevalent, soil drainage should be made as efficient as possible and the rotation should be arranged to leave 4-5 years between potato or tomato crops. Soil disinfection is impracticable in the field. Diseased tubers should not be returned to the land but may be cooked and used for fodder.

Manure from animals fed on raw infected potatoes will contain undamaged spores and should not be used for potato fields, nor should potato peelings and similar kitchen refuse be put in the compost heap. Disinfection may be practised where infected tubers have to be used on land free from the disease. They may be dipped for 3 hours in formalin solution, 1 pint of formalin in 30 gallons water, or 1: 2,000 corrosive sublimate solution. Moistening the tubers and rolling them in powdered sulphur may also be effective. Spores of closed scabs still in the pimple stage may not be killed by any of these methods.

Secondary Scab Injury

Both in common and powdery scab, especially when associated with second growth, the damage is often increased by the activity of a number of insects and other pests, such as the larvae of Sciara flies, wood lice, and millipedes which penetrate the outer layers of the tuber flesh by way of the scabs and cracks and convert it into a dry crumbling crust. The stem eelworm Anguillulina dipsaci produces extreme crust-like rotting of this kind. Secondary fungi may also play a part; even dry rot often starts at a powdery scab lesion. When storage conditions are too damp, or too warm, soft-rotting bacteria obtain easy access to the damaged tissue and the whole tuber decays.

VERTICILLIUM WILT

The symptoms of Verticillium wilt in potato usually develop only after the haulm has attained a normal size, though in extreme cases it may be stunted, with all the leaves rolled, and yields a negligible crop. More often, from July onwards, the leaves become limp and turn yellow at the tips and edges. Often one side of the leaf turns yellow and dies. Finally the leaves die and hang down brown and shrivelled against the stem, so that the whole plant gradually dries from below upwards.

Characteristic of the disease is the brown stain in the woody strands, often extending throughout the whole haulm. In autumn a delicate velvety white mould of conidiophores may appear on the base of the dying plants, and finally the stem may be blackened by the minute resting bodies of the fungus. Tubers on infected plants are usually also infected from the stolons, and if one slices them at the heel end the vascular bundles will be found to be brown, often far into the flesh. Brown vascular bundles occur also in Fusarium wilt, black-leg and other diseases, including leaf roll, and some forms of slight frost damage.

There is no natural separating layer between the tuber and the stolon so that when the crop is lifted a small wound is inevitably made at the heel end which takes a little time to heal. Before the cause of potato leaf roll was understood it was frequently confused with Verticillium wilt and there was consequently a tendency to exaggerate the prevalence and importance of the latter disease.

EFFECT OF ENVIRONMENT IN POTATO

Verticillium wilt is widespread on both sides of the Atlantic but in warm climates it tends to be superseded by Fusarium wilt. High temperatures check the growth of the fungus but the drought and excessive transpiration accompanying them usually kill all the infected potato plants. Experiments have indicated that heavy nitrogenous manuring increases the susceptibility of the crop; soil reaction has little effect. Provided a normal rotation of crops is practised the disease is unlikely to become prevalent. Crops containing many infected plants should be used for ware only.

If a few plants show Verticillium wilt in a crop grown for " seed " they should be dug out and burnt, preferably with those on each side in the drill as otherwise a few infected tubers may be left and lifted with the crop.

Also neighbouring plants may have become infected by root contact and if this occurs late in the season they may not show distinctive symptoms before the haulm begins to ripen off.

FUSARIUM WILT

It is associated with a brown discolouration of the vascular bundles throughout the plant, as in Verticillium wilt; indeed, the two diseases can only be distinguished with certainty by isolation of the fungus in pure culture. The FusaHum enters the tubers along the vascular bundles from the stolons and in the worst cases it grows through them all round the tuber so that a brown ring is visible when it is cut in half. During the winter the fungus slowly grows into the flesh and may cause rotting of the whole tuber.

If those only slightly infected are planted they give rise to infected shoots which grow only into small stunted plants. Fusarium oxysporum requires a fairly high temperature; it makes scarcely any growth at 48° F. and its optimum lies between 77° and 86° F. In cool climates it is only likely to be troublesome in potatoes forced under glass. Warm, damp soils favour infection but drought hastens the death of the infected plant. Trouble is not likely to arise even in forced potatoes if they are raised from " seed " from a normal field crop. If the disease does occur potatoes should not be grown in the same soil for several years.

BLACK DOT

This very common fungus may damage potato haulm in dry seasons. The stems are attacked just below soil level, and become marked or even girdled by dark-brown or blackish lesions from which the skin breaks away. Girdling of the stems leads to yellowing and rolling of the leaves and premature dying of the haulm. The fungus is common on the tubers where it causes silvery grey patches covered with tiny black dots like those of silver scurf. It may also girdle the stolons and penetrate some distance up the stems along the vascular bundles. The tiny black sclerotia, sometimes bearing conidia on their surface, may be found on any of the diseased tissues. King Edward, Red King and Doon Star are considered to be susceptible varieties. The fungus is cosmopolitan and has been described under several other names, of which Vermicularia variant Ducom. is that most used on the Continent. It is regarded as a serious parasite in France but is of little consequence in cooler climates. The fungus is better known as a parasite of tomato and egg plant.

DRY ROT

During storage of potatoes numerous species of Fusarium may gain access to the flesh of damaged tubers, sometimes through wounds but mainly through tissues already killed by blight. Dead patches of tissue caused by sun scald or damaged by disinfectant or other chemicals may also afford entry to weak parasites. Susceptibility of the tubers to these rots increases during the winter. True dry rot, however, is caused mainly by one easily recognized species of Fusarium coeruleum, so-called because its conidial pustules instead of being salmon pink have more or less of a blue tint. They may be covered with a white or pinkish spore powder but if this is rubbed off the blue colour will be found in the base of the pustules. It also sometimes appears in the mycelium, lining cavities in the rotting flesh. F. coeruleum is an active parasite though it may often gain access to the tuber through a scab wound or a bruise. The first sign of dry rot is a brown patch on the skin, which rapidly increases in size, becomes slightly sunken and surrounded by concentric wrinkles. The underlying flesh is deeply penetrated by a soft brown rot, full of cavities lined with white or blue mycelium, and giving off a peculiar sweetish smell. In time the rot destroys the whole tuber which becomes hard, dry, shrivelled and very light in weight. The characteristic conidial pustules burst through the dead skin.

BLACK SCURF AND STEM CANKER

This, one of the commonest and most cosmopolitan of fungi, was first recognized in connection with potatoes, with which it is almost invariably found. But it also attacks many other plants, cabbage, tomato, wheat, lettuce, asters, though sometimes in the form of a specialized strain more or less adapted to a particular host, and has been found on many weeds such as buttercup, shepherd's purse, field thistle, plantain, etc. It can also live freely in the soil. More recent studies have made it possible to sub-divide this very large genus into a number of smaller more clearly denned genera.

When this is done C. solani falls in the genus Pellicu-laria and some authors think it identical with a fungus described earlier under the name Hypochnus filamentosa Pat., hence it has been re-christened Pellicularia filamentosa. This name has not yet, however, been generally accepted.

On potato tubers one often finds hard scurfy patches to which the soil adheres. When the tubers are washed these patches show up as dark-brown or black spots and lumps. They are the sclerotia of C. solaniy sometimes described as "The dirt that won't wash off." They are attached to the skin by very fine hyphae and can be scratched off with the finger nail, leaving the uninjured skin of the tuber beneath.

Apart from making ware potatoes a little unsightly this phase of the fungus's life history does no immediate damage. Occasionally it has been found to attack tubers through the lenticels before they are lifted, causing small shallow brown pits rather like those of pit rot. When "seed" tubers carrying C. solani sclerotia are planted, however, the fungus becomes active again and many cause more or less serious injury to the sprouts. It may be found on the young sprouts even in the chitting boxes but most damage is done after planting. Then sunken brown spots appear on the sprouts below soil level. Or the tip of the shoot may be killed before it emerges above ground; it then puts out a side shoot which may escape or may also be killed.

In the worst cases groups of such dead shoots are found with the result that blanks occur in the potato drill.

Later in the summer the fungus causes dry, brown, sunken wounds on the underground parts of the stems. If these are deep and girdle the stems the haulm may be weakened and the leaves roll, somewhat as in primary leaf roll though less stiffly. When the starch cannot reach the tubers, green aerial tubers are produced in the axils of the leaves. Brown lesions also appear on the stolons, which may be killed. The plant then forms merely a cluster of small angular tubers round the base of the haulm. The roots too may be attacked, especially the fine absorbing rootlets.

In all these brown sunken lesions only the mycelium of the fungus, or occasionally Rhizoctonia sclerotia, can be found. But at the base of vigourous haulms where the air remains moist the fungus covers the stems just above soil level with a white powdery film, sometimes extending up them to a height of 6 inches. This film consists of a layer of basidia and basidiospores. No harm seems to be done to the plants by this sporing stage of the fungus but it offers special possibility for its spread by means of wind-blown spores. The effect of an attack on yield of tubers varies greatly from practically nothing to severe losses where the fungus has caused extensive gaps in the drills.

Conditions of Growth

Potato sprouts may be infected partly from the see"d tubers, partly from the soil. The fungus seems to thrive in all cultivated soils, is not much affected by soil reaction and can grow over a wide range of temperatures. The rate at which the tubers sprout determines the severity of the disease in spring because the damage is greater when potatoes are planted early in cold soil; nevertheless early planting generally pays! As a rule lavish use of dung and artificial manures helps the crop.

SILVER SCURF

Sometimes silvery patches of skin are noticeable on potato tubers, especially when they are washed. The underlying tissue may be quite normal or a little darker than usual. Silver scurf is seldom seen at lifting time but develops in the clamp and may be regarded as a slight blemish rather than a disease. In wet clamps the condition may be widespread and extensively affected tubers may tend to shrivel if stored afterwards in a dry place.

Otherwise no real harm is done. Under warm, damp conditions a black velvety layer of short conidiophores and conidia appears on the silvery patches, springing from very tiny black specks in the skin, rather like the tiny sclerotia of Colletotrichum atramen-tarium. No control measures are normally called for, but if the fungus becomes undesirably prevalent a longer interval between potato crops should be tried, as infection of the tubers is derived from the soil.

PINK ROT

The fungus, which occurs in the soil, may attack the underground parts of the haulm and the stolons, sometimes causing the plants to wilt, but this usually happens only at the end of the season. Losses from the disease are due to infection of the tubers.. sThis occurs normally at the heel end while they are still attached to the parent plant, but the fungus may also sometimes gain access through an eye or a wound. Inside the tuber it causes rather a rapid rot but the diseased potato remains fairly firm until it is completely killed. When squeezed, however, sap generally oozes from it.

If an infected tuber is cut and exposed to the air the flesh turns pink in a few minutes and within half an hour the whole diseased portion becomes salmon-coloured. Later it slowly turns purplish-brown or blackish-brown. Similar colouration may occasionally occur in healthy tubers or in those attacked by black-leg. The infected tubers decay fairly quickly and are not likely to survive until planting time, hence there is little risk of spreading the disease with the " seed." As the causal organism is a soil-borne water-mould, thorough drainage of potato fields is desirable and a long rotation should help to prevent infection of the soil being built up to a dangerous level. All infected tubers should be destroyed, not dug or ploughed back into the land.

JELLY-END ROT

This is a physiological disorder associated with a form of second growth, especially in Arran Pilot. When second growth occurs evenly over the rose end of the tuber, so that it becomes abnormally elongated, the tissue at the heel end loses its starch and becomes soft, flabby and shrunken. Ultimately it usually shrivels up and falls off leaving an irregular scar.

WET ROT

Even at lifting, tubers may be found that are completely soft and rotten; as a rule they are from a black-leg plant or have been suffocated by flooding or puddling of the soil. Potatoes that have been attacked by blight and black-leg or have been damaged during lifting and bruised by rough handling in transit, packed tightly in railway vans or in a ship's hold, or stored under ill-ventilated conditions, may be transformed in a few days into a rotten mess. Numerous species of bacteria may play a part in this decay.

If heating in the clamp is discovered in time and ventilation is supplied many of the tubers will merely develop black-heart. If not, and the temperature continues to rise, the potatoes will be suffocated and afterwards reduced to a soft, stinking, slimy mass by the common putrefactive bacteria that cannot attack living tissues.

VIRUS DISEASES

Virus diseases occur wherever potatoes are grown, though they only spread rapidly in climates favourable to their insect vectors, hence potatoes grown in some mountainous countries and in exposed wet maritime districts can be kept free from viruses without great difficulty. In commercial potato fields the virus-infected plants occur scattered throughout the crop because they arose from tubers which were already infected when they were planted. Secondary spread of the diseases within the crop is usually evident only late in the season or only in plants grown from the harvested tubers the following year.

In lowland districts the decline in productivity resulting from virus infection would render potato production uneconomic if fresh " seed " tubers were not secured every few years from a suitable " seed " producing region. Tubers from a diseased plant mostly contain the virus or viruses that have attacked it but a few may sometimes escape infection. Once a tuber has become infected, it, and the plant grown from it, always remain diseased. Hence the primary source of potato virus disease is the planting of diseased tubers. It is impossible to tell from its appearance or by any chemical test whether a tuber is virus-infected or not.

The symptoms caused by infection by a potato virus vary greatly, partly according to the variety of potato infected, partly according to the time elapsed since infection (symptoms in the second years are often very different and more severe than those in the season of infection) and partly according to environmental conditions, for heavy manuring, especially with nitrogen, and warmth may " mask " the symptoms in the haulm.

Carriers, varieties which can be or always are infected with a particular virus without showing any symptoms, are common among potato varieties. In practice potato virus diseases are usually referred to one of four categories, irrespective of the particular virus present. These are leaf roll, mild mosaic, severe mosaic and aucuba mosaic. This is the most destructive of all potato virus diseases and the most difficult to control. Rolling of the leaves may also be caused by drought, waterlogging, fume damage, Corticium solani, black-leg, insect damage to the stem, eelworm and the like, but in all these cases the rolled leaves are limp or at least pliable, and usually it is the upper young leaves that are affected.

In true leaf roll, derived from a diseased tuber, the lower leaves are rolled, point more or less upwards and are stiff and hard. Mild mosaic is defined as a mild light and dark green mottle, in which the leaves are neither distorted nor reduced in size. It may be so faint as to be visible only on a cloudy day or when the leaf is held to the light. Often it is clearest in the young haulm, and less apparent in late summer and autumn. Mottling may also result from manganese or magnesium deficiency, but then the whole haulm is usually affected throughout a field or in considerable parts of it. Aucuba mosaic, so called from a fancied resemblance to the variegated leaf of Aucuba japonica, is recognized by clearly defined, bright yellow spots scattered over the lowest leaves.

The leaves are not distorted and are of normal size, and the plant seems to suffer little from the disease. Somewhat similar variegation may result from spring frosts. This includes all diseases of the mosaic type in which the surface of the leaves is roughened, crinkled, streaked with dark lines, distorted or reduced in size and in which the haulm is more or less stunted, especially in the year after infection.

OTHER VIRUS DISEASES OF THE HAULM

Paracrinkle is a peculiarly severe form of crinkle caused in the stock when a scion of King Edward potato is grafted on certain other varieties. All King Edward plants contain the para-crinkle virus without suffering any ill effect from it. Paracrinkle is purely a laboratory disease; it has never been seen in the field and no means of transmitting it other than grafting has yet been discovered. Top necrosis begins by the appearance of numerous small brown dead spots on the youngest leaves. These rapidly spread and the shoot dies back from the tip. If any tubers were formed before the plant died, corky spots develop in them during storage and they either die before planting or, at best, give a weak shoot which soon dies.

Top necrosis is very seldom seen in a field crop but it is of practical importance in two ways. In the first place different potato varieties react by top necrosis to different viruses. Hence grafting scions from a plant under examination to a selected number of indicator varieties is a standard method of identifying the viruses it contains. This method is particularly valuable in detecting "carried" viruses. Secondly, because the progeny of a plant that reacts by top necrosis are all killed, this is a self-eliminating disease. A virus cannot be perpetuated in a potato variety in which it causes top necrosis. Hence much attention has been paid to breeding new potato varieties which react by top necrosis to as many viruses as possible.

VIRUS DISEASE OF THE TUBERS

Net necrosis is the name given to a fine brown network in the flesh of the tuber. This is a reaction of certain varieties, notably Golden Wonder, in the year they become infected with leaf roll. That is, tubers with net necrosis produce plants with primary leaf roll but these do not, as a rule, yield more tubers showing net necrosis. A somewhat similar brown network may be the result of slight frosting of the tuber.

Tuber blotch refers to small brown spots or blotches in the flesh of the tuber, rather like those known as internal rust spot. The condition may be a result of infection with Solanum Viruses. Potato varieties all react in much the same way to Solanum Virus, the cause of leaf roll, though the symptoms are more pronounced in some, e.g. President, than in others like Great Scot.

Their reaction to Solanum Virus 2 also differs in intensity rather than in kind. They react very differently, some by top necrosis, others by a mild mosaic or by showing no symptoms of disease at all.

6

Leaf and Grass

At least 20 different fungi and one bacterium are pathogenic on maple foliage. Fortunately, leaf diseases seldom detract from the aesthetic values of maples, and even on those rare occasions when they do, they do not threaten the overall health of affected trees.

Most of the fungi that cause foliage diseases are extremely sensitive to environmental conditions, and higher disease incidence can be expected in years when spring and early summer weather is cool and wet for prolonged periods of time. Leaves in lower crowns and on north sides of trees are affected more often because they remain wet longer in the morning (following dew) and after rainy periods. The powdery mildews are exceptions in that they are favored by shade and dry foliage; they are most serious in mid- to late summer.

Leaf diseases can be prevented some what by pruning or thinning to improve air circulation through crowns. In nurseries, planting trees further apart also will help speed drying of foliage after it has been wetted. Overwintering sites for many leaf disease fungi are eliminated by collecting and disposing of fallen leaves in autumn. However, because these fungi are such prolific spore producers, a few missed leaves can provide sufficient spores to start a new epidemic. Protective fungicides give good control of some maple leaf diseases, but they must be applied before infection by pathogens occurs. Timing fungicide applications to immediately precede infection periods often is difficult, but failure to do so can result in wasted chemicals, time, and money.

LEAF DISEASES

ANTHRACNOSE LEAF BLIGHT OF SHADE TREES

A number of different trees are affected by anthracnose diseases. These fungal diseases can cause severe leaf blighting and deformation, but in many cases damage to plant health is not severe. However, with sycamore anthracnose and dogwood anthracnose, the fungus regularly moves back into stem tissue and causes more significant problems. Following are profiles of some of the more common anthracnose diseases of landscape trees.

KABATIELLA APOCRYPTA

Anthracnose diseases are generally not severe on maple, but can cause considerable unsightliness from brownish leaf blotches and some leaf drop when moist weather conditions make the disease particularly severe. Extensive development of stem infections is not common on maples, as it is with sycamore anthracnose and dogwood anthracnose.

The most common symptoms include brownish discolouration along veins, varying from discrete spots to irregular patches of discolouration bordered by veins. Spore masses of the fungus can sometimes be found on lower leaf surfaces along veins during extended moist conditions. The fungus spreads from previously infected tissue in spring to new growth. Where fungicides are used, applications must be started at bud break and continued during early leaf development. When fungicides are required, use labeled products containing mancozeb, thiophanate-methyl, or chlorothalonil.

APIOGNOMONIA ERRABUNDA

This anthracnose disease is primarily a leaf blighting and blotching disease of white ash and, to a lesser extent, green ash. Small twig cankers do occur and the fungus overwinters on these twig lesions, but little damage occurs from this phase of the disease. In wet, cool spring conditions, leaves and sometimes shoots first develop water soaked areas and later large tannish blotches and leaflet distortion.

Considerable leaf drop occurs, especially from lower areas of the canopy. Though this causes concern when leaves litter the ground in late spring, damage to overall plant health is not generally severe and plants typically releaf. As leaves mature they tend to become more resistant to infection. Fungicide applications, if warranted, should be made at bud break, with several repeat applications early in the season. When fungicide is required, use a labeled material containing thiophanate-methyl, chlorothalonil, or mancozeb.

APIOGNOMONIA QUERCINA

White oaks are the most susceptible of many oak species to this leaf blotching disease. Twig infections occur but are not significant except as sources of overwintering fungal inoculum from year to year. Leaves and shoots are infected during cool, wet spring conditions causing leaf blotches that often are strictly delimited by leaf veins.

Eventually, lesions become a papery tan colour and some leaf shriveling occurs. Multiple cycles of infection can occur. Just as leaves near maturity, lesion size lessens, and once leaves mature they become fully resistant by early to mid summer. Fungicides are generally not recommended. If fungicide is required, use a labeled material containing thiophanate-methyl, chlorothalonil or mancozeb.

APIOGNOMONIA VENETA

This is a potentially serious disease of American sycamore and to a lesser extent London planetree. Susceptibility of London planetree varies considerably with seed source. Shoot blight, leaf blight and twig and branch cankers and dieback can be severe. The fungus overwinters on twig tissue on the tree with spores splashing to new buds, shoots and leaves in the spring, with disease being enhanced by cool, wet conditions during shoot and leaf development. Considerable defoliation, sometimes with complete leaf loss, occurs on many trees by late spring in some years.

Trees typically releaf by early to mid summer and are less susceptible to continued infections because of warmer, drier conditions. Also, as leaves age they become less susceptible to infection. With repeated infections over the years, cankering of twigs and branches can result in erratic shoot growth that gives an overall distorted appearance to the tree, and also witches-brooming where there are numerous side shoots that develop around a central terminal shoot that was killed by the fungus. Fungicide applications to prevent infections in the spring are sometimes warranted. If fungicide is required, use a labeled material containing thiophanate-methyl, chlorothalonil or mancozeb. Fungicide injections (which are made by tree care professionals) are also used in spring and fall to systemically control the disease.

DISCULA DESTRUCTIVA

In recent years this disease has become prominent in certain areas, especially on flowering dogwood (Cornus florida). Dogwood anthracnose is most severe where cool, moist conditions occur during the summer, such as in higher elevation areas, and in densely vegetated shady sites with poor air movement. Leaf symptoms include irregular brown blotches bordered in purple on upper leaf surfaces (tan in colour viewed from the leaf underside). Leaf lesions often are delimited by the leaf midvein.

Stem symptoms include twig dieback and stem cankering and dieback, often with visible fungal fruiting bodies on dead twigs. Attached wilted, brown leaves often persist into the next spring instead of dropping in the fall.

Plants may be killed. Fungal infections occur during moist conditions and fungicides are recommended in the spring from the period of early bud break through bract fall and through early leaf development. When fungicide is required, use a labeled product containing propiconazole or mancozeb. Flowering dogwood should be planted in sites with good soil drainage and adequate organic matter.

Partially shaded sites, such as those with just morning sun are ideal. Plants should receive a moderate fertility programme, and should be mulched to moderate fluctuations in soil temperatures. Dead branches should be promptly pruned from the plant.

Control of Anthracnose Diseases

- Overall tree care programme. Use proper fertilization, pruning, watering, and pest control practices to encourage vigorous plant growth. This aids in general tolerance of the effects of disease and in rapid refoliation in years where disease is severe.
- Fungicide applications. If significant damage occurs yearly and controls are justified, properly applied fungicides may reduce damage from these diseases. High pressure spray equipment will be needed for large tree applications, and this typically requires the hiring of a professional tree care service.

Fungicides will not be effective unless they are applied before and during infection periods. Typically, three applications are necessary, beginning in early spring, with the first application made before leaf buds open. Applications in the fall have been shown to be useful for sycamore anthracnose control. Fungicide injections have also shown promise for sycamore anthracnose control. These must be applied by professional tree care companies.

VERTICILLIUM WILT OF LANDSCAPE TREES AND SHRUBS

Verticillium wilt, caused by the fungi Verticillium albo-atrum and V. dahliae, is a serious vascular disease of hundreds of woody and herbaceous plant hosts. Food crop hosts include everything from raspberries and strawberries, to tomatoes and potatoes.

Some of the many common woody ornamental host plants include ash, barberry, catalpa, elm, magnolia, maple, Russian olive, redbud, smoketree, tuliptree, and viburnum. One group of plants not susceptible to Verticillium wilt are all the gymnosperms, including conifers such as pine and spruce. While many landscape plants are affected, Verticillium wilt is not a major problem in natural forested areas.

Diagnostic Symptoms

Wilting of leaves and dieback of branches, often one at a time or on one side of the tree, are the most severe symptoms. This can occur over a number of years, with remission of symptoms in some years, or can rapidly progress to plant death in a year or two. Other symptoms of Verticillium wilt may include: marginal browning and scorch of leaves, abnormally large seed crops, small leaves, stunting, poor annual growth, and sparse foliage.

Sometimes large areas of cambial tissue die from infections by the fungus and opportunistic fungi such as Nectria develop in elongated cankers. Late season infections may not be noticeable until plants come out of dormancy with branch dieback evident. All of the above symptoms can also be caused by other stress factors. A good field symptom that can set Verticillium wilt apart diagnostically is the discolouration of xylem and cambial tissue, visible as streaks if you cut into the wood. This discolouration is variable for different plants: generally greenish to blackish on maple, yellowish green on smoketree, and brown on ash.

This streaking is not totally diagnostic on two counts:

- Other fungi and other factors can cause discolouration; and
- On some hosts and on youngest twigs, infection is not always accompanied by discolouration.

Disease Cycle and Conditions Favouring Disease

The Verticillium fungus can survive for many years in soil, making effective crop rotation difficult. The fungus infects plant roots through wounds and in some cases direct penetration of root tissue. Verticillium also is transmitted from plant to plant by grafting and budding. From root infections, the fungus spreads upward in the plant through the vascular stream.

The results of infection are tissue damage and plugging of xylem, robbing stems and leaves of needed water and minerals. The fungus is returned to the soil as plant parts fall or die, and tiny resistant fungal microsclerotia are spread by wind, in soil and on equipment. Many weed hosts are also susceptible; therefore the cycle of contaminated soil is hard to break. Development of Verticillium wilt is favoured by factors that stress roots, including wounding and droughty conditions.

Control

Disease resistance. If Verticillium wilt is diagnosed at a particular landscape or nursery site it is prudent to replant into that area with a plant that exhibits resistance to this disease. A few common examples of plants typically free of this disease include: crabapple, mountain ash, beech, birch, boxwood, dogwood, sweet gum, hawthorn, holly, katsuratree, honeylocust, oak, pear, London planetree and sycamore, rhododendron, willow, and zelkova. The red maple cultivars Armstrong, Autumn Flame, Bowhall, October Glory, Red Sunset, Scarlet and Schlessinger have also been reported as resistant.

Keep plants as healthy as possible. Proper transplanting practices, proper water management to avoid droughts, a good fertility programme, and pruning out dead branches are all good plant health care management practices. These can help limit infections and help limit the effects of these infections to some extent. Pruning out infected branches is useful as a general horticultural practice for overall plant vigour and aesthetics, but does not eliminate Verticillium from the plant since infections spread from the roots.

Fungicides are not effective for control of this disease. Bacterial Crown Gall on Ornamentals in the Landscape Crown gall is characterized by growth of galls on roots or stems. While mostly found on woody plants, it affects some herbaceous plants as well. Although found on more than 600 plant species in over 90 families, the disease is of economic importance on relatively few ornamental plants. Some commonly affected ornamentals include rose, Prunus, (flowering cherry, flowering almond and ornamental plums), willow, and certain Euonymous species, especially wintercreeper.

Effects of Crown Gall

Crown gall can reduce the productive life of plants. Deformation of tissues due to gall formation disrupts the movement of water and nutrients between roots and leaves. Stems are weakened and growth may be reduced with a general decline in vigour. The severity of the disease depends on the size, number, and location of the galls, and also on the susceptibility of the plant and age when infected. Galls at the crown of young plants have the greatest adverse effect and can cause stunting and failure to produce healthy leaves and blossoms. This disease may have little noticeable effect on older plants.

Symptoms

Galls may develop anywhere on stems and roots, but are usually found near the soil line. They vary from pea size up to several inches in diameter. Young galls are light coloured and smooth. Older galls become discoloured, hard and woody, and eventually crack, decay and slough off. The texture at first is softer than the normal host stem or root tissue. The galls consist of disorganized host tissues. Secondary galls sometimes form above the sites of the primary gall on stems of some hosts. The secondary galls are usually smaller and occur as separate or unbroken elongated masses of tissue breaking through the bark surfaces. Unlike insect galls, crown galls are a solid mass of tissue all the way through.

Disease Development

Crown gall is caused by the soil-borne bacterium, Agrobacterium tumefaciens. The bacteria can persist in the soil for two or more years even in the absence of susceptible plants. Sometimes the bacteria are carried on seeds. Fresh wounds in stems or roots are essential for the bacteria to invade host tissues. These wounds commonly occur during planting, cultivation and pruning, and during propagation when grafting and taking cuttings. Soil insects and nematodes can also cause root wounds providing entry sites.

There are no effective chemical controls for this disease in the landscape. Cultural controls include:

- Avoid unnecessary wounding (protect from injury).
- Sanitation-remove infected plants.
- Plant resistant plants in crown gall-infested areas.
- Do not purchase plants with suspicious swelling near the soil line or on the roots.

CEDAR RUST DISEASES OF ORNAMENTAL PLANTS

There are a number of "cedar rust" diseases in which the fungus completes its life cycle on two plant hosts; one in the cypress family and one in the rose family (the rosaceous host). Discussed here are three common cedar rust diseases in the northeast U.S.

- Cedar apple rust (pathogen: Gymnosporangium juniperi-virginianae). The fungus alternates between Eastern red cedar (Juniperus virginiana) and mostly apple and crabapple.
- Cedar hawthorn rust (pathogen: Gymnosporangium globosum). The fungus alternates between junipers and hawthorn, crabapple, and apple in addition to several other rosaceous hosts.
- Cedar quince rust (pathogen: Gymnosporangium clavipes). The fungus alternates between junipers and a wide range of rosaceous hosts. The most noticeable in the landscape is hawthorn.

In some cases these diseases are minor problems, but cedar quince rust and cedar hawthorn rust can be a major problem on hawthorns and cedar apple rust is a major economic consideration in commercial apple production.

Diagnostic Symptoms

Cedar apple rust: On junipers, tan to brownish round to kidney-shaped fungal galls are present in winter and early spring. With moist weather, gaudy bright orange masses of gelatinous spores develop from these galls, and galls swell to several times their original size. Spore masses are several inches in diameter, with a central core and radiating hornlike tendrils, and are highly visible during moist weather in mid-spring. On apple and crabapple, bright orange-yellow leaf spots develop on upper surfaces of leaves in late spring, followed by light coloured, fringed cup-shaped structures on lower leaf surfaces several weeks later. Damage on junipers is generally minor and involves presence of the galls and twig dieback. On apples and crabapples, fruit infections and leaf drop also can occur. Cedar hawthorn rust: On junipers, galls are somewhat smaller than with cedar apple rust disease. Galls continue to produce spores on junipers for more than one year, compared to only one season of spore production with cedar apple rust. On hawthorn, leaf spots are similar to above and occasionally green twigs are deformed by the fungus.

Cedar quince rust: Infected areas on juniper are much less spectacular than with cedar apple rust, with a cushion-like mat of orangish fungal growth developing on spherical galls in spring. Cedar quince rust causes the greatest damage of the three rusts to ornamental rosaceous hosts, especially to hawthorns, because of extensive, unsightly fruit infestations, stunting and death of fruits and swelling and distortion of twigs. Infected leaves brown and die. Fruits become covered with orangish-pink spore horns. Unsightly spherical cankers developing on stems can last more than one year.

Disease Cycle and Conditions Favouring Disease

Rust fungi have complicated disease cycles with a number of different spore types that will not be detailed here. A crucial factor relative to control on these cedar rusts, however, is that there is no repeating spore cycle on the rosaceous hosts. In other words, spores produced on hawthorn will not reinfect hawthorns or other rosaceous plants-they will only reinfect junipers later in the season. Spores produced on juniper will not reinfect junipers-they will only infect the rosaceous host. The alternating host plant is necessary for survival of the fungus.

Spores produced on the juniper host are blown during moist weather to the rosaceous hosts in mid-spring at a time when new growth has emerged. The fungus then causes leaf spots on upper leaf surfaces and while growing in the leaf two strains of the fungus mate and emerge as a new spore form on the lower leaf surface.

These spores are then blown back to junipers in mid summer to fall, develop galled areas on the junipers over a one and a half year period and the cycle begins again. Windborne spread of spores between the hosts of several hundred yards is not unusual and spread can be a matter of miles.

Control

Application of fungicides. Protective fungicides can be applied several times starting with prebloom on hawthorn and bud break on crabapples if the disease is chronically a problem at a given site. These applications are to protect the plant from spores being disseminated from the juniper host in mid-spring. Since there is no repeating cycle of this disease on the rosaceous host, further applications after this springtime spread from juniper are unnecessary.

Commonly recommended fungicides include: Mancozeb (Fore, Dithane, Mancozeb); Chlorothalonil (Daconil*); Triadimefon (Bayleton, Strike) and propiconazole (Banner). It is the user's responsibility to follow all label instructions. When you diagnose cedar rust disease from infected hawthorn or crabapple fruits and leaves it is far too late to spray for that year. Sprays are rarely recommended to protect the juniper host from spores being disseminated from the rosaceous host in late summer and fall.

Eradication of the other host plant. One approach sometimes suggested is to eliminate junipers from around plantings of rosaceous hosts, and vice versa. Concerted efforts to eradicate junipers were historically tried in concentrated apple growing regions.

This practice is limited to some extent by practicality in terms of the widespread occurrence of junipers, long distance spread of the fungi involved, the rights of juniper lovers, and the fact that in most situations cedar diseases are not so serious that such extreme measures are needed. Nevertheless, it is prudent to separate highly susceptible junipers and rosaceous hosts to the extent possible in nursery and landscape situations. One simple practice where only a few plants are involved is to remove galls from junipers. This is easier to do with cedar apple rust and cedar hawthorn rust, since galled areas are more inconspicuous with cedar quince rust.Use plants with genetic resistance. A number of juniper species and cultivars and a number of rosaceous plant species and cultivars have varying levels of resistance and susceptibility to these three diseases and where disease pressures are historically high these plants should be used.

TIP BLIGHTS OF JUNIPERS

Phomopsis tip blight and Kabatina tip blight are two common diseases of junipers found in most states east of the Mississippi. Both diseases are caused by fungi and the damage they cause on nursery stock, transplants and certain juniper varieties in the landscape can be severe; however, most established junipers in the landscape are seldom killed. The disease is most serious on younger plants and becomes less serious as plants get older.

There are many varieties of juniper that vary from very susceptible to highly resistant. Junipers are generally considered as low maintenance because they are relatively free of major diseases and insect pests; however, these diseases can adversely affect the appearance and health of these trees in certain locations and under the proper environmental conditions. Although Phomopsis and Kabatina blights cause almost identical symptoms, aspects of their development and control do differ. Therefore, it is important to distinguish between the two diseases.

Symptoms and Causal Organisms

Phomopsis tip blight, caused by the fungus Phomopsis juniperovora, damages new growth and succulent branch tips of junipers from mid-April through September. Older, mature foliage is resistant to infection; therefore, most blighting occurs on the terminal 4 to 6 inches of the branches.

Affected foliage first turns dull red or brown and finally ash-gray. Small gray lesions often girdle branch tips and cause blighting of foliage beyond the diseased tissue. Small, black, spore-containing fungal fruiting bodies develop in the lesions. Use a hand lens to view these diagnostic fungal structures more easily. Spores of the Phomopsis fungus are produced throughout the summer, and infection can occur whenever young foliage is available and moisture or humidity are high. Most infections usually occur in April through early June and again in late August through September. Very few infections occur in mid-summer or during the winter months.

Repeated blighting in early summer can result in abnormal bunching (witches' broom) and discolouration of the foliage, stunting of young trees or shrubs, or-in severe cases-plant death. Be cautious in diagnosing witches brooming and stunting because similar damage can be caused by the dwarf tip mite. With juniper problems, it is always a good idea to have problem diagnosis confirmed by a diagnostic laboratory.

Kabatina tip blight, caused by the fungus Kabatina juniperi, first appears in February and March; and well before symptoms of Phomopsis tip blight appear. The terminal 2 to 6 inches of diseased branches throughout the juniper first turn dull green, then red or yellow.

Small ash-gray to silver lesions dotted with small, black fruiting bodies of the fungus are visible at the base of the discoloured tissue. The brown, desiccated foliage eventually drops from the tree in late May or June. Foliar blighting occurs only in early spring; it does not continue through the summer. Blighting is also restricted to the branch tips and does not cause extensive branch dieback or tree death. Be cautious in diagnosing witches brooming and stunting symptoms because similar damage can be caused by the dwarf tip mite. With juniper problems it is always a good idea to have problem diagnosis confirmed by a diagnostic laboratory.

The primary infection period for the Kabatina fungus is thought to be in autumn even though visible symptoms are not apparent until late winter or early spring. Infection often is associated with small wounds on branch tips caused by insect feeding or mechanical damage.

Control

- When purchasing new plants, select those that have been reported to have disease resistance. Table has information on relative disease resistance to Phomopsis and Kabatina for several Juniper selections.

- Space new plantings to provide good ventilation and air circulation and avoid heavily shaded areas. Avoid wounding plants, especially in spring and autumn.
- Water plants in early morning so the foliage will dry as soon as possible. Maintain adequate fertility, but do not over fertilize.
- Prune out diseased branch tips during dry summer weather and destroy them. Do so only when plants are dry and no rain or overhead irrigation is expected for several days. Avoid excessive pruning or shearing.
- Chemical control of these tip blight diseases normally is not necessary in established landscape or windbreak plantings. Occasionally, fungicide applications may be needed on susceptible junipers to control Phomopsis blight. Application of certain copper-based fungicides (Phyton-27, Kocide), thiophanate-methyl (Cleary's 3336, Domain, Fungo FLO), or mancozeb (Fore, Dithane, mancozeb) at 7- to 21-day intervals during rapid plant growth in the spring will give adequate control of Phomopsis but not Kabatina tip blight. Kabatina blight

infections occur in the fall, and there currently are no fungicides labeled for control of this disease.

SOOTY MOLDS ON TREES AND SHRUBS

Symptoms

A sooty, gray-black, velvety, often crust-like coating may develop on the leaves or needles, fruits, and branches of certain plants. The coating is actually the growth of one of several species of black-coloured fungi or molds. The coating can be removed easily by rubbing the leaf between the fingers, thus exposing the green leaf tissue below. Sooty molds grow only on the plant surface and will not kill plants. In fact, sooty molds often grow on sidewalks or fences under infested trees. Sooty molds are normally considered to be a cosmetic or aesthetic problem.

In extremely severe cases, it is possible for the black growth to block enough sunlight to interfere with photosynthesis. In such cases, leaves or needles, fruits and new shoots may be smaller, or less intensely coloured. Respiration can be reduced through the physical closure of stomates by the molds' vegetative growth.

Under drought conditions, plants affected with sooty mold will wilt more rapidly than unaffected plants. If plant vigour has been reduced, the plant may also be predisposed to further injury by other insects, diseases or environmental stresses.

Insect Association

Sucking insects are the primary cause of sooty mold growth. Many plant sap-sucking insects feed on leaves and stems of trees and shrubs. These sucking insects often produce excessive, watery excrement rich in sugars. This excrement is called honeydew. Excreted honeydew often falls on leaves or needles, branches, fruits or anything else immediately underneath the infested area of the plant. It is on this excretion that the sooty mold fungi grow. Sometimes plants not actually infested by insects may be affected if a tree above them is being attacked by a honeydew producing insect and the honeydew drops onto them.The major types of honeydew producing insects are: Aphids, soft scales, mealybugs, whiteflies, leafhoppers, planthoppers and psyllids. Occasionally, the spittle-like froth produced by spittlebugs promotes the growth of sooty molds.

Susceptible and Resistant Trees

Plants that are commonly infested by the insects mentioned above are often hosts to sooty molds. Resistance to this condition is normally a result of resistance by the plant to honeydew producing insects.

Control

Control sooty molds by controlling the honeydew producing insect. Chemical control is most commonly used to manage these sucking insects, although biological and cultural control strategies are available for some aphids and scales.One must identify the insect that is causing the problem and the plant being attacked before deciding on a method of management. Consult an appropriate up-to-date OSU Extension fact sheet or bulletin such as Bulletin 504 (Insect and Mite Control in Woody Ornamental and Herbaceous Perennials). A strong spray of water can be used to dislodge the mold growth from many plants.

POWDERY MILDEWS ON ORNAMENTAL PLANTS

Almost all landscapes have plants that become diseased with one of the powdery mildew fungi. Although the fungi that cause powdery mildew are usually different on different plants, all of the powdery mildew diseases are similar in appearance. In most cases, prompt recognition and control actions can prevent severe damage to plants from powdery mildew diseases.

Symptoms

Powdery mildews, as the name implies, often appear as a superficial white or gray powdery growth of fungus over the surface of leaves, stems, flowers, or fruit of affected plants. These patches may enlarge until they cover the entire leaf on one or both sides. Young foliage and shoots may be particularly susceptible. Leaf curling and twisting may be noted before the fungus is noticed. Severe powdery mildew infection will result in yellowed leaves, dried and brown leaves, and disfigured shoots and flowers. Although it usually is not a fatal disease, powdery mildew may hasten plant defoliation and fall dormancy, and the infected plant may become extremely unsightly. On roses, uncontrolled powdery mildew will prevent normal flowering on highly susceptible cultivars.

Hosts

Powdery mildew fungi infect almost all ornamental plants. They are commonly seen only on those plants more naturally susceptible to the disease. Susceptible woody plants include some deciduous azaleas, buckeye, catalpa, cherry, a few of the flowering crabapples, dogwood, English oaks, euonymus, honeysuckle, horse chestnut, lilac, privet, roses, serviceberry, silver maple, sycamore, tulip tree, some viburnums, walnut, willow and wintercreeper.

Powdery mildews are also common on certain herbaceous plants, such as chrysanthemums, dahlias, delphiniums, kalanchoes, phlox, Reiger begonias, snapdragons and zinnias.Remember that each species of powdery mildew has a very limited host range. Infection of one plant type does not necessarily mean that others are threatened.

Environment Favouring Powdery Mildews

Most powdery mildew fungi produce airborne spores and infect plants when temperatures are moderate (60 to 80 degrees F) and will not be present during the hottest days of the summer. Unlike most other fungi that infect plants, powdery mildew fungi do not require free water on the plant surface in order to germinate and infect. Some powdery mildew fungi, especially those on rose, apple, and cherry are favoured by high humidities. Overcrowding and shading will keep plants cool and promote higher humidity. These conditions are highly conducive to powdery mildew development.

Control of Powdery Mildews

Before using fungicides you should attempt to limit powdery mildews by other means. The following cultural practices should be beneficial for controlling powdery mildews.

- Purchase only top-quality, disease-free plants of resistant cultivars and species from a reputable nursery, greenhouse or garden centre. Horticulturists in the green industry and Extension offices should be consulted concerning the availability and performance of resistant varieties.
- Prune out diseased terminals of woody plants, such as rose and crabapple, during the normal pruning period. All dead wood should be removed and destroyed (preferably by burning). Rake up and destroy all dead leaves that might harbor the fungus.
- Maintain plants in a high vigour.
  - Plant properly in well-prepared and well-drained soil where the plants will obtain all-day sun (or a minimum of 6 hours of sunlight daily).
  - Space plants for good air circulation. DO NOT plant highly susceptible plants—such as phlox, rose, and zinnia—in damp, shady locations
  - Do not handle or work among the plants when the foliage is wet.
  - Water thoroughly at weekly intervals during periods of drought. The soil should be moist 8 to 12 inches deep. Avoid overhead watering and sprinkling the foliage, especially in late afternoon or evening. Use a soil soaker hose or root feeder so the foliage is not wetted.

Chemical Control of Powdery Mildews

In many cases, powdery mildew diseases do little damage to overall plant health, and yearly infections can be ignored if unsightliness is not a major concern. For example, lilacs can have powdery mildew each year, with little or no apparent effect on plant health. On some plants, powdery mildews can result in significant damage. Thus, fungicides must be used to achieve acceptable control.

LEAF DISEASES OF GRASSES

The more important perennial grasses that provide summer grazing in the Southern States are Bermuda-grass (Cynodon dactylon), carpetgrass (Axonopus affinis), and Dallisgrass (Paspalum dilatatum). Bermuda-grass is attacked by two species of Helminthosporium. H. giganteum causes a zonate eyespot with tan centre and brown margin. H. cynodontis causes a bleaching and withering, particularly of the leaf tips.

The leaves of carpetgrass are sometimes spotted by a species of Helminthosporium, and one species of Curvularia has also been reported from leaf spots on this grass. Dallisgrass is attacked in some areas by anthracnose (Colletotrichum graminicola). In spring the leaves sometimes are spotted by Stagonospora paspali. Neither has been severe enough to warrant intensive work by plant pathologists.

Johnsongrass (Sorghum halepense) is another perennial warm-season grass that is grazed and cut for hay in some parts of the South. It is quite susceptible to the numerous leaf diseases that attack Sudangrass and frequently suffers severe leaf injury.

Tall fescue (Festuca arundinacea) is Utilized commonly for cool-season grazing in the South. Three leaf diseases of some importance attack it. Leaf scald, caused by Rhizoctonia solani, has caused the most serious losses. It causes large, bleached, tan-coloured areas on the leaves, especially noticeable in summer.

A dark-brown, diffuse, netlike leaf discoloration (net blotch), caused by Helminthosporium dictyoides, sometimes becomes rather abundant on leaves of tall fescue during the cool months of fall, winter, and spring.

The leaf spot caused by Cercospora festucae has a gray centre and a purplish border, which differentiate it from net blotch. Cercospora leaf spot is first evident in spring and becomes more severe as summer progresses. It was first observed on tall fescue in Kentucky in 1944. It became severe on tall fescue at College Station and Temple, Tex., in 1949, and appeared to be responsible for the death of both seedling and mature plants.

Temporary winter grazing in the South is furnished largely by the early growth of winter cereals (oats, rye, barley, and wheat). Annual ryegrass (Lolium multiflorum) is also utilized throughout the South for winter grazing. Its chief foliar disease is crown rust, caused by Puccinia coronata.

Sudangrass (Sorghum vulgare var. sudanense) and pearlmillet (Pennisetum glaucum) are the grasses most widely grown for temporary summer grazing in the South.

Sudangrass is attacked by a number of bacterial and fungus diseases, which limit its usefulness. Pearlmillet is less widely grown and so far has been attacked by fewer parasites.

Bacterial stripe (Pseudomonas andropogoni) is probably the most common and destructive bacterial disease of Sudangrass. It occurs also on Johnson-grass and sorghums. It shows as stripes with blunt or jagged ends. The stripes are about one-fourth inch long when young and a foot or more when mature.

The colour, continuous throughout the lesion, ranges from purplish red to brown or tan, depending on the variety. Abundant bacterial exudate forms over the lesions and dries to form crusts or scales, especially on the lower leaf surface. The scales of exudate are the same colour as the stripes.

Bacterial streak (Xanthomonas holcicola) is another widely distributed disease of Sudangrass, Johnsongrass, and sorghums. The young lesions are narrow, water-soaked streaks 1 to 6 inches long. They bear beadlike, light-yellow drops of exudate. Red or brown margins later develop, and irregular blotches of colour appear in the streaks, breaking their continuity. The streaks may join to form irregular areas that cover much of the leaf blade. At that stage the exudate has dried to thin, white or cream-coloured scales, which distinguish this disease from bacterial stripe, which has a darker exudate.

Bacterial spot (Pseudomonas syringae) is somewhat less common than the other two bacterial diseases, but some years it occurs abundantly on the leaves of Sudangrass, Johnsongrass, pearlmillet, foxtail millet, sorghums, and corn. The spots, circular to elliptical, vary from tiny dots to almost one-half inch circles in later stages. They appear water-soaked at first. Soon they become dry and light-coloured in the centre and develop a red or brown border. The spots may unite to form large diseased areas, but they do not elongate to form stripes or streaks. Exudate does not form on the lesions.

Leaf blight, caused by the fungus Helminthosporium turcicum, is probably the most destructive disease of Sudan-grass in the Southern States. The disease occurs also on Johnsongrass, sorghums, and corn. The causal fungus is seed-borne and lives also on dead plant material on or in the soil. It may cause seed rot and seedling blight, which make it difficult to obtain a satisfactory stand.

When the leaves of older plants are attacked, the fungus causes long, elliptical lesions one-eighth to one-half inch wide and several inches long. The lesions may coalesce and kill large areas of the leaves, so that severely affected plants appear as though they had been blighted by an early frost.

The centre of the individual lesions is usually gray to straw-coloured. The border of the lesions varies from reddish purple to tan. In warm, humid weather, the lesions are covered with a dark, moldlike growth of fungus spores. Wind and rain scatter the spores and spread the disease.

Two other species of Helminthosporium attack Sudangrass, but the foliar diseases they cause are less damaging than leaf blight. Target spot, caused by the fungus Helminthosporium sorghicola, the more serious, occurs on Johnsongrass and sorghums, as well as Sudangrass. It forms small, round or oval lesions.

They consist of alternate light-tan and brown bands of tissues. The tissues have a zonate or"target spot" appearance on varieties such as Tift Sudan, which contain a tan pigment. On common Sudan, which contains a darker pigment, the lesions are purplish black and are less zonate. The disease may become more serious in the South as the acreage planted to Tift Sudan increases, because while it resists leaf blight it appears to be quite susceptible to target spot.

The second species, Helminthosporium rostratum, is primarily a parasite of corn and pearlmillet but can attack Sudan-grass, Johnsongrass, and sorghums. The leaf spots it causes are small and light brown in colour when young. Older lesions have straw-coloured centres and may coalesce to form larger necrotic areas. On sorghums and Sudangrasses having dark pigment there is some purpling around the lesions.

Zonate leaf spot (Gloeocercospora sorghi) is a conspicuous disease of Sudangrass, Johnsongrass, and sorghums. It has been reported also on sugarcane, corn, and pearlmillet. The mature spots are large and composed of alternating bands of reddish-purple and tan or straw-coloured tissue, forming a zonate pattern.

Spots near the leaf margin are semicircular. Those nearer the centre of the leaf are nearly circular with irregular, wavy margins. Black sclerotia of the fungus develop within the tissues of the older leaf lesions and the fungus spores are borne in salmon-coloured gelatinous masses (sporodochia) in and around the necrotic areas. In some seasons the disease is rather common in the lower Mississippi Valley.

Rough spot (Ascochyta sorghina) attacks Sudangrass, Johnsongrass, and sorghums. It has round or oval spots, which are yellowish brown or reddish Purple and are covered with small black fruiting bodies. The bodies usually are so abundant that the affected areas feel rough when rubbed between the fingertips.

Gray leaf spot, caused by the fungus Cercospora sorghi, is found commonly on Sudangrass, Johnsongrass, and sorghums in the Gulf States. When small, the reddish-purple to tan spots areindistinguishable as from other leaf spots, they elongate they become covered with a grayish-white fuzz, composed of fungus conidiophores and conidia. The conidia, spread by wind and rain, cause new infections.

Sooty stripe, caused by Ramulispora sorghi, occurs in the Southern States on Sudangrass, Johnsongrass, and sorghums. Mature lesions are elongate-elliptical, have a straw-coloured centre surrounded by a purple border, and usually are covered by numerous black sclerotia. In moist weather, fungus spores are produced in light-pink, gelatinous masses (sporodochia) on the lesions. The sclerotia function primarily in overwintering the fungus and the conidia produced by them are the chief source of infection in the spring.

Rust, caused by Puccinia purpurea, frequently attacks Sudangrass, Johnsongrass, and sorghums in the humid Gulf States. It causes the leaves to dry and break off, thus reducing the forage value. Rust pustules occur on both the upper and lower surfaces of the leaf. They are covered at first by a brownish coating. This soon breaks open and allows the chestnut-brown rust spores to escape. Purplish-red or tan areas develop around the rust pustules and the functional efficiency of large areas of leaf tissue is eventually destroyed.

Nonparasitic leaf discoloration caused by environmental conditions or hereditary factors also occur commonly on Sudangrass, Johnsongrass, and sorghums in the South. These lesions lack bacterial exudate and show no evidence of fungus fruiting structures, which serves to differentiate them from the parasitic disorders

Seed treatment and crop rotation help check the diseases of Sudangrass, but the most feasible control measure is the development of disease-resistant varieties.

Tift Sudan, a variety resistant to leaf blight, anthracnose, bacterial stripe, and bacterial streak, was developed through cooperative work by the Department of Agriculture and the Georgia Coastal Plain Experiment Station.

The origin and early testing of this improved variety is described by Glenn W. Burton in Georgia Circular 11, published in April 1943. Tift Sudan has become popular in the South because of its disease resistance. Plant breeders use it in attempts to improve Sudangrass still more.

Pearlmillet is susceptible to three of the diseases that attack Sudangrass; bacterial spot, zonate leaf spot, and the leaf spot caused by Helminthosporium rostratum. Eyespot, caused by Helminthosporium sacchari, also occurs on pearl-millet. The fungus infects and blackens the seed and causes a conspicuous leaf spot. Species of Curvularia have also been reported from leaf spots and seed of pearlmillet.

A more common leaf disease than any of those is caused by a species of Cercospora, which had not been named in 1953. That fungus causes a small, circular to elliptical spot with gray centre and reddish-brown border. Both the improved variety Starr and commercial pearlmillet are susceptible to it. The disease usually develops rather late in the summer, however, and so the damage is not great during the pasturing season.

SMUTS THAT PARASITIZE GRASSES

Nearly 140 different species of smuts attack approximately 300 species of grasses in the United States. The common name smut derives from words meaning to besmirch or smudge and refers to the presence of sooty, dirty, black, or brownish masses on the affected plants. All the smuts are plant parasites. Most of them occur on grasses and cereals. As with the rusts, the average person is much more familiar with the destruction wrought by smuts on cereals than on grasses. Familiar examples of destructive cereal smuts are bunt or stinking smut of wheat, oat smuts, barley smuts, sorghum smut, and boil smut on corn. In everyday practice, the name smut is used to designate the disease as well as the fungus responsible for the disease, although the latter is more correctly spoken of as the smut fungus.

The smut fungi have much less complicated life histories than do the rust fungi and generally are easier to control. The familiar dusty black smut masses are made up mostly of millions of tiny cells or groups of cells spores, which serve the same purpose to the smut fungi as seeds do to the seed-bearing plants, namely, for reproduction and dissemination.

Some smuts destroy the flowering structure. Others are restricted only to certain parts of it. Some are confined almost exclusively to the stems of grasses. Others produce galls or tumorlike structures in various parts of their host plants.

As with the rust fungi, many smut fungi display a remarkable degree of specialization not only to certain species of plants but also to certain varieties or strains within those host species. Likewise, there are often strains or races of the smut fungi to contend with. The common stinking smut, for example, has nearly 30 known strains or races, each capable of attacking different varieties of wheat and different strains or varieties of wheatgrasses and related grasses.

The smut fungi are not entirely obligate parasites as are the rust fungi. In fact, some smuts can easily complete their entire life cycle on an artificial medium if it contains the nutrients essential for growth. Some smuts apparently persist indefinitely in the soil or in old manure piles. They are fully capable, however, of attacking their host plants when the plants are available under the requisite conditions for infection.

The smut fungi have a more adverse effect directly (and perhaps indirectly) on their hosts than do the rust fungi. The smuts that attack all or parts of the flowering structures generally destroy the seeds entirely. The leaf smuts and the stem smuts, while only occasionally involving the flowering structures, do nevertheless generally suppress these structures and likewise result in a more or less complete loss of seed on affected plants.

The smuts that attack the vegetative structures (that is, the leaf smuts and stem smuts) have a decidedly weakening effect on their host plants and make them more susceptible to other sinister factors in their environment.

Many of the grass smuts are seed-borne. The wind carries millions of smut spores, which become lodged in or on the developing seeds of healthy Plants. When the seeds germinate, the smut spores also germinate and infect the young seedlings. Then the Plants that arise from the seedlings are smutted.

Some of the smut fungi are not limited to seedling infection. Apparently they can infect any succulent or rapidly growing part of their host plants and thereby make them smutty in time.

The time between infection and the appearance of smut varies rather widely. In the stripe smut of grasses, for example, seedlings often show smut within 6 weeks of the time the smut-contaminated seed is planted. Other smuts are not evident until their hosts head out. One of the stem smuts, to be described later, requires 2 to 4 years after infection before smut actually appears.

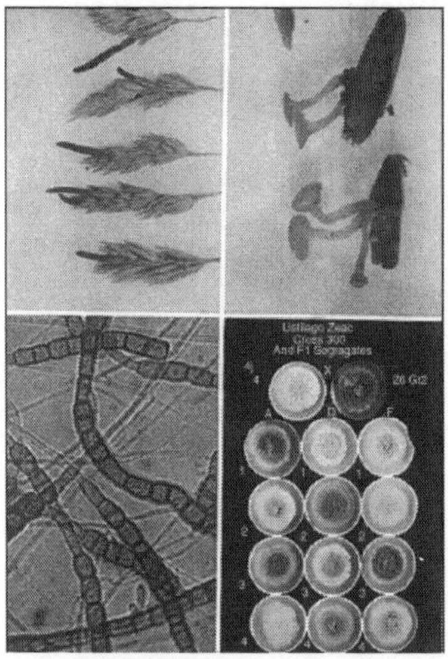

Upper left: The ergot fungus has replaced a seed in the orchardgrass flower head.

Upper right: Fruiting bodies of a fungus growing from seed of perennial ryegrass.

Lower left: Spores and mycelium of a fungus magnified by the lens of a microscope.

Lower right: Variability in progeny from a cross of two corn smut fungus cultures.

Spores of the smut fungi generally are much more durable than are those of the rust fungi. It is hard to maintain viability of rust spores for more than a year; usually it is much less than that. In the case of the smut fungi, it is unusual for viability to be maintained for less than a year. For most smuts viability is maintained for two to several years, especially if humidity is low. Some smuts have been known to retain at least some viability for 25 years. The cultivation of grasses seems to have much to do with the development of smut in them: Often cultivation practices, including harvesting and threshing, disperse the smut and contribute toward an increase in the amount of smut in succeeding crops. Any of the grass smuts therefore is a potential threat to the welfare of its grass host if the grass comes under cultivation. Some of the grass smuts are the same as those that are destructive parasites of our cereal crops.

Seed smuts or bunt (Tilletia species) are terms used here to designate the smuts of grasses in which the normal seeds are replaced by smut"balls." The balls retain somewhat the shape of the normal seed and are even encased by the seed wall; actually, though, the inside of the seed is a solid mass of spores.

About 25 of these grass seed smuts occur in the United States. Several have actual or potential importance in cultivated grasses. One of the potentially most important is the one that on wheat is commonly called stinking smut or bunt. Three species of fungi are involved in it, including what is commonly known as dwarf smut.

These smuts are well known on wheat because of the very extensive losses they have caused for a long time the world over. Besides wheat, tall oat-grass and several of the wheatgrasses are known to be susceptible, including crested wheatgrass, slender wheatgrass, and intermediate wheatgrass. Care has to be taken to keep those grasses from falling prey to the cereal smuts.

The dwarf bunt is soil-borne. It has thus far presented a knotty problem of control except when resistant varieties are used. The other two species, being mostly seed-borne, may be controlled by seed treatment and the use of resistant varieties.

Some of the bentgrasses are susceptible to another of the seed smuts, especially on the east and west coasts where considerable smut infestation is sometimes encountered in harvested seed crops. The life antiquity of this smut is not known.

Various other groups of grasses, for example the bromes, fescues, wild-ryes, hairgrasses, velvetgrass, and others, are prey to similar seed smuts.

One of the most common of the head smuts of grasses is caused by Ustilago bullata. It complicates the cultivation and production of several of our best forage grasses. More than 60 species of grasses have been reported as hosts to it, among them wheatgrasses, bromes, fescues, wild- ryes, and barley grasses. In 1946 it was thought that head smut in mountain brome, one of our most valuable forage grasses, was under control through the release of a new variety, Bromar, which was developed jointly by the Department of Agriculture and the Washington Agricultural Experiment Station. In repeated tests the new strain had remained resistant to the various races of the head smut fungus.

In 1950, however, an entirely new and very virulent strain of head smut made its appearance and caused some very badly smutted fields of Bromar mountain brome. There are 12 known races or strains of the head smut fungus, each of which is specialized to different species of the wheatgrasses, bromes, wild-ryes, and barley grasses. None of the cereals is susceptible to it.

Several dozen other head smuts of grasses constitute a potential problem among economically important forage or range grasses. Practically nothing is known concerning the life antiquity and methods of controlling most of them.

Leaf smuts are of two types: The spot or blister smuts (Entyloma species) and the stripe smuts (Urocystis and Ustilago species).

The spot or blister smuts appear as flat or slightly raised, blackish, round or oval spots in the leaves. Although rather widely distributed, they seldom cause great losses. Once in a while spot smut develops in a bluegrass lawn to such an extent as to cause premature yellowing and death of the leaves. With the stripe smuts, however, it is quite a different matter.

The stripe smuts are evident in the leaves as black stripes, which contain the smut spores. The spores are shed and dispersed into the wind. Afterwards the affected leaves take on a shredded and curled appearance and soon wither. Affected plants quite frequently are dwarfed and contorted and produce abnormal, sterile heads, if any at all. Seedlings of grasses affected with stripe smut are predisposed to drought injury and root rot. Mature plants often are so weakened that they cannot survive severe winters.

Most of the stripe smuts of grasses cannot be told apart by the unaided eye, but they are different enough under a microscope. One of the most common and most virulent is known as flag smut. Many grasses and cultivated wheat are its hosts. Flag smut has several strains, each capable of attacking different groups of grasses.

Another of the common and destructive stripe smuts is the one that has long gone under the name of stripe smut or leaf smut. It has the same effect on its grass hosts as does flag smut and affects many of the same grasses, including some of our best forage grasses the wheatgrasses, bromes, wild-ryes, fescues, and barley grasses. None of the cereals is known to be susceptible to it. Stripe smut is carried on the seed and can be controlled by seed treatment.

Still another type of leaf smut is the"sausage" smut of the grama grasses. It produces small but conspicuous blisterlike (often sausage-shaped) black Pustules on the leaves of the grama grasses, which make up a valuable component of our western ranges. It is restricted to the grama grasses, but often is widespread and undoubtedly results in reduced forage. Its life antiquity is not known. Methods of control therefore have not been developed.

Stem smuts (Ustilago species) are represented by several species that develop in significant abundance on economic grasses. All are marked by the development of conspicuous, dusty, brown or black layers of smut around the internodes of the stems. Sometimes nearly all the internodes seem to be smutty. Sometimes only the top one or two seem so. At first the smut is hidden by the leaf sheath that envelopes the stem, but as the stem elongates, the smut is exposed.

The stem smuts occur on some of our most valuable forage grasses the wheatgrasses, wild-ryes, some of the bluegrasses, the needlegrasses, Indian ricegrass, and a few of the fescues. Quackgrass is commonly infected. It might indeed furnish a supply of smut for the infection of more desirable grasses such as crested wheat-grass, big bluegrass, and blue wild-rye. A peculiar feature about the quackgrass stem smut is that an incubation period of 2 or 3 years is required after infection before the smut appears.

The smut is perennial in the plant once it becomes infected. After the incubation period, the plant will produce a crop of smutty stems each year as long as it lives. Infection takes place in the vegetative tissues and thus spreads from plant to plant in a field.

The control of grass smuts is accomplished mainly in two ways: Chemical treatment of the seed in the case of seed-borne smuts and through the use of resistant varieties or strains.

Not all of the grass smuts can be controlled by seed treatment; but most of the head smuts and the stripe smuts can be. Among the grasses that could be expected to respond favorably to seed treatment for the control of smut are the various wheatgrasses, mountain brome, rescuegrass and related bromes, tall oatgrass, Canada wild-rye and other wild-rye grasses, big bluegrass and perhaps other of the bluegrasses, and the barley grasses. Such seed treatment for the control of smut will also help protect the seed and seedlings from seed decay and damping-off.

The procedure of treating grass seed with chemicals for the control of smut is much the same as that employed with cereal seeds and thus consists in principle of thoroughly applying a certain amount of a seed-treatment chemical to a certain weight of the seed and thoroughly mixing the two. However, comparatively little is known of the effectiveness of such control for many of the grass smuts. This is probably because intensive grass cultivation is relatively recent and the need for such knowledge has not been strongly felt.

The organic mercury dusts and some of the organic sulfur dusts generally are effective in the control of some of the grass smuts. New Improved Ceresan and Ceresan M, 1 ounce to a bushel, have given excellent control. Over-dosage, however, hurts the seed and reduces the stands.

The organic sulfur dusts, Arasan, Arasan SFX, and Tersan, at 3 to 4 ounces to a. bushel, likewise have given good control but not so consistently as organic mercury materials. They have an advantage, however, in that danger of overdosage is less. In fact, these three fungicidal dusts can be applied at maximum dosage (that is, all that can be retained by the dry seed) with little or no seed injury. This tolerance of grass seed to maximum dosage of certain of the fungicides is an advantage if small lots of seed are to be treated. Then it is not practical to attempt to weigh out minute quantities of fungicide, as needed on an ounce-per-bushel basis. Therefore, it is convenient to be able to apply an excess of the fungicide to the seed and, after mixing thoroughly, shake off the excess fungicide and not have to worry about overdosage.

Others of the newer fungicides appear promising and eventually testing may show them to be as reliable. Better results are had if the seed is stored in the treated condition for a few days. As much as 8 weeks will do no harm. It is possible therefore to treat the seed well ahead of the rush of planting time.

Comparatively little progress has been made toward the control of grasssmuts through the use of resistant varieties. In the various studies that have been made of head smut, stripe smut, stinking smut, and others, and in nursery row observations, it has been noticed repeatedly that resistant lines or strains do exist, but very few attempts have been made to combine that resistance with superior agronomic qualities by the process of hybridization and selection. It is a neglected field of endeavor that merits attention, especially with regard to certain smut-susceptible species of forage grasses.

Certain it is that the smut diseases of grasses are going to come more and more into prominence as our grassland agriculture is extended. We should not delay, therefore, to make studies of the life histories of the grass smuts for which this information is lacking, because only on such a basis can intelligent control measures be devised.

LEAF DISEASES OF RANGE GRASSES

Of the troubles that beset forage grasses, the leaf diseases are the most numerous and often the most conspicuous. Although one or only a few of them may be serious on a specific grass and their individual effect on grasses may be relatively mild, their total damage can be serious.

Leaves killed by disease become weathered, low in food value, and less palatable for livestock. They cut the quantity and quality of hay and pasture. The weakened plants are less likely to withstand drought and severe winters. Even worse is the result in areas of low rainfall. There grasses may have only one chance to make their season's growth. Disease, by robbing plants of normal leaf growth, can impair the carrying capacity of a range or pasture and reduce the yields of seed to a point where self-propagation or artificial reseeding is retarded.

The more prevalent or striking types of leaf diseases are considered here. We discuss successively those of western grasses, southern grasses, and northern grasses.

Wheatgrasses (species of Agropyron) are prey to at least 70 diseases. More than half are leaf troubles, notably rusts, leaf smuts, leaf blotches and spots, bacterial chocolate spot, scolecotrichum brown stripe, rhynchosporium scald, and powdery mildew.

Powdery mildew is caused by the fungus Erysiphe graminis. It occurs throughout the northern Great Plains and the Pacific Northwest. It usually is more severe in cool, humid, cloudy climates, although it needs little moisture for spore germination. Therefore the disease also survives in drier places and attacks most of the wheat-grasses there, too. Powdery mildew occurs as white patches on the leaf blades, sheaths, and inflorescences. The fungus is conspicuous, because most of the mycelium and spores are on the surface. Small rootlike organs, haustoria, penetrate the leaf tissue and absorb nutrients at the expense of the plant. Infected leaves turn yellow and brown. The fungus may kill all the leaves in very susceptible grasses. The result is premature dormancy or unthrifty growth of the plant.

New infections start from wind-borne spores. Within a week new infections produce abundant spores, which spread to other plants. Thus a little powdery mildew rapidly can become an epidemic. The amount of loss it causes in yield of forage has not been determined, but comparable infection in barley has caused a reduction of 30 per cent in yield of grain.

Chemical dusts and sprays control powdery mildew, but they are impractical except when grass is intensively grown for seed. The development of resistant varieties of many grasses is possible.

Strains of powdery mildew that infect wheatgrasses have been found on barley, wheat, wheatgrass, and wild-rye grasses. Other mildew strains that attack barley occur on quack-grass (Agropyron repens) and a wild-rye grass (Elymus dahuricus). Grasses, therefore, can serve as sources of infection of wheat and barley. Other strains of mildew attack only wheatgrasses and wild-rye grasses. The existence of several different mildew races complicates the problem of breeding mildew-resistant wheatgrasses.

Powdery mildew is also prevalent and sometimes destructive on bluegrasses in the Pacific Northwest and northern Great Plains. A similar problem in breeding for resistance exists there, because a number of strains infect different species of bluegrass and strains within the species. Resistant plants in many species of bluegrass are known to exist, however.

Wheatgrasses in dry regions are often free from serious leaf diseases. Lack of moisture and coarse leaf texture may explain why few leaf diseases are important on those grasses.

Meadow foxtail (Alopecurusfiratensis) is attacked by at least 15 diseases. The most serious leaf troubles are scolecotrichum brown leaf stripe and rhynchosporium scald.

Meadow foxtail grows throughout the northern Great Plains and Pacific Northwest where enough moisture is available. Growth begins in early spring and is best in cool, moist weather which also favours maximum development of scald.

Scald, caused by Rhynchosporium orthosporum, makes blotches on the leaf blades and sheaths, which at first are water-soaked, ovate to irregular, and scaldlike. The colour of the blotches changes from a solid, bluish green to zonated, scalded, and brown zones. Finally the centres become pale. West of the Cascade Mountains in Oregon and Washington the disease develops throughout winter and spring and usually causes much leaf killing. A related fungus, Rhynchosporium secolis, damages barley, wheatgrasses, wild-rye grasses, western brome grasses, and sometimes reed canarygrass in the Northwest and the North Central States.

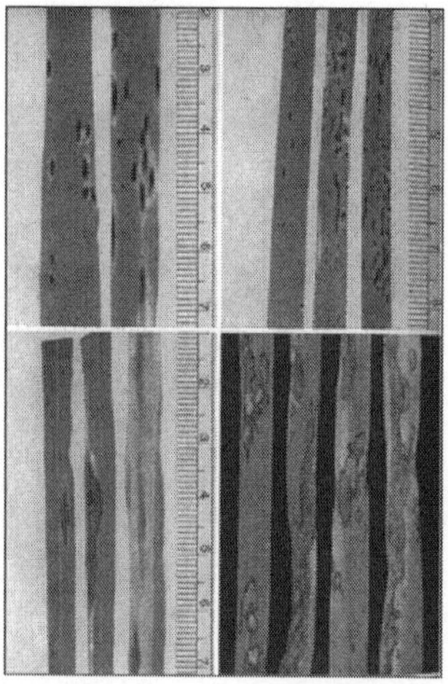

Upper left: Spots on leaves of smooth brome attacked by the fungus Helminthosporium bromi. Upper right: Orchardgrass infected by the leaf spot fungus Stagonospora maculata. Lower left: Blotching due to a bacterial disease on leaves of smooth brome. Lower right: Leaf infection on smooth brome caused by the scald fungus.

No variety of meadow foxtail is resistant to scald. Crop rotation and attention to sanitation are recommended. Careful spring burning of residues will reduce infection in some areas but would be difficult in regions where the grass grows during the wet winter and spring months.

Bluestem, or beardgrass (species of Andropogon) is attacked by a great variety of leaf disorders, including leaf rusts' black choke, anthracnose, cat-tail, leaf spots, and tar spot.

Tar spot, incited by Phyllachora luteornamlata, is of striking appearance. The fungus produces black, sunken, glossy spots on the leaves. Spores produced in organs immersed in these black masses start new infections. Many grasses are attacked by the tar spot diseases caused by similar species of this fungus. Control of tar spot has not been reported. The disease does not kill the grass, and the effect on forage and yields of seed has not been measured.

Septoria leaf spots occur from North Dakota to New Mexico and are occasionally serious. Bluestem grasses generally are subject to more injury from disease in the southern, humid part of their range.

Research to produce disease-resistant varieties of bluestem has been started in Kansas. The Kaw strain of big bluestem, Andropogon gerardi (A. furcatus), released by the Kansas State College in 1950, is relatively free from disease. Grama grasses (species of Bouteloua) are subject to 30-odd diseases. In some areas phyllachora tar spot and selenophoma eyespot are important leaf diseases. Leaf rust is often serious. Other leaf disorders include leaf spots, choke, scald, and black ring. Black ring disease gets its name from the peculiar black organs of a fungus, Balansia sirangulans, which surround grass culms with a tight collar that strangles the stem and leaves above the fungus body. The seed head is often blighted or is unable to form.

Burning could possibly help control it by destroying the fungus bodies outside the plant and thus eliminating spores that otherwise would be disserninated. New spore organs will arise from the mycelium inside the plant, however. Efforts to breed improved, disease-resistant strains of grama grasses have been started at agricultural experiment stations in Kansas and Oklahoma.

Mountain brome (Bromus marginatus) and related species are subject to at least 25 diseases. Foliage troubles include several leaf spots, anthracnose, powdery mildew, snow mold, gray leaf spot, tar spot, bacterial chocolate spot, scald, leaf rot, char spot, leaf speckle, brown blotch, brown stripe, rusts, and bacterial blight. Ordinarily the important leaf diseases are scolecotrichum leaf stripe, rhynchosporium scald, and bacterial chocolate spot.

Rescuegrass, Bromus catharticus, is subject to fewer and different diseases, including bacterial leaf streak.

Chocolate leaf spot, or bacterial blight, is caused by a bacterium, Pseudomonas coronafaciens var. atropurpurea. The lesions, circular to elliptical and water-soaked at first, later turn brown and coalesce to form purplish-brown areas on the leaf blade and sheath. Bacterial slime is absent on the surface of the leaf spots. Spots on the panicles are smaller and restricted. In severe attacks the upper nodes may be killed by secondary infections of the organism. In such plants the panicles wither and die, as though injured by frost.

The disease attacks many grasses. It is important on wheatgrasses. We do not know how to control it. The bacteria are believed to overwinter in the lesions on dead grass. Careful burning before spring growth should reduce the disease.

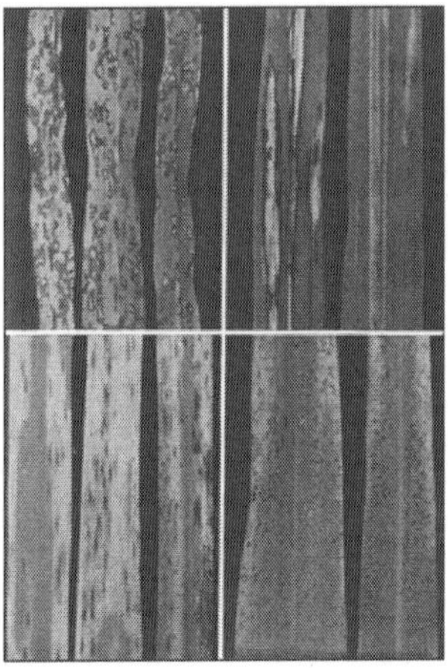

Upper left: Anthracnose (Colletotrichum graminicola) on leaves of Johnsongrass. Upper right: Sweet Sudan (tan spots) and common Sudan (red spots) infected by the leaf blight fungus. Lower left: Net blotch on tall fescue. Lower right: Leaves of Starr (wide) and common (narrower) millet affected with cercospora leaf spot. Buffalograss (Buchloe dactyloides) suffers from 11 diseases. One of them is a leaf and glume spot, frequently called false smut and caused by cercospora seminalis. The fungus forms a compact, olive-green mass held by the spines that enclose the seed spikelets. Fungus mycelium penetrates the seed and replaces it with a mass of spores. False smut occurs sporadically in dry areas, although it is abundant in wet years. The disease is especially troublesome when buffalograss is grown under irrigation for seed.

Because it reduces yields of seed, false smut has caused a shortage of seed of improved strains. Regrassing programmes in which buffalograss is the chief grass used have therefore been retarded. No strains highly resistant to false smut are available, but we hope plant breeding work at several State and Federal stations in the southern Great Plains will develop some.

Wild-rye grasses (species of Elymus) are heir to some 75 ills. Common leaf diseases are rusts, leaf smuts, powdery mildew, ascochyta leaf spot, fusarium head blight, phyllachora tar spot, scolecotrichum brown stripe, selenophoma stem speckle, bacterial chocolate spot, septogloeum tar spot, septoria leaf spots, stagonospora purple brown blotch, and epichloe choke or cattail disease.

Cattail disease is named for the whitish body of the fungus, Epichloe tvphina, which surrounds grass stems with a tight sleeve like the heads of the cattail plant. It occurs sparingly on a large number of grasses in North America. It is sometimes abundant on blue-grasses in the North Central States. Patches of wild-rye sometimes are heavily infested in Northern and Central States.

The disease is apparently restricted to sections that have cool seasons and mild winters or in places where the plants are protected by snow. It may severely damage seed-producing stands. It is much more important in Europe than in North America. It is relatively common on prairie junegrass, Koeleria cristata, over our prairies and on blue-grasses and wheatgrasses in limited regions.

The fungus produces a perennial mycelium in the crown buds. In summer the mycelium forms a white felt over the surface of late tillers and often covers the seed heads as they emerge from the sheath. The fungus body usually encloses all the seed spike or else parts of the panicle in this type of inflorescence. In late-flowering grasses, such as timothy, tillers may be trapped and delayed or destroyed. As the fungus increases in thickness, it becomes yellow, then orange, and forms the collar around the leaf sheath or stem.

The disease is transmitted in seeds of red fescue, Festuca rubra, and possibly in other grasses in which diseased plants produce seed.

The disease was introduced into Pennsylvania in red fescue seeds from Hungary. Growers of grass seed should look for cattail disease in grass-seed crops. With all the present traffic of grass seeds from domestic and foreign sources, this and other diseases could be introduced and become new problems. No adequate control for cattail disease has been developed although roguing is partly successful.

A fusarium head blight has caused serious seed losses in Russian wild-rye, Elymus junceus, in New Mexico. Bacterial leaf spots are common on the wild-rye grasses in the northern Great Plains. Powdery mildew is fairly serious on Russian wild-rye in North Dakota.

Canarygrasses (Phalaris species) have nearly 30 diseases, but most of the leaf diseases are not serious.

Reed canarygrass, Phalaris arundinacea, is adapted throughout the Western States, but it grows mainly in locations with abundant moisture, such as swampy spots, lake shores, and stream banks. Even so, it generally is free of injurious leaf diseases. A fungus, Stagonosporafohicola, causes a tawny spot on leaves. The lesions, which may be brown, wine-coloured, tawny, or buff, sometimes cover the entire leaf blade. The disease has been prevalent in late summer at Mandan, N. Dak., in years of abundant precipitation. The trouble was found in plots and native stands in the Missouri River bottom lands and is common in marshes in Minnesota and South Dakota.

Distinct differences in susceptibility of reed canarygrass plants have been noted in upland plots at the Northern Great Plains Field Station an indication that varieties resistant to the disease are possible.

Fifty recognized parasites occur on the western bluegrasses mutton bluegrass (Poa fendleriana), alkali bluegrass (P. juncifolia), Nevada bluegrass (P. nevadensis), big bluegrass (P. ampla), and related species. Their more important leaf disorders are rusts, scolecotrichum leaf stripe, selenophoma leaf spot, septoria leaf spot, and powdery mildew. Control must be sought for by breeding disease-resistant strains of bluegrass.

Gray leaf spot is common on foxtail millets in the United States; it is a minor, but sometimes destructive, leaf Spot on many grasses. Severe spotting progresses to a blighting or blasting of the foliage. The causal fungus, Piricularia grisea, is like the fungus that causes the blast disease of rice. No control has been suggested for gray leaf spot. Because the grass is an annual plant, crop rotation should help reduce the disease.

Downy mildew, Sclerospora graminicola, is probably the most serious leaf disease on foxtail millet in the United States. Affected plants are dwarfed because elongation of culms is retarded. Excessive tillering from the crown and development of branches from the axillary buds along the culm are characteristic. Leaflike malformations of the floral bracts and failure of kernel development are other common symptoms. A downy mass of spores is common on infected plants in humid areas. Leaf killing and browning are followed by splitting and shredding of the invaded leaf tissues, especially as plants approach maturity. Excessive proliferation of buds and seed heads combined with little or no kernel development causes a serious reduction in yield if infection is high.

Control of downy mildew is difficult in places where those crops are grown continually over large areas because of general soil infestation and wind-borne spores. It is difficult also when the crop is sown in areas where the wild Setaria viridis is infected. Formaldehyde, sulfuric acid, and organic mercury compounds are the best seed treatments.

Dropseeds (Sporobolus species) are attacked by 36 organisms. Leaf diseases include leaf rust, stem rust, ascochyta leaf spot, bacterial leaf spot, powdery mildew, phyllachora tar spot, selenophoma speckle, cercospora leaf spot, septoria leaf spot, stagonospora leaf mold, and false smut.

False smut or head mold, caused by Helminthosporium ravenelii, has a striking appearance. The fungus grows over the seed heads and covers the affected parts with a velvety, brownish-olive mantle, which later becomes black and crusted. Head mold is so common on Sporobolus indicus and S. poirehi that they are called smutgrasses.

It would be a good thing to treat seed to prevent spread of false smut on infected seed, but that cannot control the disease in infested areas because of contamination by wind-borne spores. Burning might help. The use of resistant varieties seems to be the best solution in places where the disease does great damage. Needlegrasses (Stipa species) suffer from 50 or more diseases. The more important are septoria leaf spots, selenophoma leaf and stem spots, stagonospora leaf blotch, and scolecotrichum brown stripe. Brown stripe disease is caused by the fungus Scolecotrichum graminis. Young leaf infections show water-soaked, circular or oval lesions, which are olive gray in the morning when they are wet with dew and dull gray when they are dry. The spots become brownish purple to ocher with gray centres. They tend to form streaks as the leaves slowly die. The spore-bearing bodies of the fungus can be seen as prominent, black dots arranged in parallel rows.

Many grasses are affected with brown stripe. The fungus causes one of the most important leaf spot diseases of timothy, orchardgrass, blue- grasses, tall oatgrasses, redtop, and needlegrasses. Early maturity of timothy and some other grasses is often forced by loss of leaves killed by the fungus.

Careful burning of dead grass reduces the spores for infection of new leaves. The relationship of infected wild grasses as sources of infection of domestic grasses needs study. Varieties resistant to the disease are needed in the needlegrasses, tall oatgrass, orchardgrass, and many others.

It is hard to control leaf diseases of the range grasses. Extensive application of chemical dusts or sprays is out of the question because of the danger of poisoning livestock. Such materials generally are too expensive for use on forage plants even when land is used intensively for pastures. The cost of treating the many low-producing acres on ranges would be prohibitive. Crop rotation, clipping, and deep plowing obviously are not feasible for range land. Early or late grazing might remove some infected leaves, but that is not wholly effective because animals avoid badly diseased and dead leaves.

Seed treatment may be helpful in preventing introduction of diseases carried on the seed to new areas in the initial reseeding of range land. Spores of many disease fungi are wind-carried into the new plantings from wild stands, however, and nullify much of the value of seed treatment.

Fire is an effective but dangerous means of destroying diseased leaves. By exercising extreme care and utilizing fire breaks and other precautions to prevent uncontrolled range fires. burning can be a cheap method of reducing initial infection by some diseases. There is, of course, a loss of organic matter and the risk of killing valuable perennial grasses, so that undesirable plants might take over the range lands.

All in all, then, the best way to control most range grass diseases is to use resistant plants. Development of disease-resistant grasses requires exact information on behaviour of the disease-producing organisms so that tests for resistance can be performed and understood. Such information is not available for many of the leaf diseases.

A good start has been made, however. Research by many workers has shown which species can be grown in various sections of the country. The identity of the organisms causing many grass diseases has been determined. Disease problems are being further clarified. Prospects are good that more and more adapted, high-yielding, disease-resistant grasses will become available eventually to increase forage on range lands.

SOME OF THE 125 RUSTS OF GRASSES

About 125 different species of rusts attack grasses in the United States. Nearly 400 species of grasses are among the hosts of the rusts. Some of the rusts attack only one or a few grasses. Others can attack a great many. Stem rust, Puccinia graminis, for example, has been recorded on nearly 200 species of grasses in the United States.

Among the rusts, which have such large numbers of hosts, we find innumerable strains or races, which look alike, even under the microscope, but differ in their comparative ability to attack species or varieties of grasses. Some of the rusts of grasses are often destructive on the cereals. Most of the so-called cereal rusts have numerous grass hosts; probably the cereal rusts originally were grass rusts that found susceptible hosts among the cereals during the centuries they have been cultivated by man.

However, since the cereals wheat, oats, barley are really only grasses whose seeds are large enough and nutritious enough to warrant intensive cultivation as food, it is only to be expected that there would be a great deal of similarity between the rusts that attack grasses and those that attack cereals. The rusts are microscopic fungi and are strictly parasites. They are among that parasitic classification known as obligate parasites; that is, they can grow only on a living plant. Indeed, many of the rust fungi require not only a certain species of grass or cereal but frequently a definite strain or variety of that species a phenomenon known as host specialization, host specificity, or physiologic specialization. It has an important part in breeding crop plants for resistance to rust.

Because the rust fungi are parasites, their development on a host plant is at the expense of that plant and the nutriments they take would otherwise go into seed, forage, or both. A light infestation of rust is not likely to cause noticeable effects on yield of seed or forage, but a heavy infestation definitely will. In grasses grown for seed, a heavy infestation will result in low test weight of the seed because of the direct effect of parasitism in sapping nutrients from the host and because of water loss through the numerous open rust pustules on the leaves and stems. Rust likewise affects the production of grasses for forage, chiefly in lower yields as a result of reduced vigour. That, however, is partly offset by the somewhat higher protein content of rust-infested grass over rust-free grass.

Secondary or indirect adverse effects should not be overlooked. Heavy attacks of rusts on grasses will make them more likely to succumb to other factors that are always more severe on the already weakened plant drought, winter injury, root rot, snow mold, and perhaps other diseases.

Reproduction and dissemination in the rust fungi, as in fungi generally, is by microscopic cells or groups of cells known as spores. Many of the rusts produce several kinds of spores during their life cycle. Very common are the familiar red uredospores, whose mass appearance accounts for the name rust. Those spores are borne throughout the summer and spread the disease rapidly during the growing season. As the plants mature, however, the red pustules gradually change to a black type. The black spores (teliospores) usually cannot germinate until the following spring; thus they insure survival of the rust fungus through fall, winter, and early spring.

In many of the rusts, especially the grass and cereal rusts, the black spores cannot infect any grass or cereal host but only some entirely different kind of plant, as the examples given later will show. Such a plant is known as the alternate host and usually is infected in the spring or early summer. The spores produced on the alternate host cannot reinfect that host; instead, they give rise to the initial red spore stage again on grasses or cereals, and thus the life cycle is completed.

Few of the 125-odd species of rust fungi that attack grasses in the United States are of economic importance: Many of the rusts are so limited geographically that they have not presented any general problem. Many are specialized to a few grasses, frequently of limited distribution and importance in the over-all range and forage picture. Another circumstance: In many wild grasses, especially of the bunch type, individual plants of a species often are separated by many other types of vegetation and by resistant grasses of other species. Susceptible individuals of one species have to be close by before rusts and leaf diseases in general can develop into an epidemic. That has been demonstrated countless times and often with disastrous results in cultivated fields of cereals and grasses.

Nevertheless, several rusts often reach economic proportions in important forage grasses and merit specific mention here. They are stem rust, leaf rust, stripe rust, crown rust, and bluegrass rust.

Stem rust of grasses (Puccinia graminis) is better known as a destructive disease of small-grain cereals than as an important disease of numerous grasses. It is evident primarily as small red pustules, chiefly on the stems, but sometimes also on the leaves, particularly on young grass plants. As the summer draws to a close and the plants mature, the red pustules gradually are replaced by black ones.

The six varieties of the stem rust fungus in the United States are differentiated mostly by the cereals and grasses they can attack. Thus the wheat variety of stem rust (Puccinia graminis tritici) attacks wheat, barley, rye, and many grasses. The oats variety (P. graminis avenge) attacks oats and various grasses. The rye variety (P. graminis secalis) parasitizes not only rye but also certain grasses. The redtop variety (P. graminis agrostidis) occurs on redtop and related grasses. The bluegrass variety (P. graminis poae) is on Kentucky bluegrass and many other bluegrasses. The timothy variety (P. graminis phlei-pratensis) attacks timothy and a few other grasses.

The wheat variety of stem rust has been found on many of the wheat-grasses (Agropyron species), orchard-grass, wild-rye grasses (Elymus species), barley grasses (Hordeum species), and a few less important grasses. The stem rust of oats occurs on tall oatgrass, sweet vernalgrass, some brome grasses, orchardgrass, a few fescues, canary-grass, timothy, a few bluegrasses, and some others of less importance. Stem rust of rye attacks many of the wheat-grasses, a few bromes, many of the wild-rye grasses, and barley grasses.

The redtop variety is practically restricted to redtop and related grasses (Agrostis species). Stem rust of blue-grasses likewise is restricted to Kentucky bluegrass and a few other of the bluegrasses. The timothy variety is virulent on tall oatgrass, orchardgrass, meadow fescue, and tall fescue. So it is apparent that three of the varieties of stem rust attack both cereals and grasses and that the other three are restricted to grasses only.

In the Southern States and other places of mild winters, stem rust usually overwinters in the red stage on grasses and on volunteer or fall-sown grain. In regions of colder winters, such overwintering is exceptional, and the rust fungus depends on the black spore stage for survival during fall and winter and for reestablishment in the following early summer. Reestablishment is impossible without intervention of a spring stage of stem rust on an entirely unrelated plant, the common barberry (species of Berberis), the alternate host.

The resulting infections on barberry bushes produce spores that set up the initial red spore stage on cereals and grasses in early summer. It is this stage that builds up in epidemic form by repeated generations during summers of frequent rains or prolonged dew.

Leaf rust (Puccinia rubigo-vera) occurs mainly on the leaves of cereals and grasses, although stem infections are encountered sometimes. Host specialization occurs, similar to that described for stem rust, so that we have six varieties, as follows: One variety of leaf rust, Puccinia rubigo-vera agroppri, common in the Rocky Mountain region, infects many of the wheatgrasses, various bromes, and several of the wild-rye grasses. It has many alternate hosts, all in the buttercup family (clematis, buttercup, columbine, larkspur, and others).

Another rust variety, P. rubigo-vera apocrypta, also occurs on a few wheatgrasses and wild-rye grasses but has alternate hosts in the waterleaf family (e. g. Hydrophyllum) and the borage family (e. g. Mertensia). Of the mountainous areas. Besides wheatgrasses, it attacks bromes, meadow foxtail, alkali-grass, mannagrass, the wild-ryes, and many others. The numerous alternate hosts are all in the buttercup family.

The wheat variety of leaf rust (P. rubigo-vera tritici) is restricted to various wheats and apparently will not infect grasses. The alternate host is meadow-rue.

The sixth variety, the leaf rust of rye (p. rubigo-vera secalis), is restricted to rye. Its alternate host is the wild forget-me-not or bugloss (Lycopsis). Leaf rust frequently is as destructive as stem rust. Occasionally infection is so heavy that the infected plants are literally dusty red with rust and may even be killed by it. As a species, leaf rust is widespread from coast to coast, although some of the varieties are limited by geography or climate.

Stripe rust (Puccinia glumarum) is quite different in appearance from stem rust and leaf rust. The individual pustules, instead of being orange red, are yellow and arranged in long rows or stripes. A cool-weather rust, it makes its best progress in the spring and early summer before hot weather sets in. It is restricted to the Rocky Mountain States and westward.

Stripe rust is found commonly on the various wheatgrasses, wild-ryes, bromes, and barley grasses, besides wheat, barley, and rye. Some grasses, such as crested wheatgrass and blue wild-rye, frequently are infected to the extent that plants are killed outright or are rendered easy prey to drought and other diseases. The alternate host of stripe rust is unknown. Being a cool-weather rust, it overwinters easily without an alternate host.

CROWN RUST (Puccinia coronata) is really a leaf rust and to the unaided eye looks just like true leaf rust. The difference between the two lies in the black spore stage and in its alternate hosts. Under the microscope its black spores (teliospores) are seen to bear a crown of long projections at the top (hence the name crown rust); these are lacking in the leaf rust spores. Also, it has only a few alternate hosts cascara buckthorn (chittum bark) and related species of buckthorn (Rhamnus).

Crown rust occurs on oats, wild oats, and many grasses velvetgrass, English ryegrass, Italian ryegrass, meadow fescue, tall fescue, orchardgrass, and some of the bentgrasses, among them. It is of economic significance more in the Mississippi Valley than east or west.

Bluegrass leaf rust (Puccinia poaesudeticae) is common only on grasses. It does not occur on any of the cereals. As the name indicates, the chief grasses affected are the bluegrasses, but occasionally others (such as meadow fescue and alpine timothy) are infected. It occurs chiefly in the leaves and produces numerous, minute, orange-red pustules, but frequently stem infections occur. Of the bluegrasses, Kentucky bluegrass is by far the most commonly infected. It rarely develops in epidemic proportion in lawns and pastures, however, probably because of too frequent mowing or grazing, but in nurseries or other undisturbed stands heavy developments often occur. Several other valuable bluegrasses are commonly infected, sometimes very badly. Bluegrass leaf rust does not have a known alternate host. It over-winters easily and effectively in the red spore stage.

Stem rust is controlled by eradicating the alternate host, the common barberry (Berberis vulgaris). In the interests of controlling stem rust on wheat, oats, barley, and rye, an active barberry eradication campaign has been in force in 18 States. The campaign also is in the interests of susceptible forage grasses. For example, in eastern Washington, before that State joined the eradication campaign in 1944, stem rust could be found on numerous grasses and sometimes in epidemic quantity. By 1951, with the barberry all but eliminated (except for numerous small seedlings), it was unusual to find stem rust in anything more than trace amounts.

In the States where crown rust is a problem, its alternate host, buckthorn, has been eradicated along with the common barberry. Those are the only rusts of importance on grasses that can thus be controlled to any practical degree. Elimination of the alternate host has another advantage: It is on that host that hybridization between strains of rust takes place, often with the result of new and more virulent strains capable of attacking varieties of grasses and cereals that already were resistant. The development or selection of grasses resistant to rust has lagged behind such projects in the cereals. Strains have been noted in timothy, orchardgrass, crested wheatgrass, blue bunchgrass, big bluegrass, and others that are resistant to their particular rusts. It is usually true, however, that those resistant strains are valid only in restricted regions and are not generally resistant to the various and numerous races or strains of rusts in all localities. The individual State colleges can best give advice on such local problems. The fact remains that genetic resistance does exist in strains of most of our forage grasses and can be used in breeding work when necessary or desirable.

ROOT AND CROWN ROTS OF THE GRASSES

Range and pasture grasses during various stages of their life are subject to attack by soil-borne parasitic fungi.

Some parasitic fungi can stand considerable drought, but most of the relatively delicate organisms need plenty of moisture. During the early life of the grass host, the fungi are well favored because the grass seeds germinate in moist soil, where the fungi are waiting. Later in its life grass may form mats of foliage, which help to keep the humidity high and therefore favour root and crown rots.

Root rots and crown rots are in total probably the most destructive group of parasites of the grass family. In parts of the Great Plains, for instance, they were one of the chief reasons why regrassing after the drought years was so difficult. Losses up to 100 per cent from seedling blight, for instance, were general.

Most of the soil-borne fungus parasites of grasses develop fine filamentous mycelium without producing any conspicuous fruiting bodies. A few develop small, hard, black sclerotic, which later give rise to small fruiting bodies about one-third inch high. A number of them produce coloured or obscure masses of spores on diseased parts. Others form microscopic or nearly microscopic fruiting bodies in diseased parts. The identification of the various root rots and crown rots must depend to some extent on microscopic examination of the diseased tissue and frequently only after isolation of pure cultures. Certain symptoms, however, aid in distinguishing some of the diseases without great difficulty.

Some of the fungi in the soil can survive alone and are called soil inhabiting. Most of them, however, depend on humus in the soil to survive during part of their life. Such fungi can grow through the soil for some distances away from the nearest particle of humus, but they must retain a life line of mycelium with the piece of humus from which they started. Such fungi are called soil invading.

Most of the root rot fungi are soil invading and can therefore be starved out by prolonged fallowing. They need nitrogen, phosphorus, and other chemicals to grow, the same as plants do. They tend to accumulate in the area next to the roots in the soil the rhizosphere. The region teems with activity from fungi, bacteria, and the plant roots. As the available supply of soil nutrients may become depleted, the fungi sometimes invade living cells in the roots of the grasses in search of food.

If they maintain a mild form of parasitism with mutual exchange of. nutrients, both host and fungus may benefit. Actually these mycorhizal fungi serve as root hairs. They grow out into the soil, seeking nutrients which they carry through their mycelial filaments into the cells of the plant. The mycorhizal fungi take from the plant but give food from the soil in exchange. If the parasitism is favorable to both fungus and plant it is called symbiosis.

Usually in grasses, however, when fungi invade the roots they are destructively parasitic. In young plants death may quickly follow. In older ones the process may be prolonged as a slow necrosis and"going-out" of old stands. All soil fungi are not parasitic. Some cannot attack living plant tissue. They are called saprophytes. Some are weakly parasitic or are starved into invading living tissue. Sometimes some of the Pythium species appear to performance in this way. Other fungi prefer the parasitic life. They are especially to be feared.

Species of grasses differ in their resistance to root rots and crown rots. Sometimes the resistance may be due to some mechanical feature of the plant, such as stout cell walls, but more likely the resistance lies in some chemical antagonism within the cytoplasm of the cell itself. We also have some instances of strain differences in grass species in their tolerance to certain fungi, but in relation to root rots these instances are all too few.

The adaptability of the host to the environment greatly influences its ability to withstand attacks by soil fungi. If the grass, for instance, is a warm-temperature-loving grass from the southern plains, it will often be wiped out by relatively weak soil-borne parasites if sown in cold, wet soil in the northern Great Plains. If the grass prefers a particular soil acidity, it may die from root rots if grown in a place where the acidity is not favorable for the growth of the grass. A desert grass such as Indian ricegrass will soon damp-off or decay if grown in areas of high humidity and frequent rain. Also, grasses that are not hardy are sometimes so weakened that they are more subject to common root rots than are vigorous ones. Winter injury, however, is not a great factor in the ecology of root rot. Much of the injury is to young spring-seeded plants. Injury to older plants is sometimes associated with winter-injured plants or with plants growing in infertile soil. These cases are usually associated with weak parasites, such as certain species of Fusarium, Curvularia, and Gloeosporium bolleyi. Some strains of those fungi, however, are strongly parasitic, so that their presence does not necessarily mean that the root rot injury is on weakened plants.

The symptoms the various fungi cause on the host are more interesting to the general reader than the exact identity of the organisms. We can classify the many rots into a few general groups on the basis of symptoms with a minimum of reference to the causal organism. It is important, however, to know something about the various species and genera of the fungi that cause the rots. The same organism may cause more than one type of decay. For instance: Helminthosporium sativum may cause a seed rot or seedling blight if it occurs on moldy, untreated seed; several years later it may be involved in a crown rot of older plants.

- *Preemergence rots*: The plant or seed is killed as the seed starts to germinate or just before it emerges from the soil. The rootlets are often rotted to short stubs or collapse in a soft decay. Seed rot in the soil is most frequent in early spring or late fall in cold, wet soil or later in the year if the seed is planted just before a heavy, beating rain. Warm-temperature grasses or grasses with small seeds are especially subject to preemergence rot. The loss of seed from this cause alone averages well above 25 per cent of all seed planted. Much of the loss is so common as to be taken for granted.

The most common causes of seed rot are certain species of bacteria and some fungi, including Pythium debaryanum, P. ultimum, Fusarium culmorum, and Rhizoctonia solani.

Control of preemergence decay includes the judicious selection of appropriate seeding dates in well-drained soil; the use of viable, clean seed of recent harvest; and seed free from seed-borne molds. The seed should be treated with some seed-treatment material such as Arasan or Ceresan M.

- Root necrosis, common root rots, and damping-off. Sometimes the plants that escape preemergence rots will develop a rapid soft rot and fall over soon after emergence. That is damping-off. Such fungi as Rhizoctonia solani and Pythium debaryanum are usually the cause of damping-off. Damping-off is common in ornamental and vegetable seedlings but less common in grasses. Sometimes one will encounter damping-off in prolonged rainy periods in thick stands that had emerged earlier during weather that was more favorable.

Grass roots are more likely to suffer from a slower decay, or necrosis. Necrosis due to Pythium debaryanum is likely in poorly drained soil or soil saturated by prolonged rains. The roots are often stubbed back by a slow and complete decay. Plants affected with pythium necrosis tend to recover rapidly when good growing conditions return.

The common root rot of maturing cereal plants has its counterpart in grasses. The grass roots are slowly killed by the action of Fusarium culmorum or Helminthosporium sativum and associated molds, sometimes alone, often competing in the roots of the same host. The Fusarium may cause pink or rosy colours on the dead roots, especially at the ground line, where masses of spores form.

Head scab of cereals and sometimes of grasses is caused by Fusarium (part of the F. roseum complex). This organism or group of organisms can also cause a seedling blight.

The associated fungus Helminthosporium sativum causes a brown blotch and root decay of wheatgrasses and, in fact, on many range and pasture grasses. Some seedling blight may result from it.

It can also cause pre-emergence rot when its spores are borne on the seed of grasses raised in areas with high rainfall in summer. Such seed should be treated before seeding. Grass seed grown in the drier western regions, however, are usually free of seed-borne parasitic molds.

- Root browning and seedling blights. In root browning, the root decay is represented by a firm, brown rot, usually of young rootlets. Its action is slow but often deadly. The diseased seedlings gradually fail to keep pace with healthy ones; about 6 weeks after seeding in the spring, they shrivel and die. They soon disappear in the winds that sweep across the plains and are replaced by weeds.

The main cause of seedling blight in grasses in the Great Plains and far West is another species of Pythium (P. graminicola). Its action differs from that of root necrosis caused by P. debaryanum in that the plants fail to recover when good weather returns. In fact, the damage often occurs during relatively favorable growing conditions. Some conditions favour its prevalence. It seems to be especially active in grass planted on old plowed sod. It outlasts the bacteria in summer fallow and can only be starved out by several years of continuous fallow. It is possibly less serious on ground that has last grown a crop of corn, oats, or potatoes.

Damage from the root browning fungus is sometimes lessened by the use of a balanced fertilizer that supplies nitrogen and phosphorus to the host and probably to the fungus. The same organism destroys the roots of mature plants in old stands, especially when the stands are sod-bound and have too little nitrogen.

Fall seeding, where practical, is helpful in checking loss from seedling blight. By the following June the plants have passed their most susceptible stage.

Seed treatment does little to check root browning. The sphere of control that seed-borne chemicals can effect is in a small zone close to the seed. Seed treatment helps control seed rot, but it is useless in controlling decay that originates on the rootlets just beyond the old seed.

In South Dakota long search for strains of grasses resistant to seedling blight has resulted in a few strains of grass said to have some tolerance to Pythium graminicola.

Other fungi besides P. graminicola cause seedling blights, but they are considerably less widespread and less often reach the devastating proportions that this disease assumes. The common root rot Fusaria, Helminthosporium, Curvularia, and Rhizoctonia sometimes kill seedlings.

Rhizoctonia solani, one of the causes of eyespot, can produce other symptoms. In closely planted turf its cobwebby mycelium spreads radially, rotting the leaves and forming brown patch areas. We sometimes find brown patch in pastures. Occasionally it also causes some stunting by attacking the roots themselves; then it is often associated with common root rot fungi, and the symptoms are blended in one complex. R. solani has at least four races that can be distinguished more or less by their capacity to attack a number of grass, cereal, and leguminous and vegetable crops. One race in western Oregon and Washington is especially virulent on the basal parts of the stems of cereals and some grasses but is scarcely parasitic on legumes. Other races in the Midwest and eastern seaboard are actively parasitic on both grasses and legumes. Crop rotation to control Rhizoctonia is difficult because of its adaptability to numerous hosts and because of the complexity of its races.

Crown rots usually develop on older plants. The interior of the crowns show brown, dry rot. Such plants are probably affected with common rot, the same as occurs in cereals. An abundance of pink Fusarium spores may be present. Sometimes the less Conspicuous brown ones of Helminthosporium are found. On Kentucky bluegrass a crown or foot rot occurs. It is caused by a distinct fungus (Helminthosporium vagans), which usually attacks the leaves and causes a dark spot.

The roots of plants suffering from crown rots usually are decayed and serve as poor anchors for the plants, which are readily removed from the ground. Old, sod-bound stands especially are subject to crown rots. They also may suffer from root browning, caused by the same fungus that causes seedling blight in young plants (Pythium graminicola). Root browning and crown rots often work together in the old stands. Sometimes the plants may be kept producing for a few more years by use of fertilizer to balance the activity of the Pythium.

- Snow molds. Some soil-borne fungi attack all above-ground parts of grasses as they lie under the snow in late winter. For many years field workers confused these diseases with winter injury, which is due to low temperature. It has been shown, however, that the elimination of the parasitic mold permitted the plants to survive without injury despite the winter weather. In other words, the parasitic snow mold fungi prefer to live at a temperature approximating that of melting snow.

There are two common groups of snow mold the pink snow mold, caused by Fusarium nivale, and the speckled snow mold, caused by species of Typhula.

Pink snow mold attacks field and turf grasses in late winter, either under the snow or during raw winter weather. The leaves in the prostrate winter rosette stage are killed and formed into pink or straw-coloured mats, which later dry to papery films. Sometimes plants recover from the disease if the crowns are not deeply injured. The colour of the dead leaves is due partly to the masses of pinkspores that are formed. The spores sometimes cause a secondary leaf spot in early spring if cold, wet weather follows melting of the snow. Pink snow mold is especially common in the Pacific Northwest on cheatgrass brome (Bromus tectorum), which serves as one of its carriers. Speckled snow mold, more restricted than pink snow mold, is a true snow mold in that it cannot thrive without the semi-refrigeration of melting snow. It causes a slimy, gray rot of grass and cereal leaves under the snow in midwinter or late winter.

The gray mold soon forms many tiny, black, hard sclerotia, which dot the white dried leaves after the snow has gone hence the name speckled snow mold. The sclerotia, which form on the leaves in March to April in the Pacific Northwest, germinate the following November. They produce small, fragile, club-shaped fruiting bodies. The bodies shoot off spores into the air.

7

Tomato

INTRODUCTION TO TOMATO

LEAF MOULD

Infection occurs mainly on the leaves, occasionally at the stalk end of the fruit. Leaf mould always appears first on the older mature leaves. The fungus enters through the stomata and the mycelium penetrates first between the leaf cells, afterwards into them. The dark conidiophores emerge in bunches through the stomata on the under-side of the leaf and bear numerous tiny elliptical conidia, mostly two-celled. They form a greyish bloom on the spots that turns a purplish brown with age.

No conidia are produced on the upper surface of the leaf but yellow blotches appear corresponding to the mould spots on the under-side. Gradually as the disease progresses the leaves turn yellow, curl and finally shrivel completely, thus greatly weakening the plants. It takes the form of a black discolouration spreading outwards over the fruit from the end of the stalk but never covering the whole surface.

The fruit may become lopsided and furrowed as a result of this attack. The fungus cannot attack the fruit directly but penetrates the stomata on the sepals or on the stalk and spreads through these into the young fruit or may prevent the fruit setting.

Seed from infected fruit may carry the fungus and not only give rise to an infected seedling but act as a source of infection for neighbouring plants in the seed boxes. The seed coat containing the fungus is carried above ground on the cotyledons, conidia are produced on it and shed on to the surrounding seedlings.As the fungus overwinters in the soil and on the interior fittings of the greenhouse the house must be disinfected after a tomato crop. This is most easily done by burning sulphur.

One should not pass straight from an infected house into one where the crop is still healthy, nor take tools, baskets, etc., from one to the other. By such means the conidia can easily be introduced into the healthy house.

It is of the utmost importance to prevent excessive atmospheric humidity. Therefore firing should be kept up at night throughout the summer and the house must be kept thoroughly ventilated. It is important to construct tomato houses so as to allow of plenty of side and end ventilation. An outbreak of leaf mould can be stopped altogether by heating and ventilating.

STEM ROT

The disease occurs mainly on the stems of medium-sized and old plants and on the fruit. It may also appear on the stems of quite small plants and sometimes causes dark spots on the leaves but this is exceptional. The rot on the stem forms a dark-brown area with a sharp boundary between it and the healthy tissue.

Dotted over the brown part are,the tiny dark pycnidia. Infections can often be seen to be centred on wounds made by defoliation or other causes. In severe attacks the whole of the plant dies above the infected part. Infection occurs not only through cracks and wounds but also directly through the uninjured skin.

The incubation period is 4 days or more. The fruit is generally attacked only in one place but the rot may spread all over it. The spot usually appears when the fruit begins to turn red. It is then much the same colour as the rest of the skin but has a granular appearance due to the crowded pycnidia.

The latter are usually very close together over the whole surface of the spot and eventually turn black so that the diseased area as a whole looks blackish. Under moist conditions pink globules of conidia ooze out of the pycnidia. Infection at the base of the fruit may cause it to fall.

ROOT ROT, FOOT ROT

The young plants become limp, the stem shrivels at soil level and they fall over. If the damage is caused by a species of Phytophthora or Pythium the shrivelled stem is greyish; if the damage is done by Corticium solani it is rather browner, but it is not always possible to distinguish the two forms of the disease without microscopic examination. Tomatoes are more often attacked by Phytophthora and Pythium than by Corticium.

That of P. cryptogea Pethybr. and Laff. is 75° F. and that of Corticium solani is 65° F. None of these fungi causes appreciable damage at temperatures below 50° F. All soil-borne fungus attacks can be prevented by sterilizing the soil by heat. Pythium and Phytophthora may also be controlled by formalin treatment of the soil before the seed is sown. Watering with Cheshunt compound can also be done to disinfect the soil before sowing and to check an outbreak of Phytophthora damping off in the early stages. Solutions of corrosive sublimate and saltpetre and proprietory preparations containing mercury may be used in the same way against Corticium solani. Drying the surface soil by raking helps to check Phytophthora but not Corticium. A few outbreaks have been reported but the disease is, no doubt, usually confused with other root rots. Affected plants wilt by day and recover at night. Usually their foliage is darker than normal and the under-side of the leaves often has a purplish tint.

The stem is thin and hard and the leaves are small and pointed. When the plant is dug up or knocked out of its pot the main root is found to be dead with a curiously pointed tip. Usually the core of the root is brown and hard. New rootlets are formed higher up, only to be destroyed in their turn, and eventually adventitious roots arise from the stem above soil level. Infection may occur in the seed box but it is seldom detected at this stage as the only symptom is blackening of one or more of the roots.

In pot plants the main root is usually destroyed and the hard appearance of the tops may develop, but often the trouble is masked by profuse development of secondary roots. Usually toe rot is first noticed after the plants have been set in the border and made considerable growth. Then, when conditions favour rapid transpiration, the damaged root system is unable to supply the necessary water and daytime wilting sets in. Cold soils encourage the disease.

FOOT ROT (COLLAR ROT) OF OLDER PLANTS

The plants are attacked at soil level where a dark, sunken, decaying patch appears on the stem. The side roots are usually dead or brown before this occurs. The main root is also often brown and rotten, its soft parts decay and only the woody core remains.

The disease may resemble stem rot but the lesions of that disease are bounded by healthy tissue above and below, whereas those made by Corticium solani start in the root and spread upwards so that they are bounded by healthy tissue at the top only. If outbreaks have occurred in previous crops the soil should be sterilized by heat or by corrosive sublimate treatment. When older plants are attacked by foot rot they can sometimes be saved by packing fresh soil round the base of the stem.

If possible soil free from the fungus should be used. The stem then puts out new roots above the diseased part. To prevent the fungus from growing into the fresh soil it should be watered occasionally with solution of corrosive sublimate and saltpetre or with a proprietary compound of mercury. Neighbouring plants should also be watered with the same solution.

Damage by this disease occurs particularly during cold springs and to weak plants, hence if the disease appears in a greenhouse the temperature should be raised. Care should be taken to see the plants make the normal rate of growth.

VERTICILLIUM WILT

Plants attacked by Verticillium wilt sometimes become stunted in growth because the stem ceases to elongate, thus causing the upper part of the plant to become rosette-like. At first the plants wilt only during the day and recover their turgidity during the night. The lower leaves develop light-orange spots, and gradually this discolouration spreads up the plant and the leaves first affected wither. Infected plants may die quickly or may remain in an unthrifty condition for a considerable period. In the latter case they may ultimately die or may recover from the attack. The vascular bundles of the stem are stained brown. Usually the fruit is not attacked but occasionally the fungus causes a soft rot. Wilting of tomatoes on hot days may also be due to root trouble, including eelworm infestation.

BROWN ROOT ROT

For several years increasing attention has been paid to this disease in indoor tomato crops. Brown or brown-spotted roots appear in association with poorly developed tops. It has not been proved that the brown roots are the cause of the poor development above ground and the low yield of fruit, but circumstantial evidence makes this highly probable. There is often a small amount of browning on the roots even of plants that arc fruiting well.

Brown roots are often seen also on melon, and the complex black root rot of strawberry seems to be a comparable condition. If plants with healthy roots are planted in " sick " soil distinct brown roots may be found after 3-4 weeks. Even earlier microscopic examination discloses spots in which the root cells have yellow thickened walls while their contents are brown and granular.

The boundary between these spots and healthy tissue is clearly denned. The brown spots or belts begin on the outer surface of the root, and gradually penetrate more deeply until they reach the vascular bundles, along which the brown discolouration spreads. When the roots are dug up one generally finds zones of brown, swollen and cracked cortex on the thicker roots alternating with zones of healthy cortex having the normal white or a light-brown colour.

In more severe attacks the roots die until only a little tuft of weak fibrous roots remains at the base of the stem; the top is very backward, the whole plant thin and lanky and the fruiting very poor. Many observations indicate that appearance of brown root rot is closely bound up with conditions of cultivation.

In experiments at Cheshunt the disease was worst on overmanured, wet and compact soil and it was concluded that great variations in soil moisture should be avoided. Brown root rot may be very prevalent in a new tomato house, and with continued cultivation of tomatoes the brown discolouration may decrease with successive crops until it almost disappears as soil conditions improve. Replacing the soil of an affected greenhouse often helps greatly but the question as to whence this soil should be taken, which previous crop is most favourable to tomatoes, requires closer investigation.

SCLEROTINIA ROT

The plants wither, sometimes the whole plant dies suddenly, in other instances the lower leaves shrivel first. A rotten area, often covered by white mycelium, is to be found on the stem near soil level. Threads of the white mycelium may grow out into the surrounding soil. Wrapped up by the mycelium or enclosed by the stem cavity from which the pith has disappeared are large sclerotia, at first soft and white but ultimately hard with a black rind.

Green tomatoes picked to ripen off may be destroyed by the same fungus if they come from infected plants and especially if they have come in contact with infected soil, or been placed on a bench where others had decayed before.

They are rapidly converted into a rotten mass overgrown by dense white mycelium containing black sclerotia. Sclerotinia rot may be destructive both out of doors and in houses once the soil has become infected and if conditions are moist enough.

BUCKEYE ROT

Symptoms and cause. The two species of Phytophthora which cause foot rot and damping off of tomato seedlings can also attack the unripe fruit. This develops a greyish spot marked with concentric brown rings round the point of entry of the fungus. Intensive work on the physiological races of potato blight has led to the recognition of a race (A) widespread throughout the world and another closely related race (T) which has a particular capacity for infecting tomato leaves.

Other races produce only larger or smaller spots on tomato leaves. In our experiments the yield of fruit has been increased and the number of diseased fruits reduced by spraying outdoor tomatoes with Bordeaux or Burgundy mixture as soon as blight is first seen on the potato crop, repeating the spray every 12 to 20 days thereafter. In experiments good results have been. obtained with copper lime dusts. Where outdoor tomatoes are picked to ripen indoors spraying definitely improves their keeping quality.

FUSARIUM FRUIT ROT

Symptoms. Infection begins at the stylar scar at the blossom end of the fruit as a small, sunken, soft spot that gradually increases in size and turns dark. From its surface break out pink conidial pustules of the Fusarium, often arranged in concentric rings.

Ultimately the entire fruit becomes permeated, turns yellow, shrivels and dries up. The disease occurs on the outdoor crop. The attack is by the above-mentioned species of Fusarium which penetrates the fruit through the tiny wound left by the fall of the style.

It cannot penetrate the unbroken skin but on picked fruit it easily enters by the stalk scar and may cause serious loss of outdoor tomatoes ripening in store. The fungus needs a high temperature and high atmospheric humidity for active development. The disease almost invariably occurs on the lower trusses of fruit. The fungi concerned inhabit the soil and attack fruit in contact with the ground, or those on to which they have been splashed during watering.

Buckeye rot is well known in many countries where tomatoes are grown and has caused great loss from time to time.

MOSAIC IN TOMATO

Symptoms vary from ill-defined, light-green spots, mainly between the veins of the leaflets, to quite a bright, clearly defined, light and dark-green mottle. The surface of the leaves may also be slightly uneven or even curled. Tomato variety, nutrition and the time of year all affect the expression of symptoms; thus, during the sunny warm days of summer the mottling is most obvious, and during spring and autumn the curling becomes apparent. At low temperatures the symptoms may be almost entirely lacking but the plants remain infected and infectious to others. Flowers of infected plants may be deformed, sterile and fall off.

There may be slight streaking of the stems and pale, slowly ripening spots on the fruit. Infection from tomato plants. The invisible infectious matter, or virus, occurs in the sap of almost all the cells of an infected tomato plant, including the cells of its numerous hairs.

These are easily broken and it is a familiar experience that one cannot handle a tomato plant without getting sap on one's hands, tools and clothes. If one touches an infected plant and then a healthy one a mere trace of sap transferred from one to the other is enough to transmit the infection. Hands, knives and other tools are the most important agents of spread. Aphides do not spread this disease. The incubation period is from 5 to 20 days or 28 days in our experiments out of doors.

It persists for a very long time in dead plants and purified virus preparations can remain viable in the laboratory for 5 years. The virus is not killed until heated for 10 minutes at 194° F. or until treated for 24 hours with 60 per cent alcohol, but it is sensitive to soap. Probably tomato sap dried on clothes can remain infectious for a long time.

Virus liberated from a plant into the soil can remain infectious for a long time if the soil is moist; freezing and drying the soil renders it non-infective. Infection from other plants and products. Common tomato mosaic is caused by the same virus as common tobacco mosaic, which is common in all tobacco-growing countries. Fermented, commercialj smoking or chewing tobacco may retain the virus in an infectious condition.

Hence chewing tobacco is a common source of infection in commercial tobacco production. Besides species of Nico-tiana this virus can infect most plants belonging to the family Solanaceae and also species in other families, notably asclepias, snapdragon, larkspur, zinnia, beans, spinach and possibly celery. Potato, black nightshade and woody nightshade (bittersweet) show no symptoms, but they are carriers of infection. From these hosts the virus can be returned to tomato.

The nightshades afford a means of carrying it over winter as also do susceptible greenhouse ornamentals like Petunia, Solanum and others. There seems little danger to the tomato crop from mosaic-infected potatoes though there is evidence of one such a transmission out of doors.

It may be supposed that the virus multiplies more luxuriantly in vigourously growing plants.

The statement that a crop can be " manured out of mosaic " only means that suitable manuring may overcome the consequences of infection; the virus in the plants is not destroyed. When nitrogen is very deficient the mottle becomes invisible; if nitrogen is then supplied it reappears. The influences of light and temperature have been mentioned above. Attacks are often found to start near doors and ventilators, which can scarcely be due to draughts but rather to infection from outside the house.

SPOTTED WILT

Then a large number of tiny bronze-coloured spots appear either in rings or scattered over the whole leaf surface. Growth stops for a time so that infected plants appear stunted. Young seedlings may be killed but more often the plant resumes growth after a time, but its leaves become distorted and have a rather conspicuous yellowish mosaic mottling. The fruit may be unaffected or it may bear pale-red, yellow or almost white markings, often in concentric rings. The virus is sap-transmissible but not to the same degree as tomato mosaic. It is not spread by aphides but only by thrips.

Curiously enough it is only in the larval stage that thrips can take up the virus from an infected plant, but once they have done so they remain infective throughout their life. Lycopersicum Virus 3 is not very resistant, it remains viable only a few hours in expressed tomato sap, is inactivated by drying, by oxidizing agents and by exposure for 10 minutes to a temperature of 108° F.

It has a very wide host range and commonly infects many popular greenhouse perennials which then form reservoirs of infection for the next tomato crop. Most of these show little sign of infection or bear only a few rather inconspicuous ring marks on their leaves.

TOMATO YELLOW LEAF

It starts as a well-marked mosaic mottle on the youngest leaves. The older leaves turn yellow, except along the main veins which remain dark-green. As the plant grows the yellow spreads until only the topmost leaves remain green. The whole picture resembles nitrogen starvation. Some evidence of seed transmission has been obtained. In properties the virus closely resembles that of common tomato mosaic. The aster yellows virus can also infect tomato and causes a certain amount of yellowing and a bushy type of growth, as it stimulates development of leafy buds and shoots in the axils of the leaflets as well.

AUCUBA MOSAIC

This disease is caused by a strain of the common tomato mosaic virus and must not be confused with aucuba mosaic of potato, caused by quite a different virus. Bright yellow spots often appear on the leaves of tomato plants infected with common mosaic. If these are punched out and used for inoculation the aucuba mosaic disease is produced. It is also sometimes found by itself in commercial tomato houses. About 5 days after inoculation the youngest leaves curl down and their surface becomes rough, wrinkled or corrugated.

By the seventh or eighth day yellow spots appear and become gradually larger, until in extreme cases the whole leaf surface is yellow, with a few raised islands of dark-green standing out on it like blisters. More often the yellow and green areas are of about equal extent and intimately intermingled. Plants are not killed by the virus but their growth is checked and the fruit may be mottled. Properties of the virus are the same as for common tomato mosaic. There is some evidence that seed-borne infection can take place in a very small number of seedlings, perhaps by virus dried on the seed coat.

LATE BLIGHT OF TOMATO

Late blight is one of the most devastating diseases of potato and tomato worldwide. It was responsible for the devastating Irish potato famine of the 1840's and has continued to be important to the present. Since 1990, late blight has caused widespread damage across the United States and Canada. If left unmanaged, this disease can result in complete destruction of potato or tomato crops.

SYMPTOMS

Late blight appears on potato or tomato leaves as pale green, water-soaked spots, often beginning at leaf tips or edges. The circular or irregular leaf lesions are often surrounded by a pale yellowish-green border that merges with healthy tissue. Lesions enlarge rapidly and turn dark brown to purplish-black. During periods of high humidity and leaf wetness, a cottony, white mold growth is usually visible on lower leaf surfaces at the edges of lesions.

In dry weather, infected leaf tissues quickly dry up and the white mold growth disappears.

Infected areas on stems appear brown to black and entire vines may be killed in a short time when moist weather persists.

On potato tubers, late blight appears as a shallow, coppery-brown, dry rot that spreads irregularly from the surface through the outer 1/8-1/2 inch or more of tissue. On tuber surfaces, lesions appear brown, dry, and sunken, while infected tissues immediately beneath the skin appear granular and tan to copper-brown. When tubers are stored under cool, dry conditions, lesion development is retarded and, upon prolonged storage, lesions may become slightly sunken and desiccated. Secondary bacteria and fungi frequently enter late-blight lesions, usually resulting in a slimy breakdown of entire tubers. Late blight can also develop on green tomato fruit, resulting in large, firm, brown, leathery-appearing lesions, often concentrated on the sides or upper fruit surfaces. If conditions remain moist, abundant white mold growth will develop on the lesions and secondary soft-rot bacteria may follow, resulting in a slimy, wet rot of the entire fruit.

Causal Organism

Late blight is caused by the fungus Phytophthora infestans. Unlike most pathogenic fungi, the late blight fungus cannot survive in soil or dead plant debris. For an epidemic to begin in any one area, the fungus must survive the winter in potato tubers (culls, volunteers), be reintroduced on seed potatoes or tomato transplants, or live spores must blow in with rainstorms. Disease development is favoured by cool, moist weather.

Nights in the 50's and days in the 70's accompanied by rain, fog or heavy dew are ideal. Under these conditions, lesions may appear on leaves within 3-5 days of infection, followed by the white mold growth soon thereafter.

Spores formed on the mold are spread readily by irrigation, rain and equipment. They are easily dislodged by wind and rain and can be blown into neighbouring fields within 5-10 miles or more, thus beginning another cycle of disease. Infection of potato tubers arises from spores that develop on foliage.

Tubers exposed by soil cracking or erosion of hills may come in contact with spores washed down from infected leaves and stems by rainfall or irrigation.

Tubers infected during the growing season may partially decay before harvest. Tuber infection may also occur at harvest when tubers contact living spores remaining on infected vines. Little if any tuber-to-tuber spread of late blight occurs during storage if tubers are kept under cool, well-ventilated conditions.

The protectant fungicides commonly used to protect plants from late blight remain fully effective with all known strains of the fungus.

- Infected cull potatoes are a major source of spores of the late blight fungus and must be disposed of properly-Do Not Make Cull Piles. Cull potatoes should be spread on fields not intended for potato production the following year in time that they will totally freeze and be destroyed during the winter. If this is not possible, they must be destroyed in some other way such as by complete chopping, burial, burning or feeding to livestock.
- Plant only certified seed potatoes. Use of "year-out" seed or seed saved from local crops is asking for trouble with late blight. Seed sources should be selected very carefully to avoid bringing in late blight on seed potatoes, especially new strains of the fungus. Look

for the characteristic coppery-brown discolouration of the potato flesh under the skin of seed tubers.

Infected tomato transplants also can be a significant source of the disease. Use only obviously healthy tomato transplants free of dark lesions on leaves or stems.

- Volunteer potatoes and tomatoes can be a significant source of spores of the late blight fungus. All volunteers should be destroyed as quickly as possible by herbicides, chopping, or cultivation.
- Growers should scout fields regularly to look for late blight. Special attention should be paid to early-planted fields because that is where the disease is likely to develop first. Scouting should be concentrated in low-lying areas, field edges along creeks or ponds, near the centre of centre-pivot irrigation rigs, in areas near woodlots or any area that is protected from wind where the leaves tend to remain wet longer.

  Any area where it is difficult to apply fungicides such as edges and corners or under power lines if using aerial application should be examined. Scouts should look for large, black or purplish lesions on stems or leaves and the telltale cottony, white mold growth, usually on the undersides. Be sure to check leaves and stems under the crop canopy as that is where the disease is most likely to begin.
- Use of a good protectant fungicide programme is necessary to fully protect any crop of potatoes or tomatoes.
- With potatoes, make sure that vines have been completely dead for 2-3 weeks prior to harvest. Fungicide applications should be continued until vines are dead.

  When foliage dies, spores of the late blight fungus that remain on the foliage also die. This practice will prevent infection of tubers during harvest and development of late blight in storage.

SEPTORIA LEAF SPOT OF TOMATOES

Septoria leaf spot is a disease of the foliage and stems. It does not affect fruit directly. The disease causes rapid defoliation when weather is warm and moist.

SYMPTOMS

Although the symptoms may appear on the leaves and stems at any stage of plant development, they usually become evident after plants have begun to set fruit in mid-July. Initially the fungus causes small, water-soaked, roughly circular spots scattered randomly over the leaf. These spots enlarge to become 1/16 to 1/8 inch in diameter with dark margins and tan centres. Small, dark, pimple-like fruiting bodies in which spores of the fungus are produced can be seen in the centre of the lesions. Older leaves near the ground usually show symptoms first. Symptoms appear rapidly on younger foliage in rainy weather. When leaves are heavily infected, they drop prematurely. Exposed fruits are subject to sunscald. The fungus which causes this disease can grow on weeds such as Jimson weed, horse nettle and nightshade.

Causal Organism

Septoria lycopersici lives between tomato crops in the soil on infested debris of tomato and weeds. Spores formed on crop debris splash onto foliage and start the disease. Wind and rain spread spores produced in the dark bodies formed in leaf spots to adjacent uninfected leaves. The fungus is most active between 60 and 80 degrees F when rainfall is abundant.

Control

- Rotate out of tomatoes for 4 years.
- Deep plow, preferably in the fall, to bury all plant refuse.
- Grow tomato transplants in sterilized soil.
- Control weeds, especially horse nettle, Jimson weed, and nightshade.

- Use of a protectant fungicide may be necessary to adequately control Septoria Leaf Spot when conditions are favourable for disease development.

FUSARIUM WILT OF VINE CROPS

Several different species of Fusarium, a soil-borne fungus, cause wilting of watermelon, muskmelon, cucumber, squash, and other vine crops. In many cases the fungus-causing wilt in a particular crop is specific to that crop. These fungi are generally capable of surviving for long periods in the soil.

SYMPTOMS

Wilting of older plants is often the first symptom of the disease. Before diseased plants totally collapse, however, they may begin to wilt during the hottest part of the day and recover during the night. Infected plants are often stunted and yellowed. Leaves often have dead areas which can mimic nutrient deficiencies. Stems of wilted plants when cut lengthwise at the soil line may show brown discolouration in the woody tissues immediately under the bark. Vines killed by Fusarium can be covered with pinkish-white fungal growth in wet weather.

Causal Organism

Fusarium oxysporum is well adapted to life in the soil. It can survive season to season in old diseased vines or it can live free in infested soil for many years in the absence of its host crop. The fungus grows at soil moisture and temperature favourable for vine crop growth. If the soil is very wet, infection is reduced. The fungus is stimulated to germinate when roots of susceptible host plants are growing nearby. It enters the plant through root tips or where some opening is present.

Control

- Plant wilt-resistant cultivars whenever possible. Degree of resistance is influenced by the populations of the fungi in the soil, and which races are present.
- Avoid introduction of the fungus into fields. Once soil is infested, crop rotation will be of little use because of the long-term survival of these fungi in soil. The fungus can be spread on equipment, tools, feet, and surface water contaminated with infested soil. Do not put compost on fields which has been made from diseased vines. Compost resulting from such piles will contain the fungus.
- Crop rotations of three to four years may be helpful in lowering the amount of Fusarium in the soil. Since the types of Fusarium-causing wilt in a crop are generally specific to that crop it is possible to rotate between vine crops in infested soil.
- In commercial production of vine crops, soil fumigation may be useful.

Anthracnose of Tomato

Anthracnose is a common and serious disease of tomato fruit. This disease can occasionally cause severe damage to peppers, especially when red fruit is allowed to develop. Anthracnose can reduce a bountiful harvest into rotted fruit in a few days in warm, moist weather.

SYMPTOMS

Small, water-soaked, circular lesions develop under the skin of fruit as it ripens. These become sunken and dark. Numerous dark specks, the fruiting bodies of the fungus, develop in the lesions in concentric rings. In moist, warm weather, these black bodies ooze gelatinous pink spore masses. In warm weather the fungus and soft rot bacteria which enter the split skin over the lesions spread internally forming a semisoft decay which renders the fruit worthless.

Causal Organism

Colletotrichum coccodes survives between crops on infested plant debris in the soil. Early in the growing season, spores from the soil splash on lower leaves of the tomato plant.

Few symptoms develop on infected leaves, but the spores produced on foliage can be carried by splashing rain to developing green fruit. Infected green fruit will not develop symptoms of anthracnose until they begin to ripen. Ripe fruit is very susceptible to this fungus.

Control

- Rotate 3 years between pepper and tomato crops.
- Plant tomatoes and peppers in well drained fields to avoid excess soil moisture as fruit ripen.
- Apply overhead irrigation during the early part of the day so that plants dry before sundown.
- Harvest and use fruit before it fully ripens.
- If conditions favour development of anthracnose, a preventative spray programme may be required to give adequate control of this disease.

Apply registered fungicides according to product label instructions when weather conditions are above 65 degrees F and the foliage is likely to remain wet longer than 6 hours. Applications to tomatoes should begin when the first fruit is larger than a walnut. Applications to peppers should be started as soon as fruit is present.

ROOT KNOT NEMATODE

Root knot first attracted attention in 1855 when it was found in a greenhouse in England. Since then it has been a cause for concern over much of the world. It affects more than 2,000 species of plants including economically important forage crops, small grains, fruits, vegetables, field crops, nursery crops, and turf grasses. Root knot nematodes are cosmopolitan in distribution and occur widely in the United States.

Symptoms

Root knot is very distinctive because of the galls or swellings produced on roots and underground portions of stems. These deformations can often completely ruin crops for sale. Plants, if infected when young, will be stunted, more susceptible to drought stress, and show symptoms of nutrient deficiency. Large and small roots may be affected with swellings varying from round sphere-like galls to elongated spindles formed from large numbers of individual galls growing together.

Root knot galls involve the entire root in the affected zone. They do not take the form of easily detached galls like those produced by nitrogen-fixing bacteria on the roots of legumes. Root knot galls should not be confused with the fungal disease, club root, on cruciferous crops. In most instances, root knot is characterized by smaller swellings, and more uniformly distributed infection on the lateral feeding roots than is typically seen with clubroot. When the galls formed by the root knot nematode are broken open, shiny white bodies about the size of a pinhead, the enlarged female nematodes, are usually found.

Also, glistening white to yellow egg masses are present on the root surface. The galls formed by clubroot do not possess this characteristic and are usually pinkish or brick coloured. Phenoxy-type herbicides such as 2,4 D can cause swellings on stems of cruciferous crops which superficially look like root knot galls. Herbicide damage on these crops will not affect the roots, however. On young potato tubers the outer surface appears rough and warty because of the enlarged females underneath the skin.

Causal Organism

Root knot is caused by a small round worm, Meloidogyne spp. There are about 40 species at the present time. Not all plants are susceptible to any one species. Juveniles emerging from eggs in the soil penetrate between and through cells to a position at the centre of the root usually near the growing tip. Feeding by the nematodes causes increases in root cell numbers and size. Enlarged cells, called giant cells, serve as food sources for female root knot nematodes. During feeding, juveniles which will become females undergo a series of molts and enlarge. The female does not move from the feeding site. Each female deposits 300-500 eggs in a protective, jelly-like matrix at the root surface. Eggs, particularly in the egg mass, can withstand unfavourable environmental conditions. They represent one means of overwintering. Root knot nematodes may also overwinter in the soil in a juvenile stage. Root knot nematodes are often introduced into a growing area in infected planting stock.

Control

- Rotate at least 3 years with non-host crops. While the feeding habits of field populations must be determined before crop rotation plans are set, the most common root knot species will not reproduce on grasses, small grains, or corn. Clean cultivation to keep down weed hosts of the nematodes is important.
- Use transplants and nursery stock certified free of root knot nematode.
- Plant resistant varieties wherever possible.
- In commercial production, soil can be treated with fumigant-type nematicides.

EARLY BLIGHT

Early blight is a very common disease of both potato and tomato. It causes leaf spots and tuber blight on potato, and leaf spots, fruit rot and stem lesions on tomato. The disease can occur over a wide range of climatic conditions and can be very destructive if left uncontrolled, often resulting in complete defoliation of plants. In contrast to the name, it rarely develops early, but usually appears on mature foliage.

SYMPTOMS

On leaves of both crops, the first symptoms usually appear on older leaves and consist of small, irregular, dark brown to black, dead spots ranging in size from a pinpoint to 1/2 inch in diameter. As the spots enlarge, concentric rings may form as a result of irregular growth patterns by the organism in the leaf tissue. This gives the lesion a characteristic "target-spot" or "bull's eye" appearance.

There is often a narrow, yellow halo around each spot and lesions are usually bordered by veins. When spots are numerous, they may grow together, causing infected leaves to turn yellow and die. Usually the oldest leaves become infected first and they dry up and drop from the plant as the disease progresses up the main stem. On tomato, stem infections can occur at any age resulting in small, dark, slightly sunken areas that enlarge to form circular or elongated spots with lighter-coloured centres.

Concentric markings, similar to those on leaves, often develop on stem lesions. If infested seed are used to start tomato transplants, seedlings may damp off soon after emergence. When large lesions develop at the ground line on stems of transplants or seedlings, the plants may become girdled, a condition known as "collar rot." Such plants may die when set in the field or, if stems are weakened, may break over early in the season.

Some plants may survive with reduced root systems if portions of stems above the canker develop roots where they contact the soil. Such plants, however, usually produce few or no fruits. Stem lesions are much less common and destructive on potato. Blossom drop and spotting of fruit stems, along with loss of young fruit, may occur when early blight attacks tomatoes in the flowering stage.

On older fruits, early blight causes dark, leathery sunken spots, usually at the point of stem attachment. These spots may enlarge to involve the entire upper portion of the fruit, often showing concentric markings like those on leaves. Affected areas may be covered with velvety black masses of spores.

Fruits can also be infected in the green or ripe stage through growth cracks and other wounds. Infected fruits often drop before they reach maturity.

On potato tubers, early blight results in surface lesions that appear a little darker than adjacent healthy skin. Lesions are usually slightly sunken, circular or irregular, and vary in size up to 3/4 inch in diameter.

There is usually a well defined and sometimes slightly raised margin between healthy and diseased tissue. Internally, the tissue shows a brown to black corky, dry rot, usually not more than 1/4 to 3/8 inch deep.

Causal Organism

Early blight is caused by the fungus, Alternaria solani, which survives in infected leaf or stem tissues on or in the soil. This fungus is universally present in fields where these crops have been grown. It can also be carried on tomato seed and in potato tubers. Spores form on infested plant debris at the soil surface or on active lesions over a fairly wide temperature range, especially under alternating wet and dry conditions. They are easily carried by air currents, windblown soil, splashing rain, and irrigation water.

Infection of susceptible leaf or stem tissues occurs in warm, humid weather with heavy dews or rain. Early blight can develop quite rapidly in mid to late season and is more severe when plants are stressed by poor nutrition, drought, or other pests. Infection of potato tubers occurs through natural openings on the skin or through injuries. Tubers may come in contact with spores during harvest and lesions may continue to develop in storage.

- Use a crop rotation that includes potatoes or tomatoes only every third or fourth year to allow infested plant debris to decompose in thc soil. Rotations with small grains, corn or legumes are preferable.
- Use tillage practices such as fall plowing that bury all plant refuse.
- Select cultivars that have a lower susceptibility to early blight.
- Use certified disease-free tomato seed and transplants.
- If producing tomato transplants, disinfest soil in plant beds and control humidity in cold frames or greenhouses. Practice good sanitation throughout the transplant production operation.
- Use appropriate measures to control weeds and volunteer potatoes and tomatoes in production areas.
- Maintain fertility at optimal levels-nitrogen and phosphorus deficiency can increase susceptibility to early blight.
- Time applications of overhead irrigation to allow plants to dry before nightfall.
- Although the above measures are important to minimize infection, it is usually necessary to apply fungicide sprays to fully protect plants from early blight.

  Applications to tomato are usually begun 2-3 weeks following emergence or soon after transplanting if a calendar schedule is followed. Timing of fungicides can also be made using the TOM-CAST system. For potatoes, fungicide applications should be initiated when plants begin to flower. Thorough coverage is important. Adjust equipment for good vine penetration.

COMBAT DISORDERS OF TOMATOES

Every tomato grower is faced with the hazard of loss from disease. Infections by fungi, bacteria, or viruses are responsible for much of the loss, but extremes of temperature and moisture or excess or deficiency of mineral elements in the soil at times may damage the crop.

The symptoms thus caused can be classified as wilts, leaf spots, fruit spots or rots, and abnormalities of growth of the foliage or fruits.

Fusarium wilt, caused by the fungus Fusarium oxysporum f. lycopersici, is serious on tomatoes. Its first symptom is a yellowing of the oldest leaves, usually on a single stem. Beginning at the base, the yellowed leaves wilt and die until all the leaves are killed. Often a single shoot dies before others are severely injured, but eventually the entire plant is affected. There is no soft decay of the stem, but if one cuts it lengthwise near the ground, he can see in the woody portion next to the outer "bark," or cortex, a brown discoloration of the water-conducting tissues; fibrovascular bundles which is characteristic of the disease.

The fungus that causes fusarium wilt can persist in the soil for many years. Infection occurs through the roots. From them the fungus passes into the water-conducting vessels of the stem. Apparently it produces a toxic substance that causes the wilting of the foliage and eventual death of the plant. The fungus is most active at temperatures between 80 and 90 F. Losses from the wilt are most common and severe in the warmer sections of the country. Clean fields can be infested by planting diseased seedlings, or by drainage water, farm implements, or any agency that carries infested soil even in small amounts to the clean field.

Other wilt diseases of tomato are caused by soil-borne bacteria and fungi. Unlike fusarium wilt, they are characterised by a decay of the stem near the ground and a wilting of the entire plant with little or no yellowing of the leaves.

Upper left: Pea streak, caused by a virus, on pea pods. Upper right: Anthracnose of cucumber Plants; the disease also affects watermelon and muskmelon growing in humid regions. Lower left: Bacterial spot of tomato on two fruits. Lower right: A plant of Great Lakes lettuce affected with rib blight, a physiologic disease.

Bacterial wilt, caused by Pseudomonas solanacearum, is an example. That organism causes a watery decay of the pith, which soon causes the wilting and death of the plant. These wilt diseases are most common in the southern United States but are of much less economic importance than fusarium wilt.

Leaf spot diseases of tomato cannot be described solely on a basis of leaf symptoms, since certain of their causal agencies also are responsible for serious spotting of the stems and spotting or rot of the fruits.

The most common and destructive leaf spots are caused by bacteria and fungi that produce spots in which the cells of the leaf have been killed. In some of the diseases an area of yellowed tissue surrounds the dead spots. With the exception of one fungus that destroys areas of tissue almost too large to be called spots, the organisms invade only a limited area around the point of infection and produce spots of characteristic sise and appearance. They may be irregular or circular and vary from one thirty-second inch to one-half inch in diametre. Both the petioles and leaflets may be spotted, and those injuries commonly cause the death of many leaves. Some viruses also cause dead spots or patches on the leaves but the spots are of a type that usually is not confused with those caused by bacteria or fungi.

The leaf spot caused by the fungus Septoria lycopersici is an example of a disease that severely injures the leaves but does no appreciable harm to the fruit. On the other hand the fungus (Alternaria solani) that causes alternaria leaf spot and the fungus (Phytophthora infestans) that causes late blight produce severe injury to the foliage and are also important because of their effect on the fruits.

Septoria leaf spot is characterised by numerous water-soaked spots that soon become roughly circular and have gray centres with dark margins. Later the centres of the spots show tiny dark specks (pycnidia), the bodies in which the fungus spores are produced. The spots are from one-sixteenth to one-eighth of an inch in diametre and may occur in such numbers as to cover the leaf. The fruits rarely are affected, but stems and blossoms may have spots.

The fungus also attacks wild solanaceous plants, such as horsenettle, jimsonweed, and nightshade. It over-winters in the soil on the remains of tomato plants, its weed hosts, and other decaying vegetation. Spores produced on such material cause the infection of tomato leaves near the soil. Spores then are produced in the spots on those infected leaves and, in wet weather, are exuded on the surface of the spot. From there they are splashed to other leaves by rain and may be carried on the hands or clothing of farm workers or on farm equipment.

The disease may occur on plants of any age, but in the field it seems to develop more rapidly after some fruit is set. If temperatures are moderately high and rains frequent, there is a progressive loss of foliage until only a few leaves may remain at the tips of the stems. When that occurs, yields are reduced and many of the fruits are injured by exposure to the sun. In hot, dry seasons the disease is much less damaging.

Septoria leaf spot causes serious loss in some sections of the Central and Atlantic States as far south as Arkansas, Tennessee, and South Carolina, but is of minor importance in the Mountain and Pacific States.

The first symptoms of alternaria leaf spot (early blight) consist of small, dark-brown spots on the older leaves. The spots may enlarge until they are one-half inch in diametre and have an irregular or circular outline. The large spots often are marked with rings in a target pattern. The tissues surrounding the spots often turn yellow and this discoloration may cover the leaflet. The disease is common on seedlings, where the spots usually are small and dark. In the field, the spotting and yellowing of the leaflets, together with spotting of the petioles, often kills much of the foliage. Plants in the field also show many spots on the stems. They are light brown, with darker margins, and from one-eighth to one-half inch in sise. On seedlings the fungus causes large, dark cankers (collar rot) that may girdle the stems. The varieties Southland and Manahill have high resistance to collar rot and some resistance to alternaria leaf spot.

Alternaria solani also causes a disease of potatoes known as early blight. Occasionally it affects peppers. It can live on decaying plant tissue in the soil. Most of the primary infection in tomatoes comes from that source, although contaminated seed may possibly cause occasional infection.

Alternaria spot is the most common leaf spot disease of tomatoes in the Central and Atlantic States and occurs in all tomato-growing regions, although it is of less importance in the Mountain and Pacific States.

Late blight is characterised by irregular, greenish-black patches, which first appear on the older leaves. They rapidly enlarge until they may cover one-fourth to one-half of the leaflet. The spots soon turn brown and many of the infected leaves wither, yet frequently remain attached to the stem. When weather conditions favour. a rapid development of the disease, so much of the foliage may be affected that the plants look as though injured. by frost. The fungus also produces water-soaked, brown streaks on the stem. In moist weather there often is a white, downy growth of the fungus on the under surfaces of the spots on the leaves and stems.

The fungus that causes late blight also causes a disease of the same name on potatoes. It is not carried in tomato seed and does not live over in the soil. It infects potato tubers, which can produce diseased plants in the spring. From them spores can be carried by the wind and infect plants in other fields.

Late blight of tomatoes is caused by a strain of the fungus somewhat different from that which ordinarily occurs on potatoes. The tomato strain can infect potatoes, however, and has been recovered from blight-infected potato tubers as a typical tomato strain. What appears to be the typical potato strain of the fungus may produce only mild symptoms when first transferred to tomatoes but can develop the virulence of a typical tomato strain after a number of passages through tomato plants.

Late blight commonly occurs on potatoes and tomatoes grown in the Gulf States during the winter and early spring. The disease works northward with those crops as the season progresses. Most of the canning tomatoes of the Central and Atlantic States are produced from seedlings grown in the South, and late blight occasionally appears in some plant fields. If the infected transplants are shipped north they become a possible source of infection to other fields. Besides that possible hazard and that of infection from diseased potato plants, there also is an occasional carry-over of the fungus on greenhouse tomatoes in winter. Seedlings grown in those houses in the spring often become infected and carry the disease into the field. Cool nights and only moderately warm days, with abundant moisture, favour the rapid development and spread of late blight.

Late blight of tomatoes was of little or no importance in many tomato-growing sections until 1945, although the disease had caused some loss in the Northeastern, Middle Atlantic, South Central, and South Atlantic States. Occasional damage also had occurred in Texas and on the Pacific coast. In most of the sections where the processing tomatoes are grown east of the Mississippi, however, the disease was almost unknown.

In 1945 there were some losses in the North Central States. Early in the season of 1946 several unusually long periods of cool, moist weather were followed by an epidemic of the disease along the Atlantic seaboard, which destroyed nearly half the crop. The damage was all the worse because the growcrs had no previous experience with the disease and were not equipped to apply the fungicides that would have prevented much of the loss. Since then, late blight has occurred to some extent each year in many tomato areas of the Central and Atlantic States, but the loss has been greatly reduced by increased use of fungicides.

A number of fruit rots are caused by bacteria and fungi that produce no other significant injuries to the tomato, plant. The most serious are due to soil-borne fungi that can infect Uninjured fruits. There also are organisms that can only enter the fruit when the epidermis is broken by growth cracks, mechanical injuries, or the lesions caused by the common fruit-spotting organisms. Such decays are unimportant in the field but may cause losses of fruits in transit, in ripening rooms, and in the markets.

Anthracnose of tomato, caused by the fungus Colletotrichum phomoides, is the most serious of the fruit rots caused by organisms that produce little or no injury to the leaves. Uninjured fruits can be infected at any stage, but in green fruits the fungus remains latent and no spotting occurs until the fruits ripen. Ripe fruits show dark, depressed spots whose centres have concentric markings. The centres are tan with dark specks (acervuli). In moist weather the masses of spores, which give the spots a salmon-pink colour, are produced in the dark specks. The spots are circular and about three-eighths inch in diametre. They penetrate a short distance into the fruit and must be removed when the fruit is processed.

Anthracnose is a serious pest of processing tomato crops in the Central and Atlantic States, but is of little importance where tomatoes are picked green for shipment to distant markets. The fungus occurs in the soil and the first infections come from that source. The spores produced on the surfaces of the fruit spots later are splashed by rain or otherwise spread to healthy fruits. In warm, moist weather many fruits are thus infected.

Fruit spots also are produced by some organisms that spot the leaves. Some of them penetrate the epidermis of the fruit and produce spots that do not extend very deeply into the flesh. The spots vary from one-sixteenth to one-half inch in diametre and have a roughened, broken surface that is brown or gray in colour.

Alternaria leaf spot and late blight, however, are characterised by rots that cover a considerable area of the fruit and extend deeply into the tissues. Spotting and ring markings of the fruits also are associated with some viruses that cause spotting of the leaves. Losses from them are not of major significance.

The fungus that causes alternaria leaf spot attacks the green fruits at the point of attachment to the stem. Here the fungus produces dark, leathery, sunken spots, which have concentric markings and may be an inch or more in diametre. A dark, dry, decay extends well in the fruit and makes it unfit for use. This fruit rot phase of the disease, however, causes less damage than the defoliation caused by the leaf spotting.

The fruit rot associated with late blight often is a cause of major loss. Fruit infection occurs at any stage of growth and is most frequent on the upper half of the surface. The grayish green, water-soaked spots enlarge until they may cover half the fruit and eventually become brown, with a firm, slightly wrinkled surface. In moist weather, a downy, white growth of the fungus often appears on the surfaces of the spots.

Tomatoes are subject to a number of diseases caused by viruses that produce a mottling or yellowing of the leaves and are accompanied by varying amounts of curling, twisting, and malformation of the leaflets. Some of them also cause a streaking of the stem and a spotting of the leaves and fruits. Most of the viruses may occur wherever tomatoes are grown in the field or greenhouse, but the destructive virus known as curly top is confined largely to the Mountain and Pacific States as it is transmitted only by a leafhopper whose breeding grounds are limited to semiarid sections in the West.

Tomato mosaic, as the name is commonly used, is the most common virus disease of tomatoes. The name refers to the disease caused by the tobacco mosaic virus (Marmor tabaci), which also affects peppers. The common green strain of the virus causes a light- and dark-green mottling of the leaves, a slight curling, and occasional malformations of the leaflets. Infected seedlings are stunted, but plants that become infected after they reach the fruiting stage show no severe check in growth although yields are reduced. There also are "yellow" strains of the virus which cause a pronounced yellow mottling of the leaves and some mottling and blotching of the stems and fruits.

The tobacco mosaic virus is rarely, if ever, transmitted in commercial tomato seed. It does not persist long in field soils, although in greenhouses, where one crop may follow another in a few weeks, some infection may occur from plant remains in the soil.

Perennial weeds, such as horse-nettle, groundcherry, and plantain, sometimes are infected with the virus and may be a source of infection. The virus remains active for years in dried tobacco leaves and is known to occur in pipe, cigar, and cigarette tobaccos. Smokers, therefore, may carry the virus on their hands, and some of the initial infection of tomato seedlings may come in that way. The virus is transmitted so readily by successive contact with mosaic-infested and healthy plants that it is almost certain to become widespread after it appears in the greenhouse or field.

Aside from its own effect on the plant, the tobacco mosaic virus is a menace to the crop because infected plants also may become infected with the virus X of potatoes (Marmor dubium). The virus is present in the tops and tubers of all the older varieties of potatoes but usually causes little visible evidence of disease. Tomatoes that are infected with both the tobacco and potato viruses develop a disease known as double-virus streak. Such plants show small, dead, brown spots on the leaves, which are mottled, dwarfed, and curled. Stems and leaf petioles develop the narrow brown streaks that give the disease its name. The plants set few fruits and those produced are often misshapen and have irregular brown spots on their surfaces. Streak can be very destructive in the greenhouse where the necessity of handling the plants in pruning and tying leads to its rapid spread.

Tomatoes also are sometimes infected with the cucumber mosaic virus (Marmor cucumeris). Such infection is much less common than that with the tobacco mosaic virus. The leaves show only a mild mottling but often are dwarfed or malformed. Frequently the leaflets are reduced to little more than a central rib, and this "shoestring" symptom is one characteristic of the disease. The plants that are infected with the cucumber mosaic virus are dwarfed and often have an abnormally compact, bushy appearance. The few fruits they set are small and often malformed.

Unlike the virus of tobacco mosaic, the cucumber mosaic virus does not withstand drying. It can be transmitted by mechanical means, but on tomatoes that occurs less readily. It is commonly disseminated by aphids, particularly the species that feed on cucumbers and melons. As they prefer to feed on plants other than tomatoes, the aphids cause less infection on tomatoes than on certain other crops. The virus is not transmitted in the seed and does not persist in the soil. It does infect a wide range of cultivated and wild plants and is common on cucumbers, muskmelons, celery, peppers, and some ornamental plants. It lives over winter in some ornamentals, such as perennial phlox, and in some perennial weeds, such as milkweed, groundcherry, and catnip. Aphids feeding on such infected plants in the spring later carry the virus to cultivated crops.

Some evidence of such diseases can be found in many fields every season. Usually the losses are minor, although the drop of blossoms, caused by hot, drying winds, sometimes is a serious factor.

Blossom-end rot, a common non-parasitic disease, usually appears on tomato fruits when they are about half-grown. It consists of a brown discoloration that enlarges until it covers one-third or more of the fruit. The dark tissues shrink and form a flattened or slightly concave area with a dry, leathery surface. There is no rot of the fruit unless the dead tissue is later invaded by fungi or bacteria. Blossom-end rot usually appears when plants that have made a rapid growth are subject to high temperatures and drought. Then the cells at the blossom end of the fruits apparently fail to receive enough moisture to maintain their growth, and the tissues break down. Plants that have had heavy applications of nitrogenous fertilizer are especially susceptible to blossom-end rot. Marked fluctuations in soil moisture increase the likelihood of injury. Plants that are pruned and staked consistently show more blossom-end rot than those growing naturally in otherwise similar conditions. That may be due largely to the restriction of the root system that results from drastic pruning of the tops.

Disease control is essential in the profitable production of tomatoes. The first step consists of measures that help to prevent the occurrence of seedling diseases. Wherever possible, seedlings should be started in soil that has not grown diseased plants. If that is not feasible, the soil can be disinfected by treatment with formaldehyde or chloropicrin or by steam.

Seed treatments are used to disinfect the surface of the seed and to coat the seed with a fungicide that will protect the seed and germinating seedling from fungi in the soil that cause seed decay and damping-off of seedlings. Tomato seed can be dusted with such materials as New Improved Ceresan, Semesan, Phygon, Arasan, or Thiram 50. They generally are used at a rate of 0.3 to 0.5 per cent of weight of seed.

Losses from wilt diseases and fruit rots caused by soil-borne organisms can be reduced somewhat by crop rotation and the avoidance of fields where such diseases have damaged previous tomato crops. Seedbeds should always be located on clean soil. If plants are purchased, they should be obtained from plantings free from disease.

In the greenhouse, wilt diseases and injury from the root knot nematode can be controlled by disinfection of the soil by chemicals or steam. In the field, the use of steam is impracticable and chemical treatments, other than those effective only against nematodes, have as yet been too expensive for large-scale use.

Resistant varieties offer the most effective means of preventing losses from wilt diseases, but we do not yet have varieties resistant to all diseases of this type.

Breeding of varieties resistant to fusarium wilt by the Department of Agriculture and State experiment stations has made it possible to maintain a profitable tomato industry in regions where the disease is prevalent. Some of the resistant varieties that have had most general use are Rutgers, Marglobe, Indiana Baltimore, Pearson, and Pritchard. They are not immune to wilt and occasionally are damaged by it. Since 1940, however, varieties have become available that have extremely high resistance. Among them are Pan America, Southland, Homestead, Cal 255, Manahill, Manasota, Fortune, Boone, Tipton, Kokomo, Tucker, Sunray, and Golden Sphere. Another such variety, Jefferson, has been introduced by a private seed company. Resistant varieties suited to greenhouse use include Ohio W-R Globe (which possesses high wilt resistance), Blair Forcing, and Michigan State Forcing. A race of the fusarium wilt fungus, which can attack plants of the highly resistant varieties, has been reported in Ohio and Missouri, but we have had no report of widespread infection of those varieties in commercial plantings.

Varieties resistant to verticillium wilt, caused by the fungus Verticillium albo-atrum, have been developed for use in sections in the West where the the disease has caused serious losses. The varieties Riverside, Essar, and Simi have tolerance of verticillium wilt but are injured when conditions are very favourable to the development of the disease. They also have moderate resistance to fusarium wilt. Two newly introduced varieties, Loran Blood and VR Moscow, are highly resistant to verticillium wilt but not to fusarium wilt. Varieties highly resistant to both diseases are now being developed.

Losses from the leaf spot diseases and certain fruit rots caused by parasitic organisms can be reduced by the timely application of fungicides. They are particularly necessary in the Central, Atlantic, and Northeastern States, where a humid climate favours the occurrence of such diseases. The use of fungicides there has become much more general because of the continued appearance of late blight in sections where it was not a problem before 1945 and 1946. The routine use of fungicides also has been accelerated by the development of the very effective dithiocarbamate compounds. which have increased the possibility of reducing losses. Proper spraying and dusting and improved cultural methods have increased tomato yields markedly since 1940.

The fungicides most commonly used on tomatoes are copper compounds and organic compounds of the dithiocarbamate group.

The neutral copper compounds (which include basic copper sulfates, copper oxychloride, copper oxychloride sulfate, and copper oxide) largely have supplanted bordeaux mixture because they are less injurious to tomato plants.

As sprays, they are generally used in formulations that give the equivalent of 2 pounds of copper to 100 gallons of water. For seedbed spraying, however, this often is reduced to 1.5 pounds to 100 gallons. Bordeaux mixture cannot be safely used on tomato seedlings, but often is employed after the fruit is set. An 8-4 100 mixture (in which the first form represents pounds of copper sulfate, the second hydrated lime, and the third water) is probably that most generally favoured, but 8-8 100, 6-6-100, and 6-3-100 preparations are used on tomatoes.

Dusts containing the neutral Coppers are formulated so as to give 5 to 7 per cent of actual copper in a suitable inert carrier.

The dithiocarbamate compounds commonly used on tomatoes are zineb (zinc ethylene bisdithiocarbamate), nabam (sodium ethylene bisdithiocarbamate), which is used with zinc sulfate, and ziram (zinc dimethyl dithiocarbamate). A newly introduced compound, manganese ethylene bisdithiocarbamate (Manzate), also appears to be effective against a number of tomato diseases. Zineb, ziram, and the manganese salt commonly are used at the rate of 2 pounds of the commercial preparation to 100 gallons of water. With nabam, 2 quarts of the commercial preparation are added to 100 gallons of water and then 1 pound of zinc sulfate is added. Zineb and ziram also are used in dust preparations containing from 6 to 8 per cent of the fungicides.

Other compounds such as Phygon (2, 3-dichloro-1, 4-naphthoquinone), captan (n-trichloromethylthio tetrahydrophalimide), Cop-O-Zink (tribasic copper sulfate and zinc sulfate), and Crag 658 (copper-zinc-chromate) also are being used. In many instances they have given satisfactory results but more experience with some of these materials is needed. New organic compounds constantly are being tested for tomato disease control.

Both the copper fungicides and compounds of the dithiocarbamate group are quite effective for the control of alternaria leaf spot. Late blight can be controlled with copper compounds and with those of the dithiocarbamate group other than ziram. Losses from gray leaf spot, caused by the fungus Stemphylium solani, and septoria leaf spot can be reduced by applying either copper or dithiocarbamate fungicides.

Manganese ethylene bisdithiocarbamate appears to be very effective against gray leaf spot. Ziram is particularly effective for control of anthracnose fruit rot but other dithiocarbamate compounds also will reduce losses from this disease. It is not satisfactorily controlled by copper fungicides.

The relative extent of the use of copper and dithiocarbamate fungicides varies with the section in which tomatoes are grown. In southern Florida, zineb and nabam have proved to be superior to the copper fungicides for late blight control and have been generally used. There has seemed to be some preference for the dithiocarbamate materials throughout the South Atlantic States, although copper fungicides also are recommended for use in tomato disease control.

In the North Central, North Atlantic, and Northeastern States, copper fungicides are commonly used for control of late blight although the dithiocarbamate materials also have been extensively used.

Seedbeds need protection from leaf spot diseases. Often they are sprayed or dusted three or four times before the plants are taken to the field. In the field, the first applications of fungicides usually can be made about 30 days after the first flower cluster blooms. Later applications can be made at 10-day intervals unless there are frequent rains, when the interval may have to be reduced to 7 days, or even less, to secure good control.

Spraying has proved to be superior to dusting in the control of tomato diseases but, when wet soil makes it impossible to use heavy spraying equipment, dusting is a very valuable adjunct. The coverage obtained with ground dusting machines has been superior to that secured from applications of dust by airplane.

We have no commercial varieties of tomatoes resistant to mosaic diseases and must depend on measures of sanitation to prevent infection. After the diseases appear in the field or greenhouse, it is hard to check their further spread. Therefore the best means of control consists of preventing infection in the seedling plants and thus delaying the appearance of the disease until a crop is well started. If that can be done, the loss is likely to be less severe.

One should never handle seedlings without first washing his hands with soap and water to remove any virus from the hands. Because manufactured tobacco may carry the virus of tobacco mosaic, no one should smoke or chew tobacco while handling the plants. Workers can stop at intervals for a smoke and then wash their hands before again touching the plants.

All perennial weeds around the seedbeds and in or near the fields should be destroyed because they may carry viruses of tobacco or cucumber mosaic.

Every effort should be made to prevent aphid infestation of the seedbed by using insecticides regularly. When seedlings are grown in a greenhouse used for commercial tomato production, the seedlings should not be handled after working with older plants unless the hands have first been washed. Anyone who has worked in a potato field or peeled or cut potatoes should wash the hands before working with tomatoes. The removal of mosaic plants in the field usually is of little value in checking the spread of mosaic diseases and often leads to further infection through brushing the infected plants against healthy ones in the course of removal. Because many nonparasitic diseases are induced wholly or partly by extremes of temperature or moisture, the grower is somewhat at the mercy of the elements where those disorders are concerned. In some diseases, however, both nutrition and weather have a part, and some losses may be avoided by care in the use of fertilizers, particularly nitrogen.

TOMATO DISTORTING OR ENATION VIRUS

This is another strain of the common tomato mosaic differing in that, in addition to causing mottling of the leaves, it stimulates the plant to excessive and unnatural growth. The leaflets may be increased so that a fern-like effect is produced with very many small leaflets crowded together, gradually diminishing in size and ending in a corkscrew-like tendril. In some cases small outgrowths (enations) are formed on the under-side of the midribs. There is a tendency to excessive growth and production of giant plants crowded with foliage.

BUSHY STUNT

This is a distinct and apparently rather uncommon virus which is easily transmitted by sap but has no known insect vector. In seedlings it causes yellow and purple colouration of the leaves, yellow spotting and death of the young leaves and often a sunken brown lesion at soil level, causing the seedlings to fall over. In older plants it causes cessation of growth by the terminal shoot and stimulation of the side shoots, hence the name " bushy stunt."

The lower leaves turn yellow or purple and often there are concentric rings of bright yellow or purple, or purple lines along the veins of a yellow leaf. Ultimately the lower leaves shrivel and drop off. This virus is particularly interesting because it has been purified and obtained in the form of minute cubical crystals.

MISSHAPEN FRUIT

The tendency to production of ridged and misshapen fruit is an inherited one, as shown by Pape. It is also, however, influenced by conditions of cultivation. Thus, Kondine Red is a variety rather prone to bear ridged fruit but it only does so when the plants are set very far apart and richly manured. To avoid this disfigurement seed should be saved only from carefully selected plants with well-shaped fruit. The seed crop should be grown under conditions conducive to misshapen fruit so that any inherited tendency to do so becomes evident. In normal commercial fruit production spacing and manuring should be that found by experience to suit the variety grown.

BLOSSOM-END ROT

The most striking symptom is a dark, more or less sunken, area at the blossom or style end of the fruit, i.e. farthest from the stalk. The trouble begins as a water-soaked spot at or near the base of the style, or the whole of that end of the fruit may look as though bruised. The affected part soon becomes leathery and usually turns black. As the rest of the fruit continues to swell the blossom end becomes slightly sunken or remains abnormally flattened. Various bacteria and fungi are commonly to be found in the affected tissues and have from time to time been described as the cause of blossom-end rot.

They are, however, purely secondary invaders, living in tissue already damaged by a physiological disturbance. Especially if the surface of the fruit remains moist these secondary organisms may enter and set up an extensive rot. Tomato varieties in which the style remains attached for a long time seem particularly susceptible to blossom-end rot, perhaps because fungi and bacteria become established on the dead style and are hence ready to invade even a small spot of true physiological blossom-end rot.

The most important preventive measure is regular watering to avoid alternate drying out and soaking of the soil. It may be worth while to pick off the dead corolla and style on varieties that retain them long after the fruit has set. Otherwise fungi or bacteria established in the dead tissue may set up secondary rots following blossom-end rot. The variety Comet seems particularly susceptible to this trouble.

HOLLOW FRUIT

Fruits divided by a single septum into two compartments are particularly prone to develop empty spaces between the septum and the fruit wall. Such fruit when shaken often makes a rustling or rattling sound.

A larger or smaller part of the seed and flesh inside may be black and dead. This unfortunate phenomenon, which appears especially towards the end of the summer, is not due to attack by any parasite. It is due especially to a period of drought during the swelling of the fruit but other growing conditions may possibly cause it. In such circumstances when there is a heavy crop only part of it will contain normal contents.

GREENBACK

Greenback appears as a hard green or yellow area at the top of the fruit, surrounding the stalk. When ripening starts this part does not turn red like the rest but remains green and then slowly goes yellow or orange. It never becomes red and soft like the rest of the flesh. Greenback, like blotchy ripening, is due to a deficiency of potassium, especially in fruit exposed to strong sunlight. Tomatoes forced to ripen at a temperature exceeding 90° F. do not turn red but yellow.

Lycopin, the red colouring matter, is not formed at such high temperatures. Greenback always occurs on the uppermost part of the fruit as it hangs on the truss, which is, of course, the part most exposed to the sun.

When defoliating tomatoes one should be careful to leave enough leaves to shade the trusses during the hottest part of the day. If the foliage is scanty, side shoots should be allowed to grow out and produce a couple of leaves before being stopped. Glasshouses should be shaded during the hottest periods. Care should be also be taken to supply enough potassium and water. Kondine Red and Tuckwood are very prone to greenback, Selandia much less so.

BLOTCHY RIPENING

In blotchy ripening larger or smaller parts of the fruit surface do not change colour with the rest as the tomato ripens. When it begins to turn red they remain green for a time but gradually turn yellow, develop a waxy appearance and a turnip-like flavour.

The vascular bundles in the blotches are often dark and show faintly through the skin as dark lines. The blotches may occur on any part of the fruit, a feature which distinguishes them from greenback which occurs only round the stalk. Blotchy ripening is seen mainly in June and July. Tomato varieties differ greatly in susceptibility to it; Kondine Red is one of the most susceptible.

Blotchy ripening is due to cultural factors or to diseased roots. In manurial experiments at Cheshunt it has been demonstrated that the greatest number of fruits with blotchy ripening occurred on unmanured plots and on plots deficient in potassium and nitrogen. If tomato roots are diseased, if they receive too much water or too little, they cannot absorb enough nutrients and this may lead to blotchy ripening. The dampness of the subsoil should therefore be taken into account. It may well happen that the top 6-9 inches of soil are fairly moist but that the deeper levels are too dry. Tomatoes seem to develop most blotchy ripening in heavily limed soil.

In Danish nurseries blotchy ripening is often prevalent where there is a large amount of phosphoric acid in the soil. If a heavy dressing of manure is given the roots may be damaged and thus less able to absorb nutrients so that the plants may starve on over-manured soil. Blotchy ripening is usually worst in new houses where growth is unusually vigourous. In summers with plenty of sunshine less potassium and more nitrogen should be supplied than in dull, cloudy seasons.

CRACKED FRUIT

Cracking of tomato fruit occurs in two chief forms, single large cracks and many small ones; both types occur mostly on the top half of the fruit. The large cracks happen especially when a dry period is suddenly followed by a damp one. They are therefore usually found in the outdoor crop, where the grower has least control over the moisture relations of the plant. Cracking may also result from a sudden acceleration of growth for other reasons, as after manuring.

The skin makes poorest growth under cool conditions and then has difficulty in keeping pace with rapid expansion of the flesh. The numerous small cracks on tomato fruit occur especially in greenhouses where there are great fluctuations in atmospheric humidity. Growers should therefore be careful not to stop night heating too early It is probably the increased root development that counteracts the effect of a fluctuating water supply. Potassium permanganate is usually used for watering, etc.

ROLLING OF THE LEAVES

Tomato leaflets sometimes roll up so much that the upper surface becomes completely overarched by the upcurled margins which may meet above the midrib of the leaflet. Such leaves feel very hard and stiff. Varieties and individual plants may differ somewhat in the degree of leaf rolling. Tomatoes, perhaps because they are more extensively stripped than the glasshouse crop. The rolling of tomato leaves has no connection with the leaf roll disease of potatoes, which is due to virus infection. Rolling up of the top leaves may occur on young, actively growing plants. It occurs mainly when the crop has been heavily manured so that there is a high concentration of nutrient elements.

Such plants have dark-green foliage and the top may have a violet tint somewhat reminiscent of spotted wilt. It occurs mainly in spring, particularly on tomatoes but also on other greenhouse plants such as pelargoniums and early forced potatoes. The outer cells become gorged with water, swell and burst the skin. The swellings then have a white powdery appearance but gradually turn brownish as the broken tissue falls away. Affected leaves have a tendency to roll. Edema occurs when the roots are absorbing more water than the leaves are able to transpire. A warm, moist soil increases the rate of water absorption but damp air, poor ventilation and shade check transpiration from the leaves. The condition may also become serious when, after a cool period with slow growth, the temperature rises and supply of water and nutrients to the foliage is suddenly increased. Such plants have relatively few leaves unable to cope with the large increased water supply resulting from the altered conditions. To check oedcma the soil should be kept fairly dry and there should be thorough ventilation. This condition arises in plants that have became much more prevalent after the adoption received too much water or excessive nitrogen of petroleum oil sprays against red spider.

The or have experienced a sudden change in con-film of oil checks transpiration from the leaves, ditions when planted out. The grower often finds a few plants which times been noticed some time after severely early attract notice by remaining short because pot-bound plants have been planted out. Once the roots have grown out into the new than in normal plants. These should be rogued soil they are able to absorb more water than out before the crop is planted out as such can be dealt with by the rather stunted tops, plants are partially or completely unfruitful. Some time after planting out the stems growth. As a rule there are only a few of these may become soft and flaccid; in bad cases the in each batch of seedlings. Like the short-plants fall over without any actual rot taking jointed plants they are practically sterile, place.

When such a stem is cut open the pith These varieties seem to be due to inherited is found to be wholly or partly wanting. Plants defects. They occur scattered amongst normal that have fallen over in this way may remain plants and should be weeded out as early as green for a long time but make no growth. possible.

8

Vegetable Gardens and Diseases

Successful vegetable gardens are not accidental. They are the results of planning, constant care, and the will to make things grow. Among the many things a vegetable garden may offer towards a satisfying experience are fresh air, exercise, sunshine, knowledge, supplemental income, mental therapy, and fresh food, rich in vitamins and minerals, harvested at the best stage of maturity.

Organic gardening differs from "conventional" gardening mainly in the areas of fertilization and pest control. The organic gardener prefers to use natural and organic materials and methods, and avoids using practices and synthetic chemicals that may be detrimental to his health or environment. The information in this publication should be beneficial to all gardeners regardless of methods of culture used; however, it is primarily intended to aid the organic gardener to employ workable methods acceptable to him and compatible with the philosophy of "organic gardening."

SOIL PREPARATION

Since organic fertilizer and soil conditioning materials are slow working in general, they should be mixed into the soil at least three weeks ahead of planting and the soil thoroughly prepared for the seed or transplants. Clumps of unrotted organic materials not only interfere with the seeding operation, but may result in nutrient deficiency and possible soil-borne diseases problems such as "damping-off" of young seedlings.

ORGANIC MATTER

A major basis for organic gardening is the use of abundant quantities of organic material applied to the soil. Usually, it is in the form of animal manures, plant manures, cover crops, compost, or mixed organic fertilizer.

Benefits of Adding Organic Matter

Improves tilth, condition, and structure of soil.
Improves ability of soil to hold water.
Improves ability of soil to hold nutrients.

Improves "buffering" capacity of soil; that is, keeps soil from "over-reacting". Supports the soil's microbiological activity (or the life of the soil).

Contributes nutrients, both minor and major.

Releases nutrients slowly.

Acids arising from the decomposition of the organic matter help to convert insoluble natural additives such as ground rock into plant-usable forms.

Helps vegetables survive stress, as from nematodes.

Helps dispose of organic waste products.

What Happens to Organic Matter Applied to the Soil or Compost Pile

Under suitable conditions, the organic matter is decomposed by micro-organisms such as fungi, algae, bacteria, molds, and earthworms. In the process, insoluble and unavailable (to plants) nutrients, such as nitrogen, are gradually changed into simple usable products. For example, *nitrogen* is converted from the unusable organic forms to a usable inorganic form through the process called nitrification. Thus, nitrification is the breakdown of protein (organic nitrogen) into ammonia and then nitrate. Some of the organic matter becomes part of the soil humus.

HISTORY OF VEGETABLES

VEGETABLES IN THE EARLY CHRISTIAN PERIOD

The early Middle Ages is a murky period for the study of vegetables, but a copy (in the Austrian State Library at Vienna) of the *Codex of Dioskorides* dating from 500 to 511 C.E. is illuminated with pictures of plants. The drawings are fairly accurate and convey the important physical characteristics of the vegetables and herbs shown. Thus it is possible to determine that a leek on folio 278 belongs to the Kurrat Group, an ancient type of salad leek mentioned earlier and still grown in the Near East.

The *Codex of Dioskorides* is medical in nature, dealing with the health and dietary aspects of the plants discussed. For a horticultural companion, the *Gheoponika* of Kassianos Bassos, a tenth-century reworking of several older agricultural treatises, provides rules for the cultivation of garden vegetables, thus offering some insights into the seasonal food cycle, both horticultural and culinary, in the old Byzantine East.

More specifically, the role of the *Gheoponika* in the provisioning of Constantinople with fresh vegetables has been studied by several historians, most importantly by Johannes Koder (1993). When taken together with the *Book of the Eparch* (prefect of Constantinople) regulating merchants and guilds during the reign of Leo VI (886–912), a relatively detailed picture of market gardening falls into place.

It is perhaps significant to note that by the 1100s many villages in Bulgaria were given imperial privileges that freed them of military duty in exchange for producing food for the court. It is for this reason that the Bulgarians have long been called the gardeners of the Balkans, a status they maintained even under later Ottoman rule.

In the West, the eighth century *Capitulare de villis* of the Holy Roman Emperor Charlemagne is quite valuable for its references to gardens. For example, the *ravocaulos* of that document is believed to refer to a variety of kohlrabi. However, the most priceless garden record is a parchment drawing of the garden plan of the Cloister of St. Gall in Switzerland surviving from the early 800s. It provides a detailed look at how the Roman kitchen garden became transmogrified into a source of both food and medical plants. Sixteen plants are discernible on the plan, including cucumbers, melons, cowpeas, bottle gourds, and smallage (celery resembling parsley). Most important, they are organized into rectangular raised beds. This is one of the earliest references extant to this common garden practice, but it was not unique.

The *Hortulus* of Walahfrid Strabo, abbot (from 838 to 849) of the Cloister of Reichenau on an island in Lake Constance, makes reference to a similar number of plants, again arranged in raised rectangular beds. Strabo's Latin poems about his garden discuss the uses of both herbs and vegetables and is the oldest surviving source on gardening written in Europe during the Middle Ages. Most interesting of all, archaeological exploration of the abbey site has revealed that it was constructed from the recycled ruins of an abandoned Roman villa and that the layout of the garden more or less followed the outlines of the ancient one.

The implication is that the Roman gardening tradition maintained by the wealthy during imperial times did not fully disappear at the outset of the Middle Ages. Many estate gardens disappeared completely due to wars and pillaging, but in some regions they simply became fewer in number and passed into non-Roman hands.

Chateau Ausone near Saint-Emilion in Bordeaux is a famous example of this continuity, although its fame rests on wine not gardens. The archaeological link is not as clear when it comes to the vegetables themselves, since botanical residues, especially seeds, impose certain limitations on what can be retrieved for science. A carrot seed is indistinguishable from a wild carrot seed and will not tell how the root was shaped or even its colour. Unfortunately, seeds are mostly what one has to work with from medieval sites, although some inferences can be revealing. Cucumber seeds show up in Polish sites in the 900s, thus establishing a bottom line for a vegetable much associated with Polish national cookery. Carbonized fava bean plants from North Germany from the same period reveal that, after the beans were harvested (as winter fare), the plants were used as straw in barns. Seeds, however, do help untangle dates of introduction, and one thing that scholars have learned from medieval archaeology is that the vegetable world was not static, as historians have led us to believe in the past.

The broad, flat fava bean, which is the preferred sort for modern cookery, did not appear until the 800s in Spain. This is only one example of vegetable breeding (probably through highly controlled selection) that took place during the Middle Ages, although innovation was indeed slow by present-day standards. Some agricultural historians have suggested that it was the Arabs who created these new types of vegetables—the cauliflower, for example. What can be documented from surviving Arab literary sources is rapid dissemination, but the westward movement of plants in general and vegetables in particular was far more complex than hitherto presumed and remains an area of research ripe for future exploration.

VEGETABLES IN EGYPT

There is a large body of published material on the history of gardening in ancient and pre-Islamic Egypt, but there are no books per se devoted exclusively to vegetables. Orchards, trees, flora, landscape gardening, and even aquatic plants have received thorough coverage, yet the vegetable stands alone in this curious neglect. Vegetables in general have been viewed as poverty food by most cultures, especially when they form a large portion of peasant diet. Egypt was no different in this regard.

The fine gardens of ancient Egypt were enclosed like those of Mesopotamia and contained trees, flowers, even ponds for fish and ducks. The gardens of the peasants were mostly simple agricultural plots devoted to a specific mix of vegetable crops associated with the local economy, as, for example, lentil or onion growing for absentee landlords in large urban centers like Alexandria. On the other hand, vegetable gardens within temple precincts were often quite elaborate and were intended to supply the priesthood with a full range of food as well as offerings for the deity. Lettuce, for example, was important to the cult of Amun-Min, thus its cultivation held both culinary and religious significance. Indeed, temple gardens were considered to be part of heaven, like the temple itself, so vegetables from those gardens achieved a purity unlike those from the common world.

Papyri and tomb paintings have provided a rich array of material dealing with the common vegetables of the day, although not much is known about their actual preparation as food. The most commonly mentioned vegetables were lentils, leeks, lotus, melons, gourds, garlic, asphodel (grown for its bulb), fava beans, chickpeas, fenugreek (ground as flour), garland chrysanthemum (now popular in Asian cooking), cucumbers, onions, lettuce, and mallow. Egypt also served as a conduit for the introduction of watermelons from tropical Africa and, during the late Ptolemaic Period, for the introduction of rice, taro, and sugar cane from Trapobane (ancient Sri Lanka). Due to their dependence on specialized irrigation and cultivation techniques, none of the last three plants spread beyond the eastern Mediterranean until after Arab conquest.

The Greek occupation of Egypt under the Ptolemys radically altered the Egyptian vegetable garden, both with new introductions and in lasting terminologies. *Molokhe* or mallow *(Malva parviflora),* which was once so important to Greek cookery both as a green sauce and as an ingredient in complex recipes, also supplied leaves used like grape leaves for making dolmas. The Egyptians transferred the Greek name to a native wild plant now known as Jews mallow *(Corchorus olitorus),* which was similarly used in green sauces. It is still called *molkhia* in Egyptian Arabic. The use of the same name for plants of a different genus or species is one of the lasting ambiguities inherited from the ancients, who were more apt to lump vegetables together according to how they were used, as in the case of the Roman propensity for treating carrots, parsnips, and parsley root as *pastinaca.*

THE VEGETABLES OF ANCIENT GREECE AND ROME

There are few surviving writings from the Greeks and Romans that do not mention food and vegetables in some manner. It is known from quotes and citations in works like the *Deipnosophists* of Athenaeus that many books on gardening and agriculture once existed but are now lost. Athenaeus himself lavished considerable attention on foodstuffs, none the least being vegetables. His interests ranged from toasted chickpeas (still a snack food in the Mediterranean) to the medical applications of beets and carrots as vermifuges or a good dish of cabbage to treat a hangover. He even cited the known varieties of lettuce, garlic, fava beans, and many other garden plants in an effort to differentiate which were the best from a connoisseur's point of view.

The surviving Roman work most easily accessible to the general reader is also by another connoisseur, an eccentric called Apicius, whose detailed recipes give specific hints about the role vegetables played in the haute cuisine of imperial Rome. For example, asparagus was baked in eggy casseroles called *patinae,* mallow was commonly added to barley soup, celery made a good stuffing for suckling pig, and turnips marry well with baked duck. There is also scattered advice on when to harvest certain vegetables, as in the case of stinging nettles, which only loose their prickly character when cooked or dried.

Many other works could be cited, such as Columella's *On Agriculture* and especially Pliny's monumental *Natural History,* but the medical writings of the imperial physician Galen are perhaps the richest in detail, since there is considerable commentary on the diet of peasants and farmers and the sorts of vegetables they ate. The aristocratic tone and intended readership of most of the writings that have survived from this period do not provide the kind of first hand observations one might expect from a true master gardener, although Pliny's eye was in fact well nuanced to such details—yet some of his botanical "facts" are obviously scrambled and second-hand. And while it is true Columella certainly knew how to run an estate, he was not the vegetable gardener.

Furthermore, aside from comments about asparagus and cabbage, Cato's treatise *On Agriculture* makes only passing reference to vegetables—be certain to grow them near cities. While this allusion does confirm the existence of well-organized market gardening, Cato's treatise is so loaded with ideology about salty Romanness *(Romanitas)* and the purity of certain rigorous lifestyles that any conclusions drawn from him must be done so with definite reservations. However, it is fairly clear from these and other ancient authors that quite a few cities had developed market gardening to a high degree and even specialized in the cultivation and export of vegetable produce to Rome and other large urban centers.

For example, Cyrene in present-day Libya was well-known in ancient times for its silphium, fragrant saffron, and a mild-tasting tuber now generally identified as taro. It was also the centre for the export of the so-called wild artichoke (*Cynara cornigera* Lindl.), whose domestication was introduced early into Cyprus, Libya, and Carthage from the Levant. This handsome plant is depicted on surviving mosaics in the House of Dionysios at Paphos, Cyprus, and in a mosaic in the Bardo Museum at Tunis. The Roman farmers of Spain and Italy evidently adapted the novel idea of harvesting the flower bud as a delicacy to their local wild cardoons because the artichoke of the western Mediterranean is a subspecies derived genetically from the cardoon (*Cynara cardunculus* L.), not from a wild artichoke ancestor. Buds of the milk thistle, blessed thistle, and safflower were also similarly harvested and eaten.

The dissemination of the artichoke, or at least of the horticultural technology required to cultivate it for food, brings up the larger question of plant exchange during the height of the Roman Empire. Commerce flowed to and from the far-flung provinces in a manner only replicated by the European Union. Archaeology has indeed confirmed that foodstuffs moved quite easily from one place to another, with such exotics as rice turning up in sites in Germany and England. There is also indisputable evidence that, among the aristocracy at least, country life on the great estates attempted to imitate the court life of imperial Rome.

Gardens excavated from villa sites have confirmed this. On the local level, however, Mediterranean cuisine and Mediterranean vegetables were not readily assimilated among the general populace. Joan Alcock's study of food in Roman Britain (2001), based on overwhelming archaeological evidence, reached the conclusion that assimilation was selective, and it was this selectivity that gave rise to the regional cookeries that eventually provided a link of continuity with the regional cookeries of the Middle Ages. This is also the growing consensus of archaeologists in other parts of Europe. Thus, the old saw that "the Romans introduced it" must be requalified, especially since quite a number of vegetables were cultivated in some regions long before the Romans arrived. Cabbage, especially the kales, originated in northern

Europe, and in fact, the English words for kale and cabbage are Celtic in origin, as are the German words *Kabbis* and *Kohl,* not to mention the Latin *brassica* and *caulis.* This is evidence in itself that the vegetable exchange during Roman times was complex and two-way, with the Romans themselves learning new things from conquered peoples.

A broader look at Roman literature of all types is especially useful in drawing general conclusions about the state of vegetable gardening from that time. For example, Pliny parodied "gastronomic prodigies," monster vegetables and fruits valued for their size alone. This would suggest that some market gardeners were well acquainted with horticultural practices based on careful seed selection, cold frame techniques, and the manuring of plants at critical periods of growth, much like the modern-day cult of the monster pumpkin or watermelon.

There is also a great deal of information concerning value judgments about the role of vegetables in the diet and their cultural significance. Many Roman satires mention garlic as a food only fit for galley slaves and peasants or as something eaten only by soldiers going off to war (garlic heats up the body and therefore creates a warlike spirit). The general drift is that anything flavoured with garlic is therefore rustic and unrefined and as much an antidote to poison as it is to the consuming flames of love (what sweet kiss is not withered by the scorpion sting of garlic breath?). Likewise, fava beans are eaten by jurymen in order to stay awake during trials, their noisy flatulency providing an echoing thunder of divine approval or of legal derision.

The most commonly mentioned vegetables in Roman literary sources include many still known, although in shape and habit they probably did not resemble modern varieties. The list includes turnips, radishes, rocket (arugula to American grocers), leeks, lentils, lettuce, orach, Old World gourds (eaten young like zucchinis), cabbage, onion, peas, chickpeas, fava beans, cucumbers, asparagus, cowpeas, beets, beet chards, sprouting broccoli, watermelon, garlic, mallow, dock, chickling vetch, and blite—otherwise known as purple amaranth *(Amaranthus lividus).*

A number of scholars have taken the liberty of translating *blitum* (blite) as spinach, and this has greatly added to the confusion about the culinary history of spinach because *blitum* is not true spinach. However, something called *barbaricum bliteum* (barbarian blite) also surfaces in Roman literature. This is either true spinach as cultivated by the Armenians and Persians or else good-king-henry, so important to the ritual cookery of the ancient Gauls—the leaves of both plants are similarly shaped. In any case, this mystery vegetable was considered insipid eating and was equated with crudeness and stupidity (insipid people were people who lacked "flavour").

Some of these vegetables also carried a great deal of symbolic baggage, especially in connection with religious cults. Mallow *(moloche)* was considered one of the purest sacrifices for Apollo Genetor at Delos, and Pythagoras himself was said to have lived on it as part of his vegetarian dietary regime because it "washes" the stomach.

Lettuce was associated with the gruesome death of Adonis, the prepubescent lover of Aphrodite, who hid among lettuce before he was gored to death by a wild boar. Thus lettuce was associated with male sterility, effeminacy, and cowardice, and generally was viewed as a suppressant of sexual performance.

Gardens of Adonis were planted in pots or baskets during the heat of summer and then allowed to die prematurely on the roofs of houses during the feast of Adonia (19 July during the Roman Empire) as symbolic evidence of the boy's sexual prowess, which produced no "seed" or fruit. Significantly, these little gardens consisted of barley, wheat, lettuce, and fennel, each plant highly symbolic of some aspect of fertility yet a total inversion of what was understood to be garden abundance.

Interestingly, a distinctive lettuce dedicated to Gauas (the Cypriot Adonis), and later known as "Cyprian" during the Byzantine period, was discovered in a Serbian monastery by the U.S. Department of Agriculture in the early twentieth century and is preserved in several American seed banks. It is physically similar to the pointed-leaf lettuce depicted in the medieval *Tacuinum Sanitatis* (Arano, 1976) of the eleventh-century Syrian Christian physician Ibn Botlan. By virtue of this continuity, at least in form and appearance, Cyprian lettuce is a true heirloom variety, a category of vegetable that will be dealt with later in this discussion.

VEGETABLES AND THE ARAB DIASPORA

The agricultural historian Andrew Watson has long promoted the idea that an agricultural revolution took place under early Islamic rule in the eastern Mediterranean, a revolution that was carried westward into North Africa and Spain. This has important implications for the movement of vegetable plants. However, other scholarship has questioned this thesis. There is growing evidence that the revolution was already taking place during the late Byzantine period and that it consisted of newer ways of irrigating land and reclaiming marshes so more intensive forms of agriculture could be undertaken. Without entering the question of who invented what, two critical points are undeniable: the technology came out of Persia and South India (the vast irrigation systems in Sri Lanka were well known even to the Greeks), and its spread westward was made possible by the political stability that Arab conquest brought to the regions under its control.

It is easy to point to the concentration of wealth in bright spots such as Syria (Damascus and Baghdad in particular), Egypt, and al-Andalus in Spain, but there was an economic implosion in other parts of the newly formed empire.

The family papers of the Ibn'Awkal merchants of eleventh-century Egypt reveal a great deal about industrial crops like Egyptian flax or high-profit goods like black pepper, indigo, and sal ammoniac, but information on common garden vegetables is rather limited.

That is, unless one looks at medical literature and cookery books. The most heavily used culinary source is also one of the oldest: the *Kitab al-tabikh,* otherwise known as the Baghdad cookery book. It was written down in 1226, although internal evidence clearly indicates that the material was compiled from several much earlier sources, some of which were not Arabic. This ambiguity is one of the difficulties in using cookbooks to pinpoint the introduction of new vegetables.

But that said, there are other Arabic cookery manuscripts equally rich in detail surviving from the Middle Ages, such as the *Manuscrito Anonimo* of Moorish Spain, and all of the recipes no matter what the source are fairly clear about the role vegetables played in the diet of the times.

There is certainly no ambiguity in the Baghdad cookery book about the use of eggplants and no doubt at all that the sort discussed had dark black skin (there are directions for removing it). The book also makes ample reference to fava beans, cardoons, rhubarb, leeks, the ridged cucumber (Armenian snake melon), carrots, gourds, taro, cultivated purslane, turnips, sweet fennel, and spinach. There are also references to a form of cabbage commonly translated into English as cauliflower.

Without a picture, one cannot be sure (it could be a type of broccoli), but since true cauliflower evidently evolved in the Dead Cities region of northwestern Syria, it is quite likely that this luxury vegetable migrated during the early 800s with its growers when they resettled elsewhere—a small group of those Syrian Christians emigrated to the Karpasia district of Cyprus, where cauliflower was first observed by pilgrims to the Holy Land later in the Middle Ages. The cauliflower is not mentioned in European scientific works until specimens are discussed by Dodonaeus in 1560. By that time Cypriot seed was being exported to northern Europe via Venice.

One is also treated with a rich array of vegetables in another work called *Kitab Wasf al-Atima al-Mutada* (Description of Familiar Foods) written in 1373. Of particular interest is the differentiation of several types of leeks, indicating not only distinct varieties but also distinct culinary uses at different stages of development—indirect evidence of a highly evolved sense of market gardening. Four sorts of leek are mentioned: the vegetable leek *(kurrath baql),* the Nabatean leek, the table leek, and the Syrian leek. The first is not a variety but rather a spring leek, young greens similar in character to Chinese garlic chives. The Nabatean leek may be equated with the modern salad leek of Iraq, a member of the Kurrat Group, short in height and rather deep-rooted. The table leek is a blanched leek similar to the Catalan Calcot onion, and indeed the cultural technique of burying them in deep trenches may be the same. The Syrian leek is the *kephaloton* of medieval Cyprus, a Greek word derived from Syrian *quaflot,* a leek with an unusually large bulb. This plant is the genetic ancestor of the modern elephant garlic.

Under the name *Porrum Syriacum,* it was first illustrated in European botanical literature by Tabernaemontanus in 1588. Arab books dealing with cookery exhibit an undeniable passion for elegant preparations, even with simple vegetables. But such food was the privilege of the aristocratic few, and the wealth that sustained that lifestyle was soon to fade with the economic upheavals caused by the Crusades. Until the late twentieth century, historians have greatly underestimated the exchanges that took place after the establishment of Latin footholds in the Levant and Byzantium or the role of large Christian minorities that persisted in Egypt and Syria during the early Muslim period.

The Nestorian or East Syrian Church, which spread into Persia, established strong trading communities in China and Malabar as well as in Cyprus, where the Nestorian Lakhan family became extremely powerful based on trade in medical aloes.

One line of trade and plant exchange went through Tabriz in Persia overland to the Caucasian kingdom of Georgia and the Greek Empire of Trebizond on the north coast of modern Turkey, all to circumvent the Arabs. That this Black Sea entry was an important route for the movement of Asian food plants westward may be inferred from an eleventh-century Byzantine reference to the "citrons" of Anatolia, a variety of lemon introduced via Georgia and Armenia and still preserved in Georgian botanical collections. Eggplants also followed this route. European contact with foods of the Arab world was not limited to the crusading troops that went to the Holy Land and returned. The Latin Kingdom of Jerusalem (1099–1291), the Principality of Achaea (1205–1430), a French feudal state established in Greece with its capital at Mistra, a Catalan principality centred on Athens, various Venetian and Genovese ports, and the sister kingdoms of Cilicia (1080–1375) in Asia Minor and on Cyprus (1192–1489) were all characterized by colonial aristocracies with highly orientalized foodways.

The last kingdoms, especially that of Cyprus due to a Papal Bull, served as conduits for the spice trade with the Muslim world. In the case of Cyprus, the kingdom lent its name to an international style of cookery mentioned in numerous medieval cookbooks. More important, the intermarriage of wealthy Latins in the Levant with European nobility, particularly with families in Aragon and in northern Italy, brought to Europe a constant influx of personal cooks, gardeners, and retainers schooled in eastern Mediterranean ways. It is not surprising that some of the earliest references to exotic vegetables like eggplants, cauliflowers, okra, and numerous sorts of Near Eastern melons show up in late medieval Italy.

VEGETABLES IN THE BAROQUE PERIOD

The seventeenth century witnessed a revolution in botanical science and the proliferation of books devoted to illustrating plants and vegetables from many parts of the world, including new introductions from Asia and the Americas. Francisco Hernandez's *Nova Plantarum* was devoted almost exclusively to the foods of Mexico and included native names for the plants. His woodcut illustrations offer a priceless look at the characteristics of common vegetables then grown in New Spain, including the lowly miltomatl or tomatillo *(Physalis ixocarpa)* now popular in Southwest American cooking. Other books containing strange designations like *Pomum amoris majus fructu luteo* (large yellow fruited love apple or, more simply, yellow tomato) remind one how much lack of order prevailed in the scientific naming of newly discovered vegetables and how much has changed since Linneaus imposed order on the world of plants in the eighteenth century.

Names like *bamia Aegypitiaca* (Egyptian okra—*bamya* is actually a Syrian word) of one author might become "ladies' fingers" of the next. Likewise the *lactuca hispanica* (Spanish lettuce) of one author was the *Cos* or Roman lettuce of another, the names more often than not reflecting the source of seed rather than the true origin and history of the vegetable. One of the most fashionable cabbages of the period was the so-called *Brassica tophosa,* better known as black Tuscan palm tree kale, "rediscovered" by American seeds-people under the new moniker "dinosaur kale." The penchant for fanciful names has not changed. If a generalization can be made about the seventeenth century, it is that the rare and exotic vegetable of the previous century gradually became the daily fare of the urban middle class by 1700.

Plant breeding, especially in Holland, brought many new sorts of vegetables onto the market. Named varieties of potatoes, carrots, celery, chicory, peas, and turnips soon proliferated in kinds and colours. Added to this roster were newly discovered Asian foods, like Malabar spinach *(Basella alba),* introduced from Java in 1688. Handbooks on plant breeding were even published, one of the earliest in English being Walter Sharrock's *History of the Propagation and Improvement of Vegetables* (1660). From this time on, the vegetable undergoes a steady refinement with emphasis on greater delicacy of flavour, more beautiful shape, and increasing tenderness.

Much of this was directly connected with shifts taking place in cookery, especially the use of vegetables in sauces and elaborately prepared dishes. Vegetables were also given ornamental value with paring knives, so turnips feathered out into birds, carrots unwound into golden fish, and the cookbooks of the day are full of illustrations showing how to do this. Most notably, however, the vegetable became a prized market commodity; growing of vegetables, a respectable line of work for the honest laborer; and period depictions of market scenes never fail to convey the impression that only the best has been laid before the eye. Aside from shifts in cookery, the virtues of country life and the pursuit of its simple pleasures helped elevate vegetable gardening as a worthy and genteel pastime. Jan van der Groen's *Den Nederlandtsen Hovenier* was extremely influential in this respect, as were Nicolas de Bonnefon's *Les delices de la campagne* and *Le jardinier francois* in France.

All of these works were translated into several languages and included specific discussions of vegetable varieties and cooking tips. Under fava beans, for example, Bonnefon recommended several different methods of preparation, including fricassees like peas or boiled plain with slices of bacon, noting that fresh green savoury went "marvelously well" with any fava bean dish.

Not the least important, from the standpoint of vegetables, was John Evelyn's *Acetaria: A Discourse on Sallets,* which discussed most of the popular types of vegetables of the day, especially ways to employ them raw or semicooked in salads. Of earth chestnuts *(Bunium bulbocastanum)* he remarked: "the Rind pard off, they are eaten crude by Rustics, with a little Pepper; but are best when boil'd like other Roots, or in Pottage rather, and are sweet and nourishing."

VEGETABLES IN THE ENLIGHTENMENT

The idea that vegetables recaptured the original wholesomeness of Eden became an underlying theme for many of the more offbeat cookbooks of the eighteenth century, with *Adam's Luxury and Eve's Cookery* considered one of the most typical.

The underlying philosophies expressed in these books may be said to represent the intellectual forerunners of true vegetarianism, which was indeed practiced in colonial North America by the so-called White Friends, a group of Quakers who wore clothing of unbleached cloth.

The most highly organized vegetarians in early North America, however, were the Bible Christians, who expanded from England in 1816. Martha Brotherton's *Vegetable Cookery* became the dietary handbook for this group. The European penchant for country life was quickly transferred to England during the 1600s and from there to colonial America. Doubtless it achieved its American apotheosis in such famous estates as William Penn's "Pennsbury Manor" along the Delaware River, Thomas Jefferson's "Monticello" in Virginia, William Hamilton's "Woodlands" near Philadelphia, and Charles Carroll's "Mount Clare" in Baltimore. Jefferson's personal garden account book, published by the American Philosophical Society in 1944, remains a lasting testimony to the central role that kitchen gardens—and vegetables in particular—played in this manorial lifestyle.

It was on such estates as these that many of the Old World exotics were first introduced to North America. Charles Norris of Philadelphia, for example, is known to have raised black-skinned eggplants, since a letter survives from

1763 imploring him for seed. Many of the most popular vegetables of this period can be found in Philip Miller's *Gardener's and Botanist's Dictionary*, and remarkable as it may seem, some of Miller's vegetables are extant, among them red celery, Spotted Aleppo and Silesia lettuces, spinach beets, and domesticated sea kale.

VEGETABLES IN THE RENAISSANCE

The *Carrara Herbal*, created sometime before 1403, was one of the first late medieval herbals to depict plants and vegetables accurately, although it may have been based on a now lost Byzantine prototype. Such illustrated handbooks of health, as well as numerous herbals, offer a rich visual record of the sorts of vegetables deemed. The beautiful gardens witnessed by travellers through the Latin East were now replicated in Italy but with the goal for reattaining a glorious Roman past. The Italian pleasure gardens of this period so impressed Casimir the Great of Poland that he installed one in Cracow during the 1360s, complete with cold frames for forcing Mediterranean vegetables. In short, the vegetable garden once again becomes an object of status.

The discovery of printing, followed quickly by the discovery of the New World and the heady harvest of its vegetable riches, only accelerated a quest for new and exotic things to ornament the gardens of the rich and powerful. Tomatoes, peppers, potatoes, sunflowers, beans, sweet potatoes, new sorts of pumpkins, and a new kind of wheat called maize fill the pages of botanical treatises and plant books of the period. The 1500s may be characterized as a century during which botanists attempted to organize the vegetable world into some type of scientific order, although that "order" by modern standards was quite chaotic. For example, a confusing observation is that the Jerusalem artichoke from North America (not from Jerusalem and not an artichoke) is known as *Flos solis Farnesianus* (Farnese sunflower) in reference to the fact that the gardens at the Villa Farnese in Rome provided several botanists with the first known specimens. Sorting out such conflicting nomenclature has plagued garden historians ever since.

However, botanical gardens were established in this century, the first in 1545 at the University of Padua, and some of the greatest botanical works of the Renaissance were issued during this era, especially those devoted to cataloging the gardens of such important plantsmen as Conrad Gesner in Switzerland (1561), Georg Fabricius in Meissen, Germany (1569), and Camerarius in Nurnberg (1588). All of these books contain valuable woodcuts depicting vegetables, and many medieval favourites like skirret *(Sium sisarum)* and monk's rhubarb *(Rumex patientia)* are shown for the first time. Vegetables also figured prominently in Renaissance art and paintings, especially the still life genre. Among the most whimsical vegetable compositions are those by the court painter Giuseppe Arcimboldo (c. 1527–1593), who used vegetables and fruits to create faces and other conceits. The most significant body of literature, however, was the garden guides that discussed not only specific vegetable varieties but also how to grow them. The French work known as *L'agriculture ou la maison rustique,* first published in Latin (1535) by the Paris printer Charles Estienne, was soon translated into most major European languages. Marco Bussato's *Giardino di agricultura* was also extremely influential, as was Johann Coler's *Oeconomica ruralis et domestica*. The great classic, however, was Oliver de Serre's *Theatre d'agriculture*, which became a standard garden book for much of the next century. This great outpouring of garden knowledge was capped in many ways by the lavishly illustrated *Hortus Eystettensis* assembled by Basilius Besler in 1613 for his patron plant collector, the bishop of Eichstatt in Bavaria. Not only did the good bishop own prize specimens of rare eggplants, balsam apple *(Momordica balsamina),* tomatoes, and domesticated asparagus, his potted prickly pear cactus from the New World required a wooden superstructure to hold the monster plant in place.

RESEARCH ON VEGETABLES

The major objectives of research on vegetables in India is improving production per unit area by solving chronic problems of production through breeding high yielding, disease & pest resistant varieties, developing F1 hybrids, standardisation of agro-techniques for different agro-ecological situations, disease and insect pest management and post-harvest studies with a view to reduce post-harvest losses.

Twenty three vegetable namely, amaranthus, bitter kgourd, bottle gourd, brinjal, cabbaage, carrot, cauliflower, chillies, coepea, cucumbefr, Dolichos, frenchbean, garlic, Luffa, muskmelon, okra, onion, peas, pointed gourd, pumpkin, sweet pepper, tomato and watermelon have been included in the national research programme on vegetable crops. The salient research achievements in vegetable research.

CROP IMPROVEMENT

(i) *New Varieties Released:* The evaluation of indigenous and exotic germplasm intP> The evaluation of indigenous and exotic germplasm introductions, and their hybridization resulted in the selection of over 30 superior varieties of different vegetables during fiftees. Of these, varieties 'Pusa Sawani' of okra, 'Pusa Ruby' and 'Pusa Early Dwarf' of tomaton, 'Pusa Purple Long' of brinjal and 'Booneville' of garden peas still continue to be the main vegetable varieties due to their high yield potential and consumer's preference. As a result of multi-disciplinary, multi-location testing of new research materials during the last two decades, 119 improved varieties in 16 major vegetable crops have been identified and recommended for cultivation in various agro-climatic regions of the country. These include 20 varieties of tomato, 22 of brinjal, 13 each of onion and cauliflower, 12 of garden pea, 9 of chillies, 8 of muskmelon 4 each of water melon, pumpkin & okra, 3 frenchbean (bush type) 2 of garlic and 1 each of Dolichos bean, cabbage, carrot, cowpea and capsicum.

(ii) It is interesting to note that out of 119 varieties recommended by All India Coordinated vegetable Improvement Project, 52 varieties/ hybrids have been released through Central Variety Release Committee for commercial cultivation in different zones of India. Moreover, the foundation and certified seeds of these varieties are being produced by the National Seeds Corporation Government of India. Besides, 74 varieties of different of India.

(iii) *F1 Hybrids Developed:* In India, even though the first report of hybrid vigour in chillies came in 1933 from Indian Agricultural Research Institute, the first F1 hybrid of tomato and capsicum was available for commercial cultivation only in 1973. Since then, there has been an increasing interest in growing hybrids in vegetable crops among the Indian farmers.

Heterosis breeding in vegetable crops in India has received serious attention only in recent years. As a result the progress in developing and popularising hybrid varieties has been very slow. The first F1 hybrid of tomato (Karnataka Hybrid) and capsaicum (Bharat) were released for commercial cultivation in 1973 by a private seed company M/s Indo-American Hybrid Seeds followed by 28 other Hybrids in 9 vegetable crops. Of the 21 F1 hybrids in 11 vegetable crops developed so far by public research institutions.

In addition to F1 hybrids, two synthetic cauliflower varieties, namely, 'Pusa Synthetic' in and 'Pusa Early Synthetic' have also been recommended for release.

The F1 hybrids developed have not been fully exploited so far due to inadequate facilities for their seed production. At present there is an urgent need to simplif production.

At present there is an urgent need to simplify the technique of hybrid seed production. Various genetic mechanisms like male sterility, self-incompatibility and sgnoecious sex forms need special attention to exploit them as female presents of the hybrids. Pioneer research work has been carried out in the Division of Vegetable Crops, IARI, New Delhi and some female parents like self-incompatible lines in cauliflower and cabbage and gynoecious sex forms in muskmelon and cucumber have been developed and are being utilized in heterosis breeding. Very good hybrid research work has been carried out at Punjab Agricultural University on muskmelon, brinjal, tomato, chilli and onion. In general, there is acute deartrh of good hybrid seeds in cauliflower, cabbnage, tomato and onion and taking up heterosis breeding in these crops is an immediate need. Work on heterosis will be strengthened after the implement of NATP project.

Several private seedsmen have also been marketing hybrid vegetable varieties, either directly imported and rebelled or developed by crossing exotic parents and hybrid seeds produced indigenously. Some of these F1 hybrids are in tomato "Rupali", "Vaishali", and "Naveen" from Bangalore, "Hybrid S-15", "Hybrid S-16" and "Samirudhi" from Jalna and SG-12" and SG-9" from Calcutta; in capsicum "Bharat" from Bangalore; 'Early Bounty' and Sutquot; from Bangalore; 'Early Bounty' and Suttons Gen Gant from Calcutta; in watermelon "Madhu and Milan" from Bangalore; in cabbage "Ganesh Gole", "No. 8" and "Hirirani" from Jalna" in cucumber "Priya" from Bangalore. There are many more being offered by other seedsmen as well but their adoiption is comparatively slow.

Disease and Pest Resistant Varieties: Research on breeding for disease/pest resistance has resulted in the release of twenty four varieties. 'Pusa Sawani' variety of okra developed as resistant to yellow-vein-mosaic virus is the first example of successful disease resistance breeding in vegetable crops in India.

REGIONAL CLIMATES AND VEGETATION

A forester faced with the practical problems of choosing what species to plant on a given site, or of selecting sites and species for the production of a particular type of timber, needs a detailed knowledge of the local climates and plant associations of his territory. This will direct him to other areas on which he might be able to draw for additional species. He will, of course, have made himself familiar with all available relevant experience whether published or to be found in the files of the various organizations concerned with natural history, land use, biological, geological, climatological and hydrological research in his country. He will also have studied the topography, soils and vegetation, both natural and artificial, of the tract in question and of other parts of the country having similar conditions.

If he believes that his purpose may be served best by the trial of exotic species, he will obviously first consider making introductions from homoclimes or climatic analogues. He will turn to zones of similar and similarly distributed rainfall and temperatures with similar latitudes and topography, and seek detailed information about the distribution and growth there of useful species, and the types of soil on which they grow.

These zones will be indicated somewhat vaguely on climatological maps of the world, and more detail about them will be available in local regional maps and in tables of climatological data published in the regions. Then the forester can generally turn to a local flora of the region to ascertain what grows there, and often he will be able to follow up the species which arouse his interest in monographs or other papers dealing with them.

If he is fortunate, he will find works such as *Applied Silviculture in the United States* and *The Silviculture of Indian Trees*, which will give him climatic, ecological and silvicultural information about the trees of considerable areas. Records of trials of species in different parts of the world such as are to be found in *Exotic Forest Trees in the British Empire* will also be useful. If he has reason to think that some members of the genus *Eucalyptus* might be of value to him, he can turn to the FAO publication *Eucalypts for Planting* the various reports of the FAO Eucalyptus Study Tour (1952) and others of the 300 or so publications listed in the bibliography of that book, and the *Forest Seed Directory*, which lists 118 eucalypt species classified according to their suitability to grow in any of 18-climatic zones. Other Australian trees besides the eucalypts are included in *A Reconnaissance of the Forest Trees of Australia from the point of view of their cultivation in South Africa.*

There is, of course, nothing new about this. Horticulturists and foresters have for many years looked to countries with climates similar to their own, visited them and brought back seed of species which they thought might make promising additions to their local floras. The only difference now is that very much more information is available, and that reliable seed can be obtained from the zones selected without difficulty or resort to smuggling as was sometimes necessary in the past.

As an example, it may be noted that in 1823 Douglas was sent to North America by the Royal Horticultural Society of London because it was realized that the Pacific Coast region was the home of a particularly rich flora growing in a climate comparable to some parts of the British Isles. This region from Oregon northwards through Washington and British Columbia to southeast Alaska and bounded on the east by the Coastal Ranges contains a far wider range of climate than does Britain, but the temperature regime at the mouth of the Columbia River around latitude 46° N., with an average in summer of 54° F. (13° C.) and an average for the year of 50° F. (11° C.), is similar to that of the English south coast, latitude about 50.5° N.; and Sitka in Alaska, latitude 57° N., closely matches the northwest coast of Scotland. The rainfall on the Pacific coast is of the winter type with midsummer the driest period, whereas in Britain spring is relatively dry. Further north up the coast the proportion of rain falling in the summer is greater, until in southeast Alaska it is close to the 22 percent commonly found in Britain. Inland, the climate becomes rapidly continental and summer temperatures are higher than in England.

The trees of the region important to forestry in Britain and parts of western Europe have been found to be Sitka spruce, Douglas fir, *Pinus contorta* Dougl., *Abies grandis* Indl., *Tsuga heterophylla* Sarg. and *Thuya plicata* Don. All penetrate into climates of much lower winter temperature than are found in Britain, and Douglas fir and the *Abies* than those of Britain, in particular grow best in warmer summer temperatures averaging 52° to 56° F. (11.1°-13.3°C.) though there is no reason to suppose that they are limited by summer temperature. In their native habitat, neither Douglas fir nor Sitka spruce appear to form part of climax forest communities, but are pioneer species giving way to *Tsuga, Thuya* and *Abies*. Sitka spruce thrives at low elevations in the British Columbian region with mean annual temperatures varying from 44° to 49° F. (6.7°-9.4°C.), summer mean of 55° to 68°F. (12.8°-20°C.), winter mean of 30° to 38° F. (1.1°-3.3° C.) and a rainfall of 40 inches (1,020 mm.) a year upwards, conditions which can easily be matched in Britain.

It is now possible to buy from government forest departments and from merchants seed certified as collected from known climatic and elevational zones in this region as from several other regions of the world. The forms of agreed international certificates of origin and quality, and the sources from which a large number of species can be obtained. One firm divides its collection area on the Pacific coast from Alaska to California into 25 climatic regions, subdivided into 127 zones, each of which is further split up into 500 foot (150 m.) elevation bands. It provides tables which give the temperatures (average annual, average summer, absolute maximum and absolute minimum), precipitation (annual and summer), and the number of frost-free days in the year, for the most representative weather station in each zone.

Another country which was drawn on early for plantation species was Australia. In 1843, several species of eucalypt were tried in the Nilgiri Hills of India, and later *Eucalyptus globulus* Labill. solved a serious fuel shortage there. In 1870, *Acacia mollissima* Willd was introduced into Natal and eastern Transvaal in South Africa and by 1952 a great tanbark industry depending on some 640,000 acres (259,000 ha.) of black wattle plantations had been built up. In 1876, *Eucalyptus saligna* Sm. was first planted for railway fuel in South Africa, and now there are some 200,000 acres (80,000 ha.) of it in eastern and northern Transvaal and on the Zululand coast. Early in the present century, the *Companhia Paulista de Estradas de Ferro*, the State railway of Sao Paulo, Brazil, imported 143 species of eucalypts and now has some 30,000 acres (12,000 ha.) of plantations, mainly of *E. camaldulensis* Dahn., *E. citriodora* Hook and *E. saligna*. The Mediterranean countries, Spain, Portugal, France, Italy and Greece, have all found *E. globulus* and *E. camaldulensis* valuable additions to their plantation species.

In California, 80 percent of the considerable eucalypt plantations are of *E. globulus*, and 15 percent of *E. camaldulensis.* Peru, Chile and Uruguay all make considerable use of *E. globulus*, while in Turkey, Cyprus, Palestine, Jordan, Tripolitania and Morocco the most popular eucalypt is *E. Camaldulensis.* Many other species are found to be suitable to particular parts of these and many other countries.

It is, therefore, worth considering the climate and vegetation of the Australian continent. Australia has a central desert zone covering nearly 40 percent of its whole area, and the rest can be divided very roughly into three main climatic zones:

1. A tropical northern zone of summer rainfall, north of about 20° S. on the west coast and about 14° S. on the east coast. The mean annual rainfall varies from about 20 inches (510 mm.) in the south of the zone to 60) inches (1,525 mm.) and more on the north and east coasts, with some areas receiving 120 inches (3,050 mm.). The mean annual temperature is in the neighborhood of 80° F. (26.4° C.), the interior being warmer than the coastal areas and the west coast warmer than the east.
2. A zone of moderate winter rainfall and dry summers in the southern parts of South Australia, Western Australia, the greater part of Victoria, and the south of New South Wales. Mean annual rainfall varies from about 10 inches (250 mm.) to about 30 inches (760 mm.) with isolated areas of up to 40 inches (1,020 mm.) on the south coast. Summer temperatures are around 70° F. (21.1° C.) and winter temperatures around 35° F. (1.7° C.)
3. A zone of more uniformly distributed rainfall on the east coast and the southeastern part of the continent with annual rainfall generally between 20 inches (510 mm.) and 60 inches (1,526 mm.). This zone includes the mountains of New South Wales, and there and on the east coast the rainfall is from 40 to 60 inches (1,020-1,526 mm.) a year, with isolated areas of 120 inches (3,050 mm.) on the coast of northern Queensland, where the summer is the wetter season. In the south (Victoria), there is a tendency towards a maximum rainfall in winter. In New South Wales, the even distribution is more noticeable, though in the north and on the east coast more rain falls in summer, and on the south coast more in winter. There are very considerable variations in temperature regimes within the zone, because of the topography.

De Beuzville (1943) considered that the whole of the east coast of Australia has a climate predominantly similar to that of Argentine, Brazil and Mexico and certain parts of South Africa, and also, in its wetter parts, in Madagascar. The north coast and its hinterland has a climate similar to those of parts of Madagascar, India and Mozambique. On the west coast and inland from it there are stations with climates similar to some found in South Africa, Algeria, Sudan, Mexico and Arizona. The climate in the south southwest is more like that of California and South Africa, and in small areas like that of Spain. The Australian Alps and the Dividing Range have cool slopes where the climate approximates to that of France and Italy. The dry centre of Australia has a climate similar to that of Egypt, Arizona, Israel and parts of the Californian desert. Robertson (1926) found that, while coastal temperatures, latitude for latitude, were very similar in Australia and South Africa, the interior of Australia was warmer than that of South Africa because of the greater elevation of the latter.

The forest formations of Australia may be roughly divided into Rain Forest (tropical, sub-tropical, and temperate), Moist Sclerophyllous Forest, pry Sclerophyllous Forest, and Open Woodland, all of which merge into each other.

The rain forests occur only in isolated relict patches. In the tropical zone their flora is Malayan without predominant species, and the natural succession is very confused.

From the Hastings River, about 30° S., in New South Wales to the north of Queensland, *Araucaria cunninghammii* Ait is found on the coast and up to 100 miles (160 km.) inland with an annual rainfall of 50 to 70 inches (1,270-1,780 mm.), falling mainly in summer. *Araucaria bidwillii* Hock, and *Agathis robusta* are found in southeast Queensland in areas with 50-60 inches (1,270-1,525 mm.) summer rain, with summer temperatures of 75° to 85° F. (24°-29° C.) and winter temperatures of 50° to 60° F. (10°-16° C.). What are apparently secondary forest formation after fires include *Tristania conferta* R. Br. and *Syncarpia laurifolia* Ten. mixed with eucalypts such as *Eucalyptus saligna*.

The sclerophyllous formations are mainly composed of eucalypts and acacias. Closed stands of Eucalyptus are not usually found where the rainfall is less than 30 inches (760 mm.) a year, below which limit open and scrubby vegetation occurs.

Many of the eucalypt species are confined to particular zones of rainfall amount and distribution, but some are very adaptable. One of the most widely distributed is *E. camaldulensis* which Boosman (1950) states can put up with 5 to 10 inches (130-250 mm.) of rain a year, is often found in zones of 22 to 28 inches (560-710 mm.), and exceptionally with 40 to 45 inches (1,020-1,140 mm.) though 35 inches (890 mm.) is regarded as its normal maximum. Actually its range is determined more by soil moisture conditions than by precipitation and it is characteristic of alluvial flats, often along river banks where water is available by inundation or percolation.

It likes warmth and extends into some of the hottest parts of the Northern Territory. It is not found in the highlands of New South Wales in which State de Beuzville (1943) gives a mean temperature of the coldest month of 46° F. (7.8° C.) as the lower thermal limit of its range. It must be remembered that the form, as well as the stand density, of eucalypt species growing in areas of their minimum rainfall is very different from what it is under optimum rainfall.

Moist sclerophyllous forest is found mainly in the southeastern coastal strip of New South Wales and Victoria, and in the southwest corner of Western Australia, in the zones of either winter or fairly uniform rainfall. In Western Australia, *Eucalyptus diversi-colour* F. V. M. is found in stands of a type approaching temperate rainforest in a climate of 40 to 60 inches (1,020-1,525 mm.) mean annual rainfall and mean annual temperatures of 62° to 65° F. (16.7°-18.6° C.) In Victoria and New South Wales, *Eucalyptus globulus* grows in the higher and cooler sites with 35 to 65 inches (890-1,650 mm.) of rain and mean annual temperatures of 44° to 49° F. (6.7°-9.4° C.) sometimes mixed with *Acacia melanoxylon* R. Br. and with an understorey of *Acacia mollissima* Wild. or *A. dealbata* Link. In the wetter range of these sites in Victoria, stands of *Eucalyptus regnas* F. v. M. are found.

Eucatyptus gomphocephala A. Dc. with an undergrowth of *Acacia cyanophylla* Lindl. is found growing on calcareous sands in the southwest of Western Australia in an annual rainfall of 30 to 40 inches (760-1,020 mm.) mainly in winter, with an annual mean temperature of 60° to 64° F. (15.6°-17.8° C.) and a summer temperature of 67° to 72° F. (19.4°-22.2° C.). There are either no frosts or only occasional light ones in places. Both species have proved valuable in the afforestation of coastal sand in South Africa, and more recently have shown considerable promise when used in combination on calcareous sand dunes in Morocco. In the dry sclerophyllous forests there is a very great variety of eucalypt species, not many of which attain timber dimensions in the lower rainfall areas. In New South Wales and Queensland, *Eucalypts crebra* F. V. M. grows with a rainfall of 20 to 26 inches (510-660 mm.) a year mainly in summer in areas of high temperature, often mixed with *Callitris glauca* R. Br. *Eucalypts sideroxylon* A. Cunn. is found in poor sites in New South Wales, Victoria and Queensland with about 20 inches (510 mm.) of rain a year.

There are also species which are characteristic of moister forests but nevertheless can grow with as little as 22 to 25 inches (560-635 mm.) a year, such as *Eucalypts marginata* Sm. in Western Australia, and *E. oblique* l'Herit. in South Australia, Victoria and New South Wales. Where there is moisture enough to permit of under this is often *Acacia pycnantha* or *A. mollissima* in the east, and *A. cyanophylla* or *A. cyclops* Cunn. in the west.

These formations merge into open woodland, particularly in western Queensland and New South Wales. *Eucalypts salmonophloia* F. V. M. grow in Western Australia in the zone of 9 to 12 inches (220-305 mm.) of rain, mainly from June to September. 'Mallee' formations consisting of a great variety of small, often bush-like, eucalypts attaining up to 20 feet (6 m.) in height with stems of 3 to 6 inches (7.6-15.2 cm.) in diameter, cover considerable areas of low rainfall.

South Africa is a good example of a country with inadequate natural forests and slow-growing indigenous species. The need to supplement the natural flora was recognized early. Conifers and hardwoods were imported from northern Europe from 1665, but did not thrive. Later some Mediterranean species, notably *Pinus pinea* L., which became naturalized in the Cape Peninsula, and *Pinus pinaster* Sol., which has been widely planted and does best in the zone with winter or all-the-year-round rainfall, were introduced. By the middle of the nineteenth century *P. radiata* had been brought from California and had proved to be very adaptable in climates similar to those favoured by *P. pinaster*, though more particular about soil. Later in the century, *P. longifolia* Roxb. was introduced from the outer ranges of the Himalayas in India and proved useful in the cool and warm temperate summer rainfall areas. A great step forward was made about 1905 when Hutchins decided that Mexico, a plateau country like the Transvaal, lying in approximately similar latitudes, having a summer rainfall and a rich flora, should be a promising source of exotics. He tried a number of species including *Pinus patula* Seem. of which there is now a bigger acreage in South Africa that of any other softwood, particularly, of course, in the summer rainfall areas. Hutchins also recommended *P. caribaea* Morelet from the southern United States of America for the sub-tropical zone, and it has shown exceptionally vigorous growth in both the temperate and sub-tropical zones with winter or all-the-year-round rainfall.

It is being planted on a large scale for paper pulp in Zululand. By 1947, some nervousness was felt about the dangers of disease in large pure blocks of these two species and an officer was sent to America to study the pines in their natural habitats and to find additional species if possible. He was particularly interested in *Pinus pseudostrobus* Lind. which had originally been tried under the name of *P. teocote* Schl. v Cham. with success, but the seed of which could not be obtained. He was able to collect 350 pounds (159 kg.) of seed in Mexico.

He was also impressed by *Pinus hondurensia* Loock in British Honduras, only lately distinguished from *P. caribaea*. This illustrates the importance of botanical identification and of securing seed of the most suitable species and varieties for use in particular localities. Where reliable local agencies for the supply of seed do not exist it may be necessary to go and collect exactly what is wanted. These conifers and others from California, Central America, India, the Mediterranean region, and Mexico now cover more than 600,000 acres (243,000 ha.) of South Africa, alongside some 640,000 acres (259,000 ha.) of acacias and 450,000 acres (186,000 ha.) of eucalypts from Australia, an example of what can be done by selection and trial of species from climates similar to those in which they are required to grow.

Reference is made earlier, in the study of which this chapter is an exerpt, to the agro-climatic analogues established at the American Institute of Crop Ecology by Nuttonson (1937-53). Up to the latter year analogues had been established between North America and Ukraine, Poland, Czechoslovakia, Yugoslavia, Greece Albania, China, Germany, Finland Sweden, Norway, Siberia, Japan, and the Ryukyu Islands. Each of these studies gives a general and comparative geography of the country covered and a brief account of its climate. There is also a varying amount of information about the natural resources of the country, its soils, major plant species, land-use, agricultural and forestry practices, etc. Relief maps show the location of the meteorological stations within the country studied and the regions of any North American climatic counterparts found. Charts give full meterological data for each station and for the counterparts. The purpose of this series of studies is "to formulate an agronomic and horticultural approach to ecology and to promote research along the lines of crop ecology as it affects plant adaptation, plant introduction, and the exchange of varietal plant material among the various agricultural areas of the worlds". Its value is not, however, confined to agriculturists. For instance, the paper on Japan (1951) points out:

"Over one half of the total land area of the country is covered with luxuriant forests of a great diversify of broadleaved and coniferous species and of dense undergrowth. These forests are found largely in the mountainous regions, as more than three-fourths of the country's land consists of rough and rugged mountains and hills topographically unsuitable for cultivation of farm crops."

PROPER CONDITIONS FOR NITRIFICATION

First, materials containing nitrogen must be present. There is a great variation in the amount of nitrogen the different organic materials contain. Then certain soil or compost conditions are necessary:

Proper soil acidity (pH) —should be about 7.0; in acid situation below 5.5 it ceases.

Proper temperature of soil — above 50°F.

Good aeration — (does not occur with wet, soggy soil or compost).

Adequate lime for use by micro-organisms and to keep the soil from being acid.

ANIMAL MANURES

Where animal manures are available, they are probably the best source of fertilizer and organic matter for the organic gardener. Use manure which has been aged for at least 30 days, or composted. Manures vary greatly in their content of fertilizing nutrients. The composition varies according to type, age, and condition of animal; the kind of feed used; the age and degree of rotting of the manure; the moisture content of the manure; and the kind and amount of litter or bedding mixed in the manure. shows average minimal amounts of nutrients to be expected. They may be as high as 4.5% N; 2% P; and 2% K in some cases. Animal manures also provide most of the micro-nutrients needed. Some manure products are composted, rehydrated or mixed with plant litter to enhance their fertility.

Before Planting

Cow, horse, hog — A minimum of 25 pounds per 100 square feet (about 5 tons per acre) of garden soil. For best results, supplement each 25 pounds of manure with 2 to 3 pounds of ground rock phosphate or raw bone meal. Use up to 1 pound per square foot.

Poultry, sheep — Apply at least 12 pounds per 100 square feet (about 3 tons per acre minimum) - or as much as 3 - 4 inches (20 tons per acre).

Other animals—Rabbit, goat, and exotic grasseaters — 10-12 pounds/100 sq ft. minimum, up to 100 lbs. per sq. ft.

After Planting (As a sidedressing) if needed

Cow, horse, hog — Sidedress with up to 5 pounds per 100 square feet of row. Poultry, sheep — Use up to 3 pounds per 100 square feet of row.

All Types — Broadcast evenly over plot and spade, roto-till or otherwise work into topsoil. Apply three or more weeks before planting. A small amount may be mixed well in the planting hole; however, plant injury may occur with 1 lb. or more placed in the hole. All Types — Scatter a band of manure down each side of the row. Place each band at the edge of the root zone and work lightly into the soil surface. For individual plants, open a furrow encircling the plant and fill with manure, then cover *mulch* is present, rake it back at the edge of the root zone in order to apply the band of manure, then re-cover with the mulch.

COMPOSTS

Acceptable manure-like organic fertilizer (artificial manure) may be obtained through the process of *composting.* Simply put, *compost* is made by alternating layers of organic materials, such as leaves and kitchen table refuse, with manure, topsoil, lime, organic fertilizer, water, and air, in such a manner that it decomposes, combines, and yields artificial manure.

How is the Compost Pile Made

The *compost* pile is made of convenient size, usually not less that 10 feet square (100 square feet) and 3 to 5 feet high. The top should be left flat or with a slight depression in the centre to catch rain or added water. Too much water eliminates air and slows the decay process. One way suggested in building the pile is to make a layer of leaves, straw, grass clippings, and other organic materials 1 foot deep, wet down and pack. Spread a layer of manure 4 to 6 inches deep over this layer of wet material.

Then spread up to 5 pounds of ground rock phosphate or 1 quart of raw bone meal per 100 square feet, and 1 pound of ground limestone. Instead of the rock phosphate and bone meal, you could use 5 pounds of a complete organic fertilizer such as Fertrell per 100 square feet. Also, a layer of topsoil is sometimes used. Then continue to repeat the process until the pile has reached 3 to 5 feet high. Compost will begin to heat after 2 or 3 days. Keep it moist, but not too wet, and do not disturb for awhile. After 3 to 4 weeks, fork it over, mixing the parts to obtain uniformity. Fatty animal wastes tend to create bad odors, draw flies and ants; so, try to avoid their use if this will be a problem.

Compost for the garden should be ready from 2 months to 1 year, depending on the time of year, type of materials added, and skill of the composter. When the compost is broken down into a homogenous mixture, and no undecomposed leaves or other material may be seen, it is ready for use.

Organic Materials Used in the Compost Pile

Most anything organic, but most popular materials are natural materials such as straw, leaves, pine straw, grass clippings, shrub clippings, garbage, fish scraps, water hyacinths, etc. A list of materials and what each might contribute to the compost is given in. In addition, certain of the materials listed as organic fertilizers (for example, tobacco stems) could also be added.

Irrigation

In irrigating the garden, it is advisable to thoroughly wet the soil once a week unless sufficient rain falls. Thus, the soil will be moistened throughout the root zone. Light sprinklings every day merely tend to wet the surface and encourage shallow root growth. Drip or trickle irrigation is encouraged as a method for conserving water. Use of organic materials as soil conditioners and fertilizers tends to improve the ability of the soil to retain moisture. Also, a good garden mulch will conserve soil moisture. Please observe all local watering regulations.

Mulching

A mulch is any material, usually organic, which is placed on the soil *surface* around the plants. Organic materials most commonly used for mulching are leaves, grass clippings, pine straw, sawdust, and wood shavings. Synthetic materials, mostly plastic sheeting, have been used quite often in recent years. Among the benefits of a mulch are (a) conserves soil moisture, (b) conserves nutrients, (c) reduces soil erosion, (d) reduces crop loss due to nematodes, (e) reduces weed growth, (f) provides barrier between fruit and soil, thus reducing soil rot on fruit, and (g) moderates the soil temperature. Apply mulch before or after seeding or transplanting. Roll back the mulch with a rake in order to wet the soil beneath when irrigating, for best results. At the end of the garden season, the mulch (except plastic) may be removed and composted, or cut into the garden soil. Most mulch is woody and should have manure or other rich organic fertilizer applied with it when cutting into the soil.

Weed Control

The primary purpose of cultivation is to control weeds. Weeds are easy to control when they are small. Shallow cultivation and hoeing are advised in order to reduce damage to the root system. A garden mulch, such as pine straw, leaves, or other material, will help to keep weeds from growing if the mulch is thick enough to exclude light.

Use of Compost in the Garden

Since compost is artificial manure, it should be used much as you would manure. Broadcast it over the entire garden three weeks or more before planting. Or if you have only a small quantity of compost, it may be mixed into the soil along each planting furrow or at each hill site. As a minimum, apply it at the rate of about 25 pounds per 100 square feet, or ¼ pound per square foot. Larger amounts are even more beneficial, up to 200 lb/100 sq ft. (2 lb/sq ft.).

Caution: If your compost is made from mostly woody materials, it may temporarily deplete the nitrogen from the soil and plants. Be sure to mix manure with it when applying.

Natural and Organic Fertilizers

Natural and organic materials which yield plant nutrients upon decomposition are often available for purchase either separately or in combination. These materials may be applied to the garden separately or combined, used in the compost pile, or mixed with manure. Many of the more commonly available materials are listed in along with the nutrients which they produce. These include both the organic materials derived from plants and animals, plus the natural deposits of rocks and minerals.

Natural Deposits (Rocks, Sands, Shells, etc.)

Such naturally occurring materials are usually not easily obtained in today's modern agriculture; however, where available they represent sources of mainly potash, phosphorus, and lime (calcium and magnesium) for organic gardeners.

Phosphorus — Rock phosphates are natural deposits of phosphate in combination with calcium. The material as dug from the earth is very hard and yields its phosphorus very slowly. When finely ground and with impurities removed, the powdery material is only slightly soluble in water, but may be beneficial to plants in subsequent seasons following application. The reaction of phosphate rock with acids from decaying organic matter in the garden or compost tend to make the phosphorus available to garden plants. Collodial phosphate is also available and widely used.

Apply both phosphates at the rate of 2-5 pounds per 100 square feet of garden soil. Or, when applying manure or compost, mix at the rate of 2½ pounds phosphate per 25 pounds manure or compost. Broadcast the material over the soil surface and work into the topsoil at least three weeks before planting. Manure or other organic fertilizer should be added at this time. Since the materials are so slowly decomposed, sidedressings are seldom beneficial.

Potash — Potassium is widely distributed in nature, occurring in rocks, soils, tissues of plants and animals, and water of seas and lakes. In gardening practice, materials such as wood ashes, tobacco stems,wool suint, seaweed, potash salts, greensand, and ground rock potash are used alone, in combinations with other materials yielding other nutrients, mixed with manure, or in compost piles. Since the potash bearing materials vary so much in composition and rate of decomposition, specific application rates must be determined for each material and its combinations. In general, ground rock potash at 5 pounds per 100 square feet may be broadcast over the soil surface three weeks prior to planting and spaded in. Langbeinite (Sul-Po-Mag) is used at 1 lb/100 sq ft.

Micro-nutrients — An advantage for using organic materials as fertilizers is that they contain many of the elements also needed by the plants in addition to N, P, and K (for example, manganese in manure). Besides the general amounts of micronutrients found in most organic materials, certain ones are concentrated into such naturally occurring materials as gypsum (calcium and sulfur), marl (calcium), dolomite (Calcium and magnesium), limestone (calcium), basic slag (iron, calcium, manganese and magnesium), and finely ground borosilicates.

Lime — Reducing the acidity of the soil is the primary purpose for using lime in the garden. However, liming materials also provide nutrients for plant use. Calcium and magnesium are the two elements most commonly provided by lime. Gypsum is used where more calcium is needed without raising the pH. Natural deposits of lime which are an organic gardener might use are limestone, dolomite, shell, and marl. All these forms must be finely ground to provide maximum benefit to the soil and plants. Dolomite is preferred due to its ocntent of both calcium and magnesium. Lime to sweeten the soil should be applied only when the needs have been established by a reliable soil test. Under most Florida soil conditions, applications of 2 to 5 pounds of finely ground dolomitic limestone per 100 square feet usually will be sufficient except on very acid soils.

Apply lime well in advance of the planting date, preferably 2 to 3 months before the garden is planted. Mix well with the soil and keep moist for best reaction. Application closer to planting time is permissible, but its benefits are delayed.

Insect and Disease Control

During periods when infestations of various garden pests are high, control by natural means becomes very difficult. However, the following practices will help to reduce losses without use of chemical pesticides.

Plant Resistant Varieties

Plant seed from disease-free plants.

Select pest-free transplants.

For cutworms, place a cardboard of tinfoil collar around plant stems at ground level.

Spade garden early so vegetation has time to rot before planting.

Use a mulch; vegetables touching the soil may rot.

Clean up crop refuse early.
Plant as early in the spring as practical.
Keep out weeds which harbor insects and diseases.
Summer fallowing (clean cultivation) helps control nematodes.
Summer flooding, where soil type permits, helps control nematodes.
Hand-pick insects.
Water in morning so plants are not wet at night.
Dispose of severely diseased plants before they contaminate others.

Some insects, like cabbage worms, may be killed by spraying with natural preparations such as *Bacillus thuringiensis*.

Rotate Garden Areas

Bake transplanting soil in oven at 160°F for 1 hour. *Crotolaria spectabalis* and marigolds, when planted as cover crops, tend to reduce some kinds of nematodes. The use of marigolds to *repel* nematodes from interplanted vegetables is not effective control. A good garden mulch tends to reduce *damage* caused by nematodes. Many organic gardeners approve of and use sprays and other preparations containing naturally occurring materials. Diatomaceous Earth comes from petrified sea life. Pyrethrin, rotenone, and ryania are examples of natural poisons from plant parts. These give some control to some insects under certain conditions. Natural predators should be encouraged wherever possible; however, predators raised in captivity, then released into the garden area are usually ineffective. Insecticidal soaps, made from fatty acids tend to work well for some insects under average conditions. Insect traps, baited with phermone lures, work well in some instances. Many of these have sticky adhesives to catch insects. Solar fumigation is effective in reducing some soil-borne problems such as nematodes.

Organic Gardening Supplies

Suitable materials for growing vegetables the organic way are not always easy to locate. The "conventional" garden supply centers carry many products, especially seeds and equipment, which may be used by the organic enthusiast. However, for the difficult-to-find items, the gardener may have to order from specialty businesses dealing in organic gardening supplies.

DESIGN OF GARDEN

Garden design is the art and process of designing and creating plans for layout and planting of gardens andlandscapes. Garden design may be done by the garden owner themselves, or by professionals of varying levels of experience and expertise. Most professional garden designers have some training in horticulture and the principles of design, and some are also landscape architects, a more formal level of training that usually requires an advanced degree and often a state license. Amateur gardeners may also attain a high level of experience from extensive hours working in their own gardens, through casual study, serious study in Master Gardener Programs, or by joininggardening clubs

ELEMENTS OF GARDEN DESIGN

Whether a garden is designed by a professional or an amateur, certain principles form the basis of effective garden design, resulting in the creation of gardens to meet the needs, goals and desires of the users or owners of the gardens. Elements of garden design include the layout of hard landscape, such as paths, walls, water features, sitting areas and decking; as well as the plants themselves, with consideration for their horticultural requirements, their season-to-season appearance, lifespan, growth habit, size, speed of growth, and combinations with other plants and landscape features.

Consideration is also given to the maintenance needs of the garden, including the time or funds available for regular maintenance, which can affect the choice of plants in terms of speed of growth, spreading or self-seeding of the plants, whether annual or perennial, and bloom-time, and many other characteristics. Important considerations in garden design include how the garden will be used, the desired stylistic genre (formal or informal, modern or traditional etc.), and the way the garden space will connect to the home or other structures in the surrounding areas. All of these considerations are subject to the limitations of the prescribed budget.

Location

A garden's location can have a substantial influence on its design. Topographical landscape features such as steep slopes, vistas, hills and outcrops etc. may suggest or determine aspects of design such as layout, and can be used and augmented in order to create a particular impression. The soils of the site will affect what types of plant may be grown, as will the garden's climate zone and various microclimates. The locational context of the garden can also influence its design; for example an urban setting may require a different design style to a rural one. Similarly, a windy coastal location may necessitate a different treatment compared to a sheltered inland site.

Soil

The quality of a garden's soil can have a significant influence on a garden's design and its subsequent success. Soil influences the availability of water and nutrients, the activity of soil micro-organisms, and temperature within the root zone, and thus may have a determining effect on the types of plants which will grow successfully in the garden. However soils may be replaced or improved in order to make them more suitable. Traditionally, garden soil is improved by amendment, the process of adding beneficial materials to the native subsoil and particularly the topsoil. The added materials, which may consist of compost, peat, sand, mineral dust, or manure, among others, are mixed with the soil to the preferred depth. The amount and type of amendment may depend on many factors, including the amount of existing soil humus, the soil structure (clay, silt, sand, loam etc.), the soil acidity/alkalinity, and the choice of plants to be grown. One source states that, "conditioning the soil thoroughly before planting enables the plants to establish themselves quickly and so play their part in the design." However, not all gardens are, or should be, amended in this manner, since many plants prefer an impoverished soil. In this case, poor soil is better than a rich soil that has been artificially enriched.

Boundaries

The design of a garden can be affected by the nature of its boundaries, both external and internal, and in turn the design can influence the boundaries, including via creation of new ones. Planting can be used to modify an existing boundary line by softening or widening it. Introducing internal boundaries can help divide or break up a garden into smaller areas. The main types of boundary within a garden are hedges, walls and fences. A hedge may be evergreen or deciduous, formal or informal, short or tall, depending on the style of the garden and purpose of the boundary. A wall has a strong foundation beneath it at all points, and is usually - but not always - built from brick, stone or concrete blocks. A fence differs from a wall in that it is anchored only at intervals, and is usually constructed using wood or metal (such as iron or wire mesh). Boundaries may be constructed for several reasons: to keep out livestock or intruders, to provide privacy, to create shelter from strong winds and provide microclimates, to screen unattractive structures or views, and to create an element of surprise.

Surfaces

In temperate western gardens, a smooth expanse of lawn is often considered essential to a garden. However garden designers may use other surfaces, for example those "made up of loose gravel, small pebbles, or wood chips" in order to create a different appearance and feel.[5] Designers may also utilise the contrast in texture and color between different surfaces in order to create an overall pattern in the design. Surfaces for paths and access points are chosen for practical as well as aesthetic reasons. Issues such as safety, maintenance and durability may need to be considered by the designer. Gardens designed for public access need to cope with heavier foot traffic and hence may utilise surfaces - such as resin-bonded gravel - that are rarely used in private gardens.

Planting design

Planting design requires design talent and aesthetic judgement combined with a good level of horticultural, ecological and cultural knowledge. It includes two major traditions: formal rectilinear planting design (Persia and Europe); and formal asymmetrical (Asia) and naturalistic planting design.

History

Persian gardens are credited in originating aesthetic planting design and used a rectilinear plan. Planting in ancient and Medieval European gardens was often a mix of herbs for medicinal use, vegetables for consumption, and flowers for decoration. Purely aesthetic planting layouts developed after the Medieval period in Renaissance gardens, as are shown in late-renaissance paintings and plans. The designs of the Italian Renaissance garden were geometrical and plants were used to form spaces and patterns. The gardens of the French Renaissance and Baroque Garden à la française era continued the 'formal garden' planting aesthetic. In Asia the asymmetrical traditions of planting design in Chinese gardens and Japanese gardens originated in the Jin Dynasty (265–420) of China. The gardens' plantings have a controlled but naturalistic aesthetic. In Europe the arrangement of plants in informal groups developed as part of the English Landscape Garden style, and subsequently the French landscape garden, and was strongly influenced by the picturesque art movement.

Application

A planting plan gives specific instructions, often for a contractor about how the soil is to be prepared, what species are to be planted, what size and spacing is to be used and what maintenance operations are to be carried out under the contract. Owners of private gardens may also use planting plans, not for contractual purposes, as an aid to thinking about a design and as a record of what has been planted. A planting strategy is a long term strategy for the design, establishment and management of different types of vegetation in a landscape or garden. Planting can be established by directly employed gardeners and horticulturalists or it can be established by a landscape contractor (also known as a landscape gardener). Landscape contractors work to drawings and specifications prepared by garden designers or landscape architects.

Garden furniture

Garden furniture may range from a *patio set* consisting of a table, four or six chairs and a parasol, through benches, swings, various lighting, to stunning artifacts in brutal concrete or weathered oak.[6] Patio heaters, that run on bottled butane or propane, are often used to enable people to sit outside at night or in cold weather. A picnic table, is used for the purpose of eating a meal outdoors such as in a garden. The materials used to manufacture modern patio furniture include stones, metals, vinyl, plastics, resins, glass, and treated woods.

Sunlight

While sunlight is not always easily controlled by the gardener, it is an important element of garden design. The amount of available light is a critical factor in determining what plants may be grown. Sunlight will, therefore, have a substantial influence on the character of the garden. For example, a rose garden is generally not successful in full shade, while a garden of hostas may not thrive in hot sun.

As another example, a vegetable garden may need to be placed in a sunny location, and if that location is not ideal for the overall garden design goals, the designer may need to change other aspects of the garden. In some cases, the amount of available sunlight can be influenced by the gardener. The location of trees, other shade plants, garden structures, or, when designing an entire property, even buildings, might be selected or changed based on their influence in increasing or reducing the amount of sunlight provided to various areas of the property. In other cases, the amount of sunlight is not under the gardener's control. Nearby buildings, plants on other properties, or simply the climate of the local area, may limit the available sunlight. Or, substantial changes in the light conditions of the garden may not be within the gardener's means. In this case, it is important to plan a garden that is compatible with the existing light conditions. Light regulates three major plant processes: photosynthesis, phototropism, and photoperiodism. Photosynthesis provides the energy required to produce the energy source of plants. Phototropism is the effect of light on plant growth that causes the plant to grow toward or away from the light.[7] Photoperiodism is a plant's response or capacity to respond to photoperiod, a recurring cycle of light and dark periods of constant length.[8]

Lighting

Garden lighting can be an important aspect of garden design. In most cases, various types of lighting techniques may be classified and defined by heights: safety lighting, uplighting, and downlighting. Safety lighting is the most practical application. However, it is more important to determine the type of lamps and fittings needed to create the desired effects.

Bibliography

A B Menan: *Introduction to Plant Anatomy*, Rajat Publication, Delhi, 2008.

A.K. Jain: *Encyclopaedia of Control of Plant Diseases*, Anmol Publication, Delhi, 2010.

Amar Tyagi: *Plant Diseases (2 Vols-Set)*, Anmol Publication, Delhi, 2006.

Archana Singh: *Plant Diseases and Their Biological Control*, Aavishkar Publication, Delhi, 2011.

Arvind Kumar: *Radioactive and Other Pollution and Their Control*, Shree Publishers, Delhi, 2011.

Ashwani Kumar and Shikha Roy: *Plant Tissue Culture and Applied Plant Biotechnology*, Aavishkar Publishers, Delhi, 2011.

Aslam Khan: *Plant Diseases*, Kalpaz Publication, Delhi, 2001.

Aslam Khan: *Plant Anatomy and Physiology*, Kalpaz Publication, New Delhi, 2001.

B A Mannan: *Encyclopaedia of Plant Anatomy (4 Vols-Set)*, Anmol Publication, Delhi, 2008.

B. P. Pandey: *Plant Anatomy*, S. Chand Publisher, Delhi, 2001.

B.B.S. Kapoor and N.K. Khatri.: *Management of Plant Diseases*, Bikaner Publication, Delhi, 2004.

B.S. Thind: *Phytopathogenic Procaryotes and Plant Diseases*, Scientific Publication, Jaipur, 2012.

Balram Sharma: *Plant Tissue Culture and Transformation Techniques*, Daya Publication, Delhi, 2008.

D.A. Evans, W.R. Sharp, P.V. Ammirato and Y. Yamada: *Handbook of Plant Cell Culture: Vol. 1 to 3*, Panima Publication, Delhi, 2009.

Endress: *Plant Cell Biotechnology*, Springer Publication, London, 2004.

F D Heald.: *Encyclopedia of Plant Diseases in Agriculture and Horticulture (4 Vols-Set)*, Asiatic Publication, Delhi, 2006.

F.C. Bawden.: *Plant Viruses and Virus Diseases*, Daya Publication, Delhi, 1995.

F.T. Bannett.: *Introduction to Fungi and Plant Diseases*, Asiatic Publication, Delhi, 2008.

G. Jahir Hussain: *Introduction to Plant Anatomy*, RBSA Publishers, Jaipur, 2011.

G.P. Gupta: *Textbook of Plant Diseases*, Discovery Publishing House, Delhi, 2004.

H.A. Modi.: *Biopesticides and Biocontrol for Green Agriculture*, Pointer Publication, Jaipur, 2012.

Horst.: *Westcott's Plant Disease Handbook, 6e*, Springer, London, 2006.

I.D. Pandian: *Botanical Analysis of Plant Cells*, A.K. Publication, Delhi, 2008.

Iqbal Hasan.: *Plant Diseases and their Biological Control*, Rajat Publication, Delhi, 2010.

J.K. Maheshwari: *Recent Researches in Plant Anatomy and Morphology*, Scientific Publication, Jaipur, 2001.

K Lindsey: *Plant Tissue Culture Manual*, Springer Publication, London, 2007.

K. Manibhushan Rao and A. Mahadevan.: *Recent Developments in Biocontrol of Plant Pathogens*, Today & Tomorrow Publication, Delhi, 1996.

K. Starr Chester.: *Nature and Prevention of Plant Diseases*, J V Publication, Delhi, 2008.

L.K. Pareek: *Trends in Plant Tissue Culture and Biotechnology*, Agrobios Publication, Jaipur, 2005.

Linskens: *Modern Methods of Plant Analysis (Plant Cell Wall Analysis)*, Springer Publication, London, 2003.

Loyala: *Plant Cell Culture Protocols*, Springer Publication, London, 2005.

M K Naik and G S Devika Rani.: *Advances in Soil Borne Plant Diseases*, New India Publication, Delhi, 2008.

M. Zahurul: *Insect Pest of Rice and Their Control*, Asiatic Publishing House, Delhi, 2010.

M.K. Adhikari and H.K. Saiju: *Research on Plant Tissue Culture*, Department of Plant Resources National Herbarium and Plant Laboratories, 2004.

Mangat Rai.: *Biocontrol of Plant Diseases*, Anmol Publication, Delhi, 2008.

Pratibha Saxena and Susheela M. Das: *A Textbook of Plant Anatomy*, Wisdom Press, Delhi, 2012.

Pravin Chandra Trivedi.: *Plant Diseases and Its Management*, Pointer Publication, Jaipur, 2010.

R C Sharma and J N Sharma.: *Plant Diseases, Pathogens and Their Vectors : An Annotated List*, Westville Publication, Delhi, 2008.

Rajaram Choyal: *Plant Anatomy and Physiology*, Sonali Publications, Delhi, 2012.

Rob Jenkins and C.K. Jain.: *Advances in Soil-Borne Plant Diseases*, Oxford Book Company, Delhi, 2010.

Index